Shakespeare
A-Z

Shakespeare A-Z

George Usher

BLOOMSBURY

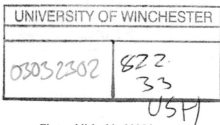
First published in 2005 by
Bloomsbury Publishing Plc
38 Soho Square, London W1D 3HB

British Library Cataloguing-in-Publication Data
A catalogue record for this book is available from the British Library

ISBN 0 7475 6999 1

1 3 5 7 9 10 8 6 4 2

Text production and proofreading
Katy McAdam, Heather Bateman, Emma Harris

All papers used by Bloomsbury Publishing are natural, recyclable
products made from wood grown in well-managed forests. The manufacturing
processes conform to the environmental regulations
of the country of origin.

Text processed and computer typeset by Bloomsbury
Printed and bound in Great Britain by Clays Ltd, St Ives plc

Contents

Introduction

A great deal of Shakespeare's language has found its way into modern English. But the social, cultural, historical, literary and linguistic connections between our age and Shakespeare's can too easily be obscured by the differences between Elizabethan and modern English. This book helps to dissolve those differences and offers us a truly accessible guide to the language of Shakespeare – not just to specific vocabulary, but also to the cultural references that are an integral part of his works.

This book is an A-Z guide to the words found in the twenty-two plays most commonly studied at school or college, or performed regularly. The explanations are written in clear, modern English, suitable for GCSE and A-Level students, as well as for the general user.

Along with descriptions of historical, mythological, fictional and Biblical people and places, the book features short essays to expand upon words of particular interest. It also illuminates the historical and cultural background, describing the various historical, mythological, fictional and Biblical people and places to which Shakespeare refers. In the supplements, you will find the full cast of characters in the plays, from the most eloquent (Lear, Hamlet, Prospero) to the most humble (Audrey, Starveling, Mopsa, Froth and Fang), as well as the historical cast of kings and queens, timelines and a filmography.

It goes without saying that the more we understand the language of Shakespeare's world the better we will understand his plays. This book will help both our education and our enjoyment.

Below is a list of the abbreviations used in the book:

Antony and Cleopatra	AC	The Merchant of Venice	MV
As You Like It	AYLI	A Midsummer Night's Dream	MND
The Comedy of Errors	CE	Much Ado About Nothing	MA
Hamlet	H	Othello	O
Henry IV Part 1	1H4	Richard II	R2
Henry IV Part 2	2H4	Richard III	R3
Henry V	H5	Romeo and Juliet	RJ
Julius Caesar	JC	The Taming of the Shrew	TS
King Lear	KL	The Tempest	T
Macbeth	M	Twelfth Night	TN
Measure for Measure	MM	The Winter's Tale	WT

A

a *preposition* **1.** of (*R2 i 3*; *CE ii 1*) **2.** on (*2H4 ii 4*) **3.** in (*R2 ii 1*) **4.** to (*MND ii 2*) ■ *verb* have (*H iv 5*) ■ *noun* **1.** he (*TS v 2*) **2.** one (*H v 2*) ■ *interjection* ah! (*2H4 ii 1*) (NOTE: 'a' is sometimes added to the end of a line in a song to complete the rhyme.)

abandon *verb* **1.** to banish someone or something (*TS Ind. 2*) **2.** to give up something completely (*O iii 3*)

abandoned *adjective* totally absorbed in (*TN i 4*)

abase *verb* to lower something (*R3 i 2*)

abate *verb* **1.** to make something blunt (*R3 v 5*; *T iv 1*; *2H4 i 1*) **2.** to deprive someone of something (*KL ii 4*) **3.** to shorten something (*MND iii 2*) **4.** to reduce someone's admiration for something (*TS Ind. 1*)

abatement *noun* **1.** a reduction (*KL i 4*; *H iv 7*) **2.** a reduction in worth or value (*TN i 1*)

abhor *verb* to disgust someone (*O iv 2*)

abhorred *adjective* abominable (*M v 7*)

abhorring *noun* something contemptible (*AC v 2*)

abide *verb* **1.** to remain briefly (*WT iv 3*) **2.** to fight or challenge someone (*MND iii 2*) **3.** to fight to defend something (*2H4 ii 3*) **4.** to suffer the consequences of something (*JC iii 1, 2*)

ability *noun* **1.** wealth (*TN iii 4*; *2H4 i 3*) **2.** strength (*WT iii 3*) **3.** strong defences (*O i 3*)

abject *adjective* servile (*MV iv 1*) ■ *noun* **1.** a humble servant (*R3 i 1*) **2.** something contemptible (*JC iv 1*)

able *verb* to vouch for someone (*KL iv 6*)

abode *noun* **1.** someone's home (*TS iv 5*) **2.** a delay (*MV ii 6*) **3.** the act of remaining (*AC i 3*) ■ *verb* to forebode

abomination *noun* a despicable act (*AC iii 6*)

abortive *adjective* **1.** born prematurely (*R3 i 3*) **2.** ugly or malformed (*R3 i 2*)

about *verb* to start working (*H ii 2*)

above *noun* upstairs (*CE ii 2*)

abridge *verb* **1.** to shorten something (*JC iii 1*) **2.** to deprive someone of something (*MV i 1*)

abridgement *noun* **1.** a short play or other form of entertainment to pass the time (*MND v 1*; *H ii 2*) **2.** a reduction (*H5 v Chor.*)

abroach *adjective* in motion or under way (*RJ i 1*; *2H4 iv 2*; *R3 i 3*)

abroad *adverb* out and about (*T iii 1*; *R3 iv 2*; *KL i 2*)

absent *adjective* (*of a period of time*) during which someone is away (*R2 ii 3*)

absolute *adjective* **1.** decided or definite (*MM iii 1*; *M iii 6*) **2.** perfect (*MM v 1*; *H5 iii 7*; *H v 2*) **3.** positive (*H v 1*) **4.** unconditional (*1H4 iv 3*)

abstemious *adjective* showing self-restraint (*T iv 1*)

abstinence *noun* the act of refraining from sexual intercourse (*H iii 4*)

abstract *noun* **1.** a summary (*R3 iv 4*) **2.** a symbol or representation of something (*AC i 4*) **3.** a short cut (*AC iii 6*)

absurd *adjective* uncalled for (*H iii 2*)

abuse *noun* **1.** an offence or injury (*H5 ii Chor.*) **2.** illegal actions (*MM ii 1*; *JC ii 1*) **3.** deception (*H iv 7*) ■ *verb* **1.** to treat someone badly (*R3 i 3*; *TS v 1*) **2.** to cheat or deceive someone (*MA v 2*; *H ii 2*) **3.** to insult someone (*AC v 2*) **4.** to make a **cuckold** of someone (*O iii 3*)

abuser *noun* a person who leads someone morally astray (*O i 2*)

abusing *adjective* causing harm or evil (*R3 iii 7*)

aby *verb* to suffer the consequences of something (*MND iii 2*)

Academe *noun* an academy, a Greek school of philosophy

accent *noun* **1.** speech or language (*RJ ii 4*; *1H4 i 1*) **2.** an echo (*H5 ii 4*)

accept *adjective* final or decisive (*H5 v 2*)

accident *noun* an event (*MND iv 1*; *MA ii 1*; *T v 1*)

accite *verb* **1.** to summon someone (*2H4 v 2*) **2.** to cause or prompt someone to do something (*2H4 ii 2*)

accommodate *verb* to provide for the needs of someone (*2H4 iii 2*; *KL iii 4*)

accommodation *noun* **1.** convenience or comfort (*MM iii 1*) **2.** the entertainment of a guest (*O i 3*)

accommodo *verb* Latin 'I accommodate' (*2H4 iii 2*)

accomplish *verb* **1.** to provide someone with something (*R2 ii 1*; *MV iii 4*) **2.** to supply someone with a complete suit of armour (*H5 iv Chor.*)

accompt *noun* **1.** the act of totalling something up (*MM ii 4*) **2.** expectation (*WT ii 3*)

accord *noun* agreement or harmony (*H5 v 2*; *AYLI i 1*)

accordant *adjective* in agreement (*MA i 2*)

according *adjective* agreeing or assenting (*RJ i 2*)

accost *verb* to flirt with or make sexual advances towards someone (*TN i 3*) [From a nautical term meaning 'to bring a ship alongside'.]

accountant *adjective* accountable (*MM ii 4*; *O i 1*)

accoutrements, accoustrements *plural noun* equipment other than weapons (*AYLI iii 2*)

acerb *adjective* bitter (*O i 3*)

Acheron *noun* **1.** the river of sorrow. In Greek mythology it was one of the five rivers in Hades, the land of the dead. (*MND iii 2*) **2.** hell (*M iii 5*)

achieve *verb* **1.** to finish something (*H5 iv 3*) **2.** to succeed in obtaining something (*TN ii 5, iii 4, v 1*) **3.** to seduce someone (*O ii 1*)

achievement *noun* **1.** something that has been achieved (*2H4 iv 5*) **2.** a heraldic design commemorating something such as an act of bravery (*H5 iii 5*)

achiever *noun* a winner (*MA i 1*)

Achilles *noun* in Greek legend, the king of the Myrmidons. He commanded troops in the siege of Troy.

acknown ◇ **be not acknown** do not admit that you know (*O iii 3*)

a-cold *adjective* chilled (*KL iii 4*)

aconitum *noun* an extract of the poisonous plant wolfsbane (*2H4 iv 4*)

acquit *verb* **1.** to take revenge for something (*H5 ii 2*; *MV v 1*) **2.** to perform your part (*AYLI i 1*)

acquittance *noun* the act of freeing someone from an obligation (*H iv 7*) ∎ *verb* to acquit or clear (*R3 iii 7*)

across *adjective* folded (*JC ii 1*)

act *noun* sexual intercourse (*O ii 1, v 2*)

action *noun* **1.** a gesture (*JC iii 2*; *H iii 2*) **2.** someone's way of standing or moving (*TS Ind. 1*)

action-taking *noun* the act of using the law for protection (*KL ii 2*)

Actium *noun* a town on the west coast of Greece. The Roman emperor Octavian defeated Antony and Cleopatra at the naval battle of Actium. (*AC iii 8*)

actor *noun* someone who does something (*MM ii 2*)

adage *noun* a saying or proverb (*M i 7*)

Adam *noun* **1.** in the Bible, the first man (*CE iv 3*) **2.** human wickedness (*H5 i 1*) (NOTE: From the sin committed by Adam and Eve in eating an apple from the forbidden tree. God expelled them from the Garden of Eden as a punishment.) **3.** an archer. Adam Bell was a famous archer. (*MA i 1*; *RJ ii 1*)

adamant *noun* a magnetic rock (*MND ii 1*)

adder *noun* a snake which was believed to be deaf

addiction *noun* a disposition or tendency (*H5 i 1*; *O ii 2*)

addition *noun* a title given to someone by tradition or in recognition of their service (*M i 3*)

addle *adjective* (*of an egg*) rotten (*RJ iii 1*)

address *verb* **1.** to direct something somewhere (*MND ii 2*; *TN i 4*) **2.** to prepare something (*AYLI v 5*) **3.** to equip someone with something (*WT iv 4*; *MND v 1*; *H5 iii 3*)

addressed *adjective* ready (*MND v 1*; *JC iii 1*)

adhere *verb* **1.** to be consistent with something (*TN iii 4*) **2.** to be congenial to someone (*H ii 2*) **3.** to be suitable for (*M i 7*)

admirable *adjective* wonderful (*MND v 1*)

admiral *noun* the flagship in a fleet. The flagship traditionally carries the admiral in command of the fleet. (*AC iii 10*)

admiration *noun* amazement (*T iii 1; KL i 4; WT v 2*)

admire *verb* to be amazed at something (*T v 1; TN iii 4*)

COMMENT: *Admire* came from the Latin 'ad-mirari', to wonder at, and therefore was not limited just to conveying approval, as it does today. It could have a neutral sense, as in **The Tempest** when Prospero addresses the court party: 'I perceive these lords/At this encounter do so much admire/That they devour their reason'. Hamlet urges Horatio to 'Season your admiration for a while', as he prepares to tell of meeting the Ghost. *Admired* carries a negative sense when Lady Macbeth rebukes her husband for disturbing the lords at his banquet: 'You have...broke the meeting/With most admired disorder'. Generally though, astonishment carries a sense of revelation, of wonder surpassing reason and opening the mind to great benefits. This is an important theme of **The Tempest**. In the play's central scene Ferdinand hears Miranda's name and puns on its meaning of 'to be wondered at': 'Admired Miranda!/Indeed the top of admiration'. This scene leads to their betrothal and finally to the pair being revealed to Alonso, who expresses wonder at being reunited with his son and at the 'goddess' who is with him.

admired *adjective* **1.** admirable (*AC ii 2*) **2.** amazing (*M iii 4*)

Adonis *noun* in Greek mythology, a beautiful youth loved by Aphrodite, the Greek goddess of love (*TS Ind. 1*)

adoptedly *adverb* by adoption (*MM i 4*)

adorning *adjective* adding to the beauty of someone or something (*AC ii 2*)

adulterate *adjective* adulterous (*CE ii 2*)

advance *verb* to lift up something (*T i 2; R3 i 2; H5 v Chor.*)

advantage *noun* **1.** the interest on a loan (*MV i 3*) **2.** chance (*T iii 3; O i 3*) **3.** an exaggeration or embellishment (*H5 iv 3*) ■ *verb* **1.** to be of benefit (*T i 1*) **2.** to derive benefit from something (*H5 iv 1*) **3.** to add to something (*R3 iv 4*)

advantageable *adjective* profitable (*H5 v 2*)

adventerous *adjective* adventurous (*H ii 2*)

adventure *noun* chance (*WT v 1; CE ii 2*) ■ *verb* to risk (*RJ ii 2; WT i 2*)

adversary *noun* a representative (*R2 i 1*)

advertise *verb* to instruct or inform someone (*MM i 1*)

advertisement *noun* **1.** news or information (*1H4 iii 2*) **2.** advice (*1H4 iv 1; MA v 1*)

advertising *adjective* attentive (*MM v 1*)

advice *noun* deliberation or consideration (*H5 ii 2; MV iv 2*)

advise *verb* to consider something (*TN iv 2; RJ iii 5; KL ii 1*)

advised *adjective* cautious (*MV i 1; RJ ii 2*)

advocation *noun* the pleading of a case by a lawyer (*O iii 4*)

Aeacides *noun* **Ajax** (*TS iii 1*)

Aegle *noun* in Greek mythology, a girl who was loved by Theseus (*MND ii 1*)

Aeneas *noun* in Greek mythology, the son of Anchises, king of Dardanus, and the goddess of love, Aphrodite. He was a Trojan, who, according to Homer, fought against the Greeks in the siege of Troy. (*H ii 2; JC i 2*)

aerial *adjective* of the sky (*O ii 1*)

Aeson *noun* in Greek mythology, the king of Iolcos. His son **Jason** led a group called the Argonauts in a search for the mythical Golden Fleece. (*MV v 1*) (NOTE: Aeson was deposed as king of Iolcus by his half-brother Pelias. Jason went on the quest to recover the Golden Fleece in an attempt to reclaim the throne.)

afar off *adverb* **1.** indirectly (*MA iii 3*) **2.** remotely (*WT ii 1*)

affability *noun* courteousness, pleasantness, or friendliness (*TS ii 1; H5 iii 2; JC ii 1*)

affect *noun* **1.** sexual desire (*O i 3*) **2.** a feeling of kindness towards someone (*R2 i 4*) ■ *verb* to love someone (*TN ii 5; KL i 1*)

affected *adjective* **1.** in love **2.** having a particular view on something (*KL ii 1; R3 iii 1*)

affection *noun* **1.** an emotion (*JC ii 1*) **2.** a natural feeling (*M iv 3*) **3.** an inclination

(T i 2; MA ii 2) **4.** sexual desire *(MND i 1; MA ii 3; TN ii 4; H i 3; RJ ii Prol.)*

affectioned *verb* to be full of affectations *(TN ii 3)*

affeer *verb* to confirm something formally *(M iv 3)*

affiance *noun* trust *(H5 ii 2)*

affied *adjective* engaged to be married *(TS iv 4)*

affined *adjective* obliged to do something *(O i 1, ii 3)*

affinity *noun* family connections *(O iii 1)*

affirm *verb* to confirm something *(H5 v 2)*

affray *verb* to frighten someone *(RJ iii 5)*

affront *verb* **1.** to meet or appear before someone *(WT v 1)* **2.** to confront someone *(H iii 1)*

affy *verb* to engage someone to be married *(TS iv 4)*

afront *adjective* alongside *(1H4 ii 4)*

after *adjective* (*of a fleet of ships*) following at the back *(O i 3)*

after-dinner *noun* the afternoon *(MM iii 1)*

after-eye *verb* to follow with the eyes

after-supper *noun* the time after the evening meal *(MND v 1)*

after-time *noun* the future *(2H4 iv 2)*

against *preposition* **1.** in preparation for *(TS iv 4; MND iii 2; MM ii 4; WT iv 4)* **2.** just before *(H ii 2; RJ iv 2)*

Agamemnon *noun* in Greek mythology, king of the ancient Greek city of Mycenae and the brother of Menelaus, Helen of Troy's husband. He led the Greeks in the siege of Troy. *(2H4 ii 4; H5 iii 6)*

agate *noun* a small person *(2H4 i 2; MA iii 1)* [From the practice of sometimes carving the semi-precious stone agate into small human figures.]

age ◇ **thy age confirmed** fully mature *(R3 iv 4)*

Agenor *noun* in Roman mythology, the son of Neptune, king of the Phoenician port of Tyre *(TS i 1)*

agent *noun* an organ of the body *(M i 7)*

aggravate *verb* to increase or add to something *(MND i 2; 2H4 ii 4)*

Agincourt *noun* a village near Calais in France. It was the site of a famous battle in 1415 in which the English, led by Henry

V, defeated the French despite being heavily outnumbered. *(H5 Prol., iv 7)*

aglet-baby *noun* a decorative female figure on the end of a lace *(TS i 2)*

agnize *verb* to acknowledge something *(O i 3)*

agone *adverb* ago *(TN v 1)*

ague *noun* a fever, possibly malaria which was common in England during Shakespeare's time *(JC ii 2; M v 5; MV i 1; T ii 2)*

a-height *adjective* on high *(KL iv 6)*

a-high *adjective* high up *(R3 iv 4)*

a-hold *adjective* (*of a ship*) kept near to the wind and so firmly under control *(T i 1)*

aid *noun* assistance formally claimed in defending a legal action *(AC v 2)*

aidance *noun* help or assistance

aidant *adjective* helpful *(KL iv 4)*

aiery, aery *noun* **1.** an eagle's nest and the young birds in it *(R3 i 3)* **2.** a group of children *(H ii 2)* (NOTE: This refers to the young choristers who sang at religious services for the English monarch and who also often acted in plays.)

aim *noun* **1.** a guess *(JC i 2)* **2.** conjecture *(O i 3, iii 1)* **3.** an object or target *(R3 iv 4)* ■ *verb* **1.** to guess *(H iv 5)* **2.** to intend *(CE iii 2)* ◇ **to cry aim** to shout encouragement to an archer

air *noun* **1.** breath *(WT v 3)* **2.** manner *(WT iv 4)* **3.** demeanour *(WT v 1)* **4.** a tune *(MND i 1)* ■ *verb* to get or be spread about *(TN iii 4)* ◇ **air'd abroad** lived abroad *(WT iv 2)*

Ajax *noun* in Greek mythology, the son of Telamon and king of Salamis *(AC iv 14; KL ii 2)* (NOTE: He was a huge, powerful but not very clever man, and a hero of the siege of Troy. When he heard that Achilles' armour had been awarded to Ulysses, he killed himself. A pun on his name is **jakes**)

alarm, alarum *noun* **1.** a call to go into battle *(R3 i 1, iv 4; O ii 3)* **2.** a loud noise or disturbance *(TS i 1; R3 i 1)* **3.** a battle *(M v 2)* **4.** excitement *(H ii 2)* ■ *verb* to spur into action *(M ii 1; KL ii 1)*

alarum-bell *noun* a bell rung as a warning of danger *(M ii 3; 2H4 iii 1)*

Albany *noun* the ancient name for the northern part of Scotland, but by Shakespeare's time it was also used of northern

Britain (*KL i 1, ii 1, iii 1, iv 3*) [From Celtic *alp*, 'a cliff'.]

Alcides *noun* same as **Heracles** (*AC iv 1; MV ii 1, iii 2; TS i 2*)

ale ◇ **in his ale** drunk (*H5 iv 7*) ◇ **sheer ale** ale drunk on its own, without food (*TS Ind. 2*)

Alecto *noun* in Greek mythology, one of the three spirits of vengeance known as the Furies. Alecto represents 'never ceasing'. (*2H4 v 5*)

Alexander the Great *noun* (356–323 BC) the son of King Philip of Macedonia, whom he succeeded in 336 BC (*AC iii 6; H v 1; H5 iv 7*) (NOTE: Alexander led a united Greek army in the conquest of Persia and captured Egypt, founding the city of **Alexandria**.)

Alexandria *noun* the main sea-port of Egypt. It was founded by **Alexander the Great** in 332 BC and was a famous centre of culture and the site of a university. (*AC ii 2, iii 1, iv 8*)

alien *noun* a stranger (*1H4 iii 2*)

a-life *adverb* dearly (*WT iv 4*)

all amort *adjective* dejected (*TS iv 3*) [From French *à la mort*.]

alla stoccata *noun* Italian a thrust in fencing (*RJ iii 1*) [From Italian, 'by the stab'.]

allay *noun* a means of alleviating something (*WT iv 2; TN i 3*) ■ *verb* to weaken or dilute something (*AC ii 5*)

alley *noun* a shaded path (*MA i 2, iii 1*)

all-hallown summer *noun* the strength of youth lasting into old age (*1H4 i 2*) [From the idea of a long period of good weather that lasts into autumn. All Hallows or All Saints' Day is 1st November, which is why 31st October is known as Hallowe'en (the day before All Hallows).]

All Hallow's Eve *noun* Hallowe'en (*MM ii 1*)

alliance *noun* marriage (*MA ii 1; RJ ii 3*)

allied *adjective* related or connected (*MM iii 2*)

allottery *noun* a share of something (*AYLI i 1*)

allow *verb* 1. to approve something (*KL ii 4; TN i 2*) 2. to concede or acknowledge something (*2H4 i 3; TN iv 2*) 3. to grant something as someone's legal due (*MV iv 1*) 4. to permit someone to do something (*KL iii 7*)

allowance *noun* 1. ability or expertise (*KL i 4, ii 2; O i 1, ii 1*) 2. acknowledgement (*H iii 2*)

allowed *adjective* acknowledged or granted (*TN i 5*)

all-thing *phrase* in every way (*M iii 1*)

ally *noun* a relative (*RJ iii 1*)

almanac *noun* a calendar with associated astronomical events happening in the year (*2H4 ii 4; AC i 2; CE i 2; MND iii 1*)

alms-drink *noun* the dregs of a drink, given to the poor (*AC ii 7*)

almshouse *noun* a home for the poor administered by a charity, often the Church (*H5 i 1*)

almsman *noun* a beggar who lives by his begging (*R2 iii 3*)

alone *adjective* unique (*AC iv 6*)

along *preposition* through all the length of (*AYLI ii 1*)

alter *verb* to exchange something with someone (*TN ii 5*)

Althaea *noun* in Greek mythology, the mother of the Greek hero Meleager (*2H4 ii 2*) (NOTE: It was prophesied that he would die when a burning brand finally burnt away but Althaea kept the brand alight)

amain *adverb* at full speed or as quickly as possible (*CE i 1*)

amaze *verb* to cause bewilderment or dismay (*1H4 v 4*)

amazement *noun* bewilderment (*H iii 4*)

Amazons, Amazonians *plural noun* a mythical race of women warriors who supposedly existed in Scythia (NOTE: According to legend, men were brought in only to conceive children. Baby girls were kept while male children were killed or returned to their fathers. The Amazons had their right breasts burnt off to enable them to use a bow more efficiently)

ambling *noun* walking in an affected or arrogant manner (*R3 i 1*)

ambuscadoe *noun* Spanish an ambush (*RJ i 4*)

amend *verb* 1. to make up for something (*T v 1; TN i 5*) 2. to improve or make someone better (*1H4 iii 1; 2H4 i 2*) 3. to recover (*M iv 3*)

amends *noun* recovery (*TS Ind. 2*)

amerce *verb* to fine someone as a punishment (*RJ iii 1*)

amiable *adjective* having a sweet, lovable nature (*MND iv 1*; *MA iii 3, v 4*; *O iii 4*)

amiss *noun* a calamity (*H iv 5*)

among *adverb* continually (*2H4 v 3*)

amort *adjective* very dejected (*TS iv 3*) [From *French*, 'to death'.]

Amurath *noun* a Turkish sultan (*2H4 v 2*)

an *conjunction* **1.** and **2.** if ■ *preposition* on (*WT iv 3*)

anatomize *verb* **1.** to dissect something for detailed study (*KL iii 6*; *AYLI ii 7*) **2.** to interpret something (*AYLI i 1*)

anatomy *noun* **1.** a corpse (*RJ iii 3*; *TN iii 2*) **2.** a skeleton (*CE v 1*)

anchor *noun* a hermit (*H iii 2*) ■ *verb* to attach firmly (*R3 iv 4*; *MM ii 4*)

anchoring *adjective* (*of a ship*) moored with an anchor (*KL iv 6*)

ancient *noun* **1.** a person who carries a military flag or standard (*O i 1, ii 1, 3*; *1H4 ii 4, iv 2*) **2.** a military flag or standard (*1H4 iv 2*)

COMMENT: Shakespeare used the adjective *ancient* in our sense of very old, as in **The Winter's Tale** when the Old Shepherd complains that young hooligans entertain themselves by 'wronging the ancientry'. But it has a different and very significant meaning as a noun in **Othello** when describing Iago's military rank. This type of *ancient* was derived from the French 'ensigne', a standard-bearer. The prose story on which Shakespeare based **Othello** refers to Iago as 'the ensign'. Iago is obsessed with what he sees as injustice: Cassio, a younger man, has become Othello's lieutenant, his second-in-command, whereas Iago remains 'the ancient'. Though the hierarchy of command is clear, Shakespeare is rather imprecise about the duties of the two soldiers. Cassio seems to perform very few officer-like duties but tends to flaunt his status, referring ostentatiously to Iago's lower rank. Iago doesn't carry a standard; he attends on Othello as a type of aide-de-camp. He is treated rather as a regimental sergeant-major, though his only act of leadership is to set the watch over the troubled town. But his role of 'ancient' is important in contributing to the play's social context of rank-distinctions.

ancient of war *noun* an experienced soldier (*KL v 1*)

ancientry *noun* **1.** traditional customs (*MA ii 1*) **2.** old people (*WT iii 3*)

angel *noun* **1.** a kind, helpful person incapable of evil (*JC iii 2*) **2.** a gold coin worth around one-third of a pound (*MV ii 7*; *TS iv 2*) **3.** a devil (*M v 8*)

angerly *adverb* angrily (*M iii 5*)

angle *noun* **1.** a fish-hook or fishing-line (*WT iv 2*; *H v 2*; *AC ii 5*) **2.** a corner (*T i 2*)

a-night *adverb* at night (*AYLI ii 4*)

Anna *noun* in Roman mythology, the sister of Dido (*TS i 1*)

annexment *noun* an appendage (*H iii 3*)

annoy *noun* harm (*R3 v 3*) ■ *verb* to harm someone (*JC i 3*)

annoyance *noun* harm (*M v 1*; *R2 iii 2*)

answer *noun* **1.** something done in retaliation (*H5 ii 2, iv 7*; *TN iii 4*) **2.** a justification for an action (*JC i 3*) ■ *verb* **1.** to suffer the consequences of an action (*JC iii 2*) **2.** to be responsible or accountable for something (*1H4 iv 2*) **3.** to be accounted for (*H iv 1*) **4.** to obey or agree to something (*T i 2*)

answerable *adjective* **1.** corresponding (*O i 3*) **2.** suitable (*TS ii 1*) **3.** accountable (*1H4 ii 4*)

Anthropophagi *noun* a tribe of cannibals (*O i 3*) [From *Greek* 'man-eating'.]

Anthropophaginian *adjective* cannibalistic (*O i 3*)

antic, antick *noun* a grotesque clown in a play (*MA iii 1*; *R2 iii 2*; *TS Ind. 1*; *1H4 i 2*; *H5 iii 2*) ■ *adjective* **1.** odd or unusual (*H i 5*; *RJ i 5, ii 4*; *M iv 1*) **2.** grotesque (*RJ i 5*)

COMMENT: Both *antic* and *antick* came from the same Latin source, meaning 'old'. The more comic *antic* was sometimes written as *antique* and meant 'bizarre or grotesque', which is how antique artefacts might appear to the archaeologists who discovered them. Shakespeare used *antic* both as an adjective and a noun. When Hamlet warns Horatio that he will adopt 'an antic disposition', he means a manner that is fantastical, not 'antique' in our sense. When the Witches perform their 'antic round', the meaning is primarily a bizarre dance, though, because they are mocking his kingly status, there may also be a secondary sense of old-fashioned in their courtly deference. In **Twelfth Night** Orsino calls for 'that old and antique song', and in **A Midsummer Night's Dream** Theseus tells Hippolyta, 'I never may believe/These antique fables, nor these fairy toys'. In both cases *antique* means 'quaint and odd' as well as old. As a noun, *antic* could be a dance or a grotesque dancer. This latter sense of figures behaving absurdly is intended when Cassandra laments Hector's death at the end of **Troilus and Cressida**. She sees 'distraction, frenzy, and amazement,/Like witless antics'. Perhaps Shakespeare's most striking image of an *antic* as jester appears in Richard II's vision of the 'hollow crown' that a king wears: within it 'Keeps Death his court and there the antic sits/Scoffing his state and grinning at his pomp'. Maybe *antic* here has the added secondary meaning of 'antique', since Richard sees this black comedy as belonging to kingship since the beginning of time.

anticked *adjective* made a fool of (*AC ii 7*)

anticly *adverb* bizarrely (*MA v 1*)

Antiopa *noun* the lover of Theseus (*MND ii 1*)

Antipodes *noun* the other side of the earth from Europe (*MA ii 1*; *MND iii 2*)

antiquity *noun* old age (*2H4 i 2*)

antre *noun French* a large cave (*O i 3*)

ape *noun* **1.** a term of affection (*2H4 ii 4*) **2.** someone who imitates someone else (*WT v 2*) ◇ **lead apes in hell** to be destined to die unmarried (*TS ii 1*)

ape-bearer *noun* a travelling showman who has performing monkeys (*WT iv 3*)

Aphrodite *noun* the Greek equivalent of **Venus**

a-piece *adverb* each (*H ii 2*)

Apollo *noun* in Greek mythology, the son of Zeus and Leto, brother to the goddess Artemis and half-brother to Hermes (*KL i 1*; *MND ii 1*; *TS Ind. 1*) (NOTE: He embodied the perfect example of manhood and was the god of poetry, music, prophecy, archery and healing. The Roman equivalent is *Helios*.)

apoplex'd *adjective* paralysed as a result of suffering a stroke, which used to be called an apoplexy (*H iii 4*)

apothecary *noun* someone who makes and sells medicines (*KL iv 6*; *RJ v 1, 3*) (NOTE: The wealth of an apothecary (whose profession merged with the occult in Elizabethan times) depended on his success in curing his patients to establish a reputation and consequently earn an income. The apothecary in Romeo and Juliet has not had this success and is forced to break the law and risk death by selling poison to Romeo.)

apparent *noun* the next in line to inherit (*WT i 2*; *1H4 i 2*)

apparently *adverb* openly (*CE iv 1*)

apparition *noun* a peculiar facial expression (*MA iv 1*)

appeach *verb* to accuse someone of something (*R2 v 2*)

appeal *noun* an accusation or charge (*R2 i 1, 3, iv 1*; *AC iii 5*)

appearance *noun* an image (*2H4 i 1*)

appellant *noun* someone who accuses someone of something and challenges them to single combat to prove their innocence (*R2 i 3, iv 1*)

appendix *noun* a bride (*TS iv 4*) [From the general idea of something that is attached to someone or something else.]

appertaining *adjective* appropriate or suitable (*RJ iii 1*)

appertinent *noun* something belonging to someone (*H5 ii 2*) ■ *adjective* belonging to someone (*2H4 i 2*)

apple *noun* the pupil of the eye (*MND iii 2*)

apple-john *noun* an apple ripening in midsummer, around the time of St John's Day (24 June), and, though shrivelled, remaining edible through the winter (*1H4 iii 3*; *2H4 ii 4*)

appliance *noun* **1.** a cure or remedy (*MM iii 1*) **2.** a device (*2H4 iii 1*)

apply *verb* to focus on someone or something (*M iii 2*)

apply for *verb* to interpret something as (*JC ii 2*)

appoint *verb* **1.** to provide or equip someone with something (*WT iv 4*; *JC iv 1*) **2.** to order someone to do something (*TS iv 4*)

appointment *noun* equipment (*R2 iii 3*; *AC iv 10*)

apprehend *verb* to imagine or think up something (*MND v 1*; *1H4 i 3*)

apprehension *noun* **1.** understanding (*H ii 2, iv 1*; *H5 iii 7*) **2.** an idea (*1H4 iv 1*) **3.** the act of sensing something (*MND iii 2*) **4.** the arrest or capture of someone (*KL iii 5*) **5.** awareness (*MM iii 1*)

apprehensive *adjective* quick to understand (*JC iii 1*)

apprenticehood *noun* an apprenticeship (*R2 i 3*)

approach *noun* an attack (*H5 ii 4*)

approbation *noun* **1.** proof (*MM v 1*) **2.** the act of putting something to the test (*TN iii 4*; *H5 i 2*) **3.** initial acceptance into a religious order, with a probationary period to be served before the final vows are taken (*MM i 2*)

approof *noun* approval (*MM ii 4*) ◊ **of very valiant approof** having proved your bravery (*AC iii 2*)

appropriation *noun* a notable feature (*MV i 2*)

approve *verb* **1.** to confirm something (*MV iii 2*; *M i 6*) **2.** to prove someone guilty (*O ii 3*) **3.** to put someone or something to the test (*MND ii 2*; *1H4 iv 1*; *TS i 1*) **4.** to recommend or endorse someone (*H v 2*)

approved *adjective* **1.** proven (*MA iv 1*) **2.** tried and tested (*R2 ii 3*)

appurtenance *noun* a characteristic (*H ii 2*)

apricock *noun* an apricot (*MND iii 1*; *R2 iii 4*)

apt *adjective* **1.** natural or likely (*O ii 1*) **2.** willing (*H5 ii 2*; *MA i 1*; *JC iii 1*) **3.** impressionable or naive (*JC v 3*)

aqua-vitae *noun Latin* brandy (*CE iv 1*; *TN ii 5*; *WT ii 4*; *RJ iii 2, iv 2*) [From *Latin* 'water of life'.]

arabian bird *noun* the phoenix, a mythical bird which was supposed to rise from the fire in which it burned at death (*AC iii 2*) (NOTE: It was also used as a Christian symbol of the Resurrection.)

arbitrement *noun* **1.** the settling of a dispute (*KL iv 7*; *TN iii 4*) **2.** a legal trial (*1H4 iv 1*; *H5 iv 1*)

arch *noun* a master (*KL ii 1*) ■ *adjective* principal or chief (*R3 iv 3*; *O iv 1*)

ardour *noun* raging lust (*H iii 4*; *T iv 1*)

argal *conjunction* therefore (*H v 1*) [From *Latin* 'ergo'.]

argosy *noun* a large merchant ship sailing from Ragusa in Sicily (*MV i 1*; *TS ii 1*)

argue *verb* to show or indicate something (*RJ ii 3*; *H v 1*)

argument *noun* **1.** proof (*MA ii 3*; *TN iii 2*) **2.** a subject for argument (*H5 iii 1*)

COMMENT: Occasionally *argument* conveyed our sense of a dispute, as when Henry V, urging his men to action, refers to their ancestors who 'sheathed their swords for lack of argument'; they would stop fighting only when there was no further quarrel to spur them on. However, *argument* probably carries this sense only because it appears in the context of warfare. Its primary meaning for the Elizabethans was more general: a motive or cause. In his Act 4 soliloquy Hamlet believes that 'Rightly to be great/Is not to stir without great argument'. Even more common is *argument* meaning 'theme or topic', as when the King of France speaking of Lear's regard for Cordelia, says that she was 'the argument of your praise'. Sometimes *argument* has this particular meaning in a story or play. King Claudius, very alert to Hamlet's subversive behaviour, sees the threatening dumbshow and asks, 'Have you heard the argument? Is there no offence in't?'. In **Henry IV Part 1** Prince Hal thinks of improvising a play about Falstaff's cowardice, 'and the argument shall be thy running away'. The word's meaning shifts slightly in **Twelfth Night** when Fabian, referring to Olivia's behaviour, urges Sir Andrew that 'this was great argument of love in her towards you'. *Argument* here means a demonstration or proof. Perhaps the closest to our meaning occurs in **Much Ado About Nothing** when Ursula praises Benedick 'for argument and valour', referring to his keenness in disputes.

Argus *noun* in Greek mythology, a god with a hundred eyes who was able to see everything (*MV v 1*) (NOTE: The goddess Hera was jealous of Io and sent Argus to watch her. Hermes charmed him to sleep by playing his lyre and then killed him. On his death his eyes were transferred to the tail of a peacock by Hera.)

Ariadne *noun* in Greek mythology, the daughter of Minos, king of Crete. She helped **Theseus** escape from the **Minotaur**. (*MND ii 1*)

Arion *noun* in Greek mythology, a musician who was saved from drowning by a dolphin that heard his music (*TN iv 3*)

arithmetic ◇ **arithmetic of memory** mental arithmetic (*H v 2*)

arithmetician *noun* a theorist (*O i 1*)

armado *noun* a fleet of armed ships (*CE iii 2*) [From *Spanish* 'to assemble'.]

arm-gaunt *adjective* fully armed and ready for battle (*AC i 5*)

aroint thee *interjection* go away! (*M i 3*; *KL iii 4, 6*)

a-row *adverb* one after the other (*CE v 1*)

arraign *verb* to put someone on trial (*MM ii 3*; *WT ii 3*; *KL iii 6, v 3*; *H iv 5*)

arrant *noun* an errand (*CE ii 1*) ■ *adjective* notorious (*H5 iii 6*)

arras *noun* a heavy tapestry hung so that there was a large gap between it and the wall, thereby providing extra insulation and warmth (*H ii 2*) [The tapestries were originally made in Arras, a town in northern France.]

arras counterpoint *noun* a tapestry bed-cover (*TS ii 1*)

arrest *noun* an order binding someone to obey the law (*H ii 2*) ◇ **I do arrest your words** I hold you to your promise (*MM ii 4*)

arrivance *noun* the people coming (*O ii 1*)

arrive *verb* **1.** to land at or on a place (*WT i 2, iv 4*) **2.** to reach a point or conclusion (*JC i 2*)

art *noun* **1.** science (*TS i 1*) **2.** magic (*T i 2*)

arter *noun* an artery (*H i 4*)

artere *noun* a ligament (*H i 4*)

Arthur's bosom *noun* a play on the biblical phrase 'Abraham's bosom', used in Luke 16:22 to describe the place where the good lie in peace after death (*H5 ii 3*)

Arthur's show *noun* a display of archery by a group of London archers known as Prince Arthur's Knights, each archer adopting the name of one of King Arthur's knights (*2H4 iii 2*)

article *noun* a clause in a legal contract (*AC ii 2*) ◇ **of great articles** very important (*H v 2*)

articulate *adjective* set out or stated (*1H4 v 1*)

artificial *adjective* **1.** artistic or creative (*MND ii 2*) **2.** produced by magic (*M iii 5*; *RJ i 1*)

artist *noun* a scholar

artless *adjective* lacking skill or control (*H iv 5*)

askance *adverb* with suspicion (*TS ii 1*) [From the literal use of *askance* meaning 'sideways'.]

aslant *preposition* diagonally across (*H iv 7*)

aspect *noun* **1.** sight or appearance (*R2 i 3*) **2.** in astrology, the position of a celestial body (*WT ii 2*; *AC i 5*) **3.** a look or glance (*CE ii 2*; *AC i 5*)

aspersion *noun* the act of sprinkling something, especially with holy water (*T iv 1*)

aspic *noun* an asp, a small poisonous snake (*AC v 2*; *O iii 3*)

aspire *verb* **1.** to be ambitious (*R2 v 2*) **2.** to climb up to (*RJ iii 1*)

assail *verb* to try to seduce a woman (*RJ i 1*)

assassination *noun* murder for political purposes (*M i 7*)

COMMENT: **Macbeth** contains the first recorded use of this word, meaning 'a murder for political purposes': 'If the assassination could trammel up the consequences'. Macbeth has left the banquet that he held to celebrate Duncan as his guest. In a soliloquy he struggles with the problems of murdering the man who is his king, kinsman, and guest; he wishes that the single act of murder could catch up in itself all the results of the action. *Assassin* was derived from 'hashisheaters', after a 13th-century sect of Arab guerrillas who attacked crusaders; their leader raised their warlike spirits by drugging them with a concoction of hashish.

assault *noun* an attempt to win someone's love (*MM iii 1*)

assay *verb* **1.** to put someone or something to the test (*MM ii 1*; *1H4 v 4*) **2.** to attempt something (*MM i 4*) **3.** to flirt with or make sexual advances towards someone (*MM i 2*) ■ *noun* **1.** an attack or assault (*H5 i 2*; *H ii 1*) **2.** a test, trial (*O i 3*) ◇ **the great assay of art** the great effort of medical science (*M iv 3*)

assemblance *noun* appearance (*2H4 v 4*)

ass-head *noun* a stupid person (*MND iii 1*; *TN v 1*)

assigns *plural noun* attachments (*H v 2*)

assist *verb* to accompany someone (*T i 1*; *WT v 1*)

assistant ◇ **and convey is assistant** transport is ready and waiting (*H i 3*)

associate *verb* to escort someone (*RJ v 2*)

assume *verb* to claim something (*MV ii 9*) ◇ **if it assume my noble father's person** if the devil takes on the form of my father (*H i 2*)

assurance *noun* **1.** confidence or security (*MA ii 2*; *M iv 1*; *MND iii 1*) **2.** guarantee (*TN i 5, iv 3*) **3.** a legal guarantee to transfer the ownership of something (*TS ii 1*)

assure *verb* **1.** to promise someone in marriage to someone else (*CE iii 2*) **2.** to transfer the legal ownership of something to someone (*TS ii 1*)

astonish *verb* to dismay or stun someone (*H5 v 1*; *JC i 3*)

astronomer *noun* someone who predicts the future from the stars

astronomical *adjective* relating to astrology (*KL i 2*)

at *preposition* at the (*MV ii 5*)

Ate *noun* mischief (*JC iii 1*; *MA ii 1*; *O iv 3*) (NOTE: Ate was the Greek goddess of mischief, strife, and their resulting effects and she had been banished to Earth by Zeus.)

Athene *noun* the Greek equivalent of **Minerva**

athwart *preposition* **1.** lying across (*AYLI iii 4*; *MA ii 2*) **2.** contrary to what might normally be expected (*MM i 3*; *1H4 i 1*)

atomy *noun* **1.** a tiny particle (*AYLI iii 2, 4*) **2.** a very small creature (*RJ i 4*) ◇ **Thou atomy thou!** a skeleton (*2H4 v 1*)

atone *verb* to reconcile or bring together (*AC ii 2*; *O iv 1*)

atonement *noun* reconciliation (*2H4 iv 1*; *R3 i 3*)

Atropos *noun* in Greek mythology, the oldest of the three **Fates**. She cuts the thread of life. (*2H4 ii 4*)

attach *verb* **1.** to affect or cause someone to be overcome by something (*T iii 3*) **2.** to arrest someone (*2H4 iv 2*; *CE iv 1*)

attached *adjective* **1.** overtaken (*CE iv 4*; *2H4 ii 2*) **2.** overcome by (*T iii 3*)

attainder *noun* a stain on someone's reputation (*R3 iii 5*)

attaint *noun* **1.** an accusation or charge (*KL v 3*) **2.** exhaustion (*H5 iv Chor.*) ■

verb to stain the reputation of someone (*CE iii 2*)

attax, attask *verb* to blame or criticise someone (*KL i 4*)

attempt *noun* an attack (*M iii 6*) ■ *verb* **1.** to tempt someone (*MM iii 1, iv 2*; *1H4 iii 2*; *M ii 2*; *O i 3*) **2.** to try to influence someone (*MV iv 1*) **3.** to try to win someone over in love (*KL ii 2*)

attend *verb* **1.** to listen to someone (*T i 2*) **2.** to carry out something (*AC ii 2*) **3.** to wait for something (*M iii 1*; *TS ii 1*)

attent *adjective* attentive (*H i 2*)

attest *verb* to confirm something (*TN v 1*; *H5 Prol.*)

attired *adjective* clothed or wrapped (*MA iv 1*)

attorney *verb* **1.** to act on the authority of someone else (*WT i 1*) **2.** to employ as a representative (*MM v 1*) ■ *noun* **1.** a lawyer (*R3 iv 4*; *CE v 1*) **2.** a legal representative (*AYLI iv 1*; *R3 iii 5*)

attorney-general *noun* a legal deputy (*AYLI iv 1*; *R3 v 3*)

attribute *noun* a reputation (*H i 4*)

attribution *noun* praise or recognition (*1H4 iv 1*)

a-twain *adverb* in two (*KL ii 2*)

audience *noun* attention (*JC iii 2*; *H i 3*)

audit *noun* an account to God of one's actions (*H iii 3*)

auger *noun* a sharp-pointed tool used for making holes in wood (*M ii 3*)

augery *noun* the practice of predicting the future by omens (*H v 2*)

augur *noun* a Roman priest who predicted the future by studying the behaviour of birds (*JC ii 2*; *M iii 4*)

aunchient *adjective* ancient (*H5 iii 2*)

aunt *noun* **1.** an old woman (*MND ii 1*) **2.** a prostitute (*WT iv 3*)

auricular *adjective* perceived via the ear (*KL i 2*)

Aurora *noun* dawn (*MND iii 2*; *RJ i 1*) (NOTE: Aurora was the Roman goddess of the dawn.)

auspicious *adjective* cheerful (*H i 2*)

austerely *adverb* clearly (*CE iv 2*)

authorize *verb* to vouch for something (*M iii 4*)

avail *verb* to benefit or profit from something (*MM iii 1*)

avaunt *interjection* go away! (*2H4 i 2*; *H5 iii 2*)

ave *noun* a greeting or shout of approval (*MM i 1*) [From Latin *Hail.*]

avert *verb* to turn away (*KL i 1*)

avise *verb* to inform someone (*MM ii 2*)

avoid *verb* **1.** to leave (*T iv 1*; *WT i 2*) **2.** to get rid of someone or something (*AYLI i 1*) **3.** to deny something formally (*AYLI v 4*)

avouchment *verb* to confirm something (*H5 iv 8*) (NOTE: This is mistakenly used instead of *avouch* 'to confirm something'.)

award *verb* to decree or decide something (*MV iv 1*; *R3 ii 1*)

away *adverb* here (*MM ii 1*; *TN ii 4*) ■ *verb* to get on or put up with someone (*2H4 iii 2*)

aweless *adjective* not inspiring respect (*R3 ii 4*)

awful *adjective* **1.** worthy of respect (*TS v 2*) **2.** respectful (*R2 iii 3*)

awkward *adjective* **1.** indirect (*H5 ii 4*) **2.** unfavourable

awl *noun* a sharp-pointed tool used by a shoemaker to make holes in leather (*JC i 1*)

axle-tree *noun* the bar on which a wheel turns (*1H4 iii 1*)

ay *interjection* **1.** yes (*used to emphasise a statement*) (*T i 2*; *WT ii 1*) **2.** why, come (*as the introduction to a question*) (*AC iii 10*) **3.** alas! (*H iii 4*)

ayword *noun* a common saying (*TN ii 3*)

B

baby *noun* a cowardly person (*M iii 4*)

Babylon *noun* the capital of the ancient empire of Chaldea in present-day Iraq (*TN ii 3*)

bacchanal *noun* **1.** a drunken party in honour of **Bacchus** (*AC ii 7*) **2.** a priest or worshipper of **Bacchus** (*MND v 1*)

Bacchus *noun* the Roman god of wine and merriment (*AC ii 7*) (NOTE: The Greek equivalent is **Dionysus**.)

back *verb* **1.** to mount a horse (*1H4 ii 3*) **2.** to have something at the back (*MM iv 1*) ■ *noun* **1.** a fallback or alternative in reserve (*H iv 7*) **2.** the rearguard of a force (*2H4 i 3*)

backare *interjection* stand back! (*TS ii 1*)

backfriend *noun* a deceptively friendly person (*CE iv 2*)

backswordsman *noun* someone who practises fencing with a stick resembling a sword (*2H4 iii 2*)

back-trick *noun* a backward step in a dance (*TN i 3, ii 3*)

backward *noun* the past (*T i 2*) ■ *adjective* thinking in the past (*H5 iv 3*)

back-wounding *noun* stabbing in the back, speaking unkindly of someone who is not present (*MM iii 2*)

badged *adjective* spotted or marred (*M ii 3*)

bad woman *noun* a prostitute (*MM ii 1*)

baes *noun* the noise made by a sheep (*MA iii 3*)

baffle *verb* to disgrace someone publicly (*TN ii 5; 1H4 i 2; R2 i 1*) (NOTE: A knight who had been convicted of perjury was disgraced by having a picture of him hanging by his heels displayed in public.)

bag and baggage *noun* all the equipment of an army (*WT i 2*) (NOTE: An army allowed to retreat or surrender with bag and baggage was being granted an honourable defeat.)

bailiff *noun* a sheriff's officer who issues writs and arrests people (*WT iv 3*)

bait *verb* **1.** to torment or tease someone cruelly (*MND iii 2; R2 iv 1*) **2.** to tempt someone (*CE ii 1*) **3.** to catch something using bait (*MM ii 2; MA iii 1*) **4.** to set dogs on a captured animal such as a bear (*M v 8*)

bake *verb* to make something become matted or stuck together (*RJ i 4*)

baked meats *plural noun* pasties or pies (*RJ iv 4*)

baker's daughter *noun* a prostitute (*H iv 5*)

balance *noun* **1.** a pair of scales for weighing (*MV iv 1*) **2.** a pan of a pair of scales (*R2 iii 4*)

bald *adjective* stupid (*1H4 i 3*)

baldrick *noun* a belt for carrying a sword, worn over the shoulder (*MA i 1*)

baleful *adjective* harmful or poisonous (*RJ ii 3*)

balk *verb* to miss a chance or fail to catch prey (*TN iii 2*) ◇ **to balk logic** to argue over something (*TS i 1*)

balked *adjective* piled in mounds (*1H4 i 1*)

ball *noun* **1.** an orb, the golden globe used as a sign of authority during the coronation of a monarch (*H5 iv 1; M v 1*) **2.** an eyeball (*MV iii 2*) **3.** a play on **basilisk** (*H5 v 2*)

ballard *noun* a song, usually about current events (*AC v 2*)

ballard monger *noun* someone who sold ballards (*1H4 iii 1*)

ballast *verb* to load a ship with cargo or heavy material designed to give added stability (*CE iii 2*)

ballow *noun* a heavy club (*KL iv 6*)

balm *verb* **1.** to anoint someone with oil (*TS Ind. 1*) **2.** to soothe or heal an injury (*KL iii 6*) ■ *noun* a healing ointment (*R2 iii 2, iv 1*)

balsam, balsum *noun* balm, a healing ointment (*CE iv 1*)

Balthazar *noun* the traditional name of one of the Three Wise Men in the biblical story of Jesus' birth (*CE iii, v 1*)

ban *verb* to prohibit something (*O ii 1*)

bandy *verb* **1.** to argue or fight (*AYLI v 1*) **2.** to throw to and fro (*RJ ii 5*) **3.** to exchange or send back and forth (*KL i 1, ii 4*; *TS v 1*)

bandying *noun* quarrelling (*RJ iii 1*)

bane *noun* **1.** destruction (*M v 3*) **2.** poison (*MM i 2*) ■ *verb* to poison someone (*MV iv 1*)

banish *verb* to refuse to have sexual intercourse with (*1H4 ii 3*)

banished ◇ **banished years** years of banishment (*R2 i 3*)

bank *noun* **1.** the seashore (*1H4 iii 1*) **2.** a sandbank (*M i 7*; *T i 2*) ◇ **awful banks** bounds of loyal disobedience (*2H4 iv 1*)

bankrout *adjective* bankrupt (*RJ iii 2*; *MND iii 2*)

banner *noun* a small piece of material hanging from a trumpet (*H5 iv 2*)

banquet *noun* fruit, wine, etc., served after the main meal (*RJ i 5*; *TS Ind. 1*; *M iii 6*)

bar *noun* **1.** an objection raised in the course of a lawsuit that is strong enough to stop it (*TS i 1*; *H5 i 2*) **2.** an obstacle or obstruction (*JC i 3*; *MV ii 7*) **3.** a law court (*H5 v 2*; *R3 v 3*)

Barbary *noun* a region in the north and northwest of Africa which exported sugar and a superior breed of horses to Europe (*R2 v 5*; *H v 2*)

Barbary cock-pigeon *noun* a term applied to non-Christians from countries in the East who kept their wives apart from other men (*AYLI iv 1*)

Barbary hen *noun* **1.** a guinea fowl, a bird originating in Africa which resembles a pheasant (*AYLI iv 1*) **2.** a prostitute (*2H4 ii 4*)

Barbason *noun* the name of an evil spirit (*H5 ii 1*)

barbed *adjective* (*of a horse*) wearing armour (*R2 iii 3*; *R3 i 1*)

barber-monger *noun* a conceited or effeminate man (*KL ii 2*) [From the idea that a man who frequently visited a barber's shop was too conscious of his appearance.]

bare *verb* to shave one's head or beard (*MM iv 2*) ■ *adjective* thin and poor (*RJ v 1*; *1H4 iv 2*)

bare-bone *noun* a thin person (*1H4 ii 4*)

barefaced *adjective* without pretence or disguise (*H iv 5*; *M iii 1*)

bare-faced *adjective* without a beard (*MND i 2*)

bare-gnawn *adjective* worn away by biting (*KL v 3*)

bareness *noun* thinness (*1H4 iv 2*)

barful *adjective* full of difficulties (*TN i 4*)

barge *noun* a boat, especially one that was highly decorated, propelled by oars, and used on state occasions (*AC ii 2*)

barked *adjective* stripped of bark, which causes a tree to die (*AC iv 12*) ◇ **bark about** to cover something with something resembling bark (*H i 5*)

barky *adjective* covered with bark (*MND iv 1*)

barley-broth *noun* ale (*H5 iii 5*)

barm *noun* yeast (*MND ii 1*)

barn, barne *noun* a child (*MA iii 4*; *1H4 ii 3*)

barnacle *noun* a black-and-white barnacle goose (*T iv 1*) (NOTE: It was once thought to develop from a barnacle, a type of shellfish.)

barren *adjective* **1.** stupid (*TN i 5*) **2.** unresponsive (*H iii 2*) **3.** having gone a long time without sexual intercourse (*AC ii 5*)

barrenness *noun* a patch of hard skin on the hand (*CE iii 2*)

barricado *noun* a barrier (*TN iv 2*)

Bartholomew boar *noun* a boar fattened for the **Bartholomewtide** fair (*2H4 ii 4*)

Bartholomew boar-pig *noun* a pig sold at the **Bartholomewtide** fair at Smithfield in London (*2H4 ii 4*)

Bartholomewtide *noun* 24 August, a traditional time for fairs (*H5 v 2*)

Basan Hill *noun* a state of terror and misery (*AC iii 13*) [In the Bible, Basan Hill was a land well known for its 'strong bulls' (Psalm 22:12).]

base *adjective* low-lying (*T iii 3*)

base court *noun* the courtyard used by the servants of a house (*R2 iii 3*)

basely *adverb* in an underhand manner (*1H4 v 2*; *AC iv 1*)

base-string *noun* the string with the lowest pitch on a musical instrument (*1H4 ii 4*)

base-viol *noun* a musical instrument similar to a modern cello (*CE iv 3*)

bashful *adjective* shy about sexual matters (*R3 iv 4*)

basilisk *noun* **1.** a mythical serpent that could kill with its gaze (*WT i 2*) *See also* **cockatrice 2.** a brass cannon firing a shot weighing about 91 kg (*1H4 ii 3*; *H5 v 2*)

basis *noun* **1.** the base of a statue (*JC iii 1*) **2.** the foot or foundation of something (*T ii 1*; *TN iii 2*)

basket hilt *noun* on a sword, a hand guard in the shape of a basket (*2H4 ii 4*) (NOTE: This was used as a term of abuse implying that the swordsman's sword and style were out of fashion.)

bass *verb* to speak in a deep voice (*T iii 3*)

basta *interjection* *Italian* Enough, no more! (*TS i 1*)

bastard *noun* **1.** a sweet Spanish wine (*MM iii 2*; *1H4 ii 4*) **2.** a product of artificial breeding (*WT iv 4*) ■ *adjective* false (*MV iii 5*)

baste *verb* to sew fabric together with large temporary stitches (*MA i 1*)

bastinado *verb* to beat someone with a stick or club (*AYLI v 1*)

bat *noun* a staff or stick (*KL iv 6*)

bate *verb* **1.** (*of a hawk*) to beat the wings when tied to the falconer's wrist (*TS iv 1*; *RJ iii 2*; *1H4 iv 1*) **2.** to lessen or reduce something (*H5 iii 2, 7*; *MV iv 1*) **3.** to weaken something (*MV iii 3, iv 1*; *1H4 iii 3*; *H5 iii 7*) **4.** to deduct an amount (*T i 2*; *H v 2*; *2H4 Epil.*) **5.** to quarrel (*2H4 ii 4*) **6.** to omit something (*MND i 1*)

bated *adjective* **1.** reduced (*T iii 3*; *MND i 1*) **2.** (*of a sword*) blunted (*H v 2*) **3.** (*of breath*) held in fear or suspense (*MV iii 3*)

bat-fowling *noun* the practice of catching birds at night using lights and nets (*T ii 1*)

batler, batlet *noun* a flat piece of wood used for beating clothes during washing (*AYLI ii 4*)

Battalia, Battalion *noun* an army drawn up for battle (*R3 v 3*; *H iv 5*)

batten *verb* to become fat (*H iii 4*)

battery *noun* unlawful assault (*TN iv 1*; *H v 1*)

battle *noun* **1.** an army or army division (*1H4 iv 1*; *H5 iv 3*) **2.** the main army (*M v 6*; *R3 v 3*) **3.** a fight between two people (*R2 i 1*)

batty *adjective* like a bat (the animal) (*MND iii 2*)

bauble *noun* **1.** a jester's stick topped with a head having donkey's ears (*RJ ii 4*) **2.** a cheap and breakable toy (*O iv 1*) **3.** a piece of cheap jewellery (*TS iv 3*)

baubling *adjective* worthless or of no importance (*TN v 1*)

baulked *adjective* **1.** frustrated **2.** overlooked **3.** omitted

bavin *noun* a bundle of dry brushwood. It would light quickly and burn away quickly. (*1H4 iii 2*) (NOTE: This is used as a term of contempt.)

bawbling *adjective* insignificant (*TN v 1*)

bawcock *noun* a fine fellow (*TN iii 4*; *H5 iii 2*) (NOTE: This is usually used as a term of rude endearment.) [From French *beau* and *coq*.]

bawd *noun* **1.** a prostitute (*MM iii 2*) **2.** a hare, a pun on 'bawd' (*RJ ii 4*)

bawdry *noun* living together when unmarried (*AYLI iii 3*)

bawl ◇ **those that bawl** testicles (*2H4 ii 2*)

bay *noun* **1.** the space between two timbers in a building (*MM ii 1*) **2.** the act of driving a hunted animal into a position where it has to defend itself (*R2 ii 3*; *R3 iv 4*) ■ *verb* **1.** to bark at (*JC iv 3*) **2.** to hold or drive a hunted animal in or into a position where it has to defend itself (*2H4 i 3*; *MND iv 1*; *JC iv 1*)

bead *noun* a small object (*MND iii 2*)

beadle *noun* a parish constable who had the authority to punish minor offences (*KL iv 6*; *H5 iv 1*)

beads *plural noun* tears, drops of liquid (*JC iii 1*) ■ *noun* a string of beads for keeping count when saying prayers (a **rosary**) (*CE ii 2*; *R2 iii 3*)

beadsman *noun* someone who is paid to say prayers for others (*R2 iii 2*)

beagle *noun* a small hound, used for hunting hares. The word is used to refer to a woman. (*TN ii 3*)

beak *noun* the decorated and pointed prow of a ship (*T i 2*)

beam *noun* **1.** the part of a pair of scales from which the two pans hung (*T ii 1*; *H iv 5*) **2.** a ray of light such as from the sun or the moon (*MND v 1*; *KL ii 2*)

bear *verb* **1.** to behave or conduct oneself (*MM i 3*) **2.** to obtain or win something (*O i 3*; *2H4 iv 1*) **3.** to contain something (*1H4 iv 1*; *AYLI iii 2*) **4.** to keep something going (*WT iv 4*; *T i 2*) **5.** to do or manage something (*MA ii 3*) **6.** to have children (*TS ii 1*; *2H4 ii 4*; *H5 iii 7*; *AC iii 7*)

bear away *verb* to sail away (*CE iv 1*)

bear back *verb* to stand back (*JC iii 2*)

beard *verb* to defy someone (*H ii 2*) ■ *noun* female pubic hair (*TN iii 1*)

bear down *verb* to be stronger than something (*MV iv 1*; *2H4 i 1*)

bearer *noun* the owner or holder of something (*2H4 iv 5*)

bear hard *verb* to dislike someone (*JC ii 1*)

bear herd, bearard, berard, berrord, bearward *noun* someone who keeps a bear to exhibit (*TS iv 4*; *MA ii 1*)

bearing *noun* **1.** behaviour or demeanour (*H5 iv 7*; *MA ii 1*) **2.** endurance (*KL iii 6*)

bearing-cloth *noun* the cloth on which a child was carried to baptism (*WT iii 3*)

bear in hand *verb* to deceive or trick someone (*MA iv 1*; *H ii 2*)

bear off *verb* to keep off or repel something (*T ii 2*)

bear out *verb* **1.** to survive or cope with (*TN i 5*; *O ii 1*) **2.** to support or back something (*2H4 v 1*)

bear up *verb* to steer a ship before the wind (*T iii 2*)

beast *noun* an ox (*KL iii 4*)

beastly *adverb* in the manner of an animal (*TS iv 2*; *AC i 5*)

beat *verb* **1.** to ponder or think about something (*H iii 1*; *KL iii 4*; *T i 2*) **2.** to flap the wings vigorously (*TS iv 1*)

beauty *verb* to decorate something (*H iii 1*)

beaver *noun* a helmet, or the part of a helmet that covers the lower part of the face (*2H4 iv 1*; *H i 2*; *R3 v 3*)

beck *verb* to summon someone with a wave of the hand (*H iii 1*)

become *verb* **1.** to make someone beautiful (*T iii 1*; *TS ii 1*) **2.** to be suitable or fitting for someone (*MV v 1*)

becomed *adjective* befitting or suitable (*RJ iv 2*)

becoming *noun* a graceful quality or action (*AC i 3*)

bed *noun* **1.** the grave (*T ii 1*) **2.** old age (*TN v 1*) **3.** marriage (*AYLI v 4*) ◇ **thrice-driven bed** a bed made of the lightest feathers, separated from the others by a draught of air (*O i 3*)

bedabbled *adjective* sprinkled (*MND iii 2*)

bedded *adjective* laid flat (*H iii 4*)

bedeck *verb* to decorate or adorn something (*RJ iii 3*)

Bedlam *noun* **1.** an asylum for people with mental disorders, originally the priory of St Mary of Bethlehem in London (*KL i 2*) **2.** a person with a mental disorder (*KL iii 7*) ■ *adjective* having a mental disorder (*H5 v 1*)

bed of Ware *noun* a famous large Elizabethan bed from Ware in Hertfordshire, now in the Victoria and Albert Museum (*TN iii 2*)

bed-presser *noun* a lazy person (*1H4 ii 4*)

bedred, bed-rid *adjective* bedridden (*H i 2*)

bed-right, bed-rite *noun* the right to have sexual intercourse with one's wife (*T iv 1*)

bed-swerver *noun* a woman who has committed adultery (*WT ii 1*)

beef *noun* **1.** cattle (*MV i 3*) **2.** the work of a prostitute (*MM iii 2*)

Beelzebub *noun* the Devil (*M ii 3*) [From Hebrew 'the lord of the flies', a god worshipped by the people of the ancient region of Philistia in modern Palestine.]

beetle *adverb* threateningly (*H i 4*) ■ *noun* a heavy piece of wood for flattening earth (*2H4 i 2*)

beetle-brows *plural noun* large, overhanging eyebrows (*RJ i 4*)

beetle-headed *adjective* stupid (*TS iv 1*)

befall *verb* to become of or happen to someone (*CE i 1*)

before *preposition* **1.** in front (*TS iii 2*; *M v 9*) **2.** rather than or in preference to something else happening (*MM ii 4*; *MV iii 2*) ■ *interjection* forward! (*2H4 iv 1*) ◇ **God before** with God's help (*H5 i 2*) ◇ **before me** Indeed! On my soul! (*TN ii 3*; *O iv 1*)

before-breach *noun* a previous offence (*H5 iv 1*)

beget *verb* **1.** to obtain something (*H iii 2*) **2.** to produce something (*TS i 1*)

beggar *verb* **1.** to reduce someone to becoming a beggar (*MV ii 6*; *R3 i 4*) **2.** to exhaust the powers of something (*AC ii 2*)

beggared *adjective* reduced to poverty (*H iv 5*)

begnaw *verb* to corrode or eat away at something (*R3 i 3*; *TS iii 2*)

beguile *verb* to disguise something (*O i 3*)

behalf *preposition* in the interests of or on the part of someone (*1H4 i 3*; *R3 iii 4*; *AYLI Epil.*)

behave ◇ **as he is behav'd** according to his behaviour (*H iii 1*)

behaviour *noun* conduct (*JC i 2*)

behests *plural noun* commands (*RJ iv 2*)

behindhand *adverb* needing to catch up (*WT v 1*)

beholding *noun* contemplating (*R3 iv 4*; *KL iii 7*)

behoof, behove *noun* advantage or benefit (*H v 1*)

behoveful *adjective* advantageous (*RJ iv 3*)

behowl *verb* to bark or howl at something (*MND v 1*)

being *noun* **1.** accommodation or a place to live (*AC ii 2*) **2.** existence (*H ii 1*; *TS i 1*; *O i 2*) ■ *conjunction* seeing that (*MA v 1*; *2H4 ii 1*)

Bel *noun* the god Baal, chief god of the people of **Babylon** (*MA iii 3*)

beldam *noun* **1.** one's grandmother (*1H4 iii 1*) **2.** a hag or witch (*M iii 5*)

be-leed *adjective* forced into the sheltered side away from the wind (*O i 1*)

Belgia *noun* a woman's pelvic area (*CE iii 2*)

belie *verb* **1.** to tell lies about someone (*2H4 i 1*) **2.** to sleep with (*O iv 1*)

bellman *noun* a town crier, especially one who announces the forthcoming death of a prisoner about to be executed and asks for prayers to be said for the dead (*M ii 2*)

Bellona *noun* the Roman goddess of war (*M i 2*)

bellows *noun* a bag, usually made of leather, that is pumped to blow air into a fire or an organ (*AC i 1*)

bell-weather, bell-wether *noun* the leading sheep of a flock. It had a bell tied to its neck so that the shepherd could find the flock. (*AYLI iii 2*)

belonging *noun* a personal quality or feature (*MM i 1*)

beloving *adjective* loving (*AC i 2*)

below *adverb* in hell (*T iv 1*) ◇ **below stairs** the servants' quarters (*MA v 2*)

bemaddening *adjective* causing madness (*KL iii 1*)

bemete *verb* to beat someone as a punishment (*TS iv 3*)

bemocked at *adjective* mocked or ridiculed (*T iii 3*)

bemoil *verb* to cover someone or something with mud (*TS iv 1*)

bemonster *verb* to make something grotesque or hideous like a monster (*KL iv 2*)

bench *verb* **1.** to sit as a judge (*KL iii 6*) **2.** to raise to a position of authority (*WT i 2*)

bench-hole *noun* the hole in the wooden plank of a primitive lavatory (*AC iv 7*)

bend *noun* a glance or look (*JC i 2*; *AC ii 2*) ■ *verb* to turn or proceed in a particular direction (*WT v 1*) ◇ **bend the brow** to frown or scowl (*RJ ii 2*)

bending *adjective* courteous or humble (*R3 iv 4*; *KL iv 2*; *O i 3*) ◇ **our bending author** the writer bowing to the audience or bowed down with the work of writing the play (*H5 Epil*)

benedicite *interjection Latin* Bless you! said by friars especially when receiving gifts of money for the poor (*MM ii 3*)

benediction *noun* the act of blessing (*KL ii 2*)

beneficial *adjective* profitable (*O ii 2*)

benefit *noun* **1.** a natural advantage (*AYLI iv 1*) **2.** a gift of property rights, etc., a legal right (*AC v 2*)

benet *verb* to trap an animal with a net (*H v 2*)

benevolence *noun* a forced loan to the king that is made out to be a gesture of good will (*R2 ii 1*) (NOTE: In fact these were first raised by Edward IV.)

benison *noun* blessing (*KL i 1*; *M ii 4*)

bent *noun* **1.** breaking point, the furthest extent to which a bow can be bent (*MA ii 2*; *H iii 2*; *TN ii 4*; *WT i 2*; *2H4 ii 4*; *JC ii 1*) **2.** a glance or look (*H5 v 2*) **3.** the act of raising the eyebrows (*AC i 3*) ■ *adjective* determined or intent upon (*MND iii 2*)

ben venuto, bien venuto *interjection Italian* Welcome! (*TS i 2*)

berattle *verb* to fill a place with noise (*H ii 2*)

bereave *verb* **1.** to take something away from someone (*O i 3*) **2.** to spoil something or someone by removing a quality such as beauty (*CE ii 1*)

bereaved *adjective* reduced or impaired (*KL iv 4*)

Bergomask *noun* a country dance associated with Bergamo in Italy, a district which was under the control of the Venetians (*MND v 1*)

berhyme, be-rime *verb* to make a rhyme about something (*RJ ii 4*; *AYLI iii 2*)

bescreen *verb* to conceal someone or something (*RJ ii 2*)

beseeched *adjective* besieged (*H5 iii 2*)

beseek *verb* to beseech (*2H4 ii 4*)

beseeming *adjective* suitable (*RJ i 1*)

beside *preposition* out of (*MA v 1*; *JC iii 1*)

besides *preposition* beyond (*CE iii 2*)

beslubber *verb* to daub or smear something with a substance (*1H4 ii 4*)

besmirch *verb* **1.** to dirty or stain something (*H5 iv 3*) **2.** to damage someone's reputation (*H i 3*)

besonian *noun* a rogue or villain (*2H4 v 3*) [From Italian *bisogno*, 'need'.]

besort *verb* to match (*KL i 4*) ■ *noun* fitting or appropriate company (*O i 3*)

bespeak *verb* to speak to someone (*TN v 1*; *H ii 2*; *R2 v 2*)

bespice *verb* to flavour food or drink with spices (*WT i 2*)

best-conditioned *adjective* having the best character (*MV iii 2*)

bestow *verb* **1.** to behave or conduct oneself (*2H4 ii 2*) **2.** to spend time (*JC v 5*) **3.** to spend money (*2H4 v 5*) **4.** to store or put something somewhere (*T v 1*; *CE i 2*) **5.** to live in a place (*M iii 1*) **6.** to give someone in marriage (*AYLI v 1*)

bestowed *adjective* stored away (*CE i 2*; *MV ii 2*; *M iii 1*; *H iv 3*)

bestraught *adjective* hysterical or beside oneself (*TS Ind. 2*)

bestride *verb* to stand over a fallen man to protect him (*CE v 1*; *M iii 3*; *2H4 i 1*)

best-tempered *adjective* of the highest quality, like the finest steel (*2H4 i 1*)

betake *verb* to take oneself to a place (*RJ i 4*; *TN iii 4*)

beteem *verb* to permit or grant something (*H i 2*; *MND i 1*)

bethink *verb* **1.** to think of something (*H i 3*) **2.** to intend something (*KL ii 3*)

betide *verb* to happen to someone or something (*R3 i 2, 3, ii 4*)

betime *adverb* early (*AC iv 4*)

betray *verb* **1.** to deceive someone (*M i 3*; *O v 2*) **2.** to expose someone to evil or punishment (*AYLI iv 1*)

better ◇ **better I** *or* **you were** it would be better for me *or* you (*AYLI iii 3*; *O iii 3*)

between *noun* the space of time between two events (*WT iii 3*)

bevy *noun* a group of women (*H v 2*)

beweep *verb* to wet something with tears (*H iv 5*)

bewhore *verb* to call someone a prostitute (*O iv 2*)

bewray *verb* to betray or reveal something inadvertently (*KL ii 1, iii 6*)

bias *noun* a natural aptitude (*KL i 2*) (NOTE: This is referring to the bowl in the game of bowls. The bowl is not spherical and curves when rolled.) ◇ **assays of bias** indirect attempts (*H ii 1*)

biddy *noun* a chicken, a term used to call or gather them in (*TN iii 4*)

bide *noun* a place to live (*AC iv 14*) ■ *verb* **1.** to endure a delay (*MND iii 2*) **2.** to insist (*WT i 2*)

big *adjective* **1.** strong or powerful (*H5 iv 2*; *O iii 3*) **2.** pregnant (*WT ii 1*) **3.** full to overflowing (*JC iii 1*)

bigamy *noun* marriage to a widow, which was against Church law (*R3 iii 7*)

biggen *noun* a soft cap worn in bed (*2H4 iv 5*) [From French *béguin*.]

bilboes *noun* a metal bar with sliding shackles to secure the ankles of prisoners, used especially on a ship (*H v 2*)

bile, byle *noun* a boil (*KL ii 4*)

bill *noun* **1.** a battleaxe with a long, usually curved blade (*MA iii 3*; *R2 iii 2*) **2.** a note of money owing (*H5 i 1*; *TS iv 3*) **3.** a public notice (*MA i 1*; *JC iv 3*) **4.** a note or written order (*JC v 2*) **5.** a list or inventory (*M iii 1*; *MND ii 2*) **6.** a label (*AYLI i 2*) **7.** a bird's beak (*AYLI iii 3*; *MND iii 1*)

billet *noun* a thick piece of wood (*MM iv 3*)

billiards *plural noun* an innuendo referring to someone's testicles (*AC ii 5*)

bird *noun* **1.** the young of a bird (*1H4 v 1*) **2.** someone who is attacked (*TS v 2*) (NOTE: This is referring to a bird hunted as game.) **3.** a term of endearment (*T iv 1*)

bird-bolt *noun* a blunted arrow used to kill birds without damaging them so that they are easier to clean for cooking (*MA i 1*; *TN i 5*)

bird lime *noun* a sticky substance for catching birds when they perch on it (*O ii 1*)

bird's nest *noun* female genitals and pubic hair (*RJ ii 4*)

birth *noun* **1.** the offspring of someone or something (*2H4 iv 4*) **2.** noble birth (*MA ii 1*) **3.** someone's character (*RJ ii 3*)

birthdom *noun* the place where one was born (*M iv 3*)

bisson *adjective* blind (*H ii 2*)

bisson rheum *noun* blinding tears (*MV i 3*; *H ii 2*)

bite ◇ **bite by the ear** to show affection (*RJ ii 4*) ◇ **bite by the nose** to treat someone with contempt (*MM iii 1*) ◇ **bite the thumb at** to flick the thumbnail away from the underside of the upper teeth as an insulting gesture (*RJ i 1*)

black gown *noun* clothes worn during mourning

Blackheath *noun* a large open common southeast of London. In the rebellions of 1381 and 1450 the rebel forces led by Wat Tyler (1381) and Jack Cade (1450) gathered there in preparation for their attacks on London. (*H5 v Chor.*)

Black Monday *noun* Easter Monday. During the Hundred Years' War, the English troops gathered outside Paris suffered considerably during a storm on Easter Monday in 1360. (*MV ii 5*)

blacks *plural noun* clothes worn during mourning (*WT i 2*)

bladed corn *noun* wheat on which the heads of grain are just forming (*MND i 1*; *M iv 1*)

blank *noun* **1.** the white part at the centre of an archery target (*H iv 1*) **2.** the aim (*O iii 4*; *WT ii 3*) **3.** something aimed at (*KL i 1*) **4.** a clean sheet of parchment bearing the king's seal, to be filled in by a royal official (*R2 ii 1*) ■ *verb* to make something pale (*H iii 2*)

blast *verb* **1.** to cause something to wither **2.** to explode (*H5 iii 1*; *H i 1, iv 7*; *KL ii 4*) **3.** to burst something (*AC iv 8*) ◇ **half blasted** sexually promiscuous (*AC iii 13*)

blastment *noun* a disease causing plants to wither (*H i 3*)

blaze *verb* to reveal or proclaim something (*RJ iii 3*; *JC ii 2*)

blazon *noun* **1.** a coat-of-arms (*TN i 5*) **2.** a description (*MA ii 1*) **3.** an announcement or proclamation (*H i 5*) ■ *verb* to

praise or describe something aptly (*RJ ii 6*)

blazoning *adjective* praising (*O ii 1*)

blear *verb* to deceive or trick someone (*TS v 1*) ■ *adjective* dim or dull (*MV iii 2*)

bleeding *adjective* running with blood (*JC iii 1*; *M v 2*) (NOTE: A sigh was thought to draw a drop of blood from the heart and hence shorten life.)

blench *verb* **1.** to flinch or turn aside (*MM iv 5*; *H ii 2*) **2.** to be inconsistent (*WT i 2*)

blent *adjective* blended (*TN i 5*; *MV iii 2*)

bless *verb* **1.** to guard or keep someone safe from harm (*R3 iii 3*) **2.** to make someone happy by receiving a gift (*T ii 1*; *CE ii 1*) **3.** to be extremely happy (*WT iii 3*; *2H4 ii 4*)

blind *adjective* **1.** heedless or reckless (*H5 iii 3*; *TN v 1*; *R3 i 4*) **2.** dark or mysterious (*R3 iii 7, v 3*)

blindfold *adjective* sightless (*R2 i 3*)

blindness *noun* concealment (*CE iii 2*)

blind worm *noun* a slow worm, a type of harmless legless lizard (*MND ii 2*; *M iv 1*)

blister *verb* to slash (*T i 2*)

Blithild *noun* the daughter of the French king Clothair (*H5 i 2*)

bloat *adjective* fat or bloated (*H iii 4*)

block *noun* **1.** a shaped piece of wood used in making hats (*MA i 1*; *RJ iii 7*) **2.** the shape of a hat (*KL iv 6*)

blood *noun* **1.** the fluid of life (*RJ iii 1*) **2.** relationship (*MND i 1*; *M ii 3*) **3.** passion or anger (*MA i 3*; *MV i 2*; *2H4 iv 4*; *KL iv 2*; *H iii 2*) **4.** lust (*T iv 1*; *O i 3*) **5.** a high-spirited person (*MA iii 3*; *JC i 2*) ◇ **in blood** in good health and spirits

COMMENT: *Blood* for Shakespeare, as for us, is the fluid in our veins and also a metaphor for our family, a guarantee of genuineness. We speak of bloodstock in cattle and in a similar way Kent in **King Lear** describes himself as 'a gentleman of blood and breeding'. There is an odd combination of these two meanings in **Richard II** when the Gardener speaks of fruit trees that are 'overproud in sap and blood'. His primary meaning is that sap in a plant is as necessary as blood in a man's body, but his overall point is that a garden is like a kingdom and therefore trees can be described as lords, men of noble *blood*, who may become dangerously ambitious. A more common Shakespearean use was connected with both these meanings: vigour, high spirits, and especially courage. Worcester in **Henry IV Part 1**, as part of a warning to Hotspur, acknowledges his 'greatness, courage, blood'. These are signs of nobility, and *blood* is also associated with the energy of life itself. However, any wise analyst, which Hotspur is not, could see that it is foolish always to live your life by acting on vigorous impulse. Hamlet, the noble prince, values his friend Horatio for his balanced temperament: 'And blest are those/Whose blood and judgement are so well commingled/That they are not a pipe for Fortune's finger/To sound what stop she please'. *Blood* denotes passion or impulse; its opposite is *judgement*, the result of a man's reason. Sometimes *blood* indicates a specific type of impulse: anger. Othello, a decisive leader, senses evasion from his officers after the brawl: 'Now, by heaven,/My blood begins my safer guides to rule'. Another frequent impulse within men and women is sexual passion and *blood* was also used in this context. Escalus, the restrained civil servant in **Measure for Measure**, is saddened by Angelo's sexual crimes: 'I am sorry one so learned and so wise,/As you, Lord Angelo, have still appeared,/Should slip so grossly…in the heat of blood'.

blood-boltered *adjective* matted with clotted blood (*M iv 1*)

blood-sucker *noun* a murderer who draws blood when killing someone (*R3 iii 3*)

bloody *adjective* **1.** indicating impending bloodshed (*JC v 1*; *H5 i 2*) **2.** bloodthirsty (*TN iii 4*; *MV iii 3*; *M iv 1*) ◇ **bloody house of life** the body (*AYLI iii 5*)

blossom *noun* someone in the prime of life (*WT iii 3*) ■ *adjective* in the prime of life (*WT v 2*; *H i 5*)

blot *verb* to tarnish or stain something (*TS v 2*)

blow *verb* **1.** to swell someone with pride (*TN ii 5*) **2.** to burst something (*1H4 ii 2*; *H5 iv 1*; *AC iv 6*) **3.** to contaminate something, as when a fly deposits its eggs (*T iii 1*; *AC v 22*; *WT iv 2*) **4.** to bloom or blossom (*MND ii 1*)

blown *adjective* **1.** swollen (*MM iii 1*; *1H4 iv 2*; *KL iv 4*) *See also* **blow 2.** contaminated (*O iii 3*) *See also* **blow 3.** past its best, like a flower that has already blossomed (*MA iv 1*; *AC iii 13*)

blow nails *verb* to wait patiently (*TS i 1*)

blow of the law *noun* enforcement of the law (*TN iii 4*)

blubbered *adjective* swollen by crying (*2H4 ii 4*)

blue *noun* the light blue colour of servants' clothing (*TS iv 1*)

blue-bottle *noun* a **beadle** (*2H4 v 4*) [From the fact that beadles wore blue coats.]

blue-caps *plural noun* Scots wearing blue bonnets, used as a term of abuse because servants wore blue caps in England (*1H4 ii 4*)

blue-eyed *adjective* having dark circles around the eyes (*T i 2*; *AYLI iii 2*)

blunt *adjective* **1.** stupid (*2H4 Ind.*) **2.** unfeeling (*R3 i 3*)

blushing *adjective* **1.** glowing, red in colour (*R2 iii 2*; *RJ i 5*) **2.** modest (*1H4 v 2*) **3.** ashamed (*R3 i 4*; *MA iv 1*)

boar *noun* the emblem of the dukes of Gloucester (*2H4 ii 2, 4*; *R3 iii 2, 4, iv 5, v 2*)

board *verb* to have sexual intercourse with someone (*MA ii 1*) [From a nautical term meaning 'to come alongside and board a ship'.] ◇ **bear up and board them** finish up your drinks (*T iii 2*)

boar of Thessaly *noun* in Greek mythology, a ferocious boar sent by Artemis to destroy the lands of Oeneus, king of Calydon, for failing to offer sacrifices to her (*AC iv 1*)

boar-pig *noun* a young pig, sold at the Bartholomew fair (an annual fair held at Smithfield in London) (*2H4 ii 4*)

boast *verb* to praise someone highly (*T iv 1*)

boat ◇ **her boat hath a leak** possibly 'she is suffering from a sexually transmitted disease' (*L iii 6*)

bob *noun* an offensive or sarcastic remark (*AYLI ii 7*) ■ *verb* **1.** to obtain something by cheating or trickery (*O v 1*) **2.** to beat or thrash someone (*R3 v 3*) **3.** to knock or collide (*MND ii 1*)

bobtail *noun* an animal's tail cut short (*KL iii 6*)

bodement *noun* a prophecy or omen (*M iv 1*)

bodkin *noun* **1.** a small dagger (*H iii 1*) **2.** a needle for making holes in cloth (*WT iii 3*) **3.** a small person (*H ii 2*)

body forth *verb* to give a mental picture of something (*MND v 1*)

bog *noun* a lavatory, latrine (*CE iii 2*)

boggler *noun* someone who is indecisive or always changing their mind (*AC iii 8 (13)*)

boiled-brains *adjective* hot-headed or reckless (*WT iii 3*)

boisterous *adjective* **1.** rough or violent (*AYLI ii 3*) **2.** hurtful (*AYLI iv 3*; *RJ i 4*)

bold *verb* to embolden or strengthen the resolve of someone (*KL v 1*) ■ *adjective* confident or certain of something (*O ii 1*)

boldness *noun* confidence (*MM iv 2*)

bolster *noun* a large pillow (*TS iv 1*) ◇ **to see them bolster** to see them in bed together (*O iii 3*)

bolt *noun* **1.** a short arrow fired from a cross-bow (*MND ii 1*; *TN ii 5*; *H5 iii 7*) **2.** a shackle or chain fastened round the ankles of a prisoner (*MM v 1*) ■ *verb* **1.** to sift or sieve something (*WT iv 4*) **2.** to put someone in shackles (*AC v 2*) ◇ **oppose the bolt** to lock the door (*L ii 4*)

bolted *adjective* sifted or sieved (*H5 ii 2*)

bolter *noun* a piece of cloth used for sifting flour (*1H4 iii 3*)

bolting-hutch *noun* a large wooden container for sifted flour (*1H4 ii 4*)

bombard, bumbard *noun* a large leather tankard (*T ii 2*; *1H4 ii 4*)

bombast, bumbast *noun* wool or cotton used for padding something (*1H4 ii 4*) ◇ **bombast circumstance** exaggerated or impressive-sounding talk (*O i 1*)

bona roba *noun* a mistress (*2H4 iii 2*)

bondage *noun* **1.** the condition of being someone's slave **2.** the state of being tied to something **3.** the state of being under an obligation to someone

bones *plural noun* **1.** flat pieces of bone rattled together to accompany a song or dance (*MND iv 1*) **2.** cylinders holding the yarn used in weaving (bobbins) (*TN ii 4*)

bonny *adjective* **1.** (*of a person*) well built (*AYLI ii 3*) **2.** happy (*MA i 3*)

bonos dies *interjection* Good day! (*TN iv 2*) [From Latin *bonos dies.*]

book *noun* **1.** a legal agreement (*1H4 iii 1*) **2.** learning or intellect (*T iii 1*) **3.** an account book (*KL iii 4*; *H i 5*) **4.** a Bible ◇

by the book by the rules (*RJ i 5*; *AYLI v 4*) ◇ **without book** from memory (*TN i 3*)

book-oath *noun* an oath taken on the Bible (*2H4 ii 1*)

book of memory *noun* a small book for noting down reminders for things to be done

boor *noun* a peasant or person of low class (*WT v 2*)

boorish *noun* unrefined or colloquial speech (*AYLI v 1*)

boot *noun* **1.** something extra or additional (*WT iv 4*; *R3 iv 4*; *M iv 3*) **2.** valuables stolen during a robbery **3.** advantage (*WT i 2*; *TS v 2*; *R3 v 3*; *AC i 1*) ■ *verb* **1.** to compensate someone with something (*AC ii 5*) **2.** to profit or be of use to someone (*R2 iii 4*) **3.** to give someone boots (*2H4 v 3*) ◇ **make boot 1.** to take advantage of something (*AC iv 1*) **2.** to carry out a raid (*1H4 ii 1*; *H5 i 2*) ◇ **no boot** no use (*TS v 2*; *R2 i 1*)

boot-hose *noun* a long stocking covering the leg like a boot (*TS iii 2*)

bootless *adjective* useless or of no benefit (*O i 3*)

border *verb* to keep something within certain limits (*KL iv 2*)

bore *noun* **1.** a drilled hole **2.** importance (*H iv 6*) ■ *verb* to make a hole in something (*MND iii 2*) [From *bore*, 'the calibre of a gun'.]

borne in hand *adjective* cheated (*M iii 1*)

borrow *noun* a loan (*WT i 2*) ■ *verb* to put on or pretend something (*KL i 4*)

borrowed *adjective* put on or pretended (*H5 ii 4*; *RJ iv 1*)

bosky *adjective* (*of an area*) covered with trees or bushes (*T iv 1*)

bosom *noun* **1.** the surface of something (*RJ ii 2*) **2.** the depths of something (*R3 i 1*) **3.** the place of emotions, secrets and intimate thoughts (*RJ v 1*; *KL iv 5*; *MM iv 3, v 1*; *JC v 1*; *O iii 1*) **4.** a small pocket in the bodice of a dress (*H ii 2*) ◇ **Abraham's bosom** heaven or paradise, a Biblical phrase used in Luke 16:22 (*R3 iv 3*)

bossed *adjective* having a raised pattern (**embossed**) (*TS ii 1*)

Bosworth, Market Bosworth *noun* a small market town in Leicestershire. The countryside nearby was the site of a battle in 1485 where Henry VII defeated Richard III to establish the Tudor dynasty. (*R3 v 3*)

botch *verb* **1.** to make a poor job of doing something such as a repair (*M iii 1*) **2.** to patch something or put something together in a haphazard way (*TN iv 1*; *H5 ii 2*; *H iv 5*)

botcher *noun* someone who mends clothes

bots *noun* a disease of horses caused by the maggot of a type of fly (*TS iii 2*; *1H4 ii 1*)

bottle-ale *adjective* low class or disreputable (*TN ii 3*; *2H4 ii 4*)

bottled *adjective* fat or swollen (*R3 i 3, iv 4*) [Referring to the shape of a bottle.]

bottle of hay *noun* a bundle of hay (*MND iv 1*)

bottom *noun* **1.** a ball of thread (*TS iv 3*) **2.** the hold of a ship (*MV i 1*; *TN v 1*) **3.** a valley (*AYLI iv 3*; *1H4 iii 1*)

bounce *noun* the noise of a cannon firing (*2H4 iii 2*)

bound *noun* **1.** a boundary or limit (*T i 2*; *H iv 7*) **2.** a territory or country (*T ii 1*; *CE i 1*; *1H4 v 4*) ■ *verb* **1.** to jump (*H5 v 2*) **2.** to rebound (*R2 i 2*) ■ *adjective* **1.** ready (*H i 5*; *KL iii 7*) **2.** intending to go (*CE iv 1*; *H iv 6*)

bounden *adjective* indebted to someone for a service (*AYLI i 2*)

bounteous *adjective* generous (*MM v 1*; *H i 3*; *O i 3*)

bounteously *adverb* generously (*TN i 2*)

bountiful *adjective* generous (*AYLI i 2*)

bounty *noun* **1.** generosity (*RJ ii 2*; *MV iii 4*) **2.** a generous gift (*AC iv 6*)

bourn *noun* **1.** a stream (*KL iii 6, iv 6*) **2.** a boundary (*T ii 1*; *H iii 1*; *WT i 2*; *AC i 1*) (NOTE: A stream often would be the boundary of a parish or other district.)

COMMENT: The English *bourn* and Scottish *burn* meaning 'stream' come from the same Anglo-Saxon origin. Because water forms natural boundaries between countries, counties, and parishes, *bourn* came to mean 'frontier or boundary'. The word survives in many place names like Broxbourne and Bournemouth, and even in cities: Tyburn, Holborn, Kilburn in London. In his soliloquy about suicide Hamlet refers to 'The undiscovered country from whose bourn/No traveller returns'. He thinks of the passage from life to death in the physical terms of a journey with such deep and mysterious implications that his *bourn* is likely to mean more than a stream. If water is implied in this boundary, then perhaps it is the River Styx of forgetfulness, or even an ocean. In **The Tempest** Gonzalo, imagining his ideal commonwealth, is more practical. He would have no 'contract, succession, bourn', meaning that boundaries of property and such legalistic concerns would be abandoned.

bout *noun* a round or fight in fencing (*TN iii 4*; *H iv 7*) ◇ **to walk** *or* **have a bout** to dance with someone (*RJ i 5*)

bow *noun* a yoke, a shaped piece of wood worn over the shoulders and used for carrying heavy loads (*AYLI iii 3*) ■ *verb* to make something bend (*TS ii 1*; *H5 i 2*)

bow-boy *noun* Cupid. He carried a bow and was the messenger of Venus, the Roman goddess of love. (*RJ ii 4*)

bow-case *noun* a thin, malnourished person (*1H4 ii 4*) [Literally the thin, flat case in which a bow was carried.]

bowels *plural noun* children (*MM iii 1*)

bower *verb* to enclose or surround something (*RJ iii 2*)

bowget *noun* same as **budget** (*WT iv 2*)

bowl *verb* to play bowls, a game that involves rolling a hard wooden ball along the ground so that it stops as close as possible to a previously rolled small white ball (*TS iv 5*; *R2 iii 4*; *H ii 2*)

bowsprit *noun* a large pole projecting from the front of a ship (*T i 2*)

boy *noun* a boy actor playing the part of a woman (*AC v 2*)

brabble *verb* to quarrel or fight (*TN v 1*)

brace *adjective* prepared to defend oneself (*O i 3*) ■ *noun* a pair (*T v 1*; *RJ v 3*)

brach *noun* a female hunting dog (*TS Ind. 1*; *1H4 iii 1*; *KL i 4, iii 6*)

brag *verb* to speak of someone or something with justified pride (*RJ i 5*)

brain *verb* to put a stop to something as if by beating out someone's brains (*MM v 1*) ◇ **bear a brain** to have a good memory (*RJ i 3*) ◇ **beat with brain** to make fun of someone or something (*MA v 4*)

brainish *adjective* impulsive or reckless (*H iv 1*)

branch *noun* a part or division of something (*CE v 1*)

branched *adjective* embroidered with a pattern like the stems and stalks of flowers (*TN ii 5*)

branchless *adjective* damaged (*AC iii 4*) [Because the branches have been removed.]

brand *verb* to mark or disfigure by burning (*H iv 5*; *KL i 2*)

brass *noun* this metal was a symbol of hardness and endurance (*MM v 1*; *H5 iv 3*)

brassed, brazed *adjective* hardened as if covered with brass (*H iii 4*; *KL i 1*)

brassy *adjective* hard as brass (*MV iv 1*)

brave *noun* defiance (*TS iii 1*) ■ *verb* **1.** to challenge or take issue with someone or something (*R3 iv 3*; *TS iv 3*) **2.** to ornament something (*R3 v 3*) ■ *adjective* **1.** beautiful (*T i 2, iii 2*; *H ii 2*; *AC v 15*) **2.** splendid or magnificent (*TS Ind. 1*) **3.** excellent or fine (*MA v 4*; *AYLI iii 4*; *1H4 iv 1*)

COMMENT: As an adjective *brave* had more meanings for Shakespeare than it has for us. One of these is 'fine or splendid'. Perhaps the most famous occurs at the end of **The Tempest** when Miranda sees the finely dressed courtiers for the first time: 'O brave new world…!', she exclaims. They are certainly not brave in our sense of 'courageous'. Her father, Prospero, treats her remark with irony perhaps because he knows that the courtiers are *brave* in the unfavourable sense of 'brash display' or showing off. Aldous Huxley borrowed Prospero's irony when he entitled his famous satire **Brave New World**, which envisages a confident but flawed future. In **The Taming of the Shrew** Tranio enters 'bravely': he is impersonating his master and enters with excessive panache, wearing fine clothes.

bravely *adverb* **1.** fearlessly (*MND v 1*) **2.** excellently or splendidly (*T iii 3*; *TS iv 3*)

bravery *noun* **1.** fine clothing (*MM i 3*; *AYLI ii 7*) **2.** a show of courage, especially when it is intended to impress someone (*JC v 1*; *O i 1*) **3.** the act of displaying or showing something (*TS iv 3*; *H v 2*)

braving *adjective* swaggering and defiant (*R2 ii 3*)

brawl *verb* **1.** to quarrel or make a disturbance (*TS iv 1*; *2H4 i 3*) **2.** (*of a stream*) to flow noisily (*AYLI ii 1*)

brawling *adjective* noisy (*RJ i 1*)

brawn *noun* a boar or pig fattened up for eating (*2H4 i 1*)

breach *noun* a break or crack in something (*H i 4*; *H5 i 2*) ◇ **breach of the sea** waves breaking on the seashore (*TN ii 1*)

bread-chipper *noun* someone who cuts the crusts off bread (*2H4 ii 4*)

break *verb* **1.** to crack open someone's head (*CE i 2*; *RJ i 3*) **2.** to crack a joke (*TS iv 5*; *MA ii 3*) **3.** to reveal someone (*MA i 1*; *H5 v 2*) **4.** to interrupt a conversation (*AC iv 14*; *2H4 iv 5*) **5.** to train or teach someone (*TS ii 1*; *CE iii 1*) **6.** to become bankrupt (*MV iii 1*; *RJ iii 2*) **7.** to be dispersed by light (*R3 v 3*) **8.** to quarrel with someone (*WT iii 2*; *MV ii 4*) ◇ **break a comparison** to indulge in word play (*MA ii 1*)

break a word *verb* to have words with or speak to someone (*CE iii 1*)

break-neck *noun* a dangerous action (*WT i 2*)

break-promise *noun* someone who breaks a promise (*AYLI iv 1*)

break the pale *verb* to avoid marriage (*CE ii 1*) [From the idea of breaking through a fence.]

break wind *verb* to become short of breath (*1H4 ii 2*)

breast *noun* a singing voice (*TN ii 3*)

breath *noun* **1.** speech (*MND iii 2*; *MA v 1*; *KL i 1*) **2.** a short time (*R3 iv 2*) (NOTE: Referring to the short length of a breath.) **3.** the ability to breathe (*CE iv 1*; *H v 2*)

breathe *verb* to speak or say something (*H ii 1*; *KL iv 2*)

breathed *adjective* strong and fit as a result of exercise (*AYLI i 2*; *TS Ind. 2*)

breather *noun* **1.** a speaker (*MM iv 4*) **2.** a living animal (*AYLI iii 2*)

breathing *noun* **1.** exercise (*H v 2*) **2.** an utterance (*AC i 3*) **3.** a delay (*MA ii 1*; *MV v 1*)

breathing while *noun* a short time (*R3 i 3*) [Referring to the short length of a breath.]

breech *noun* a husband's authority over his wife [From *breech*, 'trousers', symbolising a husband.]

breeched *adjective* covered (*M ii 3*)

breeching scholar *noun* a student young enough to be whipped (*TS ii 1*)

breed *noun* **1.** a race of people (*R2 ii 1*; *H iii 2*; *M iv 3*) **2.** children or descendants (*MV i 3*) ■ *verb* to bring up or raise someone (*KL iv 2*)

breeder *noun* a woman capable of having children (*H iii 1*)

breeding *noun* parentage (*WT iv 4*; *2H4 v 3*)

breese *noun* a type of biting fly (a gadfly) which is a pest of cattle and horses (*AC iii 10*)

breff *adjective* brief (*H5 iii 2*)

brewer's horse *noun* an old, worn-out horse (*1H4 iii 2*)

bride *noun* a bridegroom (*RJ iii 5*) ◇ **bride it** to play the part of a bride (*TS iii 2*)

brief *noun* **1.** a summary or short account (*MND v 1*) **2.** a list (*AC v 2*) **3.** a letter (*1H4 iv 4*)

briefly *adverb* soon or swiftly (*AC iv 4*)

briefness *noun* a swift act (*KL ii 1*)

brimstone *noun* sulphur. It was used to symbolise hell because of the foul-smelling and poisonous sulphur dioxide it gives off when burnt. (*O iv 1*; *TN ii 5, iii 2*)

brinded *adjective* marked with spots or streaks (*M iv 1*)

brine *noun* tears (*RJ ii 3*) [Because tears are salty.]

bring *verb* **1.** to accompany someone (*H5 ii 3*; *JC iii 2*) **2.** to inform someone about something (*H v 2*; *AC iv 13*) **3.** to give birth to (*WT ii 1*)

bring about *verb* to complete a period of time as a full cycle of day and night (*R2 i 3*)

bring forth *verb* to put someone or something on public display (*AC v 2*)

bring in *verb* to establish one's position (*O iii 1*)

bringings-forth *plural noun* achievements (*MM iii 2*)

bring on *verb* to cause something to happen (*H iii 1*)

bring out *verb* to produce something (*WT iv 3*)

bring up *verb* to raise someone or something to a higher level (*WT iv 4*)

brisk *adjective* **1.** busy (*RJ i 5*; *TN ii 4*) **2.** well dressed (*1H4 i 3*) **3.** pleasantly sharp in taste (*MND iii 1*)

brisky *adjective* lively (*MND iii 1*)

broach *verb* **1.** to pierce or impale something or someone (*MND v 1*) **2.** to open a discussion or embark on a matter (*TS i 2*; *AC i 2*)

broached *adjective* **1.** as if speared on a metal rod for roasting over an open fire (*1H4 v 1*; *H5 v Chor.*) **2.** discussed (*AC i 2*)

broad *adjective* **1.** unrestricted (*H iii 4*; *M iii 6*) **2.** widespread or disseminated (*M iii 4*) **3.** obvious (*RJ ii 4*) **4.** in full bloom (*H iii 3*)

broad-fronted *adjective* having a wide forehead (*AC i 5*)

broadside *noun* the firing of cannon from one side of a ship (*2H4 ii 4*)

broad-spreading *adjective* spreading widely (*R2 iii 4*)

brock *noun* a dirty person (used as an insult) (*TN ii 5*)

broil *noun* a confused battle (*M i 2*)

broke *verb* **1.** to haggle or bargain (*MA ii 1*; *R2 iii 1*) **2.** to cut (*R2 v 5*) ■ *noun* pawnbroking (*R2 ii 1*)

broken *adjective* **1.** imperfect or incomplete (*H5 v 1*) **2.** interrupted (*WT v 2*) **3.** bankrupt (*AYLI ii 1*)

broken delivery *noun* an incomplete account of an event (*WT v 2*)

broken meats *plural noun* food left over from a meal and eaten by the servants (*KL ii 2*)

broken music *noun* **1.** music written in parts (*H5 v 2*) **2.** a punning reference to the noise made by breaking ribs (*AYLI i 2*)

broker *noun* a go-between in a love affair (*H i 3*)

brooch *noun* someone who enhances the company they are in (*R2 v 5*; *H iv 7*) ■ *verb* to adorn or ornament something (*AC iv 13*) [From *brooch*, 'ornament'.]

brood ◇ **sits on brood** sitting like a hen on her eggs (*H iii 1*)

brook *verb* **1.** to accept something **2.** to tolerate something

broom-grove *noun* a thicket made up of bushes of the yellow-flowered broom (*T iv 1*)

brother *noun* **1.** a brother-in-law (*CE ii 2*) **2.** a step-brother (*R3 v 3*)

brow *noun* the expression on someone's face (*1H4 iv 3*; *M iv 3*; *H i 2*)

Brown *noun* the Non-conformist Robert Brown (c. 1550–1633) who led an extreme religious sect (*TN iii 2*)

brown-bill *noun* a **bill** or battleaxe painted brown (*KL iv 6*)

brow of Egypt *noun* a dark skin (*MND v 1*)

bruise *verb* to crush or press hard on something (*MM ii 1*)

bruit *noun* a rumour or report ■ *verb* to report or announce something (*H i 2*)

brush *noun* a skirmish

bubble *noun* a shallow or insubstantial person or thing (*AYLI ii 7*)

bubukles *plural noun* pimples or boils (*H5 iii 6*)

buck *noun* a male deer (*CE iii 1*)

bucket *noun* the crosspiece of a yoke or hoist (*2H4 iii 2*)

buckle *verb* **1.** to restrict or limit something (*AYLI iii 2*) **2.** to bend under pressure (*2H4 i 1*)

buckler *noun* a small shield (*1H4 ii 4*; *MA v 2*) ■ *verb* to protect or defend someone or something (*TS iii 2*) ◇ **I give thee the bucklers** I admit defeat (*MA v 2*)

buckram *noun* linen fabric stiffened with glue (*1H4 ii 4*)

bud *noun* a shoot of a plant used to form new growth on another plant (*WT iv 4*)

budding *adjective* developing (*TS iv 5*)

budge *verb* to retreat or give way (*1H4 ii 4*; *JC iv 3*)

budget *noun* a leather bag or pouch for carrying money (*WT iv 3*)

buff *noun* a type of soft leather used to make protective coats for sergeants in the army (*CE iv 2*; *1H4 i 2*)

buffet *noun* the act of hitting or striking someone or something (*AC i 4*) ■ *verb* **1.** to hit or strike someone (*CE ii 2*) **2.** to fight or strive for something (*H5 v 2*)

bug, bugbear *noun* a frightening object (*TS i 2*; *H v 2*)

COMMENT: In Shakespeare's time *bug*, and its extension of *bugbear* had a mysterious sense of 'goblin, evil spirit or ghost', something which caused terror. In **The Winter's Tale**, Hermione challenges her husband's tyranny over her: 'The bug which you would fright me with I seek'. She implies that Leontes' mind is obsessed with dark imaginings, but that she is happy to face the simplicity of death. She uses *bug* contemptuously to describe an object of fear which a frightened person is impelled to invent.

There is a similar use in **Hamlet** when the prince describes to Horatio the contents of Claudius' letter to the English king designed to discredit Hamlet: 'With, ho! Such bugs and goblins in my life…'. Our use of *bug* has removed this otherworldly sense, so that it now refers specifically to a disgusting insect or more generally to a defect as in a machine like a computer or to a virus in the body. Perhaps the original mysterious threat in the word survives when we speak of a room being *bugged*.

bugle *noun* a black glass bead (*AYLI iii 5*; *WT iv 4*)

bulk *noun* **1.** the trunk or chest of the body (*R3 i 4*; *H ii 1*) **2.** a stall or frame built so as to extend outwards from a building (*O v 1*) **3.** the main body of a ship (*TN v 1*)

bully *noun* a brave person, used as a term of affection (*T v 1*; *MND iv 2*; *H5 iv 1*)

COMMENT: *Bully* has largely changed its connotations since Shakespeare's time, though its meaning continues to be forceful. It meant 'fine fellow', a good mate, as when the workmen in **A Midsummer Night's Dream** approve of 'bully Bottom'. In a play outside our list of texts, the Host in **The Merry Wives of Windsor** greets Falstaff as 'Bully Hercules! Bully Hector', comically associating the fat knight with legendary heroes. It was a specially male word of address for noisy good fellowship. We retain this favourable meaning in the phrase, 'bully for you!'. In its distant European origins *bully* had a softer meaning of 'lover', as in old German 'buhle'. It is interesting to note that bully Bottom plays the lover in the play of Pyramus and Thisbe.

bulwark *noun* a defensive wall (*H iii 4*; *H5 iv 1*)

bum-bailey *noun* an official whose job was to follow or track down debtors and arrest them (*TN iii 4*)

bunch-backed *adjective* hunch-backed (*R3 i 3, iv 4*)

bung *noun* a pickpocket (*2H4 ii 4*)

burden, burthen *noun* **1.** birth (*CE v 1*) **2.** the refrain of a tune (*T i 2*) **3.** the bass accompaniment to a tune (*AYLI iii 2*; *TS i 2*; *WT iv 4*) **4.** the weight of a man on a woman during sexual intercourse (*RJ ii 4*)

COMMENT: This word had two distinct sources to produce two meanings. One, from the Anglo-Saxon, produced our heavy weight, sometimes used to describe childbirth or the weight of man in sexual intercourse. The second, from the French 'bourdon', the deep sound of bees humming, led to its musical context, denoting the refrain or chorus in a song, as when the sprites sing to Ferdinand in **The Tempest**. Celia in **As You Like It** uses *burden* metaphorically to mean a predictable refrain when she tries to prevent Rosalind from interrupting her story: 'I would sing my song without a burden'. The word could also describe the bass accompaniment to a song or dance. In another metaphorical use in **The Taming of the Shrew** Petruchio, tells Hortensio that 'wealth is burden of my wooing dance'. His cynical meaning is that whatever elegant niceties may be required when he courts Katherine, her money is the basic motive: his performance will be grounded there.

burdened, burthened *adjective* weighty or oppressive (*R3 iv 4*)

burdenous, burthenous *adjective* oppressive (*R2 ii 1*)

burgomaster *noun* the chief magistrate of a city (*1H4 ii 1*)

burgonet *noun* a light helmet with cheek-pieces and a flexible neck-piece (*AC i 5*)

burial *noun* a grave (*MV i 1*)

burn *verb* **1.** to be hot with sexual desire (*KL iv 6*) **2.** to heat something (*TN iii 3*) **3.** to infect someone with a sexually transmitted disease (*CE iv 3*) ◇ **burn daylight** to waste time in a pointless activity (*RJ i 4*)

burnet *noun* salad burnet, an edible plant (*H5 v 2*)

burning zone *noun* the region between the tropics of Capricorn and Cancer, areas running round the Earth parallel to the equator (*H v 1*)

burnt sack *noun* mulled wine (*TN ii 2*)

bury *verb* to conceal or keep something secret (*JC iv 3*)

bush *noun* an advertisement (*AYLI Epil.*) [From the practice of using a bunch of ivy hung outside as the sign of a tavern.]

busil'est *adjective* busiest (*T iii 1*)

business *noun* sexual intercourse (*AC i 2*)

buskined *adjective* wearing knee-length hunting boots (buskins) (*MND ii 1*)

busky *adjective* wooded (*1H4 v 1*)

buss *noun* a kiss (*2H4 ii 4*) ■ *verb* to kiss someone

butler *noun* the servant in charge of the wine cellar. This was a senior position in a household. (*T v 1*)

butt *noun* **1.** a target in archery, or the mound on which this was placed (*H5 i 2*) **2.** a goal or aim (*O v 2*) **3.** a large barrel containing 567 litres of wine or 486 litres of ale (*T ii 2*) **4.** an old barrel or tub (*T i 2*) **5.** the act of an animal striking something with its head and horns (*TS v 2*)

butt-end *noun* the last remaining part (*R3 ii 2*)

butterfly *noun* a vain, frivolous person (*KL v 3*)

butter hay *verb* to put butter on hay as a foolish kindness to one's horse (as horses would not eat hay with butter on it) (*KL ii 4*)

butter-woman *noun* a woman taking butter to market (*AYLI iii 2*)

buttery *noun* **1.** a cool room in a house where the butter and milk were kept (*TS Ind. 1*) **2.** a storeroom where various foods and alcoholic drinks are kept (*TS Ind. 1*)

buttery-bar *noun* a ledge on the half-door of a **buttery** on which to rest tankards (*TN i 3*)

button *noun* **1.** a bud (*H i 3*) **2.** a knob on top of a cap (*H ii 2*)

butt-shaft *noun* a blunt arrow used in target practice (*RJ ii 4*)

buxom *adjective* lively (*H5 iii 6*)

buy and sell *verb* to treat someone as though they were of no more importance than an item to be bought and sold (*CE iii 1*; *R3 v 3*)

buy out *verb* to pay off a debt or pay a ransom for something (*CE i 2*; *1H4 iv 2*; *H iii 3*)

buzz *noun* a rumour (*KL i 4*) ◇ **Buzz, buzz!** We know that already! (*H ii 2*)

buzzard *noun* **1.** a layabout or worthless person (*TS ii 1*) **2.** an insect that flies about in an aimless, blundering way (*TS ii 1*) [From *buzzard*, 'a bird of prey that is useless for falconry'.]

buzzer *noun* someone who spreads news or gossip (*H iv 5*) [From the idea of a buzzing insect.]

by *preposition* **1.** about (*MA v 1*) **2.** according to (*AC iii 3*)

by-drinking *noun* drinking between meals (*1H4 iii 3*)

by-gone day *noun* yesterday (*WT i 2*)

by'r Lady, by'r Lakin *noun* an oath meaning 'by Our Lady' (*T iii 3*; *MND iii 1*; *MA iii 3*; *RJ i 5*)

by-room *noun* a small side-room or private room (*1H4 ii 4*)

C

cabin *noun* a hut (*TN i 5*) ■ *verb* to enclose or confine someone (*M iii 4*)

cable *noun* the limit of action (*O i 2*) [From the idea of a rope or chain to which an anchor is attached.]

cacodemon *noun* an evil spirit (*R3 i 3*)

caddis *noun* a tape made of closely woven wool (*WT iv 4*)

caddis-garter *noun* a garter made of **caddis** (*1H4 ii 4*) (NOTE: This is used as a term of abuse, as garters could be seen when worn and were made of more showy and expensive materials than caddis.)

cadent *noun* falling (*KL i 4*)

Cadmus *noun* the founder and king of **Thebes** (*MND iv 1*)

cagion, casion *noun* occasion (*KL iv 6*)

Cain *noun* **Adam**'s elder son. He killed his brother Abel (Genesis 4). (*H v 1*)

caitiff *noun* a pitiable person (*R3 iv 4*; *O iv 1*)

COMMENT: *Caitiff* was a term of contemptuous abuse, meaning 'coward or worthless person'. It derived from the Latin and French words for 'captive'. In **Othello** it is untypically applied to a woman: Cassio, partly in sympathy, but more in contempt, says 'poor caitiff' about Bianca, who is a sort of captive in love, captivated by Cassio. In **Measure for Measure** the constable Elbow exclaims, 'O thou caitiff!' to the petty criminal Pompey, partly out of angry frustration, partly because he wants him to be imprisoned. Later Isabella uses *caitiff* as an adjective to intensify her disgust with Angelo: 'I went'/To this pernicious, caitiff deputy'. He is her social superior and a magistrate, but she knows him to be a coward and morally corrupt; more literally, the audience also knows him to be enslaved, a captive to his obsession with Isabella.

cake ◇ **my cake is dough** my plans are thwarted (*TS i 1, v 1*) ◇ **cake of roses** a compressed mass of rose petals used as perfume (*RJ v 1*)

calendar *noun* a directory (*H v 2*)

calf *noun* a stupid person (*H iii 2*)

Calipolis *noun* the heroine and wife of Muly Mahamet, a character in the play *The Battle of Alcazar* (1594) by George Peele (?1558–?97) (*2H4 ii 4*)

caliver *noun* a light firearm with a long barrel (*1H4 iv 2*; *2H4 iii 2*)

call *noun* a whistle to lure birds, or a bird trained to lure other birds by its call (*TS iv 1*) ■ *verb* to call on or visit someone (*TN iii 2*) ◇ **call in** to call someone or something back (*2H4 iv 3*)

callat, callet *noun* a prostitute (*WT ii 3*; *O iv 2*)

calling *noun* a name (*AYLI i 2*)

call on, call upon *verb* **1.** to demand payment from someone (*1H4 v 1*) **2.** to call someone to account (*AC i 4*)

call to a reckoning *verb* to have sexual intercourse with someone (*1H4 i 2*)

calm ◇ **sick of a calm** feeling nauseous or sick (*2H4 ii 4*)

calves' guts *plural noun* calves' intestines, which were used to make strings for musical instruments

cambric *noun* fine linen made at Cambrai in Flanders, France (*WT iv 2*)

Cambyses *noun* the king in the tragic play *Cambyses, King of Percia* (1570) by Thomas Preston (1537–98) (*1H4 ii 4*) □ **in Cambyses' vein** in the style of the play *Cambyses* (*1H4 ii 4*)

Camelot *noun* the legendary castle of King Arthur (*KL ii 2*)

camomile *noun* a plant that is used medicinally as a relaxant and for stomach complaints. It was also used to sow lawns. (*1H4 ii 4*)

camp *verb* to provide lodgings for someone (*AC iv 8*)

can *verb* **1.** to understand or comprehend (*T iv 1*) **2.** to be skilled at doing something (*H iv 7*)

canakin, cannakin *noun* a small metal cup (*O ii 3*)

canary *noun* **1.** a sweet white wine from the Canary Islands (*TN i 3*; *2H4 ii 4*) **2.** a lively dance said to have originated in the Canary Islands

candied *adjective* **1.** frozen together (*T ii 1*) **2.** flattering (*H iii 2*)

candle *noun* **1.** a star (*RJ iii 5*) **2.** the light of life (*M v 5*)

candle-holder *noun* an onlooker (*RJ i 4*) [From the idea of a servant who holds a candle for others to be able to see.]

candle mine *noun* a container for the animal fat (**tallow**) used to make candles (*2H4 ii 4*)

candle-waster *noun* someone who stays up late at night studying (*MA v 1*)

candy *adjective* sugared (*TN v 1*)

Candy *noun* Crete (*1H4 i 3*) [From *Candia*, an old name for Crete.]

canker *noun* **1.** an insect larva that destroys buds (*MND ii 2*; *RJ ii 3*) **2.** the wild rose (*1H4 i 3*) (NOTE: From its Latin name *Rosa canina*.)

canker bloom *noun* the flower of the wild rose (*MA i 3*; *1H4 i 3*)

canker-blossom *noun* a flower damaged by an insect larva (**canker**) (*MND iii 2*)

cankered *adjective* **1.** corroded (*2H4 iv 5*) **2.** wishing to do evil (*1H4 i 3*; *RJ i 1*)

canon, canon law *noun* the law (*H i 2*) [Canon law is strictly the legal power of the established Church.]

canonize *verb* to bury with the rites of the Church (*H i 4*) [From canonize, 'to be officially proclaimed a saint'.]

canopy *noun* the sky (*H ii 2*) ■ *verb* to provide a shelter or cover to someone or something (*TN i 1*)

canstick *noun* a candlestick (*1H4 iii 1*)

Canterbury *noun* a town in Kent on the River Stour. It has been an important centre since the foundation of the abbey by St Augustine in 597 and became a centre of pilgrimage to the tomb of St Thomas à Becket. (*1H4 i 2*; *H5 i 2*)

cantle *noun* **1.** a corner or slice of something (*AC iii 1*) **2.** a segment of a sphere (*1H4 iii 1*; *AC iii 8 (10)*)

canton *noun* a song (*TN i 5*)

canvas, canvass *verb* to beat someone severely as a punishment (*2H4 ii 4*) [From a nautical term meaning 'to be tossed in a canvas sail as a punishment'.]

cap *noun* a square cap with three folds meeting in a point at the top, worn by a Roman Catholic cardinal ◇ **throw their cap** to give up (*T iii 4*)

capable *adjective* **1.** susceptible to (*T 2*; *WT iv 4*; *2H4 i 1*) **2.** sensitive (*AYLI iii 5*; *H iii 4*) **3.** intelligent (*R3 iii 1*) **4.** comprehensive (*O iii 3*) **5.** legally able to inherit (*KL ii 1*)

capacity *noun* the ability to take in or understand information (*MND v 1*; *TN ii 5, iii 4*)

cap-a-pe, cap-a-pie *phrase* from top to toe (*H i 2*; *WT iv 4*) [From *French* 'cap-à-pie'.]

caparison *noun* **1.** an outfit or item of clothing, especially one that is flamboyant (*WT iv 3*) **2.** an ornamented covering over the saddle of a horse (*R3 v 3*)

caparisoned *adjective* dressed up (*AYLI iii 2*; *TS iii 2*)

caper *verb* to leap about (*R3 i 1*; *TN i 3*)

capital *adjective* principal (*H5 v 2*; *1H4 iii 2*)

capitulate *verb* to enter into an agreement with someone (*1H4 iii 2*)

capon *noun* a stupid man whose wife is unfaithful (*CE iii 1*) [From *capon*, 'a large castrated male chicken'.]

captain *noun* **1.** a chief or head (*R2 iv 1*; *RJ ii 4*; *O ii 1*) **2.** a subordinate officer (*R3 v 3*) **3.** a term of friendly address (with no implication of rank) (*WT i 2*)

captive *verb* to take someone captive (*H5 ii 4*) ■ *adjective* defeated (*AC ii 5*)

captived *adjective* taken captive (*H5 ii 4*)

car *noun* a chariot (*AC iv 8*; *H5 iv 4*; *R3 v 3*)

carack *noun* another spelling of **carrack** (*CE iii 2*; *O i 2*)

caraways *plural noun* small sweets made of caraway seeds covered with sugar (*2H4 v 3*)

carbonado *noun* a piece of meat slashed across and ready to cook over hot coals (*WT iii 4*) ■ *verb* to slash or cut like a **carbonado** (*KL ii 2*)

carbuncle *noun* **1.** a garnet, a red precious stone (*CE iii 2*; *H ii 2*; *AC iv 8*) **2.** a large boil on the skin (*KL ii 4*)

carcanet *noun* a jewelled collar or head ornament (*CE iii 1*)

COMMENT: 'Carcan' in Old French meant 'a bracelet or necklace'. *Carcanet* was the diminutive, and therefore more dainty word to describe an ornament for women. In **The Comedy of Errors**, Antipholus speaks to the goldsmith about 'the making of the carcanet' which he has ordered for his wife. Today it is a highly literary word for specialist uses, as in the title of a modern poetry periodical, in which the poems may be regarded as a string of pearls, delicately fashioned. The word has also been traced to a Latin origin, 'carcanum', an iron circle, which the executioner clamped round the neck of a criminal, therefore, with grim irony, a 'neck-lace'.

card *noun* **1.** a playing card **2.** a card on which the 32 points of the compass are marked (*M i 3*) **3.** a directory (*H v 1, 2*) [Literally 'to mix drinks'.] ◇ **faced it with a card** bluffed it out with something (*TS ii 1*) ◇ **pack cards** to put the cards in a particular order in the pack so as to be able to cheat (*AC iv 14*) ◇ **packed cards with** made a dishonest arrangement with (*AC iv 14*)

carded *adjective* diluted or debased (*1H4 iii 2*)

card-maker *noun* someone who makes combs for combing (carding) wool (*TS Ind. 2*)

Carduus benedictus *noun* the medicinal herb blessed thistle (*MA iii 4*)

care ◇ **have a care** to pay attention or take care (*T i 1*) ◇ **make a care, keep a care** to care for something (*T ii 1*; *WT iv 4*)

career *noun* **1.** a short gallop at full speed (*MA v 1*; *WT i 2*) **2.** a frolic or lively movement (*H5 ii 1*) **3.** a course of action (*R2 i 2*) [Literally the quick sideways movement made by a horse.]

careful *adjective* concerned or uneasy (*H5 iv 1*; *R2 ii 2*; *R3 i 3*)

careless *adjective* **1.** without worries (*H iv 7*) **2.** uncared for (*M i 4*)

carelessly *adverb* **1.** without worry (*AYLI i 1*) **2.** heedlessly (*JC i 2*)

care-tuned *adjective* anticipating sadness (*R2 iii 2*)

carkanet, carcanet *noun* a necklace (*CE iii 1*) [From French *carcan*, 'a necklace'.]

carlot *noun* a peasant (*AYLI iii 5*)

carman *noun* someone who drives a cart (*MM ii 1*; *2H4 iii 2*)

carnal *adjective* **1.** flesh-eating (*R3 iv 4*) **2.** sexual (*H v 2*)

carnation *adjective* flesh-coloured (*H5 ii 3*)

carouse *noun* a single drink from a full cup, emptying it (*AC iv 12*; *TS i 1*) ■ *verb* to take a long drink from a full cup (*AC iv 8*; *H v 1*)

carpet *noun* a tablecloth (*TS iv 1*)

carpet consideration *noun* recognition of non-military service (*TN iii 4*)

carpet-monger *noun* a man who enjoys flirting with women and is often to be found in their bedrooms rather than on the battle-field (*MA iv 2*) [From the rich furnishings of a woman's bedroom.]

carrack *noun* **1.** a large trading ship used in the Mediterranean, also equipped for war (*CE iii 2*) **2.** a prostitute (*O i 2*) (NOTE: From the frequent use of the term 'land-frigate' for a prostitute.)

carract, carat *noun* **1.** a measure of the purity of gold. 24 carat is pure gold. (*CE iv 1*) **2.** a good honest person (*2H4 iv 5*)

carriage *noun* **1.** the ability to carry something (*RJ i 4*) **2.** conduct or behaviour (*WT iii 1*; *CE iii 2*) **3.** a load (*T v 1*) **4.** the way someone moves or stands (*1H4 ii 4*) **5.** significance (*H i 1*) **6.** the strap by which a sword hangs from a belt (*H v 2*)

carrier *noun* a messenger

carrion *noun* **1.** rotting flesh or meat (*H ii 2*) **2.** living human flesh (*MV iii 1*) **3.** a term of abuse, implying that the person is no better than rotting meat (*H5 iv 2*; *RJ iii 5*) ■ *adjective* **1.** dead, rotting (*JC iii 1*) **2.** painfully thin, like a skeleton (*MV ii 7*) **3.** belonging to the body (*MV iv 1*) **4.** feeding on rotting meat (*RJ iii 3*)

carry *verb* **1.** to manage or conduct something (*KL v 3*; *MM iii 1*; *MA iv 1*) **2.** to behave (*TN iii 4*) **3.** to endure or tolerate something (*H5 iii 2*; *RJ iv 5*; *KL iii 2*) **4.** to seduce a woman (*AC ii 4*) [From a hawking term meaning 'to fly away with the game'.] ◇ **carry it** to be successful (*O i 1*) ◇ **carry it away** to be successful (*RJ iii 1*) ◇ **carry out my side** to win my game (*L v 1*) ◇ **carry through itself** to succeed (*L i 4*)

cart *noun* **1.** a cart used to take prisoners to the gallows (*1H4 ii 4*) **2.** the chariot of the sun god **Apollo** (*H iii 2*) ■ *verb* to publicly expose a prostitute (*TS i 1*)

Carthage *noun* an ancient city on the Bay of Tunis in North Africa. It was destroyed by the Romans in 146 BC. (*MND i 1*; *MV v 1*; *T ii 1*; *TS i 1*)

carve *verb* to think up a design or plan for something (*MA ii 3*; *TS iv 3*) ◊ **carve for** to make one's own choices (*H i 3*; *O ii 3*)

carver ◊ **to be his own carver** to make his own choices (*R2 ii 3*)

case *noun* **1.** a container or covering (*RJ i 4*) **2.** the body as a container for the soul (*TN v 1*; *AC iv 15*) **3.** an eye-socket (*WT v 2*; *KL iv 6*) **4.** the skin or hide of an animal (*WT iv 4*) **5.** a coat or other garment (*MM ii 4*; *1H4 i 2*) **6.** a set or collection (*H5 iii 2*) ■ *verb* to cover something (*CE ii 1*; *1H4 ii 2*)

casement *noun* a window (*AYLI iv 1*; *KL i 2*; *MND iii 1*; *MV ii 5*)

casing *adjective* enclosing or enveloping (*M iii 4*)

cast *noun* **1.** a throw of a dice (*1H4 iv 1*) **2.** the act of making (casting) a cannon (*H i 1*) **3.** a tinge of colour (*H iii 1*) ■ *verb* **1.** to dismiss someone (*O i 1*) **2.** to calculate something (*2H4 i 1*; *H ii 1*; *AC iii 2*) **3.** to throw someone in a wrestling match (*M ii 3*) **4.** to vomit or throw up something (*MM iii 1*; *H5 iii 2*) ■ *adjective* discarded or cast off (*AYLI iii 4*) ◊ **cast the water** to examine someone's urine as a way of diagnosing disease (*M v 3*)

cast away *verb* to cause a ship to be wrecked (*MV iii 1*)

castigation *noun* punishment (*O iii 4*)

Castiliano *noun* the devil in the play *The Devil and his Dame* by William Haughton (1600) (*TN i 3*)

casual *adjective* by chance (*H v 2*)

casualty *noun* **1.** a risky or unlucky event (*L iv 3*) **2.** chance or bad luck (*MV ii 9*)

cat *noun* a civet cat. Its fur was used for clothing, and it produces a substance used in perfumes. (*AYLI iii 2*; *KL iii 4*) ◊ **tear a cat** to speak aggressively (*MND i 2*)

Cataian *noun* a rogue (*TN ii 3*) [The literal meaning is 'a native of China', from Cathay, China.]

cataplasm *noun* a plaster or poultice (*H iv 7*)

cataract *noun* a large waterfall (*KL iii 2*)

catastrophe *noun* **1.** the final act or part of a play (*KL i 2*) **2.** a person's backside (*2H4 ii 1*)

catch *noun* **1.** a song for several voices (*T iii 2*; *TS ii 3*; *TN ii 3*; *RJ ii 5*) **2.** something that is caught (*TS ii 1*) ■ *verb* **1.** to snatch at something (*MA v 2*) **2.** to take or acquire something (*M i 2*)

catechism *noun* questions and answers on Christian belief which had to be learnt by constant repetition before someone was formally admitted as a full member of the Church and therefore allowed to take Communion (*AYLI iii 2*; *1H4 v 1*)

cater cousins *plural noun* close friends (*MV ii 2*)

caterpillar *noun* someone who exploits or lives off other people (*R2 ii 3*)

cates *plural noun* delicacies or fine food (*1H4 iii 1*; *CE iii 1*)

cat o' mountain *noun* a spotted wild cat (*T iv 1*) (NOTE: The reference is taken from The Bishop's Bible (Jeremiah 13, 23).)

cause *noun* **1.** the cause of a dispute (*KL iv 6*) **2.** a business or matter (*H5 i 1*; *M iii 3*; *TS iv 4*)

'cause *conjunction* because (*M iii 6*)

cautel *noun* a ploy or stratagem (*H i 3*)

cautelous *adjective* deceitful or cunning (*JC ii 1*)

caution *noun* a precaution (*M iii 6*)

cavaleiro, cavalleria *adjective* gallant (*2H4 v 3*)

caveto *interjection* *Latin* beware or be cautious (*H5 ii 3*)

caviare *noun* the salted eggs of a sturgeon (caviar), or any delicacy (*H ii 2*)

cease, cess *noun* extinction (*H iii 3*; *KL v 3*)

censer ◊ **thin man in a censer** a dish containing incense, which when it burnt, revealed a saint carved on the dish (*2H4 v 4*)

censure *noun* **1.** the opinion or judgement of someone, particularly when unfavourable (*WT ii 1*; *MM iii 2*; *AYLI iv 1*; *KL i 4*; *H i 3*) **2.** a judicial sentence (*O v 2*) ■ *verb* to give an opinion on someone (*H iii 2*; *JC iii 2*)

centaur *noun* a mythical animal, half man and half horse (*MND v 1*)

centre *noun* **1.** the centre of the Earth (*MND iii 2*; *H ii 2*) **2.** the heart or the soul (*WT i 2*)

century *noun* a hundred Roman soldiers (*KL iv 4*)

Cephalus In Greek legend, the devoted husband of Procris

cerecloth *noun* same as **cerement** (*MV ii 7*)

cerement *noun* a cloth dipped in wax and used for wrapping an embalmed body (*H i 4*)

ceremonious *adjective* attentive to the detail of formalities (*KL i 1*; *R3 iii 1, v 1*)

ceremony *noun* **1.** an omen (*JC ii 1*) **2.** a sacred symbol of state (*MM ii 2*; *H5 iv 1*)

Ceres *noun* the Roman earth goddess. She was identified with the earth and agriculture, particularly the corn harvest and had a daughter Prosperina by the god **Jupiter**. (*T iv 1*) (NOTE: The Greek equivalent is **Demeter**.)

'cern *verb* to concern oneself (*TS v 1*)

certes *adverb* certainly (*T iii 3*)

certify *verb* to assure someone (*R3 i 4*; *MV ii 8*)

cess ◊ **out of all cess** out of proportion or excessive (*1H4 ii 1*)

cestern, cesterne *noun* a water-tank (cistern) (*O iv 2*)

chace, chase *noun* **1.** the act of quibbling or disputing about someone (*H5 i 2*) **2.** a hunted animal (*WT iii 3*) [From a real tennis term referring to a ball bouncing twice where the second bounce is disputed.]

chafe *noun* anger or rage (*AC i 3*) ■ *verb* **1.** to anger or annoy someone (*TS ii 1*) **2.** to erode a river bank (*WT iii 3*; *JC i 2*; *KL iv 6*)

chaff *noun* cereal husks (*MV ii 9*)

chain *verb* to embrace something (*AC iv 8*)

chair *noun* **1.** a symbol of authority (*JC iii 2*) **2.** a sedan chair, carried by two servants (*O v 1*)

challenge *noun* a challenge to someone to fight (*MA i 1*; *RJ ii 4*) ■ *verb* **1.** to accuse someone (*M iii 4*) **2.** to challenge someone to fight (*M i 1*; *TN ii 3*) **3.** to demand something as of right (*R2 ii 3*; *O ii 1*)

challenger *noun* someone claiming something as a right (*H5 ii 4*; *H iv 7*)

Cham *noun* an emperor of China (*MA ii 1*)

chamber *noun* **1.** a small cannon (*2H4 ii 4*) **2.** a bedroom **3.** the capital city (*R3 iii 1*) ◊ **of chamber** with the job of attendant or **chamberlain** (*AYLI ii 2*; *M i 7*)

chamber-councils *plural noun* matters discussed in private (*WT i 2*)

chambered *adjective* lodged (*R2 i 1*)

chamberer *noun* a man who spends much time in women's bedrooms (*O iii 3*)

chamberlain *noun* **1.** someone who attends the king in his bedroom or private apartments (*R3 i 1*) **2.** someone in charge of the bedrooms in an inn (*1H4 ii 1*)

chamber-lye, chamber-lie *noun* urine (*1H4 ii 1*)

chameleon *noun* an African lizard that is capable of changing its colour to match its surroundings, and was believed to live on air (*H iii 2*)

champai(g)n *noun* open level country (*TN ii 5*; *KL i 1*)

champion *verb* to challenge someone to do something (*M iii 1*)

chance *noun* an unexpected event (*2H4 iv 2*; *H v 2*; *M ii 3*) ■ *adverb* possibly (*MA ii 3*; *2H4 ii 1*) ◊ **chance, how** how is that? (*2H4 iv 4*; *L ii 4*) ◊ **main chance** the most important concern (*MA ii 3*; *2H4 ii 1*)

chandler *noun* someone who makes or sells candles (*1H4 iii 3*)

change *noun* **1.** fickleness (*KL i 1*) **2.** an exchange (*MA iv 1*; *H5 iv 8*) ■ *verb* **1.** to exchange something (*T i 2*; *AYLI i 3*; *O i 3*) **2.** to change colour or alter one's expression (*MA v 1*; *H5 ii 2*) ◊ **changed eyes** glanced lovingly (*T I 2*)

changeable *adjective* varying in colour (*TN ii 4*)

changeling *noun* **1.** a child substituted for another, especially by fairies (*MND ii 1, iv 1*) **2.** one letter substituted for another (*H v 2*) **3.** an inconsistent person (*1H4 v 1*)

channel *noun* a gutter in the street (*2H4 ii 1*) ■ *verb* to plough furrows in a field (*1H4 ii 1*)

chanson *noun French* a song (*H ii 2*)

chantry *noun* a small chapel, often in a cathedral, that was funded by the bequest of a private individual and where prayers were said daily for the soul of the benefactor (*TN iv 3*)

chaos *noun* formless, disorganised matter or confusion (*RJ i 1*; *O iii 3*)

chap *noun* the cheeks and lower jaw (*T ii 2*; *2H4 ii 4*; *AC iii 5*)

chape *noun* the metal tip at the end of a scabbard (*TS iii 2*)

chapless *adjective* with the lower jaw-bone gone (*H v 1*; *RJ iv 1*)

chapman *noun* a merchant, especially one who travels around

character *noun* **1.** handwriting (*MM iv 2*; *TN v 1*; *KL i 2*; *H iv 7*) **2.** a code for secret messages (*MM i 1*) **3.** the external appearance of someone (*TN i 2*) ■ *verb* to write something (*H i 3*)

COMMENT: *Character* originally meant 'a stamped or engraved mark', and then extended its sense to include styles of handwriting. A notable example occurs at the end of **Twelfth Night** when Olivia disclaims the letter that has tricked Malvolio: 'this is not my writing/Though…much like the character'. In **Measure for Measure** the Duke comments on Angelo's fitness to rule: 'There is a kind of character in thy life/That to the observer doth thy history/Fully unfold'. He is not using *character* in our sense of inner qualities, but as the outer marks that can indicate what lies within, in this case rather like a secret code as in a primitive runic alphabet. In the next scene Claudio also uses *character* to mean 'external sign' when he refers to his girl-friend's pregnancy: 'The stealth of our most mutual entertainment/With character too gross is writ on Juliet'. In many of Shakespeare's plays, chiefly those about kings and heroes, fame is an important issue, and great exploits can be recorded in poems, chronicles, and monuments. All these require 'characters' to be read and interpreted by future generations. In a play from outside our list of texts, **Troilus and Cressida**, the heroine, expressing the enduring quality of her love, insists that it will outlive all the written records of conventional fame: 'When…mighty states characterless are grated/To dusty nothing'. It was not until the late 17th century that *character* was extended from outward marks to describe the qualities that make up the whole personality. Also at this time *character* acquired the specific sense of 'a part taken by an actor in a play'.

charactery *noun* something that is written (*JC ii 1*)

characts *plural noun* the distinguishing features of someone (*MM v 1*)

chare *noun* **1.** a job or task (*AC v 2*) **2.** occasional work (*AC iv 15, v 2*)

charge *noun* **1.** a burden or responsibility (*MA i 1*; *WT i 2*) **2.** baggage (*1H4 ii 1*) **3.** importance (*WT iv 4*) **4.** expense or cost (*R3 i 2*; *MV iv 1*) **5.** an order or command (*T v 1*; *R3 i 1*) **6.** troops under someone's command (*1H4 i 1, ii 4*; *JC iv 2*) ■ *adjective* ready to attack (*2H4 iv 1*) ■ *verb* **1.** to place a burden or responsibility on someone (*H5 i 2*; *M v 1*) **2.** to aim a weapon (*MA v 1*) **3.** to order or command someone to do something (*MV v 1*) **4.** to sexually assault someone (*2H4 ii 4*) ◇ **parcels of charge** valuables (*RJ v 2*)

chargeful *adjective* expensive (*CE iv 1*)

charge of foot *noun* a company of infantry soldiers (*JC iv 2*; *1H4 ii 4*)

chariest *adjective* most careful (*H i 3*)

Charles' wain *noun* the group of stars called the Plough (*1H4 ii 1*) [The name is a corruption of *churl's wain*, 'peasant's cart'.]

charm *noun* **1.** a bewitching person or thing (*AC iv 12*; *O v 1*) **2.** a spell (*T v 1*; *KL v 3*; *RJ ii Prol.*) ■ *verb* to call upon or beg someone to do something (*JC ii 1*) ◇ **charm my tongue** keep quiet (*JC ii 1*)

charmed *adjective* having magical properties (*M iv 1, v 8*)

charmer *noun* someone who uses magic (*O iii 4*)

charnel-house *noun* a place where bodies or bones are kept (*RJ iv 1*; *M iii 4*)

charter *noun* a granted right or privilege, permission

chary *adjective* wary or cautious (*H i 3*)

Charybdis *noun* in Greek mythology, a creature that lived under a fig tree on a rock opposite the island of Scylla. He would swallow the sea there three times a day and vomit it out again. (*MV iii 5*) (NOTE: The location is the strait between mainland Italy and Sicily that was noted for its treacherous currents.)

chase *noun* **1.** a pursuit or hunt **2.** the logic of an argument (*AYLI i 3*) ■ *verb* to harass someone (*WT v 1*) ◇ **chas'd your blood Out of appearance** caused your face to become pale (*H5 ii 2*) *See also* **chace**

chased *adjective* virginal, sexually pure (*H5 i 2, v 2*; *MV ii 6*)

chastity *noun* **1.** virginity (*AYLI iii 4*; *MM ii 4, v 1*; *RJ i 1*; *TS ii 1*) **2.** the state of being faithful to one's husband or wife (*AC i 1*; *O v 1*)

Chaucer, Geoffrey *noun* (1342/43–1400) the son of a London wine-merchant, he served in the army in France and then as a court official. One of his major works is the romance *Troilus and Cresyde* but his most famous work is the *Canterbury Tales* in which the stories told by the pilgrims from London to Canterbury are recorded.

chaudron, chawdron *noun* the intestine (*M iv 1*)

cheapen *verb* to bid or suggest a price for something (*MA ii 3*)

cheat *noun* a fraud (*WT iv 3*)

cheator, cheater *noun* an officer that controls property that falls to a feudal lord because there is no heir or that has been confiscated (*2H4 ii 4*)

check *noun* a reprimand (*AC iv 4*; *O ii 3, iii 3, iv 3*) ■ *verb* **1.** to rebuke someone (*JC iv 3*; *KL ii 2*) **2.** to no longer continue in something (*H iv 7*)

check at *verb* to slow or swerve in readiness to jump (*TN ii 5, iii 1*) [From a hawking term referring to an occasion when the hawk is distracted by unwanted prey.]

cheer *noun* **1.** the appearance of someone's face (*MND iii 2*; *MV iii 2*) **2.** happiness (*MA i 3*; *H i 2*) **3.** a warm welcome (*CE iii 1*) ■ *verb* **1.** to greet joyfully (*MND iv 1*) **2.** to encourage someone to do something

cheerly *adverb* happily or joyfully (*AYLI ii 6*; *R3 v 2*; *RJ i 5*; *T i 1*)

cherish *verb* to care for someone or something (*1H4 iii 3*)

cherry pit *noun* a children's game in which cherry stones are thrown into a small hole (*TN iii 4*)

Chertsey *noun* a town in Surrey, and the site of an ancient abbey (*R3 i 2*)

cherubin *noun* an angel (*T i 2*; *O iv 2*) [Specifically one of the nine orders of angels in the traditional Christian hierarchy.]

cheveril, cheverel *noun* a soft, flexible leather made from the skin of a young goat (*RJ ii 4*) ■ *adjective* flexible like soft leather (*TN iii 1*)

che vor' ye *interjection* I warn you (*KL iv 6*)

chew *verb* to mutter or mumble (*MM ii 4*)

chewet *noun* a pie made of minced beef and is an allusion to Falstaff's gluttony (*1H4 v 1*) (NOTE: *Chewet* is in its normal sense an alternative word for **chough**.)

chick *noun* a term of endearment (*T v 1*)

chicken *noun* a child (*M iv 3*)

chide *verb* to strike something noisily (*1H4 iii 1*)

chiding *adjective* creating a disturbance (*MND iv 1*; *AYLI ii 1*)

child *noun* **1.** a baby girl (*T v 1*; *MA iv 1*; *WT iii 3*; *KL iv 7*) **2.** a candidate for knighthood (*KL iii 4*)

child-changed *adjective* treated like a child (*KL iv 7*)

childed *adjective* having children (*KL iii 6*)

Childeric *noun* a king of the Merovingian dynasty which ruled parts of Germany and Gaul (in France) c. 500–750. (*H5 i 2*)

childing *adjective* producing fruits, abundant (*MND ii 1*)

childness *noun* the quality of being like a child (*WT i 2*)

chill *phrase* I will (*KL iv 6*)

chinks *plural noun* money (*RJ i 5*)

chip *verb* to cut the crust off a loaf of bread (*2H4 ii 4*)

chirugeonly *adverb* like a surgeon (*T ii 1*)

chivalry *noun* **1.** bravery (*1H4 v 1*; *R2 i 1*) **2.** mounted men-at-arms (*H5 i 2*)

choice *adjective* excellent (*JC iii 1*)

choice-drawn, choicely *adjective* carefully selected (*H5 iii Chor.*)

choke *verb* **1.** to smother or impede something (*R2 iii 4*; *M i 2*) **2.** to silence something (*TS ii 1*)

chop *adjective* fat cheeks (*1H4 i 2*; *2H4 ii 4*; *M i 2*) ■ *verb* to kill someone or something (*R3 i 4*)

chop-fallen *adjective* sad and miserable, with a dejected expression (*H v 1*)

chopine *noun* a high clog with a cork sole, introduced from Venice to England during the Elizabethan period (*H ii 2*)

chopless *adjective* without a lower jaw (*H v 1*)

chop-logic *noun* an argument based on a mistaken belief (*RJ iii 5*)

chopped, choppy *adjective* chapped or cracked and sore (*AYLI ii 4*; *M i 3*)

chopping *adjective* marked by constant changes to words, meanings, or an argument (*R2 v 3*)

chorus *noun* in the ancient Greek theatre the chorus was a group of singers or dancers, but by Shakespeare's time they were reduced to a single person who introduced a play or act and commented on its progress (*WT iv 1*; *H iii 2*)

chough *noun* a bird resembling a crow that lives in mountains and cliffs (*H v 2*; *KL iv 6*; *M iii 4*; *T ii 1*)

Christen *adjective* Christian (*1H4 ii 1*)

Christendom *noun* Christianity

christom child *noun* an innocent child (*H5 ii 3*) [From the idea of a child in its christening robe, *christom* being mistaken for *christening*]

chronicled *adjective* recorded in history (*MND iii 2*)

chrysolite *noun* a yellow or green semi-precious stone (*O v 2*)

chuff *noun* a surly miser (*1H4 ii 2*)

church ◇ **go to church** to be married (*MA ii 1, iii 4*; *RJ ii 5*) ◇ **like a church** slowly (*2H4 ii 4*) ◇ **old church** still in the corrupt old ways (*2H4 ii 2*)

churchman *noun* a priest (*TN iii 1*; *R3 iii 7*)

churl *noun* a loutish, ill-mannered person (*CE iii 1*; *RJ v 3*)

churlish *adjective* **1.** rough or brutal (*AYLI ii 1, v 4*; *1H4 v 1*; *H5 iv 1*; *H v 1*) **2.** miserly (*AYLI ii 4*)

cicatrice *noun* a scar formed on a wound (*AYLI iii 5*; *H iv 3*)

cinders of the elements *plural noun* stars (*2H4 iv 3*)

cinque-pace *noun* a lively dance based on five beats (*MA ii 1*; *TN i 3*) [From French *cinque pas*.]

cipher *noun* the number 0 (zero) (*AYLI iii 2*; *MM ii 2*; *H5 Prol.*)

Circe *noun* in Greek mythology, a sorceress who lived on the island of Aeaea (*CE v 1*)

circle *noun* **1.** a crown (*AC iii 12*) **2.** a boundary (*AYLI v 4*) **3.** a magic circle (a play on the female genitals) (*AYLI ii 5*; *H5 v 2*; *RJ ii 1*)

circummured *adjective* enclosed by a wall (*MM v 1*)

circumstance *noun* **1.** the use of more words than is necessary to express an idea (*CE v 1*; *RJ v 3*) **2.** an accident (*WT iii 2*) **3.** a ceremony (*TS v 1*; *WT v 1*; *H i 5*) **4.** an associated fact connected with an action and possibly forming evidence (*TN iii 4*; *MM iv 2*; *WT v 2*; *R3 i 2*; *RJ iii 3*; *H ii 2, iii 2*; *O iii 3*)

circumstanced *adjective* subject to circumstances (*O iii 4*)

circumstantial *adjective* indirect (*AYLI v 4*)

cital *noun* a mention or account of something (*1H4 v 2*)

cite *verb* to enumerate or list something (*H5 v 2*; *R3 i 4*; *MV i 3*)

city-woman *noun* the wife of a citizen (*AYLI ii 7*)

civet *noun* the perfume extracted from a substance produced by the civet cat (*AYLI iii 2*; *KL iv 6*)

civil *adjective* **1.** orderly (*H5 i 2*; *AC v 1*) **2.** of citizens (*RJ Prol.*) **3.** of civil war (*R2 iii 3*; *AC i 3*) **4.** of civil law (*MV v 1*)

clack-dish *noun* a covered dish used by beggars to collect money. They would rattle the lid to attract attention. (*MM iii 2*)

clamour *verb* to silence something (*WT iv 4*) [From a method of suddenly stopping bells ringing.]

clap *verb* **1.** to slap hands together to seal a bargain (*TS ii 1*; *WT i 2*; *H5 v 2*) **2.** to move something vigorously (*2H4 iii 2*; *R2 iii 2*) ◇ **at a clap** at one attempt (*L i 4*)

clap into *verb* to get on with or be quick about something (*MA iii 4*; *MM iv 3*; *AYLI v 3*)

clap to *verb* to shut something quickly (*1H4 ii 4*)

clap up *verb* to put someone in prison (*AC iv 2*)

claw *verb* to flatter someone (*MA i 3*)

cleanly *adjective* skilful (*1H4 ii 4*) ■ *adverb* skilfully

clear *verb* to settle a debt (*AYLI i 1*; *WT i 2, iii 1*; *MV iii 2*) ■ *adjective* **1.** innocent or without blame (*T iii 3*; *TS ii 1*; *M i 7*; *AC v 2*) **2.** bright (*MM iv 2*) **3.** cheerful (*MND iii 2*; *WT i 2*) **4.** glorious or splendid (*MV ii 9*; *KL iv 6*) ■ *adverb* happily (*M i 5*)

clearness *noun* innocence (*M iii 1*)

cleave the pin *verb* to hit a pin in the centre of a target (*RJ ii 4*)

clef *noun* a note in music (*TS iii 1*)

clepe *verb* to call something by a particular name (*M iii 1; H i 4*)

clerestory *noun* the upper storey of a building, especially a cathedral, with its own windows (*TN iv 2*)

clerk *noun* **1.** someone who can write (*MA ii 1; MV v 1; TS iv 4*) **2.** a scholar (*MND v 1*)

COMMENT: When Richard II asks ironically, 'Am I both priest and clerk?' *clerk* means 'an assistant or server at the altar'. Today the word has all but lost its strong religious meaning and indicates simply that the assistant is literate and may act as a secretary. The word's origin in the Latin 'clericus' used to carry far more status, that of a learned man, more of a rarity in medieval society; Henry I although a king and therefore with the highest status, was flattered by the epithet 'Beau-clerc'. But even in Shakespeare's time *clerk* could still convey the status of high learning. In **A Midsummer Night's Dream** Theseus tells Hippolyta, 'Where I have come, great clerks have purposed/To greet me with premeditated welcomes'. In some Celtic languages, 'clar', the harp, indicated the *clerk's* musical duties in the religious service. The relic of this meaning appears in **Much Ado About Nothing** when Margaret in the dance orders her partner to 'Answer, clerk', to say 'Amen' as a prayer-leader should.

clerk(l)y *adjective* scholarly

cliff *noun* a woman's breast (*CE iii 2*)

climate *noun* **1.** a region (*H5 iii 5; O i 1; T ii 1*) **2.** a country (*R2 iv 1; JC i 3*) ■ *verb* to live or stay in a place (*WT v 1*)

climatures *plural noun* regions or territories (*H i 1*)

climb *verb* to get to something by climbing (*RJ ii 5*)

cling *verb* to shrivel someone or something up (*M v 5*)

clip *verb* **1.** to hold someone or something firmly (*AC iv 8, v 2*) **2.** to embrace someone (*WT v 2; 1H4 iii 1; O iii 3; AC iv 8, v 2*)

clipped *adjective* shortened (*KL iv 7*)

clipper *noun* someone who cut off pieces of coins for their metal. This was a criminal offence punishable by having the ears cut off. Later, the edges of coins were marked with ridges ('milled') to prevent clipping. (*H5 iv 1*)

clisterpipe *noun* same as **clyster-pipe** (*O ii 1*)

cloak-bag *noun* a large travelling bag (*1H4 ii 4*)

clock ◇ **tell the clock** count the chimes of the clock (*T ii 1; R3 v 3*)

clodpole *noun* a stupid person (*TN iii 4*)

cloistered *adjective* confined or restricted (*M iii 2*)

cloistress *noun* a nun belonging to an order cut off from the outside world (*TN i 1*)

close *noun* **1.** the act of joining things together (*TN v 1*) **2.** a struggle (*1H4 i 1*) **3.** the final notes of a piece of music (*H5 i 2; R2 ii 1*) ■ *verb* **1.** to join together or unite (*H5 i 2; M iii 2*) **2.** to enclose something (*M iii 1*) **3.** to join hands (*RJ ii 6*) **4.** to grapple (*2H4 iv 1*) **5.** to agree (*JC iii 1; H ii 1*) ■ *adjective* tense or secret (*MM iv 3; 1H4 ii 3; R3 i 1; M iii 5*) ■ *adverb* secretly (*TS Ind. 1*)

closely *adverb* **1.** securely (*TS i 1; R3 i 1*) **2.** secretly (*RJ v 3; H iii 1*)

closeness *noun* the state of being in seclusion or on one's own (*T i 2*)

close-stool *noun* a chamber pot inside a wooden seat

closet *noun* **1.** a small private room (*H5 v 2; JC ii 1*) **2.** a small chest for private papers, etc. (*JC iii 2; KL iii 3; M v 1*)

Clothair *noun* a king of the Merovingian dynasty which ruled parts of Germany and Gaul (in France) c. 500–750. (*H5 i 2*)

clothier's yard *noun* an arrow. Cloth was measured by the clothier's yard that was 37 inches (0.93 m) rather than 36 inches (0.90 m). This was the length of the English arrow. (*KL iv 6*)

cloth of gold *noun* a fabric woven with gold thread (*AC ii 2*)

cloud *noun* a mark between the eyes of a horse, regarded as a blemish (*AC iii 2*)

clouded *adjective* maligned or spoken ill of (*WT i 2*)

clout *noun* **1.** a piece of cloth (*R3 i 3; RJ ii 4; H ii 2*) **2.** the square of cloth at the centre of a target (*2H4 iii 2; KL iv 6*)

cloyed *adjective* full or gorged (*H5 ii 2; 2H4 Epil.*)

cloyless *adjective* not full, still hungry (*AC ii 1*)

cloyment *noun* the condition of feeling full or gorged (*TN ii 4*)

clubs *interjection* a cry for help when being attacked by thieves (*RJ i 1*)

clutch *verb* to clench something in anger (*MM iii 2*)

clyster-pipe *noun* a syringe used for giving someone an enema (*O ii 1*)

coals ◇ **carry coals** to do the dirty work (*H5 iii 2*; *RJ i 1*)

coat *noun* **1.** a protective coat of mail or leather (*1H4 iv 1*; *R2 i 3*) **2.** a coat-of-arms (*MND ii 2*)

cock *noun* **1.** a weather-vane (*KL iii 2*) **2.** a small, light boat (*KL iv 6*) **3.** the trigger on a gun (*H5 ii 1 – a play on cock = penis*; *WT iv 3*) **4.** a version of 'God' used as an oath (*TS iv 1*; *2H4 v 1*; *H iv 5*)

cock-a-hoop ◇ **to set cock-a-hoop** to lose all restraints or inhibitions (*RJ i 5*)

cock-and-pie *noun* an oath (*2H4 v 1*)

cockatrice *noun* a mythical monster with a serpent's body, a cockerel's head, and a bird's wings. Its gaze was said to be fatal. (*TN iii 4*; *RJ iii 2*)

cockle *noun* a seashell (*TS iv 3*)

cockle-hat *noun* a pilgrim's hat bearing a shell as a sign of a pilgrimage made to the shrine of St James at Compostella in Spain (*H iv 5*)

cockney *noun* **1.** someone who is born in a city and who knows nothing outside it, and is therefore regarded as affected or effeminate (*TN iv 1*) (NOTE: Strictly a cockney is someone who is born within the sound of the bells of Bow Church, in East London. The term was extended by Shakespeare.) **2.** a squeamish cook who makes exaggerated expressions of fear (*KL ii 4*)

COMMENT: The word is derived from 'cockerel's egg', an egg without a yolk, written as *cockenay* in Middle English. Therefore it had a derisive meaning of 'foolish', or, in some uses, 'effeminate'. In **King Lear** the Fool urges Lear: 'Cry to it, Nuncle, as the cockney did to the eels, when she put 'em i' th' paste alive; she knapp'd 'em o' the coxcombs with a stick, and cried "Down, wantons, down!"' Folly is certainly the predominant meaning, and the Fool wants to apply this to Lear's misguided past. Effeminacy may also be implied because the woman in his story was too squeamish to kill the eels before starting to cook them. In Act 4 of **Twelfth Night** Feste mocks what he takes to be Sebastian's pedantic speech: 'I am afraid this great lubber the world will prove a cockney'. Both these examples of *cockney* convey a town-dweller's affectation and limited awareness of basic country life. *Cockney* had become attached to towns from the early 16th century, and after 1890 specifically to the speech from an area of east London. The sense of effeminacy has now gone; cockneys today are extremely street-wise.

cock-pit *noun* a round theatre (*H5 Prol.*) [Literally the small round area that was used for cock-fighting]

cock-shut time *noun* the time when chickens are shut up for the night, twilight (*R3 v 3*)

cock-sure *adverb* with absolute safety (*1H4 ii 1*)

cod *noun* this usually refers to a **codpiece** and so has a sexual connotation (*AYLI ii 4*; *O ii 1*)

codling *noun* a small or immature apple (*TN i 5*)

codpiece *noun* a pouch on the front of a man's trousers (*MA iii 3*; *MM iii 2*)

coffer *noun* **1.** a money chest (*2H4 i 1*; *H5 i 1*; *JC iii 2*; *MV iv 1*) **2.** a piece of luggage (*TS ii 1*) **3.** money (*TN iii 4*)

cog *verb* to cheat (*MA v 1*)

cogging *adjective* cheating (*O iv 2*)

cognizance *noun* a badge worn by servants or retainers (*JC ii 2*)

cohere *verb* to agree or be consistent with something (*MM ii 1*; *TN v 1*)

coherence *noun* agreement (*2H4 v 1*)

cohort *noun* a band of soldiers (*KL i 2*) [From *cohort*, 'one of the ten sections of a Roman legion'.]

coign *noun* the corner-stone of a building (*M i 6*)

coining *noun* the practice of making (minting) coins (*KL iv 6*)

coistrel *noun* a scoundrel (*TN i 3*)

Colchos *noun* Colchis, the place in Greek mythology where Jason found the Golden Fleece (*MV i 1*)

collar *noun* a hangman's noose (*2H4 v 5*)

collateral *adjective* indirect (*H iv 5*) (NOTE: The planets were thought to move in parallel orbits (**collaterally**) according to the ancient Greek astronomer Ptolemy, a theory displaced by the one now current, devised by the Polish astronomer Copernicus in 1543.)

colleagued, co-leagued *adjective* joined together, allied (*H i 2*)

collection *noun* an inference (*H iv 5*)

collied *adjective* 1. covered in soot, black (*MND i 1*) 2. overcast and troubled (*O ii 3*)

collop *noun* a term of endearment for a child (*WT i 2*) [From *collop*, 'a slice of meat', suggesting a piece of a man, i.e. his child.]

Colme-kill *noun* St Columba's cell on the island of Iona in Scotland (*M ii 4*)

coloquintida *noun* the colocynth, a plant related to the marrow which produces a bitter-tasting gourd from which a laxative was extracted (*O i 3*)

Colossus *noun* a huge statue of the Greek sun-god Helios at Rhodes (*JC i 2*) (NOTE: It is about 30m in height and one of the Seven Wonders of the World. It was completed c. 280 BC and destroyed by an earthquake in 224 BC. The description of the statue standing astride the harbour originated in the 16th century.)

colour *noun* 1. a military flag (*TN i 5*) 2. an excuse (*AC i 3*; *2H4 v 5*) 3. a type or kind (*AYLI i 2*; *KL ii 2*) ■ *verb* 1. to disguise something (*MM ii 1*; *1H4 i 3*; *H iii 1*) 2. to dye something (*TS iv 1*)

colt *noun* a young person (*MV i 2*) ■ *verb* to cheat or trick someone (*1H4 ii 2*)

comart *noun* a bargain or agreement (*H i 1*)

combat *noun* a duel or fight between two people (*H i 1*)

combinate *adjective* formally engaged to be married (*MM iii 1*)

combination *noun* a treaty (*TN v 1*; *H iii 4*)

combine *verb* to commit or oblige someone to do something (*MM iv 3*; *AYLI v 4*)

combustion *noun* a riot (*M ii 3*)

come *verb* to give way or relent (*MM ii 2*)

come about *verb* 1. to change direction (*MV ii 6*) 2. to be shown to be true (*RJ i 3*)

come away *interjection* come along! (*1H4 ii 1*)

come by *verb* to take possession of something (*T ii 1*)

come by one's own *verb* to retrieve one's property (*2H4 ii 1*)

comeddle *verb* to mix or mingle together (*H iii 2*)

comedian, commedian *noun* an actor (*TN i 5*)

come from thy ward *interjection* drop your defensive attitude (*T i 2*)

come home *verb* to drag something away from its secure base (*WT i 2*)

come in *verb* in fencing, to get behind one's opponent's guard (*2H4 iii 2*)

comely *adjective* graceful or respectable (*AYLI ii 3*; *MA iv 1, v 2*)

come near *verb* to affect someone deeply (*AYLI v 2*; *O iv 1*)

come off *verb* to get away or leave (*AYLI i 2*; *2H4 ii 4*)

come over *verb* 1. to exceed or do better than someone or something (*MA v 2*) 2. to tease someone (*H5 i 2*)

come roundly *verb* to speak plainly (*TS i 2*)

come short, come slack *verb* to fail to achieve something (*MM v 1*; *KL i 3*)

come to oneself *verb* to regain consciousness (*JC i 2*)

come up *verb* to rise to (*WT ii 1*)

comfit *noun* a small sweet or sugar-coated seed (*1H4 iii 1*)

comfortable *adjective* 1. helpful (*RJ v 3*; *KL i 4*) 2. cheerful (*AYLI ii 6*)

comfortless *adjective* 1. not able to be comforted (*CE v 1*) 2. giving no comfort (*KL iii 7*)

coming-in *noun* 1. the future (*MV ii 2*) 2. income or money (*H5 iv 1*; *MV ii 2* (*a pun on having sexual intercourse with*))

coming-on *adjective* agreeable (*AYLI iv 1*)

comma *noun* a short break or pause (*H v 2*)

commandment ◇ **at commandment** at the command or orders of someone (*2H4 iii 2, v 3*; *MV ii 2*)

commence *verb* to qualify someone for something (*2H4 iv 3*) (NOTE: Specifically 'to admit to a university degree'.)

commend *verb* 1. to entrust someone or something to the care of someone 2. to convey greetings (*MM i 4*; *MV iii 2*; *H i 5*)

commends *noun* greetings or compliments (*R2 iii 1*)

comment *noun* regard or consideration (*H iii 2*)

commenting *noun* considering or pondering (*R3 iv 3*)

commerce *noun* a discussion, or dealings about something (*TN iii 4*; *H iii 1*)

commission *noun* **1.** a document giving someone the authority to do something (*RJ iv 1*) **2.** an order (*MM i 1*; *KL v 3*) **3.** a group of people acting jointly with authority (*KL iii 6*) ◇ **in commission** given a position of authority (*2H4 iii 2*; *M i 4*)

commit *verb* to commit adultery (*MND ii 1*; *KL iii 4*)

commodity *noun* **1.** advantage or benefit (*2H4 i 2*) **2.** profit (*KL iv 1*) **3.** convenience (*WT iii 2*; *MV iii 3*) **4.** goods, especially when sold on credit and re-sold at a lower price to repay the lender (*MM iv 3*; *TN iii 1*)

common *noun* **1.** land for use by the whole community (*CE ii 2*; *JC iv 1*) **2.** the common people (*R2 ii 1*) **3.** ordinary language (*AYLI v 1*) ■ *adjective* **1.** owned or used by everyone (*MM iv 2*; *MA iv 1*; *AYLI ii 3*; *1H4 ii 1*; *M iii 1*) **2.** of the people (*CE iii 1*; *2H4 ii 3*)

commonality *noun* the common people

common bosom *noun* the opinion of the common people (*KL v 3*)

commoner *noun* a prostitute (*O iv 2*)

common-hackneyed *adjective* made common or vulgar (*1H4 iii 2*)

common house *noun* a brothel (*MM ii 1*)

commonty *noun* a comedy (*TS Ind. 2*)

commotion *noun* a riot or uprising (*2H4 ii 4*)

commune *verb* **1.** to talk (*TS i 1*; *MM iv 3*; *WT ii 1*) **2.** to share or take part in (*H iv 5*)

community *noun* familiarity (*1H4 iii 2*)

commutual *adjective* reciprocal (*H iii 2*)

compact *verb* to strengthen or support something (*KL i 4*) ■ *adjective* joined closely (*KL i 2*) ■ *preposition* **1.** made up or composed of (*MND v 1*; *CE iii 2*; *AYLI ii 7*; *TS Ind. 2*) **2.** in league with (*MM v 1*)

companion *noun* an unworthy person (*CE iv 4*; *2H4 ii 4*) (NOTE: This is used sarcastically.)

comparative *noun* an abusive person (*1H4 i 2, iii 2*) ■ *adjective* skilled at making uncomplimentary comparisons (*1H4 i 2*)

comparision *noun* an advantage when compared with something else (*MA ii 1*; *AC iii 13*)

comparisons

COMMENT: Shakespeare sometimes differed from our ways of expressing comparison. For example, he would often use two words for emphasis: 'more better' for our 'better'; 'more nearer'; 'most heaviest'; and in **Julius Caesar** 'this was the most unkindest cut of all', when Antony shows Caesar's mutilated body to the crowd. All these examples make their comparison by adding the inflection '-er' or '-est' to the adjective, and then adding the extra force of 'more' or 'most'. Sometimes he uses the inflected form on its own, where we would simply add 'more' or 'most': 'perfecter', instead of our 'more perfect'; 'quicklier', instead of 'more quickly'. In **As You Like It** Rosalind, as the boy Ganymede, describes a woman's complicated behaviour: 'the wiser, the waywarder. Make the doors upon a woman's wit, and it will out at the casement'. Her 'waywarder' feels more vivid than our 'more wayward', because it seems to convey more erratic energy. Occasionally, Shakespeare would create a comparison when our word doesn't seem to allow one: Hamlet speaks of 'worser part'; and in **Love's Labours Lost** Holofernes creates the distinctly odd 'ratherest', but he is a pedant excessively given to word-play and word-invention. Shakespeare is here using a refreshing Elizabethan freedom to adjust commonly accepted language for his immediate needs. Very often he is writing in verse and so the metre of the line sometimes calls for an extra syllable, which can often be achieved by using these unusual forms of comparison.

compass *noun* **1.** a circle (*JC v 3*) **2.** a boundary or limit (*R2 iii 4*; *O iii 4*) ■ *verb* to obtain or achieve something (*WT iv 3*; *TN i 2*; *H5 v 1*; *T iii 2*)

compassed *adjective* curved or bent (*TS iv 3*)

compeer *verb* to be as good as someone (*KL v 3*)

compel *verb* to take something by force (*H5 iii 6*)

compelled *adjective* involuntary (*MM ii 4*)

competence *adjective* sufficient to live on (*2H4 v 5*)

competency *noun* moderation (*MV i 2*)

competent *adjective* sufficient or adequate (*TN iii 4*; *H i 1*)

competitor *noun* a partner (*R3 iv 4*; *AC v 1*)

complain(t) *verb* to express sadness about something (*R2 iii 4*; *RJ ii Prol.*)

complement *noun* 1. things such as action or dress which show that someone is a gentleman (*H5 iii 2*) 2. a courteous act (*MA iv 1*; *KL i 1*)

complexion *noun* 1. behaviour (*AYLI iii 2*) 2. natural disposition or temperament (*MA ii 1*; *MV iii 1*) 3. the appearance of something, especially someone's face (*T i 1*; *CE iii 2*; *WT i 2*; *H5 ii 2*; *O iv 2*) 4. someone's general health (*H v 2*)

COMMENT: Elizabethan writers often used *complexion* in its old sense of how a person's nature is composed, or, as we would say, their temperament. Medical theory in the Middle Ages believed that the body was composed of four fluids, or 'humours'. Each person had his own mixed proportions of humours, often with one of them dominating the rest. The resulting *complexion* might be described, for example, as 'sanguine' or 'phlegmatic'. Hamlet explains to Horatio that no one can choose 'the o'er-growth of some complexion' within him, but its effects can be disturbing, 'Oft breaking down the pales and forts of reason'. Later, in a lighter satirical mood he tells Osric that the day 'is very hot and sultry for my complexion'. In **Measure for Measure**, when the Duke soothes and reassures Isabella, he declares that 'grace, being the soul of your complexion, shall keep the body of it ever fair'. Thus, Isabella's external appearance will show her inner nature. From this usage, *complexion* came to apply to the face. In **Henry V** the king shocks the traitors who go pale when they read the details of their conspiracy: 'What see you in those papers that you lose/So much complexion?'. An observer's ability to read the inner man from the outer look of him is used in simile when Scroop brings bad news to Richard II: 'Men judge by the complexion of the sky/The state and inclination of the day'. However, today we have generally limited the use of *complexion* to apply to superficial skin colouring.

complice *noun* a friend or associate (*R2 ii 3*)

complot *noun* a conspiracy (*R3 iii 1*) ■ *verb* to conspire together (*R2 i 1, 3*)

comply *verb* 1. to observe the required formalities (*H ii 2*) 2. to accomplish something (*O i 3*)

compose *verb* 1. to produce something (*MND i 1*; *M i 7*) 2. to agree (*AC ii 2*)

composition *noun* 1. an agreement or truce (*MM i 2*; *M i 2*; *AC ii 6*) 2. the nature of someone or something (*KL ii 2*) 3. consistency (*O i 3*)

composure *noun* temperament (*AC i 4*)

compound *noun* a block or lump (*1H4 ii 4*; *2H4 ii 4*) ■ *verb* 1. to make up or form something (*H5 v 2*) 2. to reach an agreement (*TS i 2*; *MM iv 2*; *R3 ii 1*) 3. to mix together (*RJ v 1*; *H iii 4*) 4. to have sexual intercourse with someone (*KL i 2*)

comprehend *verb* to arrest someone (*MA iii 3*) (NOTE: A misuse for 'apprehend'.)

compromise *noun* the settling of an argument either by making concessions or with the help of an independent advisor (*R2 ii 1*) ■ *verb* to reach agreement through compromise (*MV i 3*)

compt *adverb* in trust (*M i 6*) ■ *noun* the Day of Judgement (*O v 2*)

compter *noun* a disc used to assist in doing calculations (**counter**) (*WT iv 3*)

comptible *adjective* sensitive or easily hurt (*TN i 5*)

compulsatory *adjective* using force (*H i 1*)

compulsive *adjective* forceful or irresistible (*H iii 4*; *O iii 3*)

compunctious *adjective* regretting past actions (*M i 5*)

con *verb* 1. to learn (*MND i 2*; *JC iv 3*) 2. to learn or understand something (*TN ii 3*) See also **to con thanks** *at* **thanks**

concealed *adjective* secretly married (*RJ iii 3*)

concealment *noun* a secret (*KL iv 3*; *TN ii 4*) ◇ **profited in strange concealments** expert in magic arts (*1H4 iii 1*)

conceit *noun* **1.** an idea (*MV i 1, iii 4*; *O iii 3*) **2.** mental ability (*AYLI v 2*; *CE iv 2*) **3.** imagination (*AYLI ii 6*; *2H4 ii 4*; *R2 ii 2*) **4.** an opinion **5.** a small gift or trinket (*MND i 1*) **6.** an invention (*H v 2*) ■ *verb* to form an idea (*JC i 3*)

COMMENT: *Conceit* has slightly shifted its meaning but strikingly changed its tone since Shakespeare's time. Nowadays we use 'conceited' to show that we don't like someone showing off their cleverness. But Shakespeare and his contemporaries would be pleased if you were startled by *conceits* in their work. The word suggests imagination, brilliant comparisons, unusual ideas – the results of a very lively intellect. The Metaphysical poets of the early 17th century were noted for their inventive *conceits*. Most of the heroes and heroines in Shakespeare's comedies are also intelligent in this way: Beatrice, Benedick, Berowne, Rosalind. And clowns like Feste, Lear's Fool and Touchstone make a profession out of their *conceits*. Hamlet is impressed by the Player, who can 'force his soul so to his own conceit', meaning that the actor has a strong imaginative idea and then is totally absorbed in performing it. Occasionally the word can suggest something negative as when someone young or very sensitive is too much driven by their imagination. The child Mamilius in **The Winter's Tale** worries that his mother has died: he suffers from 'mere conceit and fear' of losing her.

conceited *adjective* **1.** formulated or thought up (*2H4 v 1*) **2.** having an idea (*TN iii 4*) ◇ **well conceited** witty (*2H4 v 1*)

conceive *verb* to understand someone or something (*MM ii 4*; *MND iv 1*)

conception *noun* an idea or fancy (*MM ii 4*; *O iii 4*)

concernancy *noun* the relevance of something (*H v 2*)

conclusion *noun* an experiment (*H iii 4*; *AC v 2*; *O i 3*)

concupiscible *adjective* desiring sexually (*MM v 1*)

condemn *verb* to discredit something (*AC v 2*)

condition *noun* **1.** a person's place in society (*T iii 1*; *2H4 iv 3*; *H5 iv 3*) **2.** a character (*MA iii 2*; *TS v 2*) **3.** temperament (*MV i 2*)

condole *verb* **1.** to grieve (*MND i 2*) **2.** to sympathise or grieve with someone (*H5 ii 1*)

condolement *noun* grief (*H i 2*)

conduct *noun* **1.** a guide or leader (*T v 1*; *RJ v 3*) **2.** guidance or leadership (*AYLI v 4*; *L iii 6*; *2H4 v 2*) **3.** an escort (*TN iii 4*; *1H4 iii 1*; *R3 i 1*)

conductor *noun* a leader (*KL iv 7*)

conduit *noun* **1.** a water-pipe (*RJ iii 5*) **2.** a channel (*CE v 1*)

conference *noun* a conversation or debate (*JC i 2, iv 2*)

confidence *noun* same as **conference** (*MA iii 5*; *RJ ii 4*)

confine *noun* **1.** a boundary or limit (*RJ iii 1*; *O i 2*) **2.** a region or country (*R2 i 3*; *R3 iv 4*) **3.** a prison (*T iv 1*; *H i 1*; *AC iii 5*) ■ *verb* to banish someone (*WT ii 1*)

confineless *adjective* having no boundaries (*M iv 3*)

confirmed *adjective* set or fixed (*MA ii 1, iv 1, v 4*)

confirmities *plural noun* infirmities (*2H4 ii 4*)

confix *verb* to join or fasten something securely (*MM v 1*)

conformable *adjective* submissive (*TS ii 1*)

confound *verb* **1.** to ruin or spoil something (*H5 iv 5*; *AC ii 5, iii 2*) **2.** to spend time (*1H4 i 3*; *AC i 1*) **3.** to form a uniform mixture (*R2 iv 1*) ■ *adjective* ruined or destroyed (*H5 iii 1*)

confusion *noun* **1.** destruction (*CE ii 2*; *KL ii 4*; *M iii 5*) **2.** a noisy disturbance (*RJ iv 5*) **3.** a mental upset (*MV iii 2*; *H iii 1*)

congee, congie *noun* a ceremonial bow, especially when leaving

conger *noun* a large eel that lives in the sea (*2H4 ii 4*)

congree *verb* to agree (*H5 i 2*)

congreet *verb* to greet one another (*H5 v 2*)

congrue *verb* to agree (*H iv 3*)

conject *verb* to give an opinion not based on evidence (*O iii 3*)

conjecture *noun* a suspicion (*MA iv 1*; *WT ii 1*; *H iv 5*)

conjuction *noun* **1.** a united force (*1H4 iv 1*) **2.** the situation in which two planets appear to be together when seen from the earth, or when they are in the same sign of the zodiac (*2H4 ii 4*)

conjunct *adjective* closely connected with someone (*KL ii 2, v 1*)

conjunctive *adjective* united (*H iv 7; O i 3*)

conjuration *noun* **1.** an appeal (*H5 i 2; RJ v 3; H v 2*) **2.** the reciting of a spell (*O i 3*)

conjure *verb* to implore someone to do something (*CE iv 4; M iv 1*)

COMMENT: *Con-jure* means, literally, 'to swear together', and so the word has a solemn and binding force, as when Macbeth in Act 4 desperately needs information from the Witches: 'I conjure you by that which you profess'. Our meaning of magic is probably not included in his *conjure*; he is trying to compel them almost by imposing an oath. But Shakespeare also uses the word in the sense of calling forth something that is powerful, possibly hidden. For example, in **Henry IV Part 1** Blunt accuses Hotspur of inciting disorder: 'You conjure from the breast of civil peace/Such bold hostility'. He has chosen this powerful verb to suggest the enormity of Hotspur's action. Here *conjure* may well be edging towards its magical sense, which it has more strongly when Benedick in **Much Ado About Nothing** overstates his aversion to Beatrice: 'I would to God some scholar would conjure her'. Scholars are skilled in the special forms of words needed for exorcism and he pretends that magic is required to drive evil spirits out of Beatrice. *Conjure* in the sense of 'bewitching or imposing a spell' makes a comic focus in Rosalind's Epilogue to **As You Like It**: 'My way is to conjure you…'. And she follows this set-piece moment with ritualistic appeals to convey a feeling of magic: 'I charge you, O women….And I charge you, O men'.

conjurer *noun* someone who drives out evil spirits (*CE iv 4*)

conscience *noun* a person's knowledge or opinion of what is right and wrong (*H5 iv 1; WT iii 2, iv 4; H iii 1; O iii 3*)

conscionable *adjective* true to your opinion of what is right and wrong (*O ii 1*)

consent *noun* harmonious agreement (*H5 i 2*)

consequently *conjunction* subsequently (*TN iii 4*)

conserve *verb* to preserve something (*MM iii 1; O iii 4*) (NOTE: Fruit used to be preserved in sugar.)

conserve of beef *noun* beef preserved in salt (*TS Ind. 2*)

consider *verb* to reward someone for something (*WT iv 2*)

considered time *adjective* appropriate or suitable (*H ii 2*)

consign to *verb* to agree to something (*2H4 v 2; H5 v 1*)

consist in *verb* to exist in something (*R3 iv 4*)

consistory *noun* a council chamber (*R3 ii 2*)

consist upon *verb* to insist on something (*2H4 iv 1*)

consonancy *noun* fellowship (*H ii 2; TN ii 5*)

consort *noun* a small group of musicians (*RJ iii 1; KL ii 1*) ■ *verb* to accompany someone (*CE i 2*)

conspire *verb* to devise a plot (*O iii 3*)

constable *noun* a high officer in the royal household with the authority to judge on matters of chivalry (*H5 ii 4, iii 7*)

constancy *noun* certainty (*MND v 1*)

constant *adjective* settled (*T ii 2*)

constantly *adverb* **1.** continuously (*TN ii 3*) **2.** confidently (*MM iv 1*) **3.** faithfully (*JC v 1; H i 2*)

constant question *noun* a sensible discussion (*TN iv 2*)

constellation *noun* a person's character and abilities as determined by the stars (*TN i 4*)

constitution *noun* **1.** the structure of something (*TN i 3*) **2.** a mental attitude (*MV iii 2*)

constrain *verb* to force someone to do something (*KL ii 2; AC iii 13*)

construction *noun* an interpretation (*M i 4; MA iii 4; TN ii 3, iii 1*)

consul *noun* a senator (*O i 1, 2*)

consummation *noun* death (*KL iv 6*)

contaminate *verb* to defile, rape (*CE ii 2; H5 iv 5*)

contemn *verb* to regard someone or something with contempt (*AC iii 6*)

contemned *adjective* rejected (*TN i 5; KL ii 2*)

contend *verb* to struggle (*MM iii 2*)

contending *adjective* engaging in war (*TS v 2*)

content *verb* **1.** to be untroubled (*TS i 1*; *JC iv 2*; *KL i 4, iii 4*) **2.** to be pleasing to someone (*TS iv 3*; *H iii 1*) **3.** to reward someone for something (*O iii 1*) ■ *noun* a wish (*R2 v 2*)

contention *noun* a battle, combat (*2H4 i 1*; *O ii 1*)

continent *noun* **1.** the total and substance of something (*MND ii 1*; *MV iii 2*; *H v 12*) **2.** a container (*AC iv 14*) **3.** a bank (*1H4 iii 1*) **4.** the Earth (*2H4 iii 1*) ■ *adjective* **1.** restrained or self-controlled (*WT iii 2*; *KL i 2*; *M iv 3*) **2.** sufficient (*H iv 4*)

continuance *noun* durability (*TN i 4*; *MM iii 1*)

continuantly *adverb* continually (*2H4 ii 1*)

continuate *adjective* uninterrupted (*O iii 4*)

continuer *noun* someone who persists with something (*MA i 1*)

contract *verb* to engage someone to be married (*WT iv 4*)

contracting *noun* an engagement to be married (*MM iii 2*)

contraction *noun* an engagement to be married (*H iii 4*)

contrariously *adverb* **1.** separately (*H5 i 2*) **2.** in different directions (*MM iv 1*) ■ *adjective* adverse (*1H4 v 1*)

contrary *adjective* wrong (*MV i 2*)

contrive *verb* **1.** to devise a plot (*R2 i 1*; *MV iv 1*; *H ii 2*) **2.** to spend time (*TS i 2*)

contriver *noun* someone who devises a plot (*AYLI i 1*; *JC ii 1*; *M iii 5*)

contriving *adjective* busy devising plots (*AC i 2*)

control *verb* **1.** to prevent someone from doing something (*T i 2*) **2.** to rebuke someone (*KL ii 4*) **3.** to overpower someone (*T i 2*)

controlment *noun* a check or curb (*MA i 3*)

controversy ◇ **hearts of controversy** a lively dispute (*JC i 2*)

contumely *adverb* insultingly (*H iii 1*)

con tutto core, ben trovato *phrase Italian* with all my heart, well met (*TS i 2*)

convenience *noun* **1.** comfort (*O ii 1*) **2.** suitability (*MM iii 1*)

conveniently *adverb* suitably (*MV ii 8*)

convent *verb* **1.** to be suitable (*TN v 1*) **2.** to agree (*MM v 1*)

conversation *noun* **1.** the act of talking together (*H iii 2*) **2.** a person's behaviour (*2H4 v 5*; *AC ii 6*; *O iii 3*) **3.** sexual intercourse (*R3 iii 5*)

converse *verb* to talk together (*H ii 1*; *O iii 1*)

conversion *noun* a change resulting in an improvement (*AYLI iv 3*)

convey *verb* **1.** to manage or carry out something (*KL i 2*) **2.** to carry out something in secret (*M iv 3*) **3.** to take someone or something away by force (*R2 iv 1*) **4.** to pretend to be someone or something (*H5 i 2*)

conveyance *noun* **1.** the transfer of the ownership of property (*H v 1*) **2.** trickery (*MA ii 1*) **3.** a convoy (*H iv 4*; *O i 3*)

convince *verb* to get the better of someone (*M i 7*)

convocation *noun* **1.** a gathering (*H iv 3*) **2.** an official gathering of clergy (*H5 i 1*)

convoy *noun* a means of transport (*H i 3*; *H5 iii 6, iv 3*; *RJ ii 4*)

cony *noun* a rabbit (*AYLI iii 2*)

cony-catching *noun* cheating or trickery (*TS iv 1*)

copatain *adjective* (*of a hat*) having a high pointed crown (*TS v 1*)

cope *verb* **1.** to meet or have dealings with someone (*AYLI ii 1*; *O iv 1*; *WT iv 4*; *H iii 2*) **2.** to repay something with something else (*MV iv 1*)

copper *adjective* worthless (*MM iv 3*) [Because copper looks like gold but is not as valuable.]

copulative *noun* someone about to be married (*AYLI v 4*)

copy *noun* **1.** a subject for discussion (*CE v 1*) **2.** an agreement or term of rental (*M iii 2*) [From *copy*, 'the minutes of a meeting'.]

coranto *noun* a fast lively dance (*TN i 3*; *H5 iii 5*)

cordial *noun* a tonic drink (*R3 ii 1*; *RJ v 1*) ■ *adjective* comforting (*WT i 2*)

Corinthian *noun* a dissolute man of fashion (*1H4 ii 4*)

corky *adjective* shrivelled or dried out like cork (*KL iii 7*)

cormorant *noun* a greedy person (*R2 ii 1*) [Because cormorants, a type of seabird, feed on large amounts of fish.]

corner ◇ **get into corners** to get someone on their own with the intention of seducing them (*MV iii 5*)

corollary *noun* an extra one (*T iv 1*) [From French *corollaire*.]

coroner's quest law, crowner's quest law *noun* the law laid down by a coroner's inquest (*H v 1*)

coronet *noun* a laurel wreath awarded as an honour by the Romans (*MND iv 1*; *H iv 7*)

corporal *noun* a senior rank in the army in Shakespeare's time (*2H4 iii 2*; *H5 ii 1, iii 2*)

correspondent *adjective* well disposed to (*T i 2*)

corrigible *adjective* **1.** correcting (*O i 3*) **2.** docile (*AC iv 14*)

corrival *noun* a rival (*1H4 i 3, iv 4*)

corse *noun* a corpse (*R3 i 2*)

costard *noun* a person's head (*R3 i 4*; *KL iv 6*) [Costards were a very large variety of apple.]

costermonger *noun* someone who sells goods, particularly fruit, from a barrow (*2H4 i 2*) *See also* **costard**

cote *noun* a cottage (*AYLI ii 4, iii 2*) ■ *verb* to overtake someone (*H ii 2*) (NOTE: From the way one dog passes another when hunting.)

cot-quean *noun* a man interested in women's affairs (*RJ iv 4*)

Cotswold, Cotsall *noun* a district in Gloucestershire famous as a place for hunting with dogs (*R2 ii 3*)

couch *verb* **1.** to crouch down or hide (*MA iii 1*; *T v 1*; *RJ ii 3*; *AYLI iv 3*) **2.** to lie down for sexual intercourse (*MV v 1*; *O iv 3*) **3.** to fix a spear in its rest on a piece of armour (*H ii 3*)

couch down *verb* to cower (*H5 iv 2*)

couching *adjective* lying down (*1H4 iii 1*) ■ *noun* an act of bowing down (*JC iii 1*)

coulter *noun* the blade in front of the main cutting blade of a plough (*H5 v 2*)

council-keeper *noun* someone who will keep a secret (*2H4 ii 4*)

count *noun* **1.** calculation (*RJ i 3*; *AC ii 6*) **2.** a lawsuit (*H iv 7*)

counted *adjective* loved or respected (*R3 iv 1*)

counter *noun* **1.** a hunting term meaning to track game backwards along the scent (*CE iv 2*; *H iv 5*) **2.** a well-known debtors' prison in London (*2H4 i 2, where it is a play on the name of the prison*) **3.** an imitation coin (*AYLI ii 7*)

counter-caster *noun* someone who adds up the amounts in accounts, used as an insult (*O i 1*)

countercheck *noun* a terse reply (*AYLI v 4*)

counterfeit *noun* **1.** a forged coin (*1H4 ii 4*) **2.** a portrait (*MV iii 2*; *M ii 3*) ■ *adjective* **1.** pretended (*TS iv 4*; *H5 iii 6*) **2.** painted as a portrait (*H iii 4*)

countermand *verb* **1.** to reverse an order previously given **2.** to reprieve **3.** to oppose **4.** to prohibit something (*CE iv 2*) **5.** to repeal a law ■ *noun* a contradictory order (*MM iv 2*; *R3 ii 1*)

counterpoint *noun* a heavy bedcover (*TS ii 1*)

counterpoise *verb* to compensate for something with something of equal value (*MA iv 1*)

countervail *verb* to weigh more than something (*RJ ii 6*)

country matters *plural noun* sexual intercourse (*H iii 2*)

county *noun* a nobleman (**count**) (*TN i 5*; *MV i 2*; *RJ i 3, iii 5, iv 1, 2, 4, v 3*)

County Palatine *noun* the territory under the control of a nobleman called a 'count palatine' (*MV i 1*)

couple ◇ **in couples** tied together (*WT ii 1*)

couple a gorge *verb French* to cut someone's throat (*H5 ii 1*) [Alteration of French *coupe la gorge*.]

couplets *noun* a couple (*TN iii 4*; *H v 1*)

course *noun* **1.** the order of events (*MA v 4*; *MM iii 1*) **2.** a way of doing something (*T ii 1*; *KL i 3*) **3.** a habit (*MM ii 1, iii 2*; *H5 i 1*; *H iii 3*; *O iv 1*) **4.** a movement (*2H4 iv 5*) **5.** a large sail (*T i 1*) **6.** in bear-baiting, an attack on the bear by dogs (*KL iii 7*) ■ *verb* **1.** to chase someone or something (*AYLI ii 1*; *KL iii 4*; *M i 6*) **2.** to set the dogs on the bear during bear-baiting (*M v 7*)

courser *noun* a fast horse (*H5 iii 7*; *R2 i 2*; *AC i 2*)

courser's hair *noun* horse hair, which when put in murky water wriggled and attracted small animals to it (*AC i 2*)

coursing *adjective* wandering (*H5 i 2*)

court-cupboard *noun* a sideboard used to display silverware (*RJ i 5*)

courtesy *noun* **1.** a greeting **2.** a curtsy **3.** good manners ◊ **courtesy of nations** civilised behaviour (*AYLI i 1*)

court holy-water *noun* flattery (*KL iii 2*)

court of guard *noun* a guardhouse (*AC iv 9*)

courtship *noun* **1.** behaviour to try and win favour with someone (*R2 i 4*) **2.** behaviour to win someone's love (*MV ii 8; O ii 1*) **3.** behaviour that is suitable for a royal court (*AYLI iii 2*)

cousin *noun* a title used out of courtesy or respect (*MM v 1; R3 iii 4*)

covenant *noun* a contract (*TS ii 1*)

Coventry *noun* a town and district in the West Midlands, near Birmingham, which in Shakespeare's time was just a small village (*1H4 iv 2*)

cover *verb* **1.** to put on your hat (*AYLI iii 3, v 1; MV ii 9*) **2.** to set a table (*2H4 ii 4; MV iii 5*) **3.** to have sexual intercourse with someone (*O i 1*)

covered goblet *noun* an empty goblet (*AYLI iii 4*) (NOTE: Ceremonial goblets were fitted with ornamental covers which were removed when the goblet was in use.) [Because goblets were usually covered when not in use.]

covert *noun* a thicket of bushes (*WT iv 4; RJ i 1*) ■ *adjective* secret (*MM v 1; 2H4 Introd; JC iv 1; L iii 2*)

coverture *noun* a shelter (*MA iii 1*)

cowish *adjective* cowardly (*KL iv 2*)

coxcomb *noun* **1.** a jester's hat (*TS ii 1; KL i 4*) **2.** a person's head (*TN v 1; H5 v 1*)

coy *verb* to caress something (*MND iv 1*) ■ *adjective* contemptuous (*TS ii 1*)

COMMENT: The word originated in Old French, where it meant 'quiet'. Therefore, it means 'to soothe or caress' when used as a verb by Titania to Bottom in **A Midsummer Night's Dream**: 'While I thy amiable cheeks do coy'. However, quietness is not always gentle, and so the adjective *coy* may take an opposite meaning – reluctant, even disdainful – as in **Much Ado About Nothing** when Hero speaks about Beatrice, knowing that she is listening: 'No Ursula, truly, she is too disdainful;/I know her spirits are as coy and wild/As haggards of the rock'.

coying *noun* pretending to be modest or shy (*RJ ii 2*)

coystril *noun* a scoundrel (*TN i 3*)

cozen *verb* to cheat or trick someone out of something (*WT iv 4; KL v 3*)

cozenage *noun* cheating or trickery (*CE i 2; H v 2*)

cozener *noun* a cheat (*WT iv 4; KL iv 6*)

cozening *adjective* cheating (*R2 ii 2; O iv 2*)

cozier *noun* someone who mends shoes (*TN ii 3*)

crab *noun* a small bitter apple (*T ii 2; KL i 5 (a play on words)*)

crabbed *adjective* bad-tempered or bitter (*WT i 2*)

crack *noun* **1.** an imperfection (*WT i 2; O ii 3*) **2.** the measured amount of gunpowder put in a cannon (*M i 2*) **3.** a cheeky boy (*2H4 iii 2*) ■ *verb* to boast ◊ **crack a quart** drink a bottle of wine (*2H4 v 3*)

cracked within the ring *adjective* having had sexual intercourse (*H ii 2*)

crack-hemp *noun* someone who deserves to be hanged (*TS v 1*) (NOTE: 'Hemp' refers to the rope used to hang people.)

craft *verb* to behave in an underhand way (*MM iii 2*) [A play on 'to be crafty']

crafty *adjective* cleverly made (*MA iii 1*) ◊ **crafty-sick** pretending to be ill (*2H4 Ind.*)

crank *verb* to twist and turn (*1H4 iii 1*) [From the idea of winding a rope.]

crants *noun* German a garland of flowers carried in front of a girl's coffin and hung over her grave (*H v 1*) [From German *Kranz*.]

crasing *noun* the act of crashing into something (*H5 iv 3*)

craven *noun* a coward (*TS ii 1; H5 iv 7*) [From *craven*, 'a cock that is trained to fight but refuses to fight'.]

craze *verb* to damage something (*R3 iv 4; KL iii 4*)

crazed *adjective* flawed, impaired (*MND i 1*)

cream *verb* to form a scum on a surface (*MV i 1*)

create *adjective* created (*MND v 1; H5 2*)

credent *adjective* **1.** believing (*H i 3*) **2.** believable (*MM iv 4; WT i 2*)

credit *noun* **1.** believability (*O ii 1*) **2.** reputation (*AYLI i 1*) **3.** a report (*TN iv 3*) ■ *verb* to honour or respect someone (*TS iv 1*)

creek *noun* a winding lane (*CE iv 2*)

crescent *adjective* becoming greater (*H i 3*)

crescive *adjective* becoming greater (*H5 i 1*)

cresset *noun* a metal basket in which a fire was lit to give light. It could be on a pole or be larger and set up on a hill as a beacon. (*1H4 iii 1*)

Cressid, Cressida *noun* a promiscuous woman (*TN iii 1*; *H5 ii 1*) (NOTE: According to medieval and renaissance accounts of the Trojan War, Cressida was a Greek woman who was captured by the Trojans. She fell in love with the Trojan prince Troilus, but when she was sent back to the Greeks she went to live with the Greek Diomedes. As a result of this story she is often depicted as the archetypal promiscuous woman.)

crest *noun* **1.** a badge or plume on a helmet (*MND iii 2*) **2.** a helmet (*M v 8*) **3.** the head or neck of a horse or other animal (*JC iv 2*) **4.** a tuft on the head of a horse or other animal (*1H4 i 1*) ■ *verb* to act as a protective cover (*AC v 2*) (NOTE: From the use of 'crest' to mean *helmet*.)

crewel *noun* a fine woollen thread used for tapestry and embroidery (*KL ii 4*)

crib *noun* a small squalid house (*2H4 iii 1*)

cribbed *adjective* hemmed in, as if living a small squalid house (*M iii 4*)

crisp *adjective* curled or curling (*T iv 1*; *MV iii 2*; *1H4 i 3*)

critic *noun* a cynical person

crone *noun* a wrinkled old woman (*WT ii 3*)

crook *verb* to bend something (*H iii 2*)

crooked *adjective* **1.** hunchbacked (*CE iv 2*) **2.** illegal (*H5 i 2*)

crooked-pated *adjective* with a curved head (*AYLI iii 2*)

crop *verb* **1.** to cut or pick something off (*R2 ii 1, v 2*; *R3 i 2*; *1H4 v 4*) **2.** to have children (*AC ii 2*)

crop-ear *noun* a horse with one of its ears cut with an identification mark (*1H4 ii 3*)

Crosby Place, Crosby Hall *noun* a house situated in what is now Crosby Square in London. It was built in 1466 by Sir John Crosby, sheriff of London, and was owned by Richard III after Crosby's death. (*R3 i 2, 3, iii 1*)

cross *noun* a coin marked with a cross (*AYLI ii 4*; *2H4 i 2*) ■ *verb* **1.** to prevent something (*MA i 3*; *MND i 1*; *TS ii 1*; *M iii 1*) **2.** to meet someone or something (*H i 1*) ■ *preposition* moving from one side to another (*JC i 3*; *KL iv 7*) ■ *adjective* tending to dispute something (*TS ii 1*; *R3 iii 1*; *RJ iv 3*) ◇ **broke cross** broken when striking an opponent's body or shield (*MA v 1*)

cross-gartered *adjective* with the garters crossed on the leg (*TN ii 5, iii 4*)

crossing *noun* a contradiction (*1H4 iii 1*)

crossly *adverb* unfavourably (*R2 ii 4*)

crossness *noun* a tendency to dispute something (*MA ii 3*)

cross-row *noun* a child's book of the alphabet (*R3 i 1*) (NOTE: In the old horn books the first row of letters was preceded by the sign of the Cross (**Christ-cross row**).)

crossways *noun* a crossroads. A crossroads was often a place where criminals were hanged and suicides buried. (*MND iii 2*)

crotchet *noun* **1.** a musical note (*RJ iv 5*) **2.** a strange idea (*MM iii 2*; *MA ii 3*)

crow[1] *noun* a crowbar (*CE iii 1*; *RJ v 2*)

crow[2] ◇ **yield the crow a pudding** be like a dead animal being pecked at by a crow (*H5 ii 1*)

crowd *verb* to crush someone (*2H4 iv 2*; *JC ii 4*)

crow-flower *noun* a flower similar to a buttercup (*H iv 7*)

crow-keeper *noun* a boy employed to keep away crows, or a dummy designed to do this (*KL iv 6*; *RJ i 4*)

crown *noun* a coin worth five shillings (25p). This might have been a month's wages for a labourer.

crown imperial *noun* a fritillary, a plant with bell-shaped, orange flowers (*WT iv 4*)

crudy *adjective* thick or semi-solid (*2H4 iv 3*)

cruel *noun* **1.** savage, merciless beings (*KL iii 7*) **2.** a **crewel** (*KL ii 4*)

cruelly *adverb* to such an excessive degree as to cause pain (*H5 v 2*)

cruelty *noun* a cruel person (*TN i 5*)

crupper *noun* a leather strap that holds a saddle in place (*CE i 2*; *TS iii 2, iv 1*)

crush *verb* **1.** to try to squeeze a meaning out of words (*TN ii 5*; *H5 i 2*) **2.** to drink something quickly (*RJ i 2*)

cruzado *noun* a Portuguese coin worth about six shillings (30p) and stamped with a cross (*O iii 4*)

cry *noun* **1.** a pack of dogs or other animals (*MND i 1*; *O ii 3*) **2.** a group of people (*H iii 3*) **3.** a rumour (*O iv 1*) ▪ *verb* to beg for or demand something (*R3 v 3*; *O i 3*)

cry on *verb* to proclaim something (*H v 2*)

cry out ◇ **cry out of sack** to shout abuse because drunk (*H5 ii 3*)

cry out upon *verb* to criticise something (*1H4 iv 3*)

crystal *noun* an eye (*H5 ii 3*)

crystal-button *noun* a button worn by wine-sellers (*1H4 ii 4*)

cry upon *verb* (*of a dog*) to bark on picking up the scent of the hunted animal (*TN ii 5*)

cry your mercy *interjection* I beg your pardon (*MM iv 1*)

cub-drawn *adjective* made extremely hungry (*KL iii 1*) [From the idea of a female dog having had all her milk sucked by her cubs.]

cubiculo *noun* an apartment (*TN iii 2*)

cuckold *noun* a man who has an unfaithful wife (*MW v 5*; *O iv 3*) ▪ *verb* to make a man's wife unfaithful (*O i 3*; *O iv 1*)

COMMENT: *Cuckold* was the mocking term given to a man whose wife was in a sexual relationship with another man. In a male-dominated society the threat of cuckoldry was the most powerful way for a woman to exercise power and to humiliate her husband. A cuckold, often an old man with a younger wife, was therefore an obvious target for much comedy and satire. And a similar situation could be the basis for tragedy, most notably in **Othello**. *Cuckold* was closely linked with 'cuckoo', from which it derives, because the cuckoo lays its eggs in another bird's nest. Both words were used as terms of mocking abuse for a fool. In **Much Ado About Nothing** Benedick, the bachelor, congratulates himself for not being a potential cuckold at the hands of a wife. In that play and elsewhere the common sign for the cuckold was a bull's horns and this sort of comedy continued to flour- ish in comedy of the Restoration period. The cuckoo and cuckold are prominent at the end of Shakespeare's **Love's Labours Lost**; marriage is the aim of the story, but not achieved within the action of the play, and so the celebration in the final song is curiously double-edged. The owl, representing wisdom and winter, competes with the cuckoo, the symbol of folly and the spring. When the meadows are alight with spring colour, 'The cuckoo then, on every tree/Mocks married men; for thus sings he/'Cuckoo!/Cuckoo,cuckoo!' O word of fear,/Unpleasing to a married ear'. With this complex mixture of melancholy and fulfilment, Shakespeare uses cuckoldry as a way of subverting the expected happy ending of a comedy.

cuckoo-flower *noun* a plant with white or pinkish flowers, related to the wallflower (*KL iv 4*)

cucullus non facit monachum *phrase* Latin 'the hood does not make the monk' – do not trust to appearances (*MM v 1*; *TN i 5*)

cudgel *verb* to beat someone with a club (**cudgel**) (*1H4 iii 2*; *TN ii 5*)

cudgelled *adjective* made by being beaten with a club (**cudgel**) (*H5 v 1*)

cullion *noun* a rogue (*TS iv 2*; *H5 iii 2*; *KL ii 2*) [From *French* 'couillon', *Italian* 'coglione'.]

cullionly *adverb* contemptibly (*KL ii 2*)

culverin *noun* a long-barrelled cannon (*1H4 ii 3*) (NOTE: Although *culverin* is mentioned in 1H4 ii 3, it is unlikely that this type of cannon had been invented by this time.)

cumber *verb* to trouble someone with something useless (*JC iii 1*)

cum privilegio ad imprimendum solum *phrase* with the sole right to print (*TS iv 4*)

cunning *adjective* **1.** clever (*MA ii 2*; *H iii 4*) **2.** knowledgeable, particularly about magic (*RJ iv 2*) ▪ *noun* **1.** knowledge (*O iii 3*) **2.** a skill (*H5 v 2*; *RJ ii 2*; *AC ii 3*)

cup *verb* to make someone drunk (*AC ii 7*)

Cupid *noun* the Roman god of love (NOTE: The blind (blindfolded) son of Venus and Mercury, depicted as a young boy carrying a bow and arrows. His gold-tipped arrows were considered to engender true love while those tipped with lead produced only lust. The Greek equivalent is **Eros**.)

Cupid's flower *noun* the violet or pansy. The flower is also known as **love-in-idleness**. (*MND ii 1, iv 1*)

cuppele gorge *verb* to cut someone's throat (*H5 iv 4*) [From French *couper la gorge*.]

cur *noun* a large dog (*M iii 1*)

curb *verb* to bend something (*H iii 4*) ■ *noun* a strap attached to the mouthpiece of a horse's bridle, used to control the horse (*AYLI iii 3*) [From French *courber*.]

curd *verb* to cause milk to form lumps as part of the process of making cheese (*H i 5*)

cure *noun* a state of good health (*KL iii 6*; *O ii 1*)

cureless *adjective* unable to be cured (*MV iv 1*)

curfew *noun* a bell rung in the the evening

COMMENT: Nowadays we occasionally speak of imposing a *curfew*, to restrict movement in the streets, usually at a time of crisis. From medieval times and during Shakespeare's life, *curfew* referred specifically to the evening bell that announced the time for damping down the fires in household hearths. The warning was to prevent uncontrolled fires spreading at night among wooden houses in narrow streets. Literally *curfew* means 'cover fire', from the French 'couvre feu'. The best-known use in Shakespeare occurs during Prospero's soliloquy of farewell to his magical powers. He refers to the spirits of the night, which, like those in **A Midsummer Night's Dream**, emerge when humans are asleep. He speaks of those 'that rejoice/To hear the solemn curfew'.

curious *adjective* **1.** careful (*RJ i 4*) **2.** carefully made (*KL i 4*) ■ particular (*TS iv 4*)

curiously *adverb* elegantly (*MA v 1*; *H v 1*)

currance *noun* a flow (**current**) (*H5 i 1*)

current *noun* a happening (*1H4 iii 3*) ■ *adjective* **1.** genuine (*1H4 ii 1*; *R3 i 2, ii 1*) **2.** usual (*R2 v 3*) ◇ **hold current** still true (*1H4 ii 1*)

curry *verb* to attempt to gain something by flattery (*2H4 v 1*)

curst *adjective* bad-tempered or savage (*TS i 1*; *MA ii 1*; *KL ii 1*; *TN iii 2*; *WT iii 3*)

curstness *noun* bad temper (*AC ii 2*)

curtain *noun* a banner (*H5 iv 2*)

curtal(l) *noun* a dog (**cur**) with its tail cut short (*CE iii 2*)

curtle-axe *noun* a short sword with a broad blade (a cutlass) (*AYLI i 3*; *H5 iv 2*)

curtsey ◇ **make curtsey** to behave respectfully (*MA ii 1*)

curvet *verb* to prance about (*AYLI iii 2*)

cushes, cuisses *plural noun* pieces of armour worn on the thighs (*1H4 iv 1*)

cushion *noun* pregnancy (*2H4 v 4*)

custard-coffin *noun* a pastry case in which to bake a custard (*TS iv 3*)

custom *noun* habitual sexual intercourse (*H iii 4*) ◇ **of custom** customary (*M iii 4*; *O iii 3*) ◇ **with a custom** as usual (*WT iv 4*)

customer *noun* **1.** a prostitute (*O iv 1*) **2.** a man who frequents brothels (*MM iv 3*)

custom-shrunk *adjective* in a situation of having fewer customers (*MM i 2*)

cut *noun* **1.** a working horse (*TN ii 3*; *1H4 ii 1*) (NOTE: This is used as a term of abuse, and derives from the fact that working horses were typically castrated.) **2.** a slash in a garment made to reveal the material underneath (*TS iv 3*; *MA iii 4*) ■ *verb* to make something impossible (*1H4 v 2*) ◇ **draw cuts** to draw lots (*CE v 1*)

cut off *verb* **1.** to put someone to death (*MM v 1*; *H5 iii 6*) **2.** to cancel something (*KL ii 4*)

cut out *verb* to cut out something from a pattern (*WT iv 4*)

cutpurse *noun* a thief who stole purses which were tied to people's belts (*2H4 ii 4*; *H5 v 5*; *KL iii 2*; *H v 5*)

cutter-off *noun* someone who interrupts (*AYLI i 2*)

cuttle *noun* a bully (*2H4 ii 4*)

Cyclops *noun* in Greek mythology, the one-eyed giants that were servants of Vulcan, the god of fire (*H ii 2*)

Cydnus *noun* a river in Egypt (*AC ii 2, v 1*)

cyme *noun* an infusion of the pods of the plant *Cassia* which was used as a laxative (*M v 3*) [Probably a misspelling of 'cynne' (senna).]

cynic *noun* someone who speaks bluntly on moral issues (*JC iv 3*) (NOTE: The Cynics believed in the philosophy developed by the Greek Antisthenes, which was based on the idea that happiness depended on moral goodness and not on material possessions.)

Cynthia *noun* the Moon (*RJ iii 5*) (NOTE: The name is often associated with the Greek goddess **Artemis** from Mount Cynthius on the island of Delos, where she is supposed to have been born.)

cypress *noun* **1.** the hard wood of the cypress tree (*TN ii 4*; *TS ii 1*) **2.** a fine black transparent fabric (*WT iv 4*; *TN ii 4, iii 1*)

Cytherea, Cythera *noun* Aphrodite, the Greek goddess of love (*TS Ind. 1*) (NOTE: Cytherea is an island off the southern tip of Greece. Its main town, of the same name, was famous for the worship of Aphrodite and so is sometimes used to refer to her.)

D

dace *noun* a small freshwater fish related to the carp (*2H4 iii 2*)

daff *verb* **1.** to take off your clothes or hat (*AC iv 4*) **2.** to put something casually to one side (*MA ii 3, v 1*; *1H4 iv 1*) **3.** to put someone off with an excuse (*O iv 2*)

dagger ◇ **dagger of lath** a wooden dagger used by Vice in the **morality plays** (*TN iv 2*; *1H4 ii 4*; *H5 v 4*) ◇ **leaden dagger** a useless weapon (*1H4 ii 4*)

Dagonet *noun* one of King Arthur's knights who was considered a fool (*2H4 iii 2*)

dainty *adjective* **1.** excessively fussy or thorough (*2H4 iv 1*; *M ii 3*) **2.** fussy about one's appearance (*MND v 1*; *T v 1*; *TS ii 1*) **3.** shy or modest (*RJ i 5*)

dalliance *noun* **1.** frivolous activity (*CE iv 1*; *H i 1*; *H5 v Chor.*) **2.** the act of flirting (*T iv 1*)

dally *verb* to treat something lightly (*TN ii 4*; *1H4 v 3*)

damask *adjective* coloured pink and white (like a damask rose) (*AYLI iii 5*; *TN ii 4*)

dame *noun* **1.** a lady of rank (*MND v 1*; *M iv 2*) **2.** a title (*AC iv 4*) **3.** the mistress of a household (*WT iv 4*) **4.** a mother (*2H4 iii 2*)

damp *noun* a mist (*AC iv 9*)

dance barefoot *verb* to be an old unmarried woman (*TS ii 1*)

dance with your heels *verb* to beat a rhythm with your heels during sexual intercourse (*MA iii 4*)

danger *noun* **1.** harm (*JC ii 1*) **2.** the range of something (*TN v 1*; *H i 3*; *M iii 2*) **3.** the power held over someone, especially by a debt that is owed (*MV iv 1*) ■ *verb* to be a danger to something (*AC i 2*)

dangerous *adjective* potentially harmful (*MA v 1*; *1H4 v 1*)

Daniel *noun* a young judge in the Bible (Ezekiel 28:3). According to the Book of Daniel he was taken captive by Nebuchadnezzar who later made him the chief minister of **Babylon**, when he was called Belteshazzar. (*MV iv 1*)

Dansker *noun* a Dane (*H ii 1*)

Daphne *noun* in Greek mythology, a woman wooed by Apollo who changed herself into a laurel bush to avoid him (*MND ii 1*; *TS Ind. 1*)

dare *noun* **1.** boldness (*1H4 iv 1*) **2.** a challenge (*AC i 2*) ■ *verb* **1.** to have the courage to do something (*MV v 1*) **2.** to challenge something (*MND iii 2*; *RJ ii 4*) **3.** to frighten someone (*H5 iv 2*) (NOTE: Larks were caught by a device made of small mirrors fastened to a cloth, called a dare.)

dark *adjective* **1.** gloomy or severe (*MV v 1*; *RJ iii 5*) **2.** evil (*R2 i 1*) **3.** vague or obscure (*T i 2*) **4.** secret (*KL i 1*) **5.** calming madness (*TN iii 4*; *CE iv 4*; *AYLI iii 2*) (NOTE: It was thought that light, especially the moon, stimulated mad people.) ■ *adverb* in the dark (*AYLI iii 5*)

darken *verb* to shade or hide something (*AC iii 1*)

darkling *adverb* in the dark (*MND ii 2*; *KL i 4*; *AC iv 15*)

darkly *adverb* **1.** unclearly (*MM v 1*) **2.** secretly (*MM iii 2*) **3.** depressingly (*TN ii 1*; *R3 i 4*)

darkness *noun* death (*MM iii 1*)

darnel *noun* a type of grass whose seeds contain a poison which is mildly narcotic (*H5 v 2*)

darting *noun* shooting arrows (*AC iii 1*)

dart of love ◇ **dribbling dart of love** possibly the penis (*MM i 3*)

dash *noun* a mark of something bad (*WT v 2*) ■ *verb* to discourage or frighten someone (*O iii 3*)

date *noun* the length of a person's life (*MND iii 2*; *CE i 2*)

dateless *adjective* endless (*R2 i 3*; *RJ v 3*)

daub *verb* **1.** to disguise something (*R3 iii 5*) **2.** to keep up a pretence of something (*KL iv 1*)

dauntless *adjective* unlikely to be frightened or discouraged (*M iii 1*)

dauphin *noun* the eldest son of the king of France (*H5 i 2, iii 3*)

COMMENT: This was the name given to the eldest son of the King of France after 1343 when the province of Dauphine was absorbed into the French kingdom. There are references to him in several of Shakespeare's history plays and he appears in **Henry V** as a rather effete counterpart to the more robust English king. Sometimes his title is written as *dolphin*, which has encouraged some philologists to search for a fish-like origin, but *dauphin* is also thought to derive from two Celtic words, 'dagh' and 'fion', meaning 'good wine', to be found in the province of Dauphine.

Daventry *noun* a town in Northamptonshire, southeast of Rugby. It was an important market town. (*1H4 iv 2*)

daw *noun* a fool (*MA ii 3; O i 1*) [From *jackdaw*, 'a bird like a crow', regarded as stupid.]

day *noun* 1. victory at the end of a day of a battle (*2H4 i 2, v 4*) 2. a length of time 3. light (*AC iv 8*) ◇ **by the day** o'clock (*1H4 ii 1*) ◇ **how's the day?** What time is it? (*T v 1*) ◇ **in my days of nature** during my lifetime (*H i 5*)

day-bed *noun* a sofa (*TN ii 5; R3 iii 7*)

dead-killing *adjective* killing (*R3 iv 1*)

deadly *adjective* like death (*CE iv 4; TN i 5; KL v 3; R3 iii 7*) ■ *adverb* unrelentingly (*MA v 1*)

dead men's finger *noun* the early purple orchid (*Orchis mascula*) (*H iv 7*)

deafening *adjective* unbearably loud (*2H4 iii 1*)

deal *verb* to make use of something (*AYLI v 1; 1H4 ii 4*)

deal in *verb* to take action on something (*MA v 1; T v 1*)

dealing ◇ **in plain dealing** I will tell you straight (*MM ii 1*)

deal on lieutenancy *verb* to act on behalf of someone else (*AC iii 11*) [From the idea of acting as a second officer.]

deal upon *verb* to act against something (*R3 iv 2*)

dear *adjective* serious (*T ii 1; H i 2*) ■ *adverb* keenly (*JC iii 1; KL i 1*)

COMMENT: *Dear* had a wider meaning for Shakespeare than it has for us. It often carried our sense of close affection, and was occasionally used as our synonym for 'expensive'. But these were particular examples within the word's wider meaning of very important. For example, it may sound odd for a modern audience to hear Henry V, just before leaving for France, refer to the traitors' 'dear offences'. Their crimes are *dear* in the sense of having great significance. *Dear* could be used as an adverb as when Antony speaks over the body of Julius Caesar: 'Shall it not grieve thee dearer than thy death/To see thy Antony making his peace…?' Again, *dear* intensifies something negative; in this example it is grief. *Dear* is a rare example of a word that has a wide and general application for Shakespeare but which has sharpened and narrowed its meaning today.

deared *adjective* more loved (*AC i 4*)

dearly *adverb* 1. earnestly (*CE ii 2; AYLI i 3*) 2. warmly (*WT v 1*)

dearn *adjective* dreadful (*KL iii 7*) ■ *noun* a secret place (*MA iii 2*)

dearness *noun* fondness (*MA iii 2*)

dearth *noun* great value on account of something's scarcity (*H v 2*)

death-marked *adjective* condemned to death by events (*RJ Prol.*)

death-practised *adjective* marked out for death by your enemies (*KL iv 6*)

death's head *noun* a skull, especially in the form of a carving or picture (*MV i 2; 1H4 iii 3; 2H4 ii 4*)

deathsman *noun* an executioner (*KL iv 6*)

debate *noun* a quarrel (*2H4 iv 4; MND ii 1*) ■ *verb* to quarrel over something (*AC ii 2; CE iv 1; H iv 4; H5 i 1; KL v 1*)

debatement *noun* discussion about someone or something (*MM v 1; H v 2*)

debitor and creditor *noun* someone who keeps financial records for someone (*O i 1*)

deboshed *adjective* 1. immoral (*T iii 2*) 2. corrupt (*KL i 4*)

decayed *adjective* financially ruined (*CE ii 1*)

decayer *noun* someone who destroys something (*H v 1*)

deceased *adjective* past (*2H4 iii 1*)

deceivable *adjective* deceptive (*TN iv 3*; *R2 ii 3*)

deceive *verb* to betray or go against something (*1H4 v 1*)

deck *verb* to cover something (*T i 2*)

decline *verb* **1.** to bend down (*KL iv 2*) **2.** to bend or tilt something (*CE iii 2*) **3.** to recite items in order (*R3 iv 4*) **4.** to fall or sink (*H i 5, ii 2*)

declined *adjective* **1.** grown old (*O iii 3*) **2.** fallen on hard times (*AC iii 13*)

declining *adjective* deteriorating (*R2 ii 1*; *KL i 2*)

decoct *verb* to heat something (*H5 iii 5*)

dedicate *adjective* devoted to (*MM ii 2*)

deeply *adverb* loudly (*TS ii 1*)

deep-mouthed *adjective* with a loud, deep-throated bark (*TS Ind. 1*; *H5 v Chor.*)

deer *noun* any small animal (*KL iii 4*)

deface *verb* to cancel something (*MV iii 2*)

default *noun* a fault (*CE i 2*)

defeat *verb* **1.** to destroy something (*MA iv 1*; *H i 2*; *AC v 1*; *O iv 2*) **2.** to disguise something (*O i 3*) **3.** to cheat someone of something (*MND iv 1*)

defeature *noun* a disfigurement (*CE ii 1, v 1*)

defect *noun* an imperfection (*M ii 1*)

defence *noun* armour (*TN iii 4*; *RJ iii 3*; *AC iv 4*)

defencible *adjective* capable of defence (*H5 iii 3*; *2H4 iii 3*)

defend *verb* to forbid something (*1H4 iv 3*; *MA ii 1*; *AC iii 3*)

defendant ◇ **means defendant** strong defences (*H5 ii 4*)

defiance *noun* **1.** rejection (*MM iii 1*) **2.** a challenge (*R2 iii 3*; *RJ i 1*; *JC v 1*)

definement *noun* a description (*H v 2*)

definite, definitive *adjective* fixed or unchangeable (*MM v 1*)

deflower *verb* to deprive a woman of her virginity (*MM iv 4*; *MND v 1*)

defunction *noun* death (*H5 i 2*)

defuse *verb* to disguise (*KL i 4*)

defy *verb* to reject someone (*MV iii 5*; *H v 2*)

defy the matter *verb* to question the meaning (*MV iii 5*)

defy the tongue *verb* to question the meaning (*1H4 iv 1*)

degree *noun* **1.** social rank (*R2 i 4*) **2.** a step in a sequence of events (*TN i 5*; *2H4 i 2*) ◇ **any fair degree** to a reasonable degree (*R2 i 1*)

COMMENT: Deriving from the Latin 'de gradus', meaning 'a step down', *degree* usually refers to levels of status in a kingdom or any social organisation. It is an important word denoting a vital concept in Elizabethan society and therefore in plays that deal with kings, princes, and government. In **Troilus and Cressida** Ulysses, the political thinker, warns against the dangers of social levelling: 'Take but degree away, untune that string,/And hark what discord follows!' He argues that human society should respect the divisions of rank, as do 'The heavens themselves'. The results of disorder would be terrifying. Elizabethans would have been very aware of the devastation caused by the Wars of the Roses and even more alarmed in the 1590s about the dangers of Queen Elizabeth leaving no heir and the possible conflicts of ambitious men in the vacuum of power that would be left. Leontes in **The Winter's Tale** just restrains himself from calling Hermione a whore; he believes that even to use that type of language to a queen would attack propriety to such an extent that 'barbarism, making me the precedent,/Should a like language use to all degrees, and mannerly distinguishment leave out/Betwixt the prince and the beggar'. Sometimes *degree* means something less significant, when it has our meaning of 'amount or extent'. France in **King Lear**, not knowing how Cordelia has offended her father, says 'her offence/Must be of such unnatural degree'; it is possible here that the king intends his *degree* to include rank as a secondary meaning.

deign *verb* to accept something graciously (*AC i 4*)

delate *verb* to talk about something at length (*CE i 1*; *H i 2*; *O i 3*)

delation *noun* an accusation (*O iii 3*)

delicate *adjective* **1.** dainty or beautiful (*T i 2*; *WT iii 1*; *O ii 3*) **2.** beautifully made (*H v 2*) **3.** sensuous (*MA i 1*) **4.** clever or subtle (*KL iv 6*; *O iv 1*)

delighted *adjective* capable of causing great pleasure (*MM iii 1*; *O i 3*)

deliver *verb* **1.** to make something plain (*WT v 2*; *CE ii 2*; *JC iii 1*) **2.** to speak (*R2 iii 3*) ◊ **be delivered** be born (*CE v 1*; *O i 3*)

delve *verb* to search for something (*H iii 4*)

demean *verb* to conduct yourself in a way that lowers your self-esteem (*CE iv 3, v 1*)

demerit *noun* what one deserves (*M iv 3*; *O i 2*)

demesnes *plural noun* the buttocks and genitals (*RJ ii 1*) [From the idea of an estate, a manor house with lands, or territories.]

Demeter *noun* the Greek equivalent of **Ceres**

demicannon *noun* a large cannon firing a ball weighing about 15kg (*TS iv 3*)

demise *verb* to transfer something to someone (*R3 iv 4*)

demi-wolf *noun* an animal that is half wolf and half dog (*M iii 1*)

demure *verb* to be serious (*2H4 iv 3*)

demurely *adverb* seriously (*MV ii 2*) ◊ **drums demurely wake** the solemn drum-beat wakens (*AC iv 9*)

demuring *adjective* presenting a modest appearance (*AC iv 13 (15)*)

denay *noun* a denial (*TN ii 4*)

denier *noun* a small French copper coin of low value (*1H4 iii 3*; *R3 i 2*)

denies his presence *phrase* refuses to attend (*M iii 4*)

denotement *noun* a sign (*O ii 3*)

denounce *verb* to declare war (*R3 i 3*; *AC iii 7*)

denunciation *noun* a public announcement (*MM i 2*)

depend *verb* **1.** to rely on something (*MM iii 2*; *KL i 4*) **2.** to be about to happen (*RJ iii 1*)

dependancy, dependency *noun* **1.** the act of giving way to someone's will or authority (*AC v 2*) **2.** something dependent on something else (*MM v 1*)

deplore *verb* to relate something with sorrow (*TN iii 1*)

depose *verb* **1.** to remove something (*R2 iii 2*) **2.** to confirm something on oath (*MM v 1*) **3.** to ask questions of someone on oath (*R2 i 3*)

depository *noun* someone you confide in (*KL ii 4*)

deputation *noun* the post of deputy (*1H4 iv 1, 3*; *MM i 1*)

depute *verb* to act for another person (*O iv 2*)

deputed *adjective* relating to a symbol of office (*MM ii 2*)

deracinate *verb* to pull something up by the roots (*H5 v 2*)

derive *verb* **1.** to be descended from someone (*MA iv 1*; *TN iii 4*) **2.** to inherit something (*AYLI i 1*) **3.** to find something out (*KL i 1*)

derogate *adjective* immoral (*KL i 1*)

descant *noun* a comment (*R3 iii 7*)

descension *noun* a descent or fall (*2H4 ii 2*)

descent *noun* **1.** the inheritance of property by heirs without there being a will (*R2 ii 3*) **2.** the lowest place (*KL v 3*)

description *noun* a type (*MV iii 2*)

descry *noun* a discovery (*KL iv 6*) ■ *verb* to find something out (*R3 v 3*)

desert *noun* something that is deserved (*CE iii 1*; *R3 ii 1*)

deserve *verb* to repay an action (*O i 1*)

deserved *adjective* worthy of reward

deserving *noun* something that is deserved (*MM v 1*; *KL iii 3, v 3*)

design *noun* a scheme (*WT iv 4*; *M ii 1*) ■ *verb* to indicate or identify something (*R2 i 1*; *H i 1*)

designment *noun* a plan of action (*R2 i 1*; *H i 1*)

desired *adjective* loved (*O ii 1*)

despair *verb* to have no hope of something (*M v 8*)

despised *adjective* scorned (*RJ iii 2*)

despite *noun* scorn or hatred

despiteful *adjective* acting with malice (*AC ii 6*; *AYLI v 2*; *TS iv 2*)

detain *verb* to keep something back (*CE ii 1*; *R2 i 1*; *KL i 2*)

detect *verb* to discover the wrongdoing of someone (*MM iii 2*)

detected for *adjective* influenced by the desire for (*MM iii 2*)

determinate *verb* to decide upon something (*R2 i 3*) ■ *adjective* **1.** fixed or unchangeable (*O iv 2*) **2.** intended (*TN ii 1*)

COMMENT: Shakespeare sometimes used *determine* in one of our senses, meaning 'to make a decision or to resolve something', but the word generally retained its core meaning of 'term', a boundary. We speak of a school term, a limited amount of time with set boundaries. The dying king, Henry IV bitterly asks for his son: 'Where is he that will not stay so long/Till his friend sickness have determined me?' meaning 'brought my life to its term or boundary'. Richard II condemns Mowbray to perpetual banishment: 'The sly, slow hours shall not determinate/The dateless limit of thy dear exile'. Here *determinate*, its sense familiar to us, came from the same source as *determine*, but in Richard's elaborate speech here it feels more formal as he tries to regain authority in public. Iago uses *determinate* as an adjective when he tells the slow-witted Roderigo that an accident will be needed to keep Othello in Venice, 'wherein none can be so determinate as the removing of Cassio'. On the surface *determinate* means 'decisive', but the irony of his words depends on 'term' as the final boundary, a euphemism for death, along with the further euphemism, 'removing'. Shakespeare rarely used *determined* in our sense of 'resolute or unflinching'.

determination *noun* a decision or intention (*1H4 iv 3*; *MM iii 2*)

determined *adjective* particular (*MM iii 1*)

detested *adjective* extremely hateful (*1H4 i 3*; *KL i 2, ii 4*; *TN v 1*)

Deucalion *noun* the survivor of a flood in classical mythology (*WT iv 4*)

devest *verb* to undress yourself (*O ii 3*)

device *noun* 1. a thought (*AYLI i 1*) 2. a plot or trick (*MND v 1*)

devise *verb* 1. to invent something (*AC ii 2*) 2. to imagine something (*RJ iii 1*) 3. to explain something to someone (*H iv 7*)

devoted *adjective* holy (*R3 i 2*)

devotement *noun* worship (*O ii 3*)

devour the way *verb* to cover a distance quickly (*2H4 i 1*)

dew *noun* 1. tears (*R2 v 1*) 2. a refreshing, gentle substance (*R3 iv 1*) ■ *verb* to moisten something (*MND ii 1*)

dewberry *noun* a large fruit resembling a blackberry. The fruit has a dew-like bloom when ripe. (*MND iii 1*)

dewlap *noun* loose folds of skin around the throat (*T iii 3*; *MND ii 1, iv 1*)

dexteriously *adverb* skilfully (*TN i 5*)

diable, diablo *noun* the devil (*O ii 3*) [From French *diable*, Spanish *diablo*.]

Diana, Dian *noun* in Roman mythology, the goddess of the Moon, hunting and fertility (*1H4 i 2*; *AYLI iii 4*; *MV i 1*) (NOTE: The Greek equivalent is **Artemis**.)

Dian's bud *noun* a type of plant (*MND iv 1*) (NOTE: It is probably the tree *Vitex agnus castus*, whose leaves and fruits were used to reduce sexual desire. It is unlikely to be one of the group of plants called **artemisia**, some of which are used to treat stomach complaints.)

dibble *noun* a tapering stick used to make holes in the earth for planting seedlings (*WT iv 4*)

dick *noun* a young lad (*TN v 1*)

Dickon *noun* King Richard (Dick) (*R3 v 8*)

diction *noun* the choice of words used in a description (*H v 2*)

die *noun* one of a pair of dice (*MND v 1*; *WT iv 3*; *R3 v 4*) ◇ **die in thy lap** to enjoy sexual intercourse (*MA v 2*)

diet *noun* a set of conditions controlling someone's conduct (*R3 i 1*)

dieted *adjective* strictly controlled

Dieu ◇ **Dieu de batailles** *French* God of battles (*H5 iii 5*) ◇ **Dieu vous garde, monsieur, Et vous aussi, votre serviteur** *French* God keep you, sir, and you too your servant (*TN iii 1*)

difference *noun* 1. an argument or disagreement (*MV iv 1*; *JC i 2*) 2. a distinctive quality (*H v 2*) 3. an alteration to a coat-of-arms to separate one branch of a family from the main one (*MA i 1*; *H iv 5*)

difficult weight *phrase* difficult to estimate (*O iii 3*)

diffused *adjective* disorderly (*H5 v 2*; *R3 i 2*)

digest *verb* 1. to organise something (*R3 iii 1*; *H ii 2*; *AC ii 2*) 2. to accept something (*MV iii 5*) 3. to take something in (*KL i 1*) 4. to get rid of something (*H5 ii Chor.*)

dignify *verb* to grant honour to someone or something (*2H4 i 1*)

dignity *noun* 1. excellence (*RJ Prol.*) 2. a position of authority (*1H4 i 1*; *2H4 v 1*; *CE i 1*; *H5 v 1*; *R3 iii 7, iv 4*; *T i 1*)

digress *verb* **1.** to deviate from a stated course (*TS iii 2*; *RJ iii 3*) **2.** to commit an offence (*R2 v 3*)

digressing *adjective* sinning (*R2 v 3*)

digt *verb* has dug (*H5 iii 2*)

dilated *adjective* extended (*H i 2*)

dilation *noun* an emotional outburst (*O iii 3*)

dildo *noun* a penis (*WT iv 4*)

diligence *noun* an earnest, industrious person (*T v 1*)

diligent *adjective* attentive (*T iii 1*)

diluculo surgere *phrase* Latin early to rise (*TN ii 3*) [From the Latin maxim *diluculo surgere saluberrimum est*, 'to rise at dawn is healthy'.]

diminutive *noun* a very small person or thing (*AC iv 12*)

dint *noun* a blow or force (*2H4 iv 1*; *JC iii 2*)

direction *noun* the ability to guide or direct (*R3 v 3*)

direct session *noun* the ordinary sitting of a court (*O i 2*)

direness *noun* horror (*M v 5*)

dirge *noun* a piece of slow music played or sung at a funeral (*RJ iv 5*; *H i 2*)

Dis *noun* the Roman god of the underworld (Hades) (*T iv 1*)

disable *verb* to regard something as being of little value (*AYLI iv 1*)

disabling *adjective* regarding something as being of little value (*MV ii 7*)

disannul *verb* to cancel something out (*CE i 1*)

disappointed *adjective* unprepared (*H i 5*)

disaster *noun* bad luck (*H i 1*; *M iii 1*) (NOTE: This was often thought to result from a planet being in an unfavourable position in relation to another.) ■ *verb* to destroy something (*AC ii 7*)

COMMENT: The scholar Horatio refers to *disasters* in the first scene of **Hamlet** when he compares the appearance of the Ghost with the horrors in Rome just before Julius Caesar's death: 'stars with trains of fire, and dews of blood,/Disasters in the sun'. He means more than our general sense of 'calamity'. He refers specifically to the word's Latin source, 'disastre', meaning 'an unfavourable star'. Elizabethans believed that the movements of the heavens could have direct effects on events in our world and that they were beyond our control, an equivalent to our 'act of God', as found in today's insurance documents. The word comes closer to our meaning when the First Murderer tells Macbeth that he is 'so weary of disasters, tugged with fortune'.

disbranch *verb* to cut something off (*KL iv 2*)

discandy *verb* to melt or dissolve something (*AC iii 11 (iv 12)*)

discase *verb* to remove your clothes (*T v 1*; *WT iv 4*)

discernings *plural noun* the faculties needed for judging something or someone (*KL i 4*)

discharge *noun* a performance (*T ii 1*) ■ *verb* **1.** to play a part (*MND iv 2*) **2.** to pay off a debt (*MV iii 2*) **3.** to release someone or something from doing something (*MA v 1*; *RJ v 1*) **4.** to ejaculate semen (*2H4 ii 4*)

discipline *noun* teaching (*H5 iii 2*; *R3 iii 7*)

disciplines of war *plural noun* military tactics (*H5 iii 2*)

disclaim *verb* to refuse to have anything to do with someone (*R2 i 1*; *KL i 1, ii 2*)

disclaiming *noun* a refusal to have anything to do with something (*H v 2*)

disclose *noun* a chick emerging from its shell (*H iii 1*) ■ *verb* to hatch (*H v 1*)

disclosed *adjective* unfolded (*H i 3*)

discolour *verb* to make something blush (*2H4 ii 2*)

discomfited *adjective* **1.** completely defeated (*1H4 iii 2*) **2.** discouraged (*TS ii 1*)

discomfort *noun* **1.** discouragement (*R2 iii 2*; *M i 2*) **2.** sadness (*2H4 i 2*; *M iv 2*; *AC iv 2*) ■ *verb* **1.** to discourage someone (*JC v 3*) **2.** to grieve (*H iii 2*)

discomfortable *adjective* discouraging (*R2 iii 2*)

discommend *verb* to disapprove of something (*KL ii 2*)

discontent *noun* someone who is dissatisfied with their conditions (*1H4 v 1*; *AC i 4*)

discontented *adjective* full of expressions of dissatisfaction (*O v 2*)

discontenting *adjective* dissatisfied (*WT iv 4*)

discontinue *verb* to give up something (*MA v 1*; *MV iii 4*)

discourse *noun* the power or process of reasoning (*MM i 2*; *H i 2*, *iv 4*; *O iv 2*) ■ *verb* to produce something (*H iii 2*)

discover *verb* **1.** to recognise something (*MM iv 2*; *JC ii 1*) **2.** to reveal the truth about someone (*KL i 1*) **3.** to find something out by spying or observation (*CE i 1*; *R2 ii 3*; *AC iv 10*)

COMMENT: *Discover* often had a more literal meaning in Shakespeare's time than it has for us. For example, it was used in a specific way in the theatre to indicate that a character begins the scene on stage rather than making an entry. Literally, the cover – or curtain – is raised to reveal him/her to the audience. Within the plays, *discover* is often associated with conspiracies or furtive behaviour. In **King Lear** Edmund's plot is to persuade Gloucester that Edgar is plotting: 'with curst speech/I threatened to discover him', meaning that he will reveal the 'truth' about him. In **Othello**, Roderigo tells Brabantio, 'I think I can discover him', i.e. reveal where he is. Again, this is a plot about another supposed plot. Sometimes *discover* meant simply 'to recognise'. In **Measure for Measure** the Provost worries about a plot to substitute one condemned man for another: 'Angelo hath seen them both and will discover the favour', i.e. recognise the face. But here again the context is of furtive behaviour.

discoverer *noun* an army scout (*2H4 iv 1*)

discovery *noun* a revelation (*H ii 2*)

discreet *adjective* indiscreet (*2H4 ii 4*)

discretion ◇ **do your discretion** do as you think fit (*O iii 2*)

disease *noun* trouble or worry (*AYLI v 4*; *KL i 1*) [From *dis+ease*, the idea of having no ease.]

disgrace *noun* **1.** dishonour **2.** contempt **3.** bad luck ■ *verb* to insult someone

disgracious *adjective* disliked (*R3 iii 7*, *iv 4*)

disguise *noun* a state of being drunk (*AC ii 2*)

dishonest *adjective* **1.** unreliable (*MM v 1*; *TN iii 4*) **2.** not a virgin (*AYLI v 3*; *TN i 5*; *H5 i 2*)

disjoin *verb* to separate something from something else (*JC ii 1*)

disjoint *verb* to fall apart (*M iii 2*) ■ *adjective* harassed (*H i 2*)

dislike *noun* a disagreement (*1H4 v 1*; *KL i 4*) ■ *verb* to displease someone (*RJ ii 2*; *O ii 3*)

disliken *verb* to disguise something (*WT iv 4*)

dislimn *verb* to blur something (*AC iv 12 (14)*)

dismissed *adjective* **1.** rejected (*T iv 1*) **2.** forgiven (*MM ii 2*)

dismission *noun* the act of dismissing someone from an official position (*AC i 1*)

dismount *verb* to draw a sword from its scabbard (*TN iii 4*)

disnatured *adjective* unnatural (*KL i 4*)

dispark *verb* to open up to public use an area of parkland where game animals used to be kept (*R2 iii 1*)

dispatch *noun* **1.** speed (*H5 ii 4*; *O i 3*) **2.** a settlement (*MM iv 4*) **3.** permission to leave (*KL ii 1*) **4.** the control or arrangement of something (*M i 5*) ■ *verb* **1.** to kill someone (*R2 iii 1*; *R3 i 2*) **2.** to conclude a business transaction (*MM iii 1*; *AC iii 2, v 2*) **3.** to deprive someone of something (*H i 5*)

dispense *verb* to pardon something (*CE ii 1*; *MM iii 1*)

dispense with *verb* **1.** to accept (*CE ii 1*; *MM iii 1*) **2.** to do without something (*MM iii 1*)

displace *verb* to remove something (*M iii 4*; *2H4 iv 5*)

displant *verb* to move something from one place to another (*RJ iii 3*; *O ii 1*)

disponge *verb* to pour out like water being squeezed from a sponge (*AC iv 9*)

disport *noun* a pastime (*O i 3*) ■ *verb* to amuse oneself

dispose *noun* a way of behaving (*O i 3*) ■ *verb* **1.** to accept (*H5 iii 3*, *iv 1*) **2.** to stow something away (*RJ v 1*)

disposed *adjective* in a good mood (*TN ii 3*)

disposition *noun* arrangements made for someone (*O i 3*)

disprise *verb* to regard something with contempt (*H iii 1*)

disproportioned *adjective* disfigured (*O i 3*, *iii 3*; *T v 1*)

disputable *adjective* argumentative (*AYLI ii 5*)

disputation *noun* a conversation (*1H4 iii 1*; *H5 iii 2*)

dispute *verb* **1.** to discuss something (*WT iv 4*; *RJ iii 3*) **2.** to resist something (*M iv 3*)

disquantity *verb* to make something smaller (*KL i 4*)

disseat *verb* to dethrone someone (*M v 3*)

disseise *verb* to dispossess (*M v 3*)

dissemble *verb* to disguise something (*TN iv 2*)

dissembling *noun* falseness (*AC i 3*) ■ *adjective* false (*CE iv 4*)

dissembly *noun* a gathering (*MA iv 2*)

dissipation *noun* the act of breaking something up (*KL i 2*)

dissolution *noun* **1.** melting **2.** destruction (*MM iii 2*; *R2 ii 1*; *KL i 2*)

dissolve *verb* **1.** to melt (*MND i 1*; *R2 iii 2*; *KL v 3*) **2.** to stop working (*T iv 1, v 1*) **3.** to loosen something (*R2 ii 2*)

distaff *noun* **1.** a short stick for holding the wool, etc. when spinning (*KL iv 2*) **2.** a penis (*TN i 3*)

distance *noun* **1.** hostility (*M iii 1*) **2.** the space between two people fencing (*RJ ii 4*)

distaste *verb* to taste unpleasant (*O iii 3*)

distemper *noun* **1.** bad temper (*WT i 2*; *H iii 2*) **2.** drunkenness (*H5 ii 2*) **3.** illness (*H ii 2*) ■ *verb* to upset something (*TN ii 1*)

distemperature *noun* a spell of bad weather (*MND ii 1*; *1H4 v 1*)

distempered *adjective* **1.** bad tempered (*H iii 2*) **2.** unwell (*TN i 5*)

distempering *adjective* sedating (*O i 1*)

distill *verb* **1.** to fall in small drops (*RJ v 1*) **2.** to melt (*AYLI iii 1*)

distinctly *adverb* in separate parts (*T i 2*)

distinguishment *noun* the act of distinguishing between things (*WT ii 1*)

distract *verb* **1.** to separate something (*AC iii 7*; *O i 3*) **2.** to confuse someone (*O ii 3*) **3.** to make someone mentally disturbed (*2H4 ii 1*) ■ *adjective* **1.** mentally disturbed (*TN v 1*; *KL iv 6*; *H iv 5*) **2.** confused (*CE iv 3*; *JC iv 3*; *H i 5*)

distractedly *adverb* in a confused manner (*TN ii 2*)

distraction *noun* a group (*AC iii 7*)

distrain *verb* to seize goods as payment of a debt (*R2 ii 3*)

distressful *adjective* earned by hard work (*H5 iv 1*)

disvouch *verb* to contradict something (*MM iv 4*)

ditch-dog *noun* a dog lying dead in a ditch (*KL iii 4*)

divers *adjective* many (*1H4 i 1*; *2H4 iii 1*; *MV iii 1*)

divine *noun* a priest (*WT iii 1*) ■ *adjective* immortal (*R2 i 1*)

divinely *adverb* invoking God (*R3 iii 3*)

diviner *noun* a fortune-teller (*CE iii 2*)

division *noun* **1.** a musical term referring to one long note being replaced by many short ones (*1H4 iii 1*; *RJ iii 5*) **2.** variation (*M iv 3*) **3.** the positioning of the sections of an army (*2H4 i 3*; *O i 1*)

doctrine *noun* learning or knowledge (*AC v 2*; *RJ i 1*; *TN i 5*)

document *noun* an instruction (*H iv 5*)

do de *phrase* representing the sound of someone shivering with cold (*KL iii 4*)

doer *noun* someone who commits adultery (*MM iv 3*)

doff *verb* to take something off (*TS iii 2*; *RJ ii 2*) See also **daff**

dog-ape *noun* a male ape or dog-faced baboon (*AYLI ii 5*)

dog-hearted *adjective* cruel (*KL iv 3*)

dog weary *adjective* exhausted (*TS iv 3*)

doing *noun* sexual intercourse (*H5 iii 7*)

doit *noun* something insignificant (*T ii 2*) [From *doit*, 'a small Dutch coin of little value'.]

dole *noun* misery (*MND v 1*; *AYLI i 2*; *H i 2*)

doleful *adjective* miserable (*2H4 ii 4*; *RJ iv 5*)

dollar *noun* a large silver German coin (*T ii 1*; *M i 2*) [From German *thaler*.]

domesday *noun* Judgement Day, the end of the world (*1H4 iv 1*; *R3 v 1*; *RJ v 3*)

domineer *verb* to have a wild party (*TS iii 2*)

don *noun* sir or master (*MA v 2*)

done *adjective* lost or finished (*R2 i 1*; *H iii 2*)

doom *noun* **1.** death (*R2 iii 2*; *R3 iv 4*) **2.** a punishment (*R2 i 3*) ◊ **Great Doom** the day of death and the Last Judgement (*RJ ii 2*; *M iv 1*)

door particulars *plural noun* personal and private concerns (*KL v 1*)

dormouse *adjective* sleeping (*TN iii 2*) [Because a dormouse was noted for the length of time during which it hibernates.]

dotage *noun* an infatuation (*MA ii 3*; *MND iv 1*; *O iv 1*)

double *verb* to repeat oneself (*2H4 iii 1*) ■ *adjective* approved by two people (*H v 1*) ◇ **as double** twice as powerful (*O i 2*)

double-dealing *noun* cheating (*TN v 1*)

doublet and hose *noun* the typical characteristics of a man (*AYLI ii 3*) [Because doublet and hose were the normal items of dress of a man.]

dough ◇ **cake's dough** failure (*TS I 1, v 1*)

dout *verb* to put out a fire (*H5 iv 2*; *H iv 7*)

dovehouse *noun* a dovecote (*RJ i 3*)

Dover *noun* a port on the coast of Kent. It has always been important as the nearest port to the French coast. (*KL iii 1, 6, 7, iv 1*)

dower *noun* a dowry, the money and property given by the bride's father to the bridegroom on their marriage (*KL i 1*; *MM i 1*; *T iii 1*; *TS ii 1, iv 2*)

dowlas *noun* a coarse linen cloth which was originally from the town of Doulais in Brittany, France (*1H4 iii 3*)

dowle *noun* down, the small soft feathers from a duck or goose (*T iii 3*)

down-gyved *adjective* covering the ankles like chains (*H ii 1*)

downright *adverb* **1.** straight down (*RJ iii 5*) **2.** definitely (*AYLI iii 4*; *MND ii 1*)

down-roping *adjective* hanging down in sticky strings (*H5 iv 2*)

down sleeves *plural noun* sleeves that hang down (*MA iii 4*)

doxy *noun* a prostitute (*WT iv 3*)

drab *noun* a prostitute (*H ii 2*; *M iv 1*; *MM ii 1*)

drabbing *noun* associating with prostitutes (*H ii 1*)

drachma *noun* a silver coin or weight used in ancient Greece (*JC iii 2*)

draff *noun* scraps fed to pigs (*1H4 iv 2*)

draw *verb* **1.** to pull something out (*AYLI v 2*; *TN ii 3*) **2.** to empty something (*MM ii 1*) **3.** to impose a fine (*MV iv 1*) **4.** to meet someone (*M ii 2*) **5.** to entice someone (*MV v 1*) **6.** to act together (*TC v 5*; *O iv 1*) **7.** to gather something together (*1H4 iii 1*) **8.** to play a violin (*MA v 1*) **9.** to withdraw from doing something (*2H4 ii 1*) **10.** to win something (*WT i 2*; *KL i 1*; *H iv 5*) **11.** to write something (*MND i 1*; *TS iii 1*; *MV iv 1*)

drawbridge *noun* a bridge across a moat that can be pulled up in the event of attack (*R3 iii 5*)

draw dry-foot *verb* to hunt an animal by following its scent (*CE iv 2*)

drawer *noun* someone who serves beer in an inn (*1H4 ii 4*)

drawn *adjective* **1.** drunk quickly and in large amounts (*T ii 2*) **2.** (*of a hunted animal*) forced from its hiding place (*1H4 iii 3*) **3.** ready with a drawn sword (*MND iii 2*; *T ii 1*; *RJ i 1*)

dread-bolted *adjective* accompanied by lightning (*KL iv 7*)

dreg *noun* the remains of something (*T ii 2*; *R3 i 4*)

dressing *noun* the special clothes worn by someone holding a particular official position (*MM v 1*)

dribbling *adjective* (*of an arrow*) falling short of the target (*MM i 3*)

drive at *verb* **1.** to attack someone (*1H4 ii 4*) **2.** to rush at someone (*H ii 2*)

driven *adjective* (*of snow*) formed into drifts (*WT iv 4*)

driving *adjective* (*of a boat*) drifting (*TN i 2*)

drollery *noun* **1.** a puppet show (*T iii 3*) **2.** an amusing picture (*2H4 ii 1*)

drone *noun* a pipe on a bagpipe that emits one continuous note (*1H4 i 2*)

dropping *adjective* dripping (*H i 2, i 5*)

drossy *adjective* worthless (*H v 2*) (NOTE: Dross is the scum formed on molten metal.)

drovier *noun* someone who drives cattle from place to place (a drover) (*MA ii 1*)

drum *noun* a meeting place (*1H4 iii 3*)

dry-beat *verb* to beat someone severely but without drawing blood (*RJ iii 1, iv 5*)

dry bones *plural noun* a supposed symptom of a sexually transmitted disease (*AC i 4*)

dry convulsions *plural noun* rheumatism (*T iv 1*)

dub *verb* to make someone a knight or give someone some other title of rank (*2H4 v 3*; *H5 ii 2*)

ducat *noun* **1.** a gold coin which was widely used in Europe (*H ii 2, iii 4*; *MM iii 2*) **2.** a silver coin used in Italy (*MV ii 8*; *TN i 3*)

ducdame *noun* a call to attract attention (*AYLI ii 5*) [Possibly from *duc ad me* Latin 'bring to me', or *dewch da mi* Welsh 'come to me'.]

dudgeon *noun* the handle of a dagger (*M ii 1*)

duello *noun* the laws regulating duelling (*TN iii 4*)

duer paid *adjective* more acceptable to (*2H4 iii 2*)

dugs *plural noun* nipples (*AYLI ii 4*; *R3 ii 2*)

dump *noun* a slow dance (*MA ii 3*; *RJ iv 5*)

dumps *noun* low spirits (*RJ iv 5*)

dun *adjective* of a grey-brown colour (*M i 5*) ◇ **to draw dun from the mire** a game involving lifting a log that represented a horse stuck in mud (*RJ i 4*) ◇ **dun's the mouse** keep still! (*RJ i 4*)

dungy *adjective* vile (*WT ii 1*; *AC i 1*)

dup *verb* to open something (*H iv 5*)

durance *noun* **1.** prison dress (*CE iv 3*; *TN v 1*; *2H4 v 5*) **2.** imprisonment (*MM iii 1*)

duty *noun* **1.** respect (*AYLI v 2*; *MND v 1*; *TN iii 1*; *1H4 v 2*) **2.** what is deserved (*TS iv 1*)

dwindle *verb* to gradually decrease (*M i 3*; *1H4 iii 3*)

E

eager *adjective* **1.** bitter (*R2 ii 1*; *H i 5*) **2.** keen physically or mentally (*R2 i 1*; *H i 4*) **3.** without thought for the consequences (*R2 v 3*)

eale *adjective* evil (*H i 4*)

ean *verb* (*of a sheep*) to give birth (*MV i 3*)

eanling *noun* a young lamb (*MV i 3*)

ear *verb* to plough land (*AC i 2*; *R2 iii 2*) ◇ **by the ears** quarrelling ◇ **in the ear** so everyone can hear (*H iii 1*; *1H4 iv 5*) ◇ **o'er eared** drowned (being in water so deep that it is above the ears) (*T iv 1*) ◇ **shake your ears** to act like a donkey (*TN ii 3*)

ear-bussing *noun* whispering in the ear (*KL ii 1*) [From *buss*, 'to kiss'.]

earn *verb* **1.** to grieve (*JC ii 2*) **2.** to feel compassion (*H5 ii 3*)

earnest *noun* a payment given in advance (*WT iv 4*; *CE ii 2*; *H5 v 1*)

earth *noun* **1.** an estate or kingdom (*R2 ii 1*; *RJ i 2*) **2.** anything dull and heavy (*R2 iii 4*; *KL v 3*) (NOTE: May refer to the element 'earth' – one of the elements, earth, fire, wind and water – which has these properties.)

earthed *adjective* (*of a dead body*) buried (*T ii 1*)

earthy *adjective* **1.** concerned with material and practical things (*T i 2*; *CE iii 2*) **2.** dull and colourless

eastern star *noun* the star seen by the Three Wise Men which guided them to the place where the baby Jesus lay (Matthew 2) (*AC v 2*)

eat ◇ **eat the air** to be given promises or hopes of things that are unlikely to happen (*2H4 i 3*; *H ii 2*)

ebb *verb* **1.** to lose force or energy (*T ii 1*; *AYLI ii 7*; *AC i 4*; *O iii 3*) **2.** to be dry (*T i 2*)

ebon *adjective* black like ebony, the wood of a tropical tree (*2H4 v 5*)

Ebrew *noun* Hebrew (*1H4 ii 4*)

ecce signum *phrase Latin* behold the sign (*1H4 ii 4*)

ecstasy *noun* a trance (*O iv 1*)

edge *noun* **1.** a sword or dagger (*2H4 iii 2*; *H5 ii 1*) **2.** a keen desire, often sexual (*TS i 2*; *MM i 4*; *T iv 1*; *H iii 2*) **3.** a dangerous path on a ridge (*2H4 i 1*) ◇ **to give an edge** to encourage someone to do something (*H iii 1*)

education *noun* general upbringing rather than teaching (*AYLI i 1*; *O i 3*; *TS Ind. 1, ii 1*)

effect *verb* to result in something ■ *noun* a result ◇ **prove effects** to be fulfilled (*L iv 2*)

effeminate *adjective* **1.** weak or cowardly (*RJ iii 1*) (NOTE: Literally 'like a woman'.) **2.** inconsistent (*AYLI iii 2*) **3.** gentle (*R3 iii 7*)

effigies *plural noun* images (*AYLI ii 7*)

eftest *noun* the fastest (*MA iv 2*)

egally *adverb* equally (*R3 iii 7*)

egg *noun* something that is worthless (*WT i 2*; *M iv 2*)

egg-shell *noun* same as **egg** (*H iv 4*)

eglantine *noun* the sweet-smelling wild rose (*MND ii 1*)

egregious *adjective* extraordinary (*H5 ii 1*)

egregiously *adverb* outrageously (*O ii 1*)

Egyptian thief *noun* Thyamis, who tried to kill his captive Chariclea before she was taken by his captors (*TN v 1*)

eight and six *noun* the common metre of ballads of the time was alternating lines of eight and six syllables (*MND iii 1*)

eight-penny *adjective* trivial (*1H4 iii 3*)

eisel, eysel *noun* vinegar (*H v 1*)

eke *verb* to add to something (*MV iii 2*) ■ *conjunction* also (*MND iii 1*)

Elbe *noun* a major river in Germany which starts at Reisengebirge in the Czech Republic and flows into the North Sea at Cuxhaven in Germany (*H5 i 2*)

elbow [From the old belief that happiness made your elbow itch.] ◇ **to rub the elbow** to be happy (*1H4 v 1*)

eld *noun* **1.** old times (*T v 1*) **2.** old age (*MM iii 1*)

elder-gun *noun* a toy gun made from a twig of an elder tree (*H5 iv 1*)

element *noun* the night sky (*2H4 iv 3*)

eleven and twenty *adjective* exactly right (*TS iv 2*) [Referring to an old card game similar to pontoon (vingt-et-un, 21 up) in which a winning hand had to add up to 3.]

elf *verb* to make the hair tangled and matted (*KL ii 3*) (NOTE: This was supposed to be caused by the work of elves.)

elfish-marked, elvish-marked *adjective* having a birthmark (*R3 i 3*)

elflocks *plural noun* tangled, matted hair (*RJ i 4*)

elf skin, eel skin *noun* a very thin person (*1H4 ii 4*)

ell *noun* a length of 1.125 m (*1H4 iii 2; CE iii 2; RJ ii 4*)

elm *noun* elm branches, which do not rot readily, were used to support vines (*MND iv 1; CE ii 2*)

Elysium *noun* paradise (*H5 iv 1; TN i 2*) (NOTE: In Greek mythology, Elysium was the place where certain heroes went after death.)

embassage *noun* a message or errand (*MA i 1, ii 1; R3 ii 1*)

embattle *verb* to put forces in a position ready for battle (*H5 iv 2; AC iv 9*)

embayed *adjective* (*of a ship*) trapped in or sheltered by a bay (*O ii 1*)

embossed *adjective* **1.** swollen (*AYLI ii 7*) **2.** foaming at the mouth like a horse after a hard run (*TS Ind. 1; AC iv 11*)

embowel *verb* to cut out someone's internal organs (*1H4 v 4; R3 v 2*)

embrace *verb* **1.** to accept someone or something **2.** to surround something **3.** to cherish something **4.** when used in the usual sense of clasping someone closely, there is always a sexual connotation

eminence *noun* **1.** high rank (*KL v 1*) **2.** a special honour (*M iii 2*)

emmew *verb* to confine someone like a horse in a stable (*MM iii 1*)

emper *noun* a kingdom or empire (*H5 i 2*)

empery *noun* **1.** an empire (*R3 iii 7*) **2.** complete rule over a country (*H5 i 2*)

employ *verb* to send someone on a mission (*AC v 2*)

empoison *verb* to have a destructive effect on something (*MA iii 1*)

emulate *adjective* ambitious (*H i 1*)

emulation *noun* **1.** an attempt to equal someone's achievements (*AYLI iv 1*) **2.** ambition (*JC ii 3; R3 ii 3*)

emulator *noun* someone who is jealous of another person or thing and treats them with contempt (*AYLI i 1*)

enact *verb* **1.** to act a part in a play (*H iii 2*) **2.** to cause something (*R3 v 4*) **3.** to decree something (*MV iv 1*)

enacture *noun* an action (*H iii 2*)

enamelled *adjective* hard, smooth and shiny (*MND ii 2; CE ii 1*)

enchafed *adjective* furious (*O ii 1*)

enchanted *adjective* having magical powers (*T v 1; MV v 1*)

enchanted trifle *noun* a magic trick (*T v 1*)

enchantingly *adverb* by magic (*AYLI i 1*)

enchantment *noun* a woman with magical powers (*WT iv 4*)

enclog *verb* to obstruct something (*O ii 1*)

enclouded *adjective* covered completely as if in a cloud (*AC v 2*)

encompassment *noun* the act of talking about a subject indirectly (*H ii 1*)

encounter *noun* behaviour (*TS iv 5; WT iii 2; H ii 2*) ■ *verb* to make love (*MM iii 1*)

encumbered *adjective* folded (*H i 5*)

end *noun* **1.** death (*2H4 iv 4; R3 ii 1*) **2.** a purpose **3.** a cause **4.** a quotation (*MA i 1; R3 i 3*)

endart *verb* to fire an arrow into something (*RJ i 3*)

endeared *adjective* indebted to someone (*2H4 ii 3*)

endue, indue *verb* to provide someone with something (*TN i 5*)

endurance *noun* patience (*MA ii 1*)

endure *verb* to last (*TN ii 3*)

Endymion *noun* in Greek mythology, a shepherd who was loved by the moon-goddess Selene (*MV v 1*) (NOTE: Zeus gave Endymion eternal youth and beauty by allowing him to sleep every night on Mount Latmus. Here he was visited nightly by Selene by whom he had fifty daughters.)

enew *verb* to chase an animal into a river or lake (*MM iii 1*) [From a term used in falconry meaning 'to drive into water'.]

enfeoff *verb* to give yourself up to be made a slave (*1H4 iii 2*)

enfoldings, infoldings *plural noun* clothing (*WT iv 4*)

enforce *verb* to rape a woman (*MND iii 1*)

enforcement *noun* **1.** compulsion (*2H4 i 1*; *R3 iii 7*) **2.** rape (*R3 iii 7*)

enfranched *adjective* freed (*AC iii 13*)

enfranchise *verb* **1.** to free someone (*MA i 3*) **2.** to grant someone political freedom (*AC i 1*)

engage *verb* **1.** to promise something as a guarantee (*1H4 ii 4*; *AYLI v 4*; *O iii 3*) **2.** to use something as security for a loan (*1H4 iv 3*) **3.** to undertake something (*AC iv 7*)

engagement *noun* an undertaking (*JC ii 1*)

engaol *verb* to put someone in jail (*R2 i 3*)

engild *verb* to make something bright like gold (*MND iii 2*)

engine *noun* **1.** a large piece of military equipment (*O iii 3, iv 2*) **2.** an instrument of torture (*KL i 4*) **3.** a device (*T ii 1*)

COMMENT: *Engine* has narrowed its meaning since 1600 to our limited sense of 'a machine'. Shakespeare remained closer to the word's Latin origin of 'ingenium', meaning 'an inborn capacity or skill'. Our 'genius' is connected to 'ingenium'. Therefore *engine* could have a general meaning of anything cleverly contrived, like a plot or a device. In **The Two Gentlemen of Verona** the *engine* or device is a rope ladder used to help a girl escape from a high window. In **Othello**, Iago, protesting his loyalty, invites the general to 'devise engines for my life' if he breaks his promise. Here, *engines* has the broad sense of 'means or plans', perhaps edging towards something more specific like machinery for torture.

engineer *noun* an inventive person (*H iii 4*; *O ii 1*)

englut *verb* **1.** to consume something (*O i 3*) **2.** to engulf something (*H5 iv 3*)

engraff *verb* to attach something firmly (*2H4 ii 2*; *JC ii 1*)

engross, ingross *verb* **1.** to accumulate, build up (*1H4 iii 2*) **2.** to make a corrected copy of something (*R3 iii 6*) **3.** to make something fat (*R3 iii 7*)

engrossing *adjective* taking over completely (*RJ v 3*)

engrossment *noun* the total accumulated (*2H4 iv 5*)

enguard *verb* to protect someone or something (*KL i 4*)

enjoin *verb* **1.** to order someone to do something on oath (*MA v 1*; *RJ iv 2*; *T iii 1*) **2.** to bind someone by an oath (*MV ii 9*)

enkindle *verb* to tempt someone to do something (*M i 3*)

enlarge *verb* to free someone (*TN v 1*; *H5 ii 2*)

enlargement *noun* freedom (*1H4 iii 1*)

enlink *verb* to join something to something else (*H5 iii 3*)

enmesh *verb* to snare someone (*O ii 3*)

enormous *adjective* riotous (*KL ii 2*)

enraged *adjective* **1.** passionate (*MA ii 3, iii 2*) **2.** heated (*2H4 i 1*)

enrol *verb* to record something on a roll of parchment (*MM i 2*; *JC iii 2*)

enrooted *adjective* mixed closely together (*2H4 iv 1*)

enround *verb* to surround someone (*H5 iv Chor.*)

enschedule *verb* to write something down (*H5 v 2*)

ensconce *verb* to hide behind something (*CE ii 2*)

enseamed *adjective* creased and soaked after sexual intercourse (*H iii 4*)

enshied *adjective* protected (*MM ii 4*)

ensign *noun* **1.** a military banner (*JC v 1*; *RJ v 1*) **2.** someone who carries a military banner (*JC v 3*)

ensinewed, insinewed *adjective* joined together firmly (*2H4 iv 1*)

enstate, instate *verb* to give money or property to someone (*MM v 1*)

ensteeped *adjective* lying under water (*O ii 1*)

enteasured *adjective* preserved (*2H4 iii 1*)

enter *verb* **1.** to bind yourself to a contract (*CE iv 4*; *MA ii 3*; *R2 v 2*; *O iii 3*) **2.** to bring a legal action (*2H4 ii 1*) **3.** to introduce someone (*AC iv 14*)

entertain *verb* **1.** to employ someone (*MA i 3*; *JC v 5*) **2.** to draw attention to something (*WT iv 4*) **3.** to engage an enemy (*H5 i 2*) **4.** to maintain something (*MM iii 1*; *MV i 1*) **5.** to accept something as being true (*CE iii 1*; *AYLI iii 2*; *R3 i 4*)

entertainer *noun* someone who clings on to hope or an idea (*T ii 1*)

entertainment *noun* **1.** accommodation and food for guests **2.** employment (*AC iv 6*) **3.** a way of spending time ◇ **mutual entertainment** mutual caressing ending in sexual intercourse (*MM I 2*)

entire *adjective* **1.** sincere (*TS iv 2*) **2.** pure (*2H4 ii 4*; *KL i 1*)

entirely *adverb* **1.** sincerely (*MA iii 1*; *MV iii 2*) **2.** without stopping (*MM iv 2*)

entrance *noun* **1.** an entrance fee (*TS ii 1*) **2.** an opening (*1H4 i 1*)

entreat *verb* **1.** to pass time (*RJ iv 1*) **2.** to handle someone (*R2 iii 1*) **3.** to negotiate (*AYLI iv 3*; *KL iii 3*)

entreatment *noun* a favour asked (*H i 3*)

envenom *verb* to poison someone (*AYLI ii 3*; *H iv 7*)

enwheel *verb* to encircle someone (*O ii 1*)

Ephesian *noun* a drinking companion (*2H4 ii 2*) (NOTE: Why Shakespeare used this as a description of a drinking companion is not clear.)

Ephesus *noun* one of the great cities of the Eastern Mediterranean, it was situated about 5 km from the sea on the bank of the Cayster River and was one of the main transport junctions between East and West. It is now a ruin in modern Turkey. (*CE i 1, ii 2, iv 1, 4*)

epicure *noun* a lover of luxury and the easy life (*M v 3*; *AC ii 7*)

epicurean *adjective* devoted to luxury (*AC ii 1*)

epicurism *noun* luxury (*KL i 4*)

Epicurus *noun* a Greek philosopher (c. 341– c. 270 BC) who believed that omens had no meaning and that the pursuit of pleasure was the absolute aim of life. This pleasure was absolute peace of mind. (*JC v 1*) (NOTE: Although the idea of luxurious living and excessive material pleasures is now associated with his teaching, this is a corruption of his philosophy.)

Epidamnum, Epidamnus *noun* a port on the coast of Illyria (modern Albania) (*CE i 1, 2, iv 1, v 1*)

epigram *noun* a short poem expressing a satirical or witty point (*MA v 4*)

epithet *noun* an idiom (*MA v 2*; *O i 1*)

equal *verb* to manage to deal with someone (*2H4 i 3*)

equinoctial *noun* the equator (*TN ii 3*)

equinox *noun* a counterbalance (*O ii 3*)

equity *noun* justice (*1H4 ii 2*; *KL iii 6*)

equivocal *adjective* having two or more possible meanings (*O i 3*)

equivocate *verb* to attempt to deceive someone by using a statement with more than one possible interpretation (*M ii 3*)

equivocation *noun* the attempt to deceive someone by using a statement with more than one possible interpretation (*M v 5*; *H v 1*)

equivocator *noun* someone who swears to a statement while mentally denying it (*M ii 3*)

COMMENT: *Equivocate*, meaning literally 'to speak on both sides', makes its only Shakespearean appearance in **Macbeth**, but it is very significant for the play's theme. It appears in the Porter's drunken soliloquy when he imagines himself as porter of Hell-gate facing a queue of offenders looking for admission: 'Faith, here's an equivocator, that could swear in both the scales against either scale, who committed treason enough for God's sake, yet could not equivocate to heaven. O, come in, equivocator!' Shakespeare is referring specifically to a Jesuit, Father Garnet, who was accused of complicity in Catholic plots against the king and was executed in 1606. At his trial 'he was found shifting and faltering in all his answers', as a result of the practice of Jesuit priests to mislead their interrogators without technically lying. *Equivocation* is relevant to the play as a whole because Macbeth's life becomes corrupted by lies and evasions as he succumbs to temptation, and, in particular, he relies on the Witches who mislead him and play with his expectations. Eventually, when Macduff reveals their final piece of trickery, Macbeth attacks these expert *equivocators*: 'And be these juggling fiends no more believed/That palter with us in a double sense,/That keep the word of promise to our ear/And break it to our hope'. It is one of Shakespeare's intriguing techniques to embed one of the play's central issues in a short scene, like the Porter's, which has virtually no impact on the plot.

Erebus *noun* **1.** in Greek mythology, the region between Earth and Hades (*2H4 ii 4*; *JC ii 1*) **2.** darkness personified (*MV v 1*)

ergo *conjunction Latin* therefore (*CE iv 3*; *MV ii 2*; *TS iv 3*)

Eros *noun* the Greek equivalent of **Cupid**

erring *adjective* wandering (*AYLI iii 2*; *H i 1*; *O i 3*)

erroneous *adjective* behaving wrongly, either criminally or by being misled (*R3 i 4*)

error *noun* **1.** a wrongdoing **2.** a lie **3.** an act of wandering off course

erst *conjunction* previously (*AYLI iii 5*; *H5 v 2*)

escape *noun* a freak (*O i 3*)

escote *verb* to provide for someone (*H ii 2*)

espial *noun* a spy (*H iii 1*)

espirance *noun* **1.** a hope (*KL iv 1*) **2.** Percy's battle-cry (*1H4 v 2*)

esquire *noun* someone next below a knight in rank, often a young man who was being trained as a knight. He was entitled to bear heraldic arms. (*2H4 iii 2*)

COMMENT: *Esquire* came from the French for 'shield-bearer', but its status increased during the Middle Ages until it described a rank just below that of a knight. In Chaucer's **The Canterbury Tales** the Squire accompanies his father, the Knight, as a pilgrim. He is depicted as elegant, cultured and devoted to 'fin amour', or courtly love. Shakespeare uses *squire* in this sense when in **Much Ado About Nothing** Don John refers to Claudio as 'A proper squire!' The sneering tone here befits the speaker, but the audience appreciates that Claudio, a very young man, has distinguished himself in war and is trying to acquire the social graces of a lover with the help of an aristocratic mentor. A similar use has survived: until recently *squire* was used as a verb, when a young man might, for example, squire a lady to a social event. In **The Winter's Tale** Leontes describes his child as 'this young squire'; Mamilius is too young to be a Claudio but the word here carries a teasing affection as the father sees his son as the companion he hopes for in about 10 years' time. Elsewhere Shakespeare uses *esquire* more formally to denote rank. In **Henry IV Part 2** when the knight Sir John Falstaff arrives in Gloucestershire, Shallow introduces himself in a mixture of pride and deprecation: 'I am Robert Shallow, sir, a poor esquire of this county, and one of the King's justices of the peace'. Squires were country landowners, often with substantial houses and estates and holding great influence over local families; they played important roles in the life of many 18th- and 19th-century novels about marriage where social distinctions influence relationships. The use of *esquire*, through the abbreviation 'Esq'. as a general term of respect, has survived in the way we often address a formal letter, though it does not now indicate a precise social rank.

essay *noun* a test (*KL i 2*)

essence *noun* existence (*MM ii 2*; *O iv 1*)

essential *adjective* real, fundamental qualities (*O ii 1*)

establish *verb* **1.** to agree something (*MV iv 1*; *H5 i 2*) **2.** to give property to someone through a will or contract (*M i 4*)

estate *noun* **1.** possessions (*MV i 1*; *2H4 i 3*) **2.** government (*WT iv 4*) ■ *verb* to give property to someone through a will or contract (*T iv 1*; *MND i 1*; *AYLI v 2*)

esteemable *adjective* **1.** valuable (*MV i 3*) **2.** admiring (*TN ii 1*)

estimate *noun* someone's reputation (*R2 ii 3*)

estimation *noun* guessing (*1H4 i 3*)

estridge *noun* **1.** an ostrich (*1H4 iv 1*) **2.** a type of hawk (a goshawk) used for hunting geese and other large birds (*AC iii 13*)

et cetera *plural noun* the female genitals (*RJ ii 1*)

eterne *adjective* eternal (*M iii 2*; *H ii 2*)

Ethiope, Ethiop *adjective* black (*AYLI iv 3*) [From *Ethiopia*.]

et tu Brute *phrase Latin* You, too, Brutus (*JC iii 1*)

Euphrates *noun* the longest river in Southwest Asia (1780 km). It rises in Armenia and joins the River Tigris, entering the Persian Gulf at Shatt-al-Arab. The Tigris-Euphrates basin was the centre of ancient civilisations. (*AC i 2*)

Europa *noun* in Greek mythology, the daughter of Agenor and his wife Telephassa (*MA v 4*) (NOTE: Europa bore Zeus three sons, Minos, Rhadamanthys and Sarpedon.)

even Christian *noun* a fellow Christian (*H v 1*)

even pleached *adjective* evenly intertwined (*H5 v 2*)

event *noun* the consequence of an action (*T i 2*; *MM iii 2*; *TS iii 2*)

ever-fired *adjective* continually burning (*O ii 1*)

everlasting *adjective* durable (*CE iv 2*)

every *determiner* 1. each one of (*T v 1*) 2. all (*AYLI v 4*; *AC i 2*)

evidence *noun* a witness (*MA iv 1*; *R3 i 4*)

evil *noun* 1. a disease, infection, etc. (*WT ii 3*; *AYLI ii 7*; *M iv 3*) 2. a brothel (*MM ii 2*)

ewer *noun* a large jug with a wide spout (*TS Ind. 1, ii 1*)

exactly *adverb* 1. completely (*R2 i 1*; *H i 2*) 2. accurately (*T i 2*; *AC v 2*)

examination *noun* a statement in answer to close questioning (*MA iii 5, iv 2*)

exasperate *verb* to anger someone (*TN iii 2*; *M iii 6*; *KL v 1*)

exceed *verb* to be the very best (*MA iii 4*)

excellently *adverb* very much (*MA iii 4*)

except *conjunction* unless (*CE v 1*; *R3 v 3*) ■ *verb* 1. to object to something (*R2 i 4*; *JC i 2*; *H ii 2*) 2. to raise an objection (*TN i 3*; *R2 i 1*)

excepted *adjective* excluded (*JC ii 1*; *MA iii 1*; *TN i 3*)

exception *noun* an objection (*1H4 i 3*; *H5 ii 4*; *O iv 2*; *TN i 3*)

excess *noun* the charging of excessive interest on money loaned (**usury**) (*MV i 3, iii 2*)

exchange flesh *verb* to have sexual intercourse (*WT iv 3*)

excitement *noun* a stimulus (*H iv 4*)

exclaim *noun* a plea (*R2 i 2*)

exclaim on *verb* to make loud accusations against something (*MV iii 3*; *R3 iii 3*)

exclamation *noun* a noisy rebuke (*R3 iv 4*)

excrement *noun* any growth on the body, including hair (*CE ii 2*; *MV iii 2*; *WT iv 3*; *H iii 4*)

excursion *noun* a rush (*H5 iv 4*) (NOTE: This is used as a stage direction.)

excuse *noun* a pardon (*TS Ind. 2*) ■ *verb* 1. to justify something (*MND v 1*; *CE iii 1*) 2. to prove yourself innocent (*R3 i 2*)

execute *verb* to perform something (*T i 2*; *R3 i 4*)

execution *noun* 1. the performance of something (*KL i 1*; *O iii 3*) 2. slaughter (*M i 2*)

executioner *noun* a murderer (*R3 i 2*)

executor *noun* 1. an agent (*T iii 1*) 2. an executioner (*H5 i 2*)

exempt *adjective* separated from (*AYLI ii 1*; *CE ii 2*; *R3 ii 1*)

exercise *noun* 1. an activity (*WT i 2*) 2. an act of worship (*WT iii 2*; *R3 iii 7*; *O iii 4*) 3. a skill (*H iv 7*) 4. a speech or sermon (*R3 iii 2*)

exhalation *noun* a meteor (*JC ii 1*)

exhale *verb* 1. to draw something out (*R3 i 2*; *RJ iii 5*) 2. to draw out a sword (*H5 ii 1*)

exhibit *verb* to propose something (*MM iv 4*; *MV ii 3*)

exhibiter *noun* someone who proposes a parliamentary bill (*H5 i 1*)

exhibition *noun* money given as a gift or allowance to provide for someone (*KL i 2*; *O i 3, iv 3*)

exigent *noun* an emergency (*JC v 1*) 2. the end (*AC iv 12 (14)*)

exion *noun* an action (*2H4 ii 1*)

exorcist *verb* someone who invokes the spirits of the dead, especially to remove any evil (*JC ii 1*)

expect *verb* to wait for something (*MV v 1*)

expectancy *noun* someone in whom hopes are placed (*H iii 1*; *O ii 1*)

expectation *noun* hope (*1H4 ii 3*) See also **note of expectation** *at* **note**

expedience *noun* 1. haste (*R2 ii 1*; *H5 iv 3*) 2. an expedition (*1H4 i 1*; *AC i 2*)

expedient *adjective* hasty (*R2 i 4*)

expediently *adverb* as hastily as possible (*AYLI iii 1*)

expedition *noun* progress (*H5 ii 2*; *R3 iv 4*)

expense *noun* an extravagance (*KL ii 1*)

experimental *adjective* relating to experience (*MA iv 1*)

expiate *adjective* arrived (*R3 iii 3*)

expire *verb* to finish (*RJ i 4*)

expostulate *verb* **1.** to put forward an idea (*H ii 2*) **2.** to argue with someone about something (*O iv 1*; *R3 iii 7*)

express *adjective* true to a divine pattern (*H ii 2*)

expressure *noun* description (*TN ii 3*)

exsufflicate *adjective* inflated (*O iii 3*)

extemporal, extemporally *adverb* on the spur of the moment (*AC v 2*)

extend *verb* **1.** to stretch something (*MV ii 7*) **2.** to demonstrate something (*O ii 1*) **3.** to increase something (*AC v 1*; *M iii 4*) **4.** to offer something (*KL i 1*; *MV i 1*; *TN ii 5*)

extent *noun* **1.** an assault (*TN iv 1*) **2.** a favour (*H ii 2*) **3.** an act of taking property with legal authority (*AYLI iii 1*)

extenuate *verb* **1.** to reduce a legal sentence (*MND i 1*) **2.** to belittle something (*JC iii 2*)

extenuation *noun* the reduction of a legal sentence (*1H4 iii 2*)

extermine *verb* to destroy something (*AYLI iii 5*)

extern *adjective* outward (*O i 1*)

extinct *adjective* extinguished (*R2 i 3*; *H i 3*; *O ii 1*)

extirp *verb* to root something out (*T i 2*; *MM iii 2*)

extirpate *verb* to remove something completely (*T i 2*)

extort *verb* to obtain something by threats or torture (*TN ii 1, iii 1*)

extravagancy *noun* the act of going beyond set limits (*TN ii 1*; *H i 1*)

COMMENT: Our meaning of 'lavish or wasteful' did not appear in the language until 1711, a hundred years after Shakespeare. For him the meaning was closely connected with its derivation from 'extra' and 'vagrant', a wandering beyond accepted boundaries. It implies something alarming and uncontrolled, as in **Hamlet** where 'the extravagant and erring spirit hies/To his confine' at dawn, when worrying darkness is replaced by the sun rising. The black general Othello can also be seen as disturbingly alien: Iago discredits him to Brabantio as 'an extravagant and wheeling stranger/Of here and everywhere'. In **Twelfth Night** Sebastian, in low spirits, has no evident purpose, but wanders around in a foreign country: 'my determinate voyage is mere extravagancy'.

extravagant *adjective* wandering (*O i 1*; *H i 1*)

eyas *noun* a young hawk in training (*H ii 2*)

eye *noun* a shade of colour (*T ii 1*) ■ *verb* to appear (*AC i 3*)

eye-glass *noun* the lens of the eye (*WT i 2*)

F

fable *noun* a lie (*CE iv 4*)

face *verb* **1.** to deceive or lie blatantly (*TS iv 3*; *TN iv 2*) **2.** to brave out (*CE iii 1*; *H5 iii 7*) **3.** to trim or ornament a garment (*TS iv 3*; *1H4 ii 3, v 1*)

faced *adjective* patched (*1H4 iv 2*)

face-royal *noun* the face of the monarch on a gold coin (*2H4 i 2*)

facing *noun* trimming on a garment (*MM iii 2*)

fact *noun* **1.** a crime (*MM iv 2*) **2.** what had to be done (*M iii 6*) **3.** a way of acting (*WT iii 2*)

COMMENT: For us *fact* is a neutral and generally abstract word, whereas Shakespeare used it more closely related to its source: the Latin 'facere', 'to do', and therefore from 'factum', 'something done'. In his plays the sense is negative and means 'an evil action or crime'. In **Measure for Measure** the Provost says that Barnardine's 'fact' has only just been proved. Later the Duke pretends to warn Isabella not 'to kneel down in mercy of this fact' because Angelo's fact, or crime, is so serious. Leontes accusing Hermione in **The Winter's Tale** slightly shifts the sense: 'As you were past all shame,/(Those of your fact are so) so past all truth'. He uses *fact* near to the sense of 'faction', a secret sect of evil-doers, in this case, of women who commit adultery. In **Henry VI Part 2** some conspirators are 'apprehended in the fact', or, as we would say, 'in the act' of committing the crime. Our use of 'act', or doing something, is similar to the Latin 'factum'.

faction *noun* a group, especially one disagreeing with another (*AYLI v 1*; *H v 2*; *JC ii 1*; *R3 i 3*)

factious *adjective* rebellious

factor *noun* an agent (*AC ii 6*)

faculty *noun* a personal quality (*H ii 2*; *H5 i 1*)

fadge *verb* to work out or end up (*TN ii 2*)

fading *noun* **1.** a dance (*CE v 1*) **2.** the refrain of a song or dance, the part that is repeated (*MV iii 3*; *WT iv 4*)

fail *noun* **1.** something someone failed to do (*WT ii 3*) **2.** a fault ■ *verb* **1.** to make a mistake (*MM iii 2*; *MND iii 2*) **2.** to fail to do something (*KL ii 4*; *M iii 6*)

fain *adjective* **1.** willing **2.** fond **3.** glad ■ *verb* to wish

fain to *adjective* obliged to someone (*KL iv 7*)

fair befall you *phrase* good luck to you (*R3 iii 5*)

fairest-boding *adjective* containing good omens (*R3 v 3*)

fairly *adverb* **1.** beautifully (*TS i 2*; *R3 iii 6*) **2.** favourably (*MND i 1*; *1H4 iv 3*; *H5 v 2*) **3.** completely (*TS i 1*; *RJ ii 4*) **4.** with honour (*MV i 1*) **5.** courteously (*CE v 1*)

fairy *noun* a woman with magical powers (*AC iv 8*)

fairy gold *noun* money given by the fairies that rapidly disappeared (*WT iii 3*)

fairy time *noun* the time when the fairies were active, between midnight and the rising of the morning star (*MND v 1*)

fairy toy *noun* a fairy tale (*MND v 1*)

faith-breach *noun* a treacherous act (*M v 2*)

faithed *adjective* believed in (*KL ii 1*)

faithless *adjective* **1.** disloyal **2.** treacherous (*MM iii 1*) **3.** not believing in the religion you claim to follow (*MV ii 4*)

faitor *noun* a cheat (*2H4 ii 4*)

falchion *noun* a short broad sword with a curved blade (*R3 i 2*; *KL v 3*)

fall *noun* **1.** a group of notes descending in pitch at the end of a piece of music (a cadence) (*TN i 1*) **2.** a round in wrestling (*AYLI i 2*)

fall backwards *verb* (*of a woman*) to offer sexual intercourse (*RJ i 3*)

67   **fardel**

fall from *verb* **1.** to desert someone (*MA i 1*) **2.** to have fallen out of favour with someone (*H ii 2*)

fallible *adjective* **1.** likely to be misplaced (*MM iii 1*) **2.** incapable of being wrong (*AC v 2*) (NOTE: This is a deliberate mistake for the work **infallible**.)

falling sickness *noun* epilepsy (*JC i 2*)

fall off *verb* to withdraw your support for someone (*1H4 i 3*; *KL i 2*)

fallow *noun* ground that has been ploughed but not sown or planted with any crops (*MM i 4*; *H5 v 2*)

falourous *adjective* brave (*H5 iii 2*)

false *adjective* (*of strings*) badly made and so producing a poor sound (*JC iv 3*)

false fire *noun* an act of firing a gun that isn't actually loaded (*H iii 2*)

false gallop *noun* a canter (*MA iii 4*)

false generations *plural noun* illegitimate children (*WT ii 1*)

falsely *adverb* **1.** wrongly (*O v 2*) **2.** treacherously (*T ii 1*; *MM ii 4*) **3.** mistakenly (*R3 v 3*)

falsify *verb* to prove to be not based on fact (*1H4 i 2*)

falsing *adjective* false, artificial (*CE ii 2*)

fame *noun* **1.** someone's reputation (*AC iii 1*) **2.** a rumour (*MA ii 1*; *AC ii 2*)

familiar *noun* a close friend (*2H4 ii 2*) ■ *adjective* **1.** belonging to a family (*H5 ii 4*; *O iii 3*) **2.** usual or ordinary (*MA v 4*; *MM i 4*)

fancy *noun* **1.** love (*AYLI iii 5*; *TN ii 4*; *MV iii 2*) **2.** a song, especially a love-song (*TS iii 2*; *2H4 iii 2*) ■ *verb* to fall in love with someone (*TS ii 1*; *TN ii 5*)

COMMENT: In all its various shades of meaning *fancy* was connected with the way the imagination works or the results of imagining. Its origins were shared with 'fantasy', something unreal, but often more exciting than what is revealed to human reason or to the basic senses. It could carry the sense of 'a dangerous illusion', as in the song in Act 3 of **The Merchant of Venice** while Bassanio is choosing the casket. Much depends on his choice for both his and Portia's fortunes, and the song echoes his uncertainty: 'Tell me where is fancy bred/Or in the heart or in the head?' The answer is that 'fancy dies/In the cradle where it lies'. The pun on 'lies' indicates that fancy is childish and

deceitful and that true love is far more than merely a superficial something 'engender'd in the eye'. Sometimes the connotations of *fancy* are more positive. Hamlet praises Yorick, the clown, as being 'A fellow…of most excellent fancy', meaning that he had a very fertile imagination with which to entertain the court. However, extreme fancy can be eccentric and make a fantastical man a subject for mockery: in **Love's Labours Lost** the King describes Armado as 'this child of fancy'. Generally, *fancy* was associated with the heightened imagination of a lover, who could be liable to foolish infatuation. In **A Midsummer Night's Dream** *fancy* is personified: lovers engage in 'thoughts and dreams and sighs, / Wishes and tears, poor Fancy's followers'. Sometimes the slightness of *fancy* brought the word to our meaning of 'a whim', as in **Much Ado About Nothing** when Don Pedro speaking of Benedick, recently in love, refers to 'a fancy that he hath to strange disguises'. Around 1800 Romantic poets and theorists speculated on how much status they should give to *fancy*; in his **Biographia Literaria**, Coleridge drew a philosophical distinction between fancy and the imagination.

fancy-monger *noun* someone who sells love-potions or is a match-maker (*AYLI iii 2*)

fancy-sick *adjective* lovesick (*MND iii 2*)

fane *noun* a temple (*CE iv 2*)

fantastic *adjective* **1.** elaborate (*H iv 7*) **2.** strange (*MM ii 2*)

fantastical *adjective* **1.** imaginary (*M i 3*) **2.** imaginative (*TN i 1*) **3.** incredible (*MM iii 2*; *MA ii 1*; *O ii 1*)

fantasticoes *plural noun* conceited men who like fine clothes (*RJ ii 4*)

fantasy *noun* **1.** imagination (*1H4 v 1*; *2H4 v 1*; *RJ i 1*) **2.** a whim (*RJ ii 4*; *H i 1, iv 4*; *O iii 3*) **3.** love (*AYLI ii 4, v 1*) **4.** thoughts prompted by worry (*JC ii 1*)

far *conjunction* farther (*WT iv 3*)

farced *adjective* padded out to appear dignified (*H5 iv 1*) [From French *farce*, 'stuffing'.]

fardel *noun* a cumbersome bundle (*WT iv 4*; *H iii 1*) [From Italian *fardello*.]

farm *verb* **1.** to rent something from someone (*H ii 2, iv 4*; *H5 v 2*) **2.** to lease the right to collect taxes on something (*R2 i 4*) ◇ **in farm** on a lease (*R2 ii 1*)

farrow *noun* a litter of a specified number of piglets (*M iv 1*)

farthingale *noun* a hooped petticoat designed to give a wide shape to a woman's skirt (*TS iv 3*)

fashion *noun* **1.** a type (*WT iii 2*; *MV i 2*) **2.** a pretence (*MV iv 1*) ■ *verb* **1.** to make something happen (*MND iii 2*; *O iv 2*) **2.** to bring something about for your own purposes (*MA iii 3*; *JC ii 1*) **3.** to forge or alter something illegally (*MA i 3*; *H5 i 2*) **4.** to adapt someone to something (*MA iv 4*; *CE ii 2*) ◇ **out of fashion** strange (*H5 iv 1*; *O ii 1*)

fashion-monger *noun* a fashionable person (*RJ ii 4*)

fashion-monging *adjective* fashionable (*MA v 1*)

fashions *noun* a disease of horses (**glanders**) with symptoms including swollen glands (*TS iii 2*)

fast *adverb* irrevocably (*MM i 2*; *O i 2*) ■ *adjective* close (*WT iv 4*)

fast and loose *noun* a cheating game in which someone was challenged to bet on whether they could put a stick into a coiled belt so that it could not be pulled away (*AC iv 12*)

fasted *adjective* forced (*O ii 3*)

fasten'd *adjective* determined (*KL ii 1*)

fat *noun* a vat (*AC ii 7*) ■ *adjective* **1.** hot (*1H4 ii 4*) **2.** heavy and dull (*TN v 1*; *H i 5*) [From the idea of feeding someone delicacies.]

fat-brained *adjective* stupid (*H5 iii 7*)

Fates in both Greek and Roman mythology the three Fates (Clotho, Lachesis and Atropos) controlled the birth, life and death of every person without considering individual wishes

father *noun* someone who gives away the bride at wedding (*MA v 4*) (NOTE: The 'father' at wedding could be any friend or relative.) ◇ **fathers herself** shows who is her father by her resemblance to him (*MA i 1*)

fathered *adjective* given as a father (*KL iii 6*)

father-in-law *noun* a stepfather (*R3 v 3*)

fathom *noun* **1.** depths (*WT iv 4*) **2.** ability or intelligence (*O i 1*) [From *fathom*, 'the distance between the finger tips of the outstretched arms (1.8 metres)'.]

fathom-line *noun* a line to test the depth of the sea, a river, etc. (*1H4 i 3*)

fat-witted *adjective* stupid (*1H4 i 2*)

fault *noun* a hunting term for when the dogs are unable to find the scent or the scent disappears (*TN ii 5*; *TS Ind. 1*)

faulty *adjective* guilty (*1H4 iii 2*)

favour *noun* **1.** someone's facial features (*MM iv 2*; *1H4 iii 3, v 1*; *KL iii 7*; *JC i 3, ii 1*) **2.** a token of goodwill or love (*1H4 v 4*; *R2 v 3*; *H5 iv 7*) **3.** mercy (*AC iii 8*) **4.** charm (*O iv 3*) **5.** the female genitals (*H ii 2*)

COMMENT: Sometimes Shakespeare's meaning of *favour* was similar to ours. In **The Winter's Tale** Polixenes is the closest friend of King Leontes – they show each other great signs of favour. When he senses coldness, Polixenes worries that his 'favour here begins to warp'. The word is also used as a term of politeness, as when Macbeth attempts courtly graciousness when he apologises to his guests: 'Give me your favour', meaning 'kind indulgence'. In **Richard II** the word carries our sense of benefit or gesture of regard when the King says, 'I well remember the favours of these men'. But, knowing the speaker's caustic wit, we may sense a pun that reveals Shakespeare's more common meaning of *favour*. It means 'face or appearance'. Richard regards the courtiers as hypocrites whose favours, in the sense of giving the King graceful benefits, were matched by their favours as (smiling) faces. The pun is more grim in **Hamlet**. The Prince finds Osric's skull in the graveyard and speaks to it as to a messenger who will go to the Queen: 'Now get you to my lady's chamber, and tell her, let her paint an inch thick, to this favour she must come'. The skull's face will speak to the lady's face, thick with make-up to retain her illusion of youth, and warn her that she can't avoid eventually having his fleshless face. Hamlet also implies in this bleak pun that death is an unavoidable benefit (or *favour*). A *favour* is also a token of love or friendship. The ladies in **Love's Labours Lost** receive this type of favour, i.e. gifts from the four young men who love them. Henry V honours Fluellen by giving him a glove: 'wear thou this favour for me, and stick it in thy cap'.

favourable *adjective* noble or kind (*2H4 iv 5*; *R3 iii 7*)

favouring *adjective* kind (*AC iv 8*)

fawn *verb* to flatter someone (*JC i 2, iii 1, v 1*; *MND ii 1*) ■ *noun* a one-year-old male deer (*AYLI ii 7*)

feat *adjective* neat (*T ii 1*)

feather *noun* a shallow self-opinionated person wearing feathers in his hat (*TS iii 2*; *H iii 2*)

feathered *adjective* having wings (*1H4 iv 1*; *O i 3*)

featly *adverb* neatly or with agility (*T i 2*; *WT iv 4*)

feature *noun* **1.** someone's looks and appearance (*T iii 1*; *H iii 1*) **2.** shapeliness (*MA iii 1*; *R3 i 1*)

featured *adjective* shaped (*MA iii 1*)

feazed, fazed *adjective* worn out or frayed (*1H4 iv 2*)

fedary *noun* a partner in wrongdoing (*MM ii 4*; *WT ii 1*) (NOTE: This word is linked to the modern word **confederate**.)

fee *noun* **1.** a payment for services (*MA ii 2*; *MV iv 1*; *R3 i 2*; *KL i 1*; *H ii 2*) **2.** a payment for sexual intercourse ■ *verb* **1.** to use something (*MV iii 1*; *M iii 4*) **2.** to see someone (*TN i 5*) ◇ **sold in fee** sold with total and perpetual ownership (*H iv 4*)

feed *noun* land for animals to graze on (*AYLI ii 4*)

feeder *noun* **1.** a shepherd (*AYLI ii 4*) **2.** someone who is dependent or relies too heavily on someone else (*2H4 i 3, v 5*; *MV ii 5*) **3.** a servant (*AC iii 13*)

feeding *noun* land for animals to graze on (*WT iv 4*)

fee grief *noun* a personal grief that is not shared (*M iv 3*)

feel *verb* to find out about something (*H5 iv 1*; *KL i 2*)

fee simple *noun* ownership of a property that is total and allows you to dispose of it as you wish (*RJ iii 1*; *H i 4, iv 4*)

feeze, pheeze *verb* to complete the business of someone (*TS Ind. 1*)

feign *verb* to tell the story (*MV v 1*)

COMMENT: *Feign* generally carried the negative sense of 'pretending in order to deceive'. Sometimes it was used by country people to criticise the sophisticated ways of the court. In **As You Like It** Amiens' song welcomes the winter wind because it is more honest than human behaviour, in which 'Most friendship is feigning, most loving mere folly'. However, creative artists also *feign*, in the sense of imitating or inventing. In **The Merchant of Venice** Lorenzo refers to Ovid's magical stories: 'Therefore the poet/Did feign that Orpheus drew trees and stones and floods'. 'Drew' means that he lured inanimate things away from their natures. The Greek philosopher Plato disapproved of the feigning poets for their dishonesty, and placed them below the truth-seeking historian and philosopher. Sir Philip Sidney, one of the greatest Elizabethan poets and literary critics, answered Plato in his **Apology for Poetry**, arguing that creative literature instructs its readers by enriching the imagination and 'that a feigned example hath as much force to teach as a true example...since the feigned may be tuned to the highest key of passion'. Shakespeare's Theseus describes the poet's intensity in the last act of **A Midsummer Night's Dream**: 'The poet's eye, in a fine frenzy rolling,/Doth glance from heaven to earth, from earth to heaven'. This *feigning* is akin to madness but is an elevated state of mind as it 'bodies forth the forms of things unknown'.

feigning *adjective* **1.** pretending (*MND i 1*) **2.** imaginative (*AYLI iii 3*)

felicitate *adjective* made happy (*KL i 1*)

fell *noun* an animal skin with the hair attached (*AYLI i 2*; *M v 5*; *KL v 3*) ■ *adjective* **1.** angry (*MND ii 1*) **2.** ruthless or fierce (*MND v 1*; *TN i 1*; *O v 2*)

fellow *noun* a servant (*R3 iii 3*; *RJ i 2*)

fellowly *adjective* sympathetic (*T v 1*)

fellowship *noun* **1.** a friendly relationship (*H ii 2*) **2.** an alliance (*H5 iv 3*; *MM iii 2*)

fence *verb* to protect someone or something (*AYLI iv 3*) ■ *noun* the skill of sword-fighting (fencing) (*MA v 1*)

fennel *noun* an aromatic herb *Foeniculum vulgare* used in cookery. It is a symbol of flattery. (*2H4 ii 4*; *H iv 5*)

fenny *adjective* living in a low-lying marsh (a fen) (*M iv 1*)

fen-sucked *adjective* drawn out of a low-lying marsh (a fen) (*KL ii 4*)

fere *noun* a husband or wife

fernseed *noun* the spores of ferns (*1H4 ii 1*) (NOTE: The spores were supposedly visible only on midsummer eve. If collected, they were supposed to make the person collecting them invisible.)

ferret *verb* to chase and attack someone (*H5 iv 4*)

fertile *adjective* **1.** plentiful (*TN i 5*) **2.** giving fertility (*2H4 iv 3*)

fervency *noun* eagerness (*AC ii 5*)

festinate *adjective* hurried (*KL iii 7*)

festival *adjective* joyful (*MA v 2*)

fet *adjective* fetched (*H5 iii 1*; *R3 ii 2*)

fetch *noun* **1.** a trick (*H ii 1*; *KL ii 4*) **2.** a plant resembling clover, used to feed animals (*T iv 1*) ∎ *verb* **1.** to make something (*MV v 1*) **2.** to come from something (*MM iii 1*; *H5 ii 2*; *O i 2*)

fetch in *verb* **1.** to cheat or trick someone (*MA i 1*) **2.** to capture someone (*AC iv 1*)

fetch off *verb* **1.** to kill someone (*WT i 2*) **2.** to outwit someone (*2H4 iii 2*)

fettle *verb* to get something ready (*RJ iii 5*)

fewness *noun* conciseness (*MM i 4*)

fico *noun* a sign of contempt made by placing the thumb between first and second fingers, with sexual connotations (*2H4 v 3*)

field *noun* **1.** a battle (*MV ii 1*; *JC v 5*; *1H4 v 5*) **2.** a green cloth on a writing table, in the building where the money and records of a person or business were kept (*H5 ii 3*)

field bed *noun* a simple bed on the ground (*RJ ii 1*)

fierce *adjective* wild (*MND iv 1*)

fife *noun* a small flute (*MA ii 3*; *MV ii 5*; *O iii 3*)

figure *noun* **1.** the true shape (*MA i 1*) **2.** an expression (*H ii 2*) **3.** something imagined (*JC ii 1*) (NOTE: Hot lead used to be poured into water and the resulting random forms resembling figures were used to tell fortunes.) **4.** writing (*O i 1*) **5.** a character in a play (*T iii 3*) ∎ *verb* **1.** to imagine something (*MM i 2*) **2.** to show something (*R3 i 2*) **3.** to represent something (*MND i 1*; *2H4 iv 1*)

filch *verb* to steal something (*MND i 1*; *O iii 3*)

file *noun* **1.** a row of soldiers (*2H4 i 3*; *AC i 1*, *iv 1*) **2.** a group of people (*MM iii 2*) **3.** a list (*M iii 1*) ∎ *verb* to tarnish something (*M iii 1*)

fill a bottle with a tun-dish *verb* to have sexual intercourse (*MM iii 2*)

fill-horse *noun* a carthorse (*MV ii 2*)

fillip *verb* to throw something in the air (*2H4 i 2*)

film *noun* a piece of cobweb (**gossamer**) (*RJ i 4*) ∎ *verb* to cover something with a very thin fabric (*H iii 4*)

find *verb* **1.** to feel something (*MM iii 1*) **2.** to find out about something (*1H4 i 3*; *O ii 1*) **3.** to provide something (*H5 i 2*)

finder of madmen *noun* a member of a jury appointed to determine whether the accused was sane (*TN iii 4*)

find-fault *noun* someone who finds mistakes (*H5 v 2*)

find forth *verb* to find someone out (*CE i 2*; *MV i 1*)

fine *noun* money paid by a tenant to the landlord for permission to transfer his tenancy to someone else or to a **fee simple** (*CE ii 2*; *H v 1*) ∎ *adjective* **1.** delicate or beautiful (*T i 2*; *RJ ii 1*; *H ii 2*) **2.** subtle (*MA iii 4*; *1H4 iv 1*) **3.** skilful (*TS i 2*; *JC i 1*; *AC ii 6*) **4.** pure (*2H4 iv 5*) **5.** (*of wine*) clear (*2H4 v 3*) ∎ *verb* **1.** to pay something as a punishment (*H5 iv 7*) **2.** to punish someone (*MM ii 2*; *R2 ii 1*) **3.** to improve (*H5 i 2*) ◇ **in fine** at last (*H iv 7*, *v 2*)

fineless *adjective* without end (*O iii 3*)

finger *noun* the width of a finger (*1H4 iv 2*) ∎ *verb* to steal something in the manner of a pick-pocket (*H v 2*) ◇ **put one's finger in the eye** to make oneself cry (*TS i 1*)

finical *adjective* fussy about your clothes (*KL ii 2*)

Finsbury *noun* Finsbury Fields were on the outskirts of London (at what is now Finsbury Circus) and were used as a place for recreation (*1H4 iii 1*)

firago *noun* an aggressive woman (*TN iii 4*) [From *virago*, 'a violent woman'.]

firk *verb* to beat, possibly to copulate (*H5 iv 4*)

first *noun* **1.** the beginning (*H ii 2*; *M v 5*) **2.** the colour first mentioned when describing a coat of arms (*MND iii 2*)

firstlings *plural noun* the things first produced (*M iv 1*)

fish *noun* a prostitute (*RJ i 1*) (NOTE: Any reference to 'fish' has a sexual connotation)

fishmonger *noun* a pimp (*H ii 2*)

fit *noun* a sudden attack of an illness (*H iv 1*)

fitchew *noun* a prostitute (*KL iv 6*; *O iv 1*) [Literally 'a polecat', an animal noted for its smell and sexual activity.]

fitness *noun* willingness (*H v 2*) ◇ **my fitness** what is right for me (*L iv 2*)

fives, vives *noun* a disease of horses with symptoms including swollen glands in the lower jaw (*TS iii 2*) [From French *avives*.]

fixture *noun* stability (*WT v 3*)

flag *noun* a reed, or possibly an iris (*AC i 4*)

flamen *noun* in ancient Rome, a priest who served one particular god

flap-dragon *noun* a burning raisin floating in an alcoholic drink, swallowed while burning (*2H4 ii 4*) ■ *verb* to swallow something quickly as though swallowing a snapdragon (*WT iii 3*)

flap-eared *adjective* with broad drooping ears (*TS iv 1*)

flask *noun* a container for gunpowder (*RJ iii 3*)

flat-long *adjective* with the flat side of the blade of a sword downwards (*T ii 1*)

flatness *noun* completeness (*WT iii 2*)

flats *plural noun* 1. large areas of shallow water (*T ii 2*) 2. hidden sandbanks (*MV i 1*)

flattering *adjective* anticipating pleasure to come (*TS Ind. 1*; *RJ ii 2*)

flattery *noun* pleasant deception (*O iv 1*)

flaunts *plural noun* fine clothes (*WT iv 4*)

flaw *noun* 1. a crack (*KL ii 4*; *AC iii 10*) 2. an outburst (*MM ii 3*; *M iii 4*) 3. small pieces of ice (*2H4 iv 4*)

flawed *adjective* damaged

flax *noun* male pubic hair (*TN i 3*)

flax-wench *noun* a woman working with the fibres of a plant used to make the fabric called linen (**flax**) (*WT i 2*)

flay *verb* to beat someone (*KL i 4*) [From the idea of removing the skin by flogging.]

flayed *adjective* undressed (*WT iv 4*)

flecked, fleckl'd *adjective* spotted (*RJ ii 3*)

fledge *adjective* not mature enough to grow a beard (*2H4 i 2*) [Referring to a bird's feathers growing when it is mature.]

fledged *adjective* (*of a young bird*) having all its feathers and so ready to fly (*MV iii 1*)

fleer *noun* a sneering grin (*MA v 1*; *RJ i 5*)

fleet *adjective* quick (*TS Ind. 1*) ■ *verb* 1. to disappear (*MV iii 2*) 2. to go quickly (*MV iv 1*) 3. to while away time (*AYLI i 1*) 4. to be at sea (*AC iii 13*)

Fleet *noun* a prison in London on the bank of the River Fleet just below the City wall (*2H4 v 5*)

flesh *noun* the female body ■ *verb* to introduce a new soldier to battle for the first time (*KL ii 2*) [From the idea of giving hounds the flesh of the prey to eat to make them keen to pursue it.]

fleshed *adjective* 1. fed with meat (*2H4 i 1*) 2. made ready for a fight (*TN iv 1*; *H5 iii 3*) 3. accustomed (*R3 iv 3*) 4. initiated (*1H4 v 4*)

fleshment *noun* the satisfaction of a first success (*KL ii 2*)

flesh-monger *noun* someone who has sexual intercourse when not married (*MM v 1*)

flewed *adjective* having large drooping cheeks like a bloodhound (*MND iv 1*)

flexure *noun* the act of bending or bowing (*H5 iv 1*)

flibbertigibbet *noun* one of the five fiends which possessed Tom (*KL iii 4, iv 1*) (NOTE: Shakespeare got the names of the fiends in this passage from Harsnet's *Declaration of Egregious Popish Impostures* in which it is declared that the Jesuits cast out forty fiends, including the five mentioned in this passage. A flibbertigibbet was a mischievous gossip, and was sometimes synonymous with Puck.)

flickering *adjective* twinkling (*KL ii 2*)

flight *noun* a long light arrow, used for shooting over long distances (*MA i 1*)

flighty *adjective* swift (*M iv 1*)

fling *verb* to charge or rush (*M ii 4*)

flirt-gill *noun* a promiscuous woman (*RJ ii 4*)

flock *noun* wool (*1H4 ii 1*)

flood ◇ **at the flood** at the peak (*JC iv 3*)

Florence *noun* a city in Tuscany in northern Italy. It was an ancient centre of commerce and culture and during Shakespeare's time was ruled by the Medicis. (*O i 3*; *TS iv 2*)

Florentius *noun* a knight in Gower's *Confessio Amantis*, who married an old hag who could answer his riddle (*TS i 2*)

flote *noun* the sea, a wave (*T i 2*)

flourish *verb* 1. to ornament something excessively (*MM iv 1*; *R3 i 3*; *H ii 2*) 2. to wave a sword aggressively (*JC iii 2*; *RJ i 1*)

flower *noun* beauty (*R2 iii 3*)

flowered *adjective* decorated with a pattern cut through the material (*RJ ii 4*)

flowing *adjective* plentiful (*H5 iv 3*; *O ii 3*)

flush *adjective* thriving (*AC i 4*; *H iii 3*)

flux *noun* 1. a secretion (*AYLI iii 2*) 2. the flow (*AYLI ii 1*)

fly off *verb* to leave hurriedly (*KL ii 4*; *AC ii 2*)

foil *noun* 1. a sword blunted to practise swordfighting (*MA v 2*; *H ii 2, v 2*) 2. the setting of a jewel showing off its beauty (*1H4 i 2*; *R3 v 3*; *H v 2*) 3. disgraceful behaviour (*AC i 4*) 4. a setback rather than total defeat (*T iii 1*; *AYLI ii 2*) ▪ *verb* to reverse the effect of something (*O i 3*) [From a wrestling term meaning 'to be partially thrown'.]

foin *noun* a thrust (*KL iv 6*) ▪ *verb* to thrust in swordfighting (*MA v 1*)

follow *verb* 1. to copy someone or something (*MND ii 1*; *WT v 2*) 2. to carry out something (*TN v 1*; *2H4 i 1*) 3. to carry on an occupation (*TN i 3*; *KL ii 2*)

fondly *adverb* foolishly (*TS iv 2*; *R2 iii 3*; *2H4 iv 2*)

food ◇ **in food** while eating (*CE v 1*)

fool-begged *adjective* foolish (*CE ii 1*)

foolish Greek *noun* a foolish merry person (*TN iv 1*)

foot *verb* to walk (*KL iii 4*) ▪ *adjective* in a place (*H5 ii 4*; *KL iii 3*) ▪ *verb* 1. to kick someone (*MV i 3*) 2. to seize someone as if with a hawk's talons 3. to have sexual intercourse ◇ **at foot** a little way behind (*H iv 3*; *AC i 5*) ◇ **have secret feet** to have landed secretly (*L iii 1*) ◇ **set on your foot** to be on your way (*JC ii 1*) ◇ **upon the foot of fear** running away in fear (*1H4 v 5*) ◇ **upon the foot of motion** ready to show itself (*M ii 3*)

foot and hand *adverb* lunging and striking a blow at the same time (*1H4 ii 4*)

footboy *noun* a servile follower (*TS iii 2*)

foot-cloth *noun* a decorative covering for a horse that reached down to its feet (*R3 iii 4*)

footing *noun* 1. the act of landing in a place (*O ii 1*) 2. dancing (*T iv 1*)

foot-landraker *noun* a robber on foot who attacked travellers (*1H4 iv 2*)

foot-land-rakers *plural noun* thieves (*1H4 ii 1*)

foot-licker *noun* a person who flatters someone in a servile way (*T iv 1*)

footman *noun* any person walking (*WT iv 3*)

fop *noun* a fool, especially one who dressed outlandishly (*KL i 2*) ▪ *verb* to fool someone (*O iv 2*)

foppery *noun* foolish behaviour (*KL i 1*; *MM i 1*; *MV ii 5*)

foppish *adjective* foolish (*KL i 4*)

forage *verb* to eat like a wild animal (*H5 i 2*)

forbid *adjective* cursed (*M i 3*)

forbiddenly *adverb* without permission (*WT i 2*)

force *verb* to stuff someone with something (*H5 ii Chor.*)

fordo, foredo *verb* to destroy something violently (*KL v 3*; *H v 1*; *O v 1*)

fordone *adjective* 1. destroyed (*KL v 3*) 2. exhausted (*MND v 2*)

foredoom *verb* to condemn someone before an event has actually taken place (*KL v 3*)

fore-hand *noun* the advantage (*H5 iv 1*) ▪ *adjective* anticipated (*MA iv 1*)

fore-hand shaft *noun* an arrow for shooting at point blank range (*2H4 iii 2*)

forehead *noun* the place from which a cuckold's horns grow (*O iii 3*) (NOTE: It was popular myth at the time that a man would grow horns when his wife was unfaithful.)

foreign *adjective* not related ▪ *noun* a stranger to ▪ *adjective* unfamiliar

fore-rank *adjective* most important (*H5 v 2*)

forerun *verb* to anticipate something (*MM v 1*; *R2 ii 4*; *RJ v 1*)

forespeak, forspeak *verb* to speak against something (*AC iii 7*)

forespent, forspent *adjective* finished with (*2H4 i 1*)

fore-spurrer *noun* someone who rode ahead (*MV ii 9*)

fore-stall *verb* **1.** to prevent someone from doing something (*H iii 3, v 2*; *2H4 iv 5*) **2.** to discredit someone (*2H4 v 2*)

forester *noun* someone who looks after a forest (*AYLI iii 2, iv 2*; *MND iii 2, iv 1*)

forest of Arden *noun* a forest area near Stratford-on-Avon, Shakespeare's birthplace (*AYLI i 1, 3, ii 4*)

foreward *noun* the troops at the front of an army (*R3 v 3*)

forfeit in a barber's shop *noun* a list of punishments for various minor offences which was displayed in barbers' shops (*MM v 1*)

forfeiture *noun* the time when a debt payable under the terms of a contract became due (*MV i 3, iii 2, 3, iv 1*)

forfended place *noun* the female genitals (*KL v 1*)

forge *verb* to invent a story (*R2 iv 1*; *M iv 3*)

forgery *noun* an invented story (*MND ii 1*; *H ii 1, iv 7*)

forgetive *adjective* inventive (*2H4 iv 3*) [Possibly from 'forge', i.e. to make.]

fork *noun* **1.** a person's crotch (*KL iii 4, iv 6*) **2.** the tongue of a snake (*MM iii 1*; *M iv 1*) **3.** a barbed arrow-head (*KL i 1*)

forked *adjective* **1.** (*of a man*) whose wife has committed adultery (*WT i 2*) *See also* **forehead 2.** two-legged (*KL iii 4*) [Literally 'with two horns'.]

fork heads *plural noun* barbed arrows (*AYLI ii 1*)

forks *plural noun* combs worn to keep the hair in place (*KL iv 6*)

forlorn *adjective* abandoned or wretched (*2H4 iii 2*; *KL iv 7*)

form *noun* **1.** a military formation (*2H4 iv 1*) **2.** behaviour (*TN v 1*; *JC i 2*) **3.** rank (*H5 iv 1*) **4.** ceremony (*MA iv 1*; *MM v 1*; *RJ ii 2*)

formal *adjective* **1.** sane (*CE v 1*; *TS ii 2*; *TN ii 5*; *AC ii 5*) **2.** accurate (*AYLI ii 7*) **3.** traditional (*R3 iii 1*)

former *adjective* the one in front (*JC v 1*)

formerly *adverb* just now (*MV iv 1*)

Forres *noun* a royal borough on the Findhorn River, near the Moray Firth in Scotland (*M i 3*)

forsake *verb* **1.** to give something up (*CE iv 3*) **2.** to refuse something (*O iv 2*)

forted *adjective* fortified (*MM v 1*)

forth *adjective* **1.** out (*T v 1*; *CE iv 4*; *MM v 1*; *MV i 1*; *JC iii 3*; *R2 iii 2*) **2.** not at

home (*CE ii 2*; *JC i 2*) **3.** on the battlefield (*AC iv 11*) ■ *adverb* forward (*TS iv 1*)

forthcoming *adjective* arrested and ready to be brought to trial (*TS v 1*)

forthrights *plural noun* straight paths (*T iii 3*)

fortify *verb* **1.** to strengthen something (*H5 iii 3*) **2.** to uphold something (*2H4 i 3*)

fortitude *noun* strength (*O i 3*)

fortune *verb* to control the fortune of (*AC i 2*)

COMMENT: The Roman goddess Fortuna was thought to preside over the chance and luck in people's lives. She was pictured with a large wheel, to whose rim all were bound. Half a rotation could raise beggars at the bottom to the position of kings, who would be cast down into misfortune and poverty. Shortly before the battle of Agincourt in **Henry V**, there is great apprehension among the soldiers, who know that Fortune will destroy some of them and preserve others. Captain Fluellen, with his great experience, is calm in the tense situation. He refers to a standard emblem book and recalls that 'Fortune is painted blind, with a muffler afore her eyes, to signify to you that Fortune is blind: and she is painted also with a wheel, to signify to you, which is the moral of it, that she is turning, and inconstant, and mutability and variation'. Fortune itself may bring equally either gain or loss, but the single word *fortune* generally implies 'benefit'. In **Romeo and Juliet** Friar Laurence rebukes Romeo for focusing exclusively on his exile and not on the ways in which *fortune* has been kind: 'But like a mishaved and sullen wretch,/Thou pouts upon thy fortune and thy love'. Elizabethans drew a distinction between nature and fortune. Nature gives her gifts and disadvantages at birth: these determine the personality, but Fortune gives and withholds erratically on many occasions during a lifetime. Therefore, *fortune* comes to imply material possessions and continues this sense up to the present day. It was a prominent word and issue in many 19th-century novels when young men and women prepared to marry; there was much discussion about the value of money and lands that their families could contribute. Shakespeare often used *fortune* in this sense: at the end of Othello Gratiano is told to 'keep the house and seize upon the fortunes of the Moor'. The possessions come to him because he is related to Desdemona.

Forum *noun* a public meeting-place between the Palatine and Capitoline Hills in Rome. It was surrounded by various public buildings, including temples and was enclosed by colonnades. (*JC iii 2*)

forward *adjective* 1. at the front (*T ii 2*) 2. eager (*TS i 1, ii 1, iii 1*; *R2 iv 1*; *R3 iii 2*) 3. early (*R3 iii 1*; *H i 3*)

forwardness *noun* recklessness (*AYLI i 2*)

foundation *noun* a charitable institution, e.g. one involved in the care of sick people (*MA v 1*)

founded *adjective* sure (*M iii 4*)

founder *verb* to cause a horse to go lame (*T iv 1*; *2H4 iv 3*)

four *noun* used to indicate any unknown number (*1H4 ii 2*; *AC ii 7*)

four-inched *adjective* four inches (10 cm) wide (*KL iii 4*)

foutra *noun* something worthless, a fig. A term of contempt as in 'I don't give a fig'. (*2H4 v 3*) [From French *foutre*, 'to have sexual intercourse'.]

fowler *noun* someone who catches birds (*MND iii 2*)

fox *noun* a type of sword with a broad blade, some makes of which were marked with a wolf's head, mistaken for a fox (*H5 iv 4*) (NOTE: The fox is frequently used as a symbol of deceit and ingratitude.) ◇ **hide fox** a children's game of hide and seek (*H iv 2*)

fracted *adjective* broken (*H5 ii 1*)

frailty *noun* a moral failing causing someone to easily give way to sexual temptation (*TN ii 2*; *H i 2*; *O iv 3*)

frame *noun* 1. order 2. a pattern 3. a structure ◇ **out of frame** distorted (*H i 2*)

franchised *adjective* (*M ii 1*)

frank *adjective* 1. open or unconcealed (*H5 i 2*; *O i 3*) 2. generous (*O iii 4*) ■ *noun* a pen in which pigs are kept (*2H4 ii 2*) ■ *verb* to shut up in a pigpen (*R3 i 3, iv 5*)

franked in hold *phrase* shut up in custody (*R3 iv 5*)

franklin *noun* a freeholder who was not bound to an overlord (*1H4 ii 1*)

Frateretto *noun* the name of a demon (*KL iii 6*)

fraud *noun* faithlessness (*MA ii 3*)

fraught *noun* a load or cargo (*TN v 1*; *O iii 3*) ■ *adjective* loaded (*WT iv 4*; *MV ii 8*; *KL i 4*)

fraughtage *noun* a cargo (*CE iv 1*)

fraughting *adjective* constituting the cargo (*T i 2*)

free *adjective* 1. innocent (*AYLI ii 7*; *TN i 5*; *WT i 2*; *H ii 2*) 2. generous (*O iii 3*) ■ *verb* 1. to release someone from being blamed for something (*WT iii 2*; *H v 2*) 2. to remove something (*M iii 6*; *T Epil.*)

COMMENT: Shakespeare used the adjective *free* more widely than we do. For example, he inherited its important medieval meaning of 'generous or magnanimous': *freedom* was an important aspect of noble behaviour when Chaucer explored this theme in some of his Canterbury Tales. In **Twelfth Night** Olivia uses the word in the same sense when she describes Orsino as 'free, learned and valiant'. Its original Old English meaning was 'beloved', and perhaps the intimacy implied in this reinforces the Duke's request to Isabella in **Measure for Measure** when he says, 'And now, dear maid, be you as free to us'. as he anticipates making a proposal of marriage. The word moves a little way towards its more familiar sense of 'liberated' when Hamlet imagines the effect of his own suffering if performed by the Player: he would 'Make mad the guilty and appal the free'. Here *free* means innocent. Iago, speaking of Desdemona, asks Othello to 'hold her free, I do beseech you'. He is pretending that he wants Desdemona to be considered innocent. *Free* combines at least two meanings when Macbeth asks Banquo, 'Let us speak/Our free hearts each to other'. On the surface *free* means 'uninhibited, frank, open', with the generous intimacy of the word's original meaning, but both men know of the guilty thoughts that are gathering beneath. Macbeth's *free* is therefore ironic or it implies a wish that his heart could return to innocence.

freely *adverb* without any conditions or restrictions (*TN i 4*; *MV iii 2*)

freestone coloured *noun* of a light yellowish-brown, the colour of sandstone (*AYLI iv 3*)

French crown *noun* **1.** a French coin (*2H4 iii 2*; *H5 iv 1*) **2.** a bald head caused by the sexually transmitted disease syphilis (*MND i 2*; *MM i 2*)

French hose *noun* wide loose breeches that came to the middle of the thigh and were often stuffed to make them stand out (*H5 iii 7*; *M iii 3*)

French slop *noun* **French hose** (*RJ ii 4*)

French velvet *noun* the clitoris ◊ **piled for a French velvet** to have been infected with the sexually transmitted disease syphilis (*MM i 2*)

fresh *noun* a spring of fresh water (*T iii 2*)

fret *noun* a crossbar on a lute which regulates the effective length of the string (*H iii 2 (a pun)*) ■ *verb* **1.** to decorate something with carving (*JC ii 1*; *H ii 2*) **2.** to be angry (*TS iii 2*) **3.** to wear something away (*KL i 1*) **4.** to worry (*1H4 ii 2*; *CE ii 1*; *H iii 2*; *JC iv 3*; *M v 5*; *MND iv 1*)

fretten *adjective* worn away (*MV iv 1*)

frieze *noun* a rough woollen fabric (*O ii 1*)

frippery *noun* a shop selling old clothes (*T iv 1*)

fro *preposition* from (*RJ iv 1*)

frolic *adjective* merry (*MND v 1*) ■ *adverb* merrily (*TS iv 3*)

front *noun* **1.** the forehead or face (*R3 i 1*; *M iv 3*) **2.** a lock of hair hanging over the forehead (*O iii 1*) **3.** the beginning (*WT iv 4*) **4.** the troops at the front of an army (*AC v 1*) ■ *verb* to challenge someone or something (*2H4 iv 1*; *AC ii 2*)

frontier *noun* **1.** an outer fortification (*1H4 i 3, ii 3*) **2.** a fortress on a frontier (*H iv 4*)

frontlet *noun* a frown (*KL i 4*) [From the idea of a band worn around the forehead.]

frosty *adjective* white-haired

froward *adjective* disobedient (*TS i 1, ii 1, v 1*)

fruitless *adjective* not having or unable to have children (*MND i 1*; *M iii 1*)

frutify *verb* to notify (*MV ii 2*) (NOTE: This is a mispronunciation.)

fubbed *adjective* put off with excuses (*2H4 ii 1*)

fulfil *verb* to carry something out (*CE iv 1*)

fuller *noun* someone who cleans wool or cloth (*JC iv 3*; *O ii 1*)

full-fraught *adjective* well balanced (*H5 ii 2*)

full-gorged *adjective* fully fed (*TS iv 1*)

fullness *noun* prosperity (*M i 4*)

fully *adverb* to the full (*KL iii 5*)

fulsome *adjective* **1.** disgusting (*O iv 1*; *R3 v 3*; *TN v 1*) **2.** pregnant (*MV i 3*)

fume *noun* **1.** a vapour that confuses the brain, said to come from the stomach (*T v 1*; *M i 7*) **2.** a bad temper **3.** an act of breathing out (*RJ i 1*)

fumitory, fumiter *noun* a weed which was used to treat scurvy (*H5 v 2*; *KL iv 4*)

function *noun* **1.** virility (*O ii 3*) **2.** action (*H ii 2*) **3.** an occupation (*TN iv 2, v 1*)

functional shift

COMMENT: This is a technical term in grammar to indicate that a word has changed its part of speech: for example, an adjective or noun may be used as a verb. Shakespeare often used the technique, chiefly to draw attention to the action or idea described. In **Richard II**, Henry Bolingbroke, who is about to commit treason, greets his uncle York: 'My gracious uncle'. York angrily dismisses these glib words: 'Grace me no grace, nor uncle me no uncle'. 'Grace' and 'uncle' have shifted from noun to verb, so emphasising two important values which Bolingbroke will damage. In **King Lear** Kent reassures Cordelia after their mutual banishment: 'Thou losest here, a better where to find'. He has turned adverbs into nouns and the usage has made the line extremely compact in the balance of monosyllables, as well as indicating a hint of mystery in the 'where' of her future in France. Edgar achieves a similar neatness when he sees the mad king and realises that the two main families are both suffering: 'He childed as I fathered'. The odd word 'childed' draws attention to the unnatural relationships developing within the families. Sometimes the functional shift gives an extra vivid and physical sense. Caliban in **The Tempest** is treated like an animal: he protests, 'here you sty me/In this hard rock'. The noun, a 'sty' for pigs, has become an aggressive verb. Cleopatra, aware of her physical power over men, almost seduces the messenger:

'and here/My bluest veins to kiss – a hand that kings/Have lipp'd, and trembled kissing'. Shakespeare probably wanted to avoid using 'kiss' three times, but the effect of 'lipp'd' as a verb emphasises that even kings have been captivated. Shakespeare's widespread use of functional shift should be seen in the context of a very language-conscious Elizabethan culture in which words were constantly invented and adapted. Perhaps now we are more inclined to accept unthinkingly the language we are given; Elizabethan writers questioned and relished it and their rough and individual treatment of words may, paradoxically, indicate their greater respect.

Furies *plural noun* in Greek mythology, the three goddesses of vengeance, the daughters of Earth and Night. They were Tisiphone, Alecto and Megaera. They were depicted as having blood dripping from their eyes and snakes entwined in their hair. (*2H4 v 1*; *MND v 1*; *R3 i 1*) (NOTE: The Greek equivalent is **Erinyes**.)

furlong *noun* a distance of 220 yards (198 metres) (*T i 1*; *WT i 2*)

furnace *noun* any place where a fire was kept going (*AYLI ii 7*)

furnish *verb* 1. to supply someone with something (*MV ii 4*; *2H4 i 2*; *H i 2*; *AC i 4*) 2. to dress someone (*MA iii 1*; *RJ iv 2*)

furniture *noun* equipment, decorations, etc., especially relating to horses (*1H4 iii 2*; *TS iv 3*)

furrow *noun* ploughed land (*T iv 1*)

furrow-weeds *plural noun* weeds in a ploughed field (*KL iv 4*)

fust *verb* to become mouldy (*H iv 4*)

fustian *noun* a coarse fabric made of cotton and flax (*TS iv 1*) ■ *adjective* 1. nonsense (*TN ii 5*) 2. pompous speaking (*2H4 ii 4*; *O ii 3*)

COMMENT: *Fustian* was coarse cloth such as servants wear. The Act 4 servants in **The Taming of the Shrew** are dressed in fustian. But this implication of low status led to its use as metaphor: for example, in **Othello** Cassio, disgusted with himself after recovering from too much wine, says that a drunkard is debased to 'discourse fustian with one's own shadow'. Here *fustian* means 'absurd or nonsensical speech', and Cassio is generally very conscious of his elegance and social status. The word has an appropriately clumsy sound and Cassio may be using its thickness of sound, as well as its original meaning, to suggest the slurred speech of a drunkard. *Fustian* is also used as an adjective, as in **Henry IV Part 2** when the prostitute gets irritated with the braggart Pistol: 'I cannot endure such a fustian rascal'.

fustilarian *noun* a dirty, fat, smelly person (*2H4 ii 1*)

fut *interjection* God's foot! (*KL i 2*)

G

gaberdine *noun* a long loose cloak, as traditionally worn by Jews (*MV i 3*; *T ii 2*)

gad ◇ **upon the gad** on the spur of the moment (*L i 2*)

gage *noun* **1.** an object given as a sign of trust (*H5 iv 1*) **2.** a glove thrown down as a pledge to combat (*R2 i 1, iv 1*) ■ *verb* **1.** to be involved in something (*MV i 1*) **2.** to commit someone to something by an oath (*1H4 i 3*) **3.** to promise something (*H i 1*)

gain *verb* to obtain something (*2H4 iv 4*)

gain-giving *noun* misgiving (*H v 2*)

gainsaying *noun* a refusal (*WT i 2*)

gait *noun* a course of action (*H i 2*)

Galen *noun* a Greek physician to the Roman emperor Marcus Aurelius whose writings were the medical authority in Shakespeare's time (*2H4 i 2*) (NOTE: He based his medicine on the belief that everything was created by God for a purpose so that medical investigation was unnecessary. Through his influence, medical progress was held back for centuries.)

gall *noun* the quality of aggression (*H ii 2*; *O iv 3*) ■ *verb* **1.** to hurt or chafe something (*2H4 i 2*; *H v 1*) **2.** to harass someone (*1H4 i 3*; *O i 1*) [Because bile is produced by the liver which was considered to be the site of courage and resentment.]

gallant-springing *adjective* growing well and potentially handsome (*R3 i 4*)

gall at *verb* to make fun of someone (*H5 v 1*)

galled *adjective* **1.** made sore by rubbing, as when crying (*R3 iv 4*; *H i 2*) **2.** diseased (*H iii 2*) **3.** made smaller by the action of the sea (*H5 iii 1*)

galley *noun* a large fast, flat-bottomed ship, propelled by sails and oars (*AC ii 6*)

Gallia *noun* Gaul, an ancient region in France (*H5 i 2, v 1*)

galliard *noun* a lively dance (*H5 i 2*; *TN i 3*)

gallimaufry *noun* an absurd mixture or group (*WT iv 4*)

gallow *verb* to terrify someone (*KL iii 2*)

gallow-glasses *plural noun* heavily armed Irish mercenary foot-soldiers (*M i 2*)

gallows *noun* someone who deserves to be hanged (*T i 1*) (NOTE: This is a shortening of *gallows-bird*.)

gambol *noun* a leap (*MND iii 1*; *MV iii 2*) ■ *adjective* playful (*2H4 ii 4*) ■ *verb* to skip about (*H iii 4*)

gambold *noun* a frolic (*TS Ind. 2*)

game *noun* **1.** a sport (*MND i 1*) **2.** love-making (*O ii 3*)

gamesome *adjective* lively (*TS ii 1*)

gamester *noun* a playful person (*AYLI i 1*; *TS ii 1*)

gamut, gamoth, gamouth *noun* all the notes in a musical scale (*TS iii 1*)

Ganymede *noun* the son of Laomedon (Tros), king of Troy (*AYLI i 3, iii 2, iv 3, v 2*) (NOTE: According to myth, because of his exceptional beauty he was carried off by Zeus, disguised as an eagle, to be his cup-bearer. He was identified with the constellation Aquarius.)

gap *noun* a pause in a song where a male singer interjects some obscenity (*WT iv 4*)

gape *verb* to wish longingly (*RJ ii Prol.*) ◇ **gaping pig** a whole cooked pig served with an apple in its mouth (*MV i 1*)

garb *noun* fashion (*H5 v 1*; *KL ii 2*; *H ii 2*)

garboil *noun* a disturbance (*AC i 3, ii 2*)

garden-house *noun* a summerhouse (*MM v 1*)

Gargantua *noun* a giant (*AYLI iii 2*) (NOTE: Gargantua was the main character in the satire *Gargantua* by the French writer **Rabelais**.)

garish *adjective* gaudy (*R3 iv 4*; *RJ iii 2*)

garland *noun* **1.** the monarch's crown (*2H4 v 2*; *R3 iii 2*) **2.** a reward for something in the form of a crown (*AC iv 15*)

garner *noun* a storehouse for grain (*T iv 1*) ■ *verb* to store something (*O iv 2*)

garnish *noun* clothing (*MV ii 6*)

garnished *adjective* equipped (*MV iii 5*)

Garter *noun* Order of the Garter, a very prestigious English order of chivalry formed by Edward III in 1348 (*1H4 ii 2*; *R3 iv 4*)

gaskins *plural noun* wide loose trousers (*TN i 5*)

gasted *adjective* frightened (*KL ii 1*)

gastness *noun* signs of fright (*O v 1*)

gate *noun* **1.** the main vein of the body, the *vena cava* (*H i 5*) (NOTE: Formerly known as the gate-vein.) **2.** the vulva (*WT i 2*)

gather *verb* to obtain information (*H ii 2*)

gaud *noun* a trinket (*MND iv 1*)

gaudy *adjective* festive or bright (*AC iii 11 (iii 13)*)

gaudy-night *noun* a night of celebration (*AC iii 13*)

gauge *verb* to judge somebody (*MV ii 2*)

gauntlet *noun* a heavy leather glove sometimes reinforced with steel (*2H4 i 1*; *KL iv 6*)

gay *adjective* sexually promiscuous (*O ii 1*)

gaze *noun* the centre of attraction (*M v 8*)

gear *noun* **1.** business matters (*R3 i 4*; *RJ v 1*) **2.** frivolous conversation (*MV i 1, ii 2*)

geck, geek *noun* someone who has a trick played on them (*TN v 1*)

gelded *adjective* reduced in value (*R2 ii 1*)

gender *noun* a type (*H iv 7*; *O i 3*) ■ *verb* to mate (*O iv 2*)

general *noun* the public (*JC ii 1*; *H ii 2*)

generally *adverb* **1.** by all; universally (*R2 ii 2*) **2.** as a whole (*AYLI iii 2*; *TS i 2*; *H5 i 1*)

generation *noun* **1.** the offspring of a person or animal (*WT ii 1*; *KL i 1*) **2.** a breed (*T iii 3*; *MM iv 3*) **3.** reproduction (*2H4 iv 2*) ◇ **work of generation** breeding (*MV i 3*)

generative *adjective* capable of reproducing (*MM iii 2*)

generous *adjective* of good birth (*MM iv 6*; *H iv 7*; *O iii 3*)

genius *noun* **1.** a spirit who watches over someone (*M iii 1*) **2.** one of the two spirits (good and evil) that are part of a person's personality (*T iv 1*) **3.** a person's

personality (*TN iii 4*) **4.** the embodiment of something (*2H4 iii 2*)

COMMENT: *Genius* meant an inborn spirit that guides a person and gives him/her an identity. Therefore when Macbeth complains that in Banquo's presence 'My genius is rebuk'd; as, it is said,/Mark Antony's was by Caesar', he feels an inhibition as though his very nature is thwarted.

gennet *noun* same as **jennet** (*O i 1*)

Genoa *noun* a sea port in Italy which has been a major trading centre in the Mediterranean since medieval times (*MV iii 1*; *TS iv 4*)

gentility *noun* good birth (*AYLI i 1*)

gentle *noun* people of good birth (*H5 Prol.*) ■ *adjective* **1.** noble, honourable (*R3 i 3*) **2.** of noble birth (*WT i 2*) **3.** cultivated (*WT iv 4*) ■ *verb* to raise in rank (*H5 iv 3*)

COMMENT: This is a very common Shakespearean word, used mainly as an adjective, but also as a noun or verb. In its French origin, 'gentil', it referred to social class and meant 'nobly born'. It came to describe the behaviour that should accompany high birth: generosity, duty, loyalty, social concern and honouring one's word. In the late 14th century Chaucer makes 'gentilesse' a major theme of his tales and aims to show that noble conduct can appear in any class of society, not just in the upper ranks. Conversely, 'cherlyshe' behaviour, a boorishness that may be expected from churls, or peasants, may be found among aristocrats. When Holofernes in **Love's Labours Lost** rebukes the young male courtiers for their mockery, he refers specifically to what should be expected of high birth when he says, 'This is not generous, not gentle, not humble'. Our 'gentleman', continues these moral and social meanings of *gentle*. Shakespeare's noblemen often use the word as a general compliment when addressing each other, though when Richard II addresses 'Gentle Northumberland' he is ironically implying that Northumberland lacks these qualities. In **Henry V** the Chorus uses *gentle* as a noun: 'Pardon, gentles all'. He is showing respect to the audience, regardless of the mixture of classes in the public playhouse. In Act 4 the King rouses his troops' morale before the battle, promising them gentlemanly status when they return home; most are common soldiers but 'this day shall gentle their condition'. Here *gentle* serves as a verb. Perhaps the closest to our limited use of *gentle*, meaning the opposite of violent, occurs in **Macbeth**: 'Blood hath been shed ere now I'the olden time/Ere humane statute purged the gentle weal'. His *gentle* means that civilisation has brought order and peace to the state.

gentleman *noun* **1.** a man of good birth acting as an attendant to a person of noble rank (*TN v 1*; *1H4 i 2*) **2.** an officer (*1H4 iv 2*; *H5 iv 1*)

gentlewoman *noun* a woman of good birth acting as an attendant to a person of noble rank (*MA ii 3*; *O iii 1*)

gentry *noun* **1.** a courtesy (*H ii 2*) **2.** good breeding (*H v 2*)

George *noun* a jewel decorated with the figure of St George, the insignia of the Order of the Garter (*R3 iv 4*)

german, germane *noun* a blood relative (*O i 1*) ■ *adjective* related to what is happening (*H v 2*)

germen *noun* seeds (*M iv 1*; *KL iii 2*)

gest *noun* **1.** *French* an appointed time (*WT i 2*) **2.** military exploits (*AC iv 8*) [From French *giste*, *gite*, 'a stopping-place on a royal progress'.]

gesture *noun* a person's attitude or bearing (*AYLI v 2*; *H5 iv Chor.*)

get *verb* to learn something (*WT iv 2*; *H iii 1*)

getting-up *noun* sexual penetration (*MV iii 5*)

ghost *noun* a corpse (*H i 4*) ■ *verb* to haunt someone as a ghost (*AC ii 6*)

ghostly *adjective* spiritual (*RJ iii 3*)

gib *noun* an old male cat (*1H4 i 2*; *H iii 4*)

gibber *verb* to babble (*H i 1*)

gibbet *verb* to hang from something (*2H4 iii 2*)

gig *verb* to walk carelessly (*H iii 1*)

giglet, giglot *noun* a silly flirtatious girl (*MM v 1*)

gild *verb* **1.** to make something more beautiful (*1H4 v 4*; *2H4 i 2*; *AC i 5*) **2.** to smear something (*M ii 2*) **3.** to supply someone with money (*MV ii 6*)

gilded *adjective* **1.** made happy by drinking (*T v 1*) **2.** golden (*AC i 4*) **3.** supplied with money (*H iii 3*)

gillyvor, gillyflower *noun* a garden plant whose flowers smell of cloves, related to the wallflower (*WT iv 4*)

gilt *noun* **1.** money (*H5 ii Chor.*) **2.** ornamentation (*TN iii 2*; *H5 iv 3*)

gimmaled *adjective* (*of two similar pieces*) hinged together (*H5 iv 2*)

gin *noun* a trap for animals (*TN ii 5*; *M iv 2*) ■ *verb* to begin (*T iii 3*; *M i 2, v 5*)

gipsy *noun* an Egyptian (*AC iv 12*)

gird *noun* a sarcastic remark (*TS v 2*) ■ *verb* **1.** to mock someone (*2H4 i 2*) **2.** to encircle something (*H5 iii Chor., v 2*)

girdle ◇ **put a girdle around the earth** To go completely around the world (*MND ii 1*) ◇ **to turn the girdle** to swallow your anger and put up with something (*MA v 1*)

Gis *interjection* 'By Jesus' (*H iv 5*)

give *verb* **1.** to consider something (*WT iii 2*) **2.** to represent someone or something in a particular way (*AC i 4*) **3.** to give someone the title of something (*RJ iv 5*; *M i 3*)

give away *verb* to hand over the bride at a marriage (*AYLI iii 3*)

give out *verb* to claim (*H i 5*; *O iv 1*)

giving-out *noun* a claim (*MM i 4*)

Glamis *noun* a village in Angus, Scotland (*M i 3, 5, iii 1*) (NOTE: The castle is now famous as the birthplace of Queen Elizabeth, the Queen Mother.)

glance *noun* a witty satirical remark (*AYLI ii 7*)

glanders *noun* a disease of horses which affects the lungs, nose, etc., and causes swelling of the glands (*TS iii 2*)

glass *noun* **1.** an hourglass, a device for telling the time, consisting of two connected spheres of glass which contain sand that takes an hour to flow from one to the other (*T i 2, v 1*; *WT i 2*) **2.** a crystal ball or a magic mirror (*M iv 1*)

glasses of the eye *plural noun* the pupils of the eye (*R2 i 3*)

glass eyes *plural noun* a pair of spectacles (*KL iv 6*)

glass-gazing *adjective* vain (*KL ii 2*) [From the idea of constantly looking at yourself in a mirror.]

glassy *adjective* reflected, or brittle and easily destroyed (*MM ii 2*)

glaze *verb* to glare (*JC i 3*)

glean *verb* to collect things up (*H iv 2*)

gleaned *adjective* cleared of everything (*H5 i 2*)

gleek *noun* **1.** a joke at someone else's expense (*MND iii 1*) **2.** a scornful remark (*RJ iv 5*) ■ *verb* to joke (*H5 v 1*)

glib *verb* to castrate a person or animal (*WT ii 1*)

globe *noun* the head (*H i 5*)

glooming *adjective* gloomy (*RJ v 3*)

gloss *noun* a deceptively good appearance (*M i 7*)

gloze *verb* **1.** to use flattery (*R2 ii 1*) **2.** to interpret something to be something (*H5 i 2*)

glut *verb* to swallow someone or something up (*T i 1*)

glutted *adjective* full up with food (*1H4 iii 2*)

gnarling *adjective* snarling (*R2 i 3*)

goal ◇ **get goal for goal** to get even with someone (*AC iv 6*)

goatish *adjective* lustful (*KL i 2*)

God-a-mercy *interjection* 'God have mercy!' (*1H4 iii 2*; *H ii 2*; *H5 iv 1*; *TS iv 3*)

Godden *interjection* 'Good day, God give you good even' (*RJ i 2*)

godfather *noun* a member of a jury who condemns a person to death (a joke) (*MV iv 1*)

God's bread *noun* the bread used in the Christian ceremony which commemorates the Last Supper. The term is used as an oath. (*RJ iii 5*)

God's me *interjection* 'God save me!' (*1H4 ii 3*)

gog *noun* God (*TS iii 2*)

gold *noun* gold thread (*TS ii 1*)

golden *adjective* favourable (*TN v 1*)

golden care *noun* the responsibility of governing as part of being a monarch (*2H4 iv 5*)

Golgotha *noun* the place outside Jerusalem where Jesus was crucified (*M i 2*) [From Aramaic 'skull'.]

gone *adjective* lost (*MM v 1*; *MV iii 5*)

good *adjective* wealthy (*MV i 3*)

good cheap *adjective* cheap (*1H4 iii 3*)

good deed *interjection* indeed (*WT i 2*)

goodness *noun* success (*M iv 3*)

good-night *noun* a serenade (*2H4 iii 2*)

good now *interjection* 'Let there be good will amongst us' (*CE iv 4*; *H i 1*; *AC i 2*)

good-year *interjection* 'What the devil!' (*2H4 ii 4*; *KL v 3*; *MA i 3*)

goose *noun* an iron with a handle shaped like a goose's neck, used by a tailor (*M ii 3*)

COMMENT: Shakespeare followed earlier writers who found human virtues and vices replicated in birds. Like 'snipe' and 'woodcock', *goose* is an emblem for stupidity. Macbeth sneers at his servant's pale-faced fear: 'Where got'st thou that goose look'. The inventive Berowne in **Love's Labours Lost** points to the would-be scholars' folly: 'The spring is near when green geese are a-breeding'. He is also referring to the Whitsun festival when young geese were sold to be eaten, therefore indicating too that his companions are over-confident about their future. Later he overhears Longaville's love-sonnet to Katherine and comments: 'This is the liver vein, which makes flesh a deity;/A green goose a goddess'. Here the woman is the goose, also implying naivety, but he also implies the coarser meaning of *goose* for 'prostitute'. If a goose can become a goddess it proves that love can transform something to its opposite and so make a fool of the starry-eyed lover. An unpleasant extension of this meaning was expressed in 'Winchester goose', a swelling in the groin caused by venereal disease. The last speech of **Troilus and Cressida**, a play full of squalor and disillusion, is given to the bawd, Pandarus, who speaks of his sexual diseases, including 'some galled goose of Winchester'.

goose-pen *noun* a quill pen (*TN iii 2*)

gorbellied *adjective* pot-bellied (*1H4 ii 2*)

Gorboduc *noun* a legendary British king. He divided his kingdom between his two sons Ferrex and Porrex. Porrex drove Ferrex into exile. When Ferrex returned with an army he was killed, but soon afterwards Porrex was torn to pieces by his mother and her servants. The story was recorded by Geoffrey of Monmouth (1100–54) and was the subject of the tragedy *Gorboduc or Ferrex and Porrex* by Thomas Norton and Thomas Sackville (1562). (*TN iv 2*)

Gordian knot *noun* a problem that seems impossible to resolve (*H5 i 1*) (NOTE: From the legend of Gordian, a peasant who was elected king of Phrygia. To mark this honour he dedicated his wagon to **Jupiter** and fastened it to a beam by a knot that no one could untie. **Alexander the Great** was told that whoever undid the knot would rule over all the east. Alexander promptly cut it through with his sword.)

gored *adjective* seriously wounded (*KL v 3*)

gorge *noun* **1.** the throat (*WT ii 1*) **2.** swallowed food (*H ii 1*; *O ii 1*)

Gorgon *noun* a hideous person, especially a woman (*AC ii 5*) (NOTE: In classical mythology, the three gorgons were women who had snakes instead of hair on their heads. They had enormous teeth and jaws made from brass. Anyone they looked at was turned into stone.)

gospelled *adjective* religious and following the teachings of the Gospels in the Bible (*M iii 1*)

goss *noun* gorse, a prickly bush with yellow flowers that typically grows on moors and heaths (*T iv 1*)

gossamer *noun* fine strands of cobweb floating in the air (*RJ ii 6*; *KL iv 6*)

gossip *noun* a woman who is a friend and may attend at a birth or be a godparent at a christening (*WT ii 3*)

COMMENT: *Gossip* came from 'god' and 'sib' ('sib' meaning 'relative', hence our word 'sibling') and meant 'a godparent'. In **The Winter's Tale** Paulina bursts into Leontes' room with his baby demanding to discuss 'some gossips' at the baptism. At the end of **The Comedy of Errors** the Abbess celebrates the reunion by asking for a sort of second nativity with a 'gossip's feast', at which the Duke plays on the word, turning it into a verb: 'With all my heart I'll gossip at this feast'. He has introduced the next meaning of *gossip*: idle chatter. Women often take charge at such occasions and talk enthusiastically, and so *gossip*, as a noun, came to describe them. Puck in **A Midsummer Night's Dream** tells the First Fairy, 'sometimes lurk I in a gossip's bowl'. A particularly disparaging usage occurs in **Much Ado About Nothing**, when Benedick is being mocked by

Claudio and Don Pedro. He takes an impatient male attitude to their laughter, treating them as tiresome old women: 'I will leave you now to your gossip-like humour'.

gossiping *noun* merry-making (*CE v 1*)

go through *verb* to bargain for something (*MM ii 1*)

Goths *plural noun* a warlike tribe from eastern Europe. They originated in southern Sweden and migrated south. They sacked Rome in 410. During the 5th and 6th centuries they were the dominant rulers in Europe. (*AYLI iii 3*)

goujeres, goujeers, goodyear *noun* a sexually transmitted disease (*KL v 3*) (NOTE: Also known as the French disease.) [From French *goujère*, a spurious word.]

gout *noun* a drop (*M ii 1*) [From French *goutte*.]

governess *noun* a woman who controls something (*MND ii 1*)

government *noun* **1.** self-control (*1H4 iii 1*; *O iii 3*) **2.** control (*RJ iv 1*) **3.** the command of an army (*1H4 iv 1*; *O iv 1*) ◇ **in government** in accordance with musical requirements (*MND v 1*)

governor *noun* a military commander (*O ii 1*)

Gower, John *noun* (1325–1408) an English poet. He was a contemporary of Chaucer. His major work was *Confessio Amantis* which is the source of Shakespeare's *Pericles*.

gown *noun* a nightdress (*2H4 iii 2*; *JC iv 3*)

grace *noun* **1.** God's forgiveness **2.** an answer to a prayer **3.** honour **4.** the form of address to a duke **5.** an attendant on **Venus** ■ *verb* to give a good appearance

COMMENT: Shakespeare's characters use *grace* in various contexts, all denoting approval. It may mean something as slight as Portia's promise in **The Merchant of Venice** to 'wear my dagger with the braver grace', denoting elegance. Often it refers to the favour or protection of a powerful patron, as when Lear understands why Oswald is so confident in his insolence: 'This is a slave whose easy borrowed pride/Dwells in the fickle grace of her he follows'. But the fundamental meaning of *grace* is theological, meaning the divine influence that can operate in men and women to regenerate and sanctify them. **The Winter's Tale**, though ostensibly a non-Christian play, with the god Apollo presiding, uses the Christian concept of *grace*, chiefly through the forgiving and regenerating influence of Hermione. She uses *grace* several times when Leontes is recalling his youth. When he grew from innocent childhood into the complicated feelings and temptations of adulthood, she hopes that her decision to be his wife was 'Grace indeed'. Leontes abuses this gift of grace when he destroys his wife and family, but grace still exists in the lost daughter, Perdita. After sixteen years, she has 'grown in grace,/Equal with wondering'. Before wife and daughter can be restored, 'It is required you do awake your faith', as Paulina instructs Leontes, acting as his religious mentor. Then, finally, grace is given to him a second time. Perdita is the daughter of grace, but has grown up in a shepherd's cottage under the influence of nature. The play is showing that God's providence works through nature and grace which combine in their process of healing. In **Romeo and Juliet**, Friar Laurence, picking herbs at the dawn of a new day, a time which symbolises regeneration, reflects on the diversity of earth's gifts: 'O mickle is the powerful grace that lies/In plants, herbs, stones and their true qualities'. In **Hamlet** Ophelia, an abused innocent, gives flowers to the corrupted court, including rue, which is associated with suffering and penance. She tells them, 'you may call it herb o'grace o'Sundays', the time for reflection when the heart may open to receive God's grace.

graceful *adjective* blessed with God's forgiveness (*WT v 1*)

gradation *noun* **1.** seniority (*O i 1*) **2.** gradual movement forward (*MM iv 3*)

graff *verb* to join a shoot from one plant to the growing stem of another (to **graft**) (*AYLI iii 2*; *R3 iii 7*)

graffing *noun* grafting (*2H4 v 3*)

graft *adjective* firmly joined like a plant grafted on to another (*R3 iii 7*)

grafters *plural noun* the trees from which shoots have been taken to join to another tree (*H5 iii 5*)

grain [From *grain*, 'a red dye produced by grinding the bodies of female coccus insects, *Kermes ilicis*, which live on oak trees'.] ◇ **in grain** permanent (*TN i 5*)

grained *adjective* **1.** permanently stained (*H iii 4*) **2.** wrinkled (*CE v 1*)

grand *adjective* **1.** chief (*T i 2*; *R2 v 6*; *R3 iv 4*) **2.** principal (*AC iii 12*)

grand captain *noun* a commander-in-chief (*AC iii 1*)

grand jurors *plural noun* men who owned sufficient property, etc., to enable them to serve on a jury (*1H4 ii 2*)

grandsire *noun* an old man (*TS iv 5*) ■ *adjective* ancient (*RJ i 4*)

grange *noun* an isolated country house (*MM iii 1*; *WT iv 4*; *O i 1*)

grate *verb* to annoy someone (*2H4 iv 1*; *H iii 1*; *AC i 1*)

gratify *verb* **1.** to reward someone (*O v 2*) **2.** to pay someone (*MV iv 1*)

gratillity *noun* a small reward for something done (*TN ii 2*)

gratulate *adjective* gratifying (*MM v 1*) ■ *verb* to greet someone (*R3 iv 1*)

grave *verb* **1.** to engrave something (*MV ii 7*; *R3 iv 4*) **2.** to bury someone (*R2 iii 2*)

gravel *adjective* hard (*MM iv 3*)

gravelled *adjective* at a loss, stuck for words, an idea, etc. (*AYLI iv 1*) [From the idea of a ship stranded on a sandbank.]

graves *plural noun* greaves, pieces of armour for a person's lower legs (*2H4 iv 1*)

gravy *noun* sweat (*2H4 i 2*) [Referring to the juices that come from cooking meat.]

greasy *adjective* fat (*AYLI ii 1*)

great-belly doublet *noun* a well-padded jacket (*H5 iv 7 – where Falstaff is the stuffing!*)

great chamber *noun* the great hall of a house (*RJ i 5*)

greatly *adverb* nobly (*H5 Epil.*)

great morning *noun* broad daylight

green *adjective* immature (*WT iii 2*; *2H4 iv 5*; *H i 3*; *AC i 5*) [With reference to a young shoot on a tree.]

COMMENT: Apart from its obvious meaning of colour, especially of vegetation, *green* had contradictory symbolic meanings. In the magical plays **The Tempest** and **A Midsummer Night's Dream** *green* is part of the natural world which fairy and white magic use for their strange effects on human life. Prospero speaks of 'you demi-puppets that/By moonshine do the green sour ringlets make' and Titania of 'the quaint mazes in the wanton green'. These both have positive connotations, but because of green's association with spring and youth, the word comes to denote naivety. Cleopatra refers to 'My salad days/When I was green in judgement'. The soldier Henry V half-despises the behaviour of a young lover he has to adopt when he woos the French princess: 'I cannot look greenly, nor gasp out my eloquence'. In the punning play **Romeo and Juliet** Shakespeare gives his heroine a grisly pun in her most serious moment. She is alone in the tomb and wakes to see the body of her cousin: 'Where bloody Tybalt, yet but green in earth,/Lies festering'. *Green* is literally the colour of a decaying body, but it has also been 'greenly', or recently, interred. No matter for the distraught Juliet, that the *green* of festering would not begin until long after the *green* of recent burial!

green-eyed *adjective* jealous (*MV iii 2*; *O iii 3*)

greenly *adjective* lacking judgement, like an immature person (*H5 v 2*; *H iv 5*)

green-sickness *noun* **1.** anaemia (*AC iii 2*) **2.** a general lack of interest in doing anything (*2H4 iv 3*; *RJ iii 5*)

greet the time *verb* meet the occasion (*KL v 1*)

greymalkin *noun* the **familiar** of a witch, often a cat (*M i 1*)

grief *noun* **1.** suffering (*MA i 1*; *1H4 v 1*; *2H4 i 1*) **2.** a complaint (*1H4 iv 3*; *JC i 3*)

grievance *noun* **1.** an inconvenience (*2H4 iv 1*; *O i 2*) **2.** someone or something causing grief or annoyance (*RJ i 1*)

grievous *adjective* very (*1H4 iv 1*; *R2 i 4*)

grievously *adverb* **1.** with regret or sorrow (*O v 1*) **2.** at great cost (*JC iii 2*)

griffin *noun* a mythical animal with the body of a lion and the head of an eagle (*1H4 iii 1*; *MND ii 1*)

gripe *verb* to grip something (*1H4 v 1*; *H5 iv 6*; *M iii 1*; *O iii 3*)

griping *adjective* painful (*RJ iv 5*)

grise, grize *noun* a pace (*TN iii 1*; *O i 3*)

Grissel, Griselda *noun* the model wife in Chaucer's *The Clerk's Tale* (*TS ii 1*)

grizzle *noun* a few grey hairs (*TN v 1*)

grizzled *adjective* (*of a person's hair*) streaked with grey (*H i 2*; *AC iii 3*)

groat *noun* a small silver coin worth four old pence (*2H4 i 2*; *H5 v 1*)

gross *noun* the total amount (*MV i 3*) ■ *adjective* stupid (*MND v 1*; *CE iii 2*; *H5 iv 1*) ■ *adverb* plainly (*MM ii 4*; *H5 ii 2*)

gross in sense *adjective* clear to see (*O i 2*)

grossly *adverb* **1.** openly (*AC iii 10*; *KL i 1*; *CE ii 2*) **2.** stupidly, foolishly (*O iii 3*; *MM iii 1*; *R3 iv 1*) **3.** substantially (*TN v 1*; *MV v 1*) **4.** indecently (*MV v 1*) **5.** in a condition where sins have not been absolved (*H iii 3*)

ground *noun* **1.** the area covered or under control (*MV ii 2*; *2H4 ii 3*) **2.** the basic bass part of a tune on which variations are made (*R3 iii 7*) **3.** the bottom of the sea, a river, etc. (*1H4 i 3*; *2H4 iv 1, 4*) **4.** the base coat of a painting (*1H4 i 2*)

grounded *adjective* firmly established (*AYLI i 2*; *R3 i 3*)

groundlings *plural noun* the poorer people who stood in the pit of a theatre to watch a play (*H iii 2*)

grow *verb* to become due (*CE iv 1, 4*)

grow on, grow upon *verb* **1.** to go forward (*MND i 2*) **2.** to become worse (*H5 iii 3*; *KL v 3*) **3.** to come to take advantage of (*AYLI i 1*) **4.** to gain ground on (*JC ii 1*)

grow to *verb* **1.** to become closely joined to something (*AC i 3*; *JC i 2*) **2.** to arrive at a point (*MV ii 2*; *RV ii 6*)

grow to a point *verb* to come to the point (*MND i 2*)

grudge *noun* a complaint (*T i 2*)

grudging *noun* the action of complaining (*MA iii 4*) ■ *adjective* unwilling (*R3 ii 1*)

guard *noun* **1.** the custody of someone (*CE v 1*; *MV i 3*; *AC v 2*) **2.** a decorative trimming (*MM iii 1*) ■ *adjective* trimmed (*MV ii 2*)

guardage *noun* the care and responsibility for someone (*O ii 1*)

guards *plural noun* the two stars in the constellation of Ursa Minor (Little Bear) said to guard the North Pole (*O ii 1*)

gudgeon *noun* a gullible person (*MV i 1*) [From *gudgeon*, 'a small freshwater fish, *Gobio*, that is easily caught'.]

guerdon *noun* compensation for something (*MA v 3*)

guidon *noun* a small flag (*H5 iv 2*)

guilder *noun* an old Dutch gold coin, or any coin of value (*CE i 1*)

guiled *adjective* treacherous (*MV iii 2*)

guilts *plural noun* crimes (*KL iii 2*)

guinea-hen *noun* a prostitute (*O i 3*) (NOTE: A guinea fowl is a type of bird.)

guise *noun* clothes worn (*M v 1*)

gules *noun* the heraldic name for red (*H ii 2*)

gulf *noun* **1.** a whirlpool that draws everything into it (*H5 ii 4*; *R3 iii 7*; *H iii 3*) **2.** an enormous stomach that can hold any quantity (*M iv 1*)

gull *noun* a young bird before it has grown its feathers (*1H4 v 1*)

COMMENT: Elizabethans used *gull* both as a verb and a noun: to trick, the trick itself and a simpleton who is easily tricked. The word survives in our adjective 'gullible'. The gull was thought to be a bird easily deceived and trapped. Malvolio in **Twelfth Night** discovers that he has been 'the most notorious geck and gull,/That ere invention played on'. The perpetrator was Maria, whom Sir Toby celebrates as 'my noble gull-catcher'. Gulls and gulling are often the basis of both the humour and the plot in comedy, but their effects can be darker in tragedy, as where Iago deceives Othello. When Emilia discovers the truth she is appalled at how the hero has been undermined: 'O gull, O dolt,/ As ignorant as dirt'. Other easily trapped birds were also emblems of stupidity. Iago scorns the idea that he 'would time expend with such a snipe': Roderigo is the 'snipe', the first victim of deceit in **Othello**. In **Much Ado About Nothing** Claudio tries to be witty by implying that Benedick has been duped: at the feast 'Shall I not find a woodcock too?' The world of nature provided writers with many images of animals and birds to stand for human characteristics, as shown by the popularity of emblem books in the 16th century.

gull-catcher *noun* a cheat (*TN ii 5*)

gum *noun* **1.** a glue used for stiffening cloth (*H ii 2*; *O v 2*) **2.** a discharge from the eyes or nose (*H5 iv 2*)

gummed velvet *noun* velvet stiffened with glue (*1H4 ii 2*)

gun-stones *plural noun* a cannon ball (*H5 i 2*) (NOTE: Cannon balls were sometimes made of stone.)

gurnet *noun* a small fish with a large head and three spines in front of the front fin which it uses to walk on. 'Soused gurnet' is a term of abuse. (*1H4 iv 2*)

gust *verb* **1.** to taste something (*TN i 3*) **2.** to know of something (*WT i 2*)

guts *noun* a very fat person (*1H4 ii 4*; *H iii 4*)

guttered *adjective* worn by the action of water (*O ii 1*)

gyves *plural noun* shackles (*1H4 iv 2*; *H iv 7*; *MM iv 2*; *RJ ii 2*)

H

haber-de-pois *noun* a system of weights in which one pound = 16 ounces (454g) (avoir-du-pois) (*2H4 ii 4*)

habiliment *noun* clothing (*TS iv 3*)

habit *noun* attitude (*AYLI iii 2*)

COMMENT: Shakespeare rarely used *habit* in our sense of a custom. In his plays it generally means clothes, relating back to the Latin 'habere', to have or hold. Nowadays we restrict this meaning of *habit* to the garments of monks and nuns, who own very few personal possessions. In **The Taming of the Shrew** Tranio identifies Vincentio as 'a sober, ancient gentleman by your habit'. *Habit* can also extend to a person's general bearing. Gratiano assures Bassanio in **The Merchant of Venice** that he will not embarrass him at Belmont: 'If I do not put on a sober habit…never trust me more'. He probably means clothes, but he also uses the metaphor of putting on clothes for adopting a serious manner, and in this play on the word he mocks Bassanio's anxiety. *Habit* became associated with 'habiliments', also clothes, but came from a different source, the French 'abiller', meaning 'to fit out or prepare'. Caesar refers to Cleopatra dressed 'In th'habiliments of the goddess Isis'.

hack *verb* to cut or chop at something (*JC ii 1; M v 1; R3 iii 3; 1H4 ii 4*)

Hades *noun* a place of despair and gloom and repose of the souls of the dead (NOTE: The Roman equivalent is **Tartarus**.)

hag *noun* **1.** an ugly witch (*R3 i 1; T i 1*) **2.** an evil fairy (*RJ i 1*)

Hagar's offspring *noun* Ishmael, an aggressive person. In the Bible, Hagar was Abraham's wife (Genesis 16:15) and mother of Ishmael who was prophesied to be an aggressive person (Genesis 16:11). (*MV ii 5*)

haggard *noun* **1.** an adult female hawk that was caught and is being trained (*MA iii 1*) **2.** an unfaithful or disobedient woman (*TS iv 1, 2*) ■ *adjective* wild (*O iii 3*)

haggled *adjective* with many wounds (*H5 iv 6*)

hag-seed *noun* the children of a witch (*T i 2*)

hai *noun* the cry made by a fencer when he strikes his opponent with his sword (*RJ ii 4*) [From Italian *hai*, 'you have it!']

hair *noun* **1.** the nature of something (*1H4 iv 1*) **2.** the hair of a fast horse used in hunting that was supposed to come to life when placed in water (*AC I 2*)

halcyon *noun* a kingfisher (*KL ii 2*) (NOTE: When free to move the bird turns into the wind, so the dead bird was used as a weather cock. The Sicilians believed that the kingfisher laid its eggs in the sea where they incubated for fourteen days during the winter solstice.) [From Greek 'kingfisher'.]

hale *verb* to haul something (*MA ii 3; TN iii 2*)

half *noun* a husband or wife (*TS v 2; JC ii 1*)

half-achieved *adjective* half won (*H5 iii 3*)

half-blooded *adjective* having only one parent of noble birth (*KL v 3*)

half-can *noun* a drinking cup used in ale-houses, etc., that is larger than the usual type (*MM iv 3*)

half-cheeked bit, half-checked bit, half-chequed bit *noun* insufficient control (*TS iii 2*) [Because when the side pieces attaching a bit on a horse to the bridle are broken, the horse cannot be controlled properly.]

half-face *adjective* **1.** miserable-looking (*2H4 iii 2*) **2.** half and half (*1H4 i 3*)

halfpenny *noun* a small piece (*MA ii 3*) [Because a halfpenny is a small silver coin.]

half sword *adverb* closely engaged in a fight (*1H4 ii 4*)

hall ◇ **a hall!** an interjection asking for room for dancers on the floor (*RJ i 5*)

hallow¹, halloo *noun* a shout to attract someone, used especially when hunting (*2H4 i 2*; *KL iii 4*; *WT iii 3*)

hallow² *verb* to make something holy (*H i 1*; *MND v 1*; *O iii 4*)

Hallowmas *noun* All Saints' Day (1 November) (*R2 v 1*)

halter *noun* a noose placed around the neck, especially for hanging a person or leading a horse (*1H4 ii 4*; *AC iii 1*; *MV iv 1*; *O iv 2*)

hammered of *adjective* thought about (*WT ii 2*)

handfast ◇ **in handfast** in custody (*WT iv 3*)

handsaw *noun* **1.** a small saw used with one hand (*1H4 ii 4*) **2.** a heron (*H ii 2*) (NOTE: 'heronshaw' and 'handsaw' were dialect terms for a heron.)

handy-dandy *phrase* take your choice (*KL iv 6*) [From the children's game during which one player has to guess in which hand of the other player a small object is hidden.]

hangers *plural noun* the straps attaching the scabbard of a sword to a belt (*H v 2*)

hanging *adjective* miserable (*MM iv 2*)

hang off *interjection* let go! (*MND iii 2*)

Hannibal *noun* (247–103 BC) a Carthaginian general famous for his several victories over the Romans (*MM ii 1*)

haply *adverb* perhaps, by chance (*TN i 2, iii 3*; *R3 iv 4*)

happily *adverb* **1.** fortunately (*TS i 2, iv 4*) **2.** perhaps (*H ii 2*; *MM iv 2*; *O iii 3*; *TS iv 4*)

happiness *noun* appropriateness (*MA ii 3*; *H ii 2*)

happy *adjective* appropriate (*1H4 v 4*)

hard-favoured *adjective* ugly (*AYLI iii 3*)

hardiment *noun* bravery (*1H4 i 3*)

hardly *adverb* **1.** with difficulty (*M v 3*) **2.** severely (*R3 ii 1*)

hardock *noun* burdock, a weed that has strong hooks on its seed cases (*KL iv 4*)

hardy *adjective* bold (*TN ii 2*; *M i 2*)

hare *noun* a prostitute (*MA i 1*; *RJ ii 4*)

Harfleur *noun* a town in France on the Seine estuary which was the site of Henry V's landing and first victory over the French (*H5 iii Chor., 3, 6*)

hark *noun* a hunting cry calling the dogs (*T iv 1*)

harlot *adjective* unworthy (*WT ii 3*; *CE ii 2*)

harlotry *noun* **1.** a prostitute (*O iv 2*) **2.** a silly young girl (*1H4 iii 1*; *RJ iv 2*) ■ *adjective* useless (*1H4 ii 4*)

harmony *noun* pleasant music (*T iii 3*; *H iii 2*)

harness *noun* armour (*1H4 iii 2*; *AC iv 8*; *M v 5*; *TS Ind. 2*)

harp *verb* **1.** to focus on something and keep on talking about it (*MM v 1*; *R3 iv 4*) **2.** to guess something (*M iv 1*)

harpier *noun* somebody who is like a harpy (*M iv 1*)

harpy *noun* a mythological creature with the face of a woman and the body of an eagle (*MA ii 1*; *T iii 3*)

harrow *verb* to distress someone (*H i 1, 5*)

harry *verb* to harass someone (*AC iii 3*)

hart *noun* a male deer over five years old (*AYLI iii 2*; *H iii 2*; *JC iii 1*; *TN i 1*)

hasted *adjective* quick (*MV ii 2*)

hasty-witted *adjective* acting without thinking (*TS v 2*)

hatch *noun* a door with upper and lower sections that can be opened separately (*CE iii 1*; *KL iii 6*)

hatches *plural noun* planks that can be moved to give access to a ship's hold (*R3 i 4*; *T i 2, v 1*)

hatchment *noun* a tablet bearing the heraldic arms of a person (*H iv 5*) (NOTE: Usually a hatchment was a black diamond-shape with the arms on it. This was placed on the door of the house of a person who had died.)

haught *adjective* arrogant (*R2 iv 1*; *R3 ii 3*)

haughty *adjective* **1.** noble (*1H4 v 2*) **2.** ambitious (*R3 iv 2*)

haunch *noun* the later part of something (*2H4 iv 4*)

hautboy *noun* a wind instrument similar to an oboe (*2H4 iii 2*)

have at him *noun* a fencing thrust (*2H4 i 2*)

have to't *verb* to battle (*TS i 1*)

having *noun* a desire (*MV i 1*; *O iv 3*)

havoc *noun* the indiscriminate killing of a large number of people (*H v 2*) ◇ **to cry 'havoc'** to show no mercy (*JC iii 1*)

hawk *noun* a hoe or a farming tool resembling a pickaxe (**mattock**) (*H ii 2*)

hazard *noun* **1.** a risk (*H5 iii 7*) (NOTE: Hazard was an old game of dice.) **2.** a winning shot (*H5 i 2*) [From a real tennis term meaning 'the side of the court into which the ball is served'. A point was won if the ball is not returned by the opponent.]

head *noun* **1.** face (*MND i 1*; *MA v 1*; *MM iv 3*) **2.** the beginning (*R2 i 1*; *H i 1*) **3.** a unit of soldiers (*1H4 iv 4*; *H iv 5*) ■ *verb* to behead someone (*MM ii 1*)

headed *adjective* matured or fully grown (*AYLI ii 7*)

headier *adjective* impetuous (*KL ii 4*)

headland *noun* the edges of a field left unploughed until the end to allow the plough to be turned (*2H4 v 1*)

head-lugged *adjective* pulled by the ears and otherwise roughly treated (*KL iv 2*)

headly *adjective* main (*H5 iii 3*)

headpiece *noun* **1.** a helmet (*H5 iii 7*; *KL iii 2*) **2.** the head (*WT i 2*)

headstall *noun* a horse's bridle (*TS iii 2*)

heady-rash *adjective* hasty (*CE v 1*)

health *noun* a toast drunk to someone or something (*TN i 3*)

heap ◇ **on heaps** in ruins (*H5 v 5*)

hearing *noun* news (*TS v 2*)

hearken *verb* to inquire about something (*MA v 1*; *R3 i 1*)

hearsed *adjective* in a coffin (*MV iii 1*; *H i 4*)

heart ◇ **for his heart** to save his life (*MV v 1*) ◇ **out of heart** discouraged (*1H4 iii 3*) ◇ **with all heart** a greeting (*O iv 1*)

heart-burned *adjective* deeply affected (*MA ii 1*; *1H4 iii 3*)

hearted *adjective* deeply felt (*O i 3*)

heartiness *noun* good-heartedness (*WT i 2*)

heartless *adjective* without the desire to live (*RJ i 1*)

heart's ease *noun* absence of stress (*H5 iv 1*)

heart-strings *plural noun* in the anatomical view of the time, the tendons that hold and control the heart (*R3 iv 4*)

heart-struck *adjective* causing stress to the heart (*KL iii 1*)

heart-whole *adjective* not involved in a romantic relationship (*AYLI iv 1*)

heat *noun* the amount of drink needed to comfortably warm the body (*TN i 5*) ■ *verb* to ride swiftly over something (*WT i 2*) ◇ **seven years' heat** until seven years have passed (*TN i 1*)

heave *noun* a deep sigh (*WT ii 3*; *H iv 1*) ■ *verb* to utter something (*AYLI ii 1*; *KL iv 3*)

heavily *adverb* sadly (*R3 i 4*; *M iv 3*)

heavy *adjective* **1.** slow (*MND v 1*; *AC i 7*) **2.** important or serious (*1H4 ii 3*; *KL v 1*) **3.** stupid (*O ii 1*) **4.** wicked (*MM ii 3*; *WT iii 2*; *H iv 1*)

heavy-gaited *adjective* sluggish (*R2 iii 2*)

heavy-headed *adjective* drunken (*H i 4*)

hebonon, hebenon, hebona *noun* any plant or fruit with a poisonous juice, possibly henbane or yew (*H i 5*) [From German *Eibenbaum*, 'yew tree'.]

Hecate same as **Diana**

hectic *noun* a persistent fever (*H iv 3*)

Hector *noun* one of the Trojan princes mentioned in Homer's *Iliad*. The name is used to represent bravery. (*2H4 ii 4*; *MA iii 3*) (NOTE: Hector was the son of King **Priam**. Having held out in Troy for ten years, he was killed by **Achilles** who tied his body to his chariot and dragged it in triumph around the walls of Troy.)

Hecuba *noun* the wife of **Priam**, king of Troy, and the mother of **Hector** (*H ii 2*) (NOTE: After the fall of Troy, she was taken by **Ulysses** and finally changed into a dog. When she found that she could only bark, she threw herself into the sea.)

hedge *verb* to protect (*H iv 5*)

hedge in *verb* to keep inside or outside a place by force (*JC iv 3*)

hedge-pig *noun* a hedgehog (*M iv 1*)

heel *verb* to dance ◇ **at heel of** after that (*AC ii 2*) ◇ **out at heels** penniless (*L ii 2*)

heft *verb* to retch (*WT ii 1*)

heifer *noun* a sexually promiscuous woman (*WT i 2*)

height *noun* social rank (*R2 i 1*; *R3 i 3*)

heinously *adverb* badly (*1H4 iii 3*)

heir *noun* a woman's genitals (*CE iii 2*) [From a pun on 'hair'.]

Helen *noun* in Greek mythology, the daughter of Zeus and Leda, considered the archetype of female beauty (*RJ ii 4*; *MND v 1*; *2H4 v 5*) (NOTE: She was the wife of Menelaus of Troy but eloped with Paris, thus bringing about the Trojan War and the destruction of Troy.)

Helios *noun* the Roman equivalent of **Apollo**

hell *noun* a debtor's prison (*CE iv 2*)

Hellespont *noun* the ancient name for the Dardanelles, a narrow sea passage leading from the Mediterranean to the Sea of Marmara (*AYLI iv 1*; *O iii 3*)

hell-hated *adjective* hated as much as hell (*KL v 3*)

hell-hound *noun* a fiend (*R3 iv 4*; *M v 8*)

hell-kite *noun* an excessively cruel person (*M iv 3*) [From the idea of a terrible bird of prey.]

helm *noun* a helmet (*KL iv 2*; *AC ii 1*) ■ *verb* to steer something (*MM iii 2*)

help *noun* a cure (*CE v 1*) ◇ **at help** is favourable (*H iv 3*)

helpless *adjective* of no use or benefit (*R3 i 2*)

hem *verb* to cough (*2H4 ii 4*)

hemlock *noun* a poisonous weed (*H5 v 2*; *KL iv 4*; *M iv 1*)

hemp *noun* the fibre used to make a hangman's rope (*H5 iii 6*)

hemp-seed *adjective* destined to be hanged (*2H4 ii 1*) *See also* **hemp**

henchman *noun* a respected attendant (*MND ii 1*)

hent *noun* an intention (*H iii 3*) ■ *verb* **1.** to seize something (*MM iv 6*) **2.** to jump over something (*WT iv 2*)

Hera *noun* the Greek equivalent of **Juno**

Heracles The son of Zeus and Alcmene. He was born with super-human strength. (NOTE: Being made mad by **Juno**, he killed his wife and children. For this he was condemned by **Apollo** to serve Eurystheus for twelve years. During this time he completed twelve seemingly impossible tasks. Afterward Heracles was granted immortality. The Roman name is *Hercules*.)

herb of grace *noun* rue, a plant which was traditionally the symbol of repentance (*R2 iii 4*; *H iv 5*)

Hercules and his load *noun* the Globe theatre in London, from its sign (*H ii 2*)

here-approach *noun* the arrival of someone (*M iv 1*)

here-remain *noun* a stay in a place (*M iv 3*)

Hermes *noun* in Greek mythology, the god who charmed Argus to sleep by playing his magic pipe (*H5 iii 7*) (NOTE: The Roman equivalent is **Mercury**.)

hermit *noun* someone who is paid to say prayers for others, a **beadsman** (*M i 6*)

Hero in Greek mythology, a priestess of **Venus** who fell in love with Leander. He swam the **Hellespont** (a distance of about 6.5km) every night to be with her. One night Leander drowned and Hero drowned herself. (*AYLI iv 1*)

Herod *noun* the ruler of the Jews at the time of Jesus Christ (*H iii 2*) [In the mystery plays he was depicted as a blustering villain, so to *out-Herod* means 'to bluster more than Herod'.]

hest *noun* an order (*1H4 ii 3*; *T iii 1, iv 1*) [Shortening of 'behest'.]

hewgh *noun* a representation of the sound of an arrow whizzing past (*KL iv 6*)

hic est Sigeia tellus *phrase Latin* here is the Sigeian land (**Sigeum**) (*TS iii 1*)

hic et ubique *phrase Latin* here and everywhere (*H i 5*)

hic ibat Simois *phrase Latin* here ran the river Simois (*TS iii 1*) (NOTE: Simois is a small river near Troy, mentioned in Greek mythology.)

hic steterat Priami regia celsa senis *phrase Latin* here would have stood the lofty palace of old King Priam (*TS iii 1*)

hide *verb* **1.** to sheath a sword (*AYLI ii 7*; *R3 i 2*) **2.** to protect someone (*JC ii 1*)

hide-fox and all after *noun* the game of hide-and-seek (*H iv 2*)

Hiems *noun Latin* winter personified (*MND ii 1*) (NOTE: Hiems was the Roman god of winter.)

high-battled *adjective* at the head of a victorious army (*AC iii 11*)

high cross *noun* the market cross in a town (*TS i 1*)

high day *noun* a religious holiday (*MV ii 9*)

high-engendered *adjective* born in heaven (*KL iii 2*)

high-gravel-blind *adjective* almost completely blind (*MV v 1*)

high lone *adjective* alone on your own two feet, like a baby taking its first steps (*RJ i 3*)

high-proof *adverb* to a great degree (*MA v 1*)

high-sighted *adjective* seeing from a height (*JC ii 1*)

high-stomached *adjective* proud (*R2 i 1*)

hight *adjective* named (*MND v 1*)

hilding *noun* a despicable immoral person (*RJ i 5, ii 4, iii 5*) ■ *adjective* cowardly (*2H4 i 1*; *H5 iv 2*)

hind *noun* a farm labourer or peasant (*1H4 ii 3*; *AYLI iii 2*; *CE iii 1*; *R3 ii 4*)

hint *noun* 1. an opportunity (*T ii 1*; *AC iii 4*) 2. an occasion (*O i 3*; *T i 2*)

hip ◇ **upon the hip** at a disadvantage (*MV i 3*; *O ii 1*)

hipped *adjective* lame due to an injured hip bone (*TS iii 2*)

Hiren *noun* Irene, the mistress of Sultan Mahomet II (in a lost play by Peele) (*2H4 ii 4*) (NOTE: Used as a pun on 'iron'.)

hit *verb* 1. to achieve something (*MV iii 2*) 2. to agree (*KL i 1*) ■ *adjective* reflected (*WT v 1*) ■ *noun* it (*M i 5*) ◇ **hit of** hit upon something (*CE iii 2*)

hive *verb* to live with someone (*MV ii 5*)

hizz *verb* to hiss (*KL iii 6*)

hoar *adjective* 1. mouldy (*RJ ii 4*) 2. whitish (*H iv 7*)

hob, nob *phrase* hit or miss (*TN iii 4*)

hobbididence *noun see* **flibbertigibbet** (*KL iv 1*)

hobby-horse, hoby-horse *noun* 1. a stick with a horse's head on it, used as a children's toy and also in morris dancing (*H iii 2*) 2. a prostitute (*MA iii 2*; *O iv 1*)

hobgoblin *noun* a mischievous fairy (*MND ii 1*)

hogshead *noun* a wine cask holding about 240 litres (*2H4 ii 4*; *T iv 1*)

hold *noun* a stronghold (*2H4 Ind.*) ■ *verb* to bet someone something (*MV iii 4*)

hold in *verb* to keep silent about something (*1H4 ii 1*)

holding *noun* the theme of a song (*AC ii 7*)

hole ◇ **find a hole in his coat** find his weak spot (*H5 iii 6*)

holidame, holidam *noun* holiness (*TS v 2*)

holla *interjection* whoa! (*KL v 1*) ■ *verb* to shout something (*1H4 i 1*; *MND iv 1*)

hollo *verb* to shout something (*TN i 1*; *R2 iv 1*; *1H4 i 3*)

Holmedon *noun* a battlefield where the Percy and Douglas families fought (*1H4 i 1, 3, v 3*)

holy ◇ **court holy water** to make promises that you don't intend to keep (*L ii 2*)

Holy Rood Day *noun* Holy Cross Day (14 September) (*1H4 i 1*) (NOTE: **Rood** is another name for a crucifix.)

homager *noun* a servant (*AC i 1*)

home *verb* to hit a target ■ *adjective* all the way ■ *adverb* to the full ■ *adjective* domestic (*R2 i 1*) ◇ **to feed from home** to be unfaithful (*CE ii 1*; *AC iii 12*) ◇ **near at home** nearly at home (*MM iv 3*)

homely *adjective* plain or unattractive (*CE ii 1*; *WT iv 4*)

homespun *noun* a yokel (*MND iii 1*)

homily *noun* a sermon (*AYLI iii 2*)

honest *adjective* virginal (*H iii 1*; *O iii 3*)

honesty *noun* 1. honour (*CE v 1*; *JC iv 3*) 2. decency (*TN ii 3*; *O iv 1*) 3. virginity (*H iii 1*)

honeybag *noun* a specialised stomach of the honey bee which carries the honey (*MND iii 1*)

honeying *noun* talking sweetly and affectionately (*H iii 4*)

honey-seed *adjective* murderous (*2H4 ii 1*) (NOTE: This is a mistake for 'homicidal'.)

honey-suckle *adjective* murderous (*2H4 ii 1*) (NOTE: This is a mistake for 'homicidal'.)

honour *noun* a noble deed (*KL v 3*)

honour-flawed *adjective* no longer a virgin (*WT ii 1*)

honour-owing *adjective* honourable (*H5 iv 6*)

hood *verb* 1. to disguise or hide something (*MM v 1*) 2. to put a hood on a hawk's head to stop it bating (*H5 iii 7*; *RJ iii 2*)

hoodman-blind *noun* the game of blindman's buff (*H iii 4*)

hoodwink *verb* 1. to blindfold someone (*RJ i 1*) 2. to deceive someone (*M iv 3*) 3. to conceal something (*T iv 1*)

hoop *noun* a ring (*MV v 1*) ■ *verb* 1. to encircle something (*WT iv 4*) 2. to shout out in astonishment (*H5 ii 2*)

hooted at *adjective* laughed at (*WT v 3*)

horn *noun* 1. an ox horn carried by beggars to take any drink that is offered (*KL iii 6*) 2. a horn used to symbolise a situation of having large amounts of food and other essentials (*2H4 i 2*) **3.** a horn used to symbolise a man whose wife has been unfaithful to him (*MA i 1*; *AC i 2*)

horn beasts *plural noun* cuckolds (*AYLI iii 3*) (NOTE: The whole of Touchstone's speech here has a double meaning.)

horn-mad *adjective* furious, like an enraged bull (*CE ii 1*; *MA i 1*)

horn-maker *noun* something that makes a **cuckold** of a man (*AYLI iv 1*)

horologue, horologe *noun* a clock (*O ii 3*)

horse *verb* to put one thing on top of another, with a sexual connotation (*WT i 2*)

host *verb* to stay at an inn (*CE i 2*)

hot at hand *adjective* not to be held back (*JC iv 2*)

hot-house *noun* a place providing hot baths for the public (a euphemism for a brothel) (*MM ii 1*)

hound of Crete *noun* a shaggy breed of dog (*H5 ii 1*)

hour *noun* a moment (*MV iv 1*)

housekeeper *noun* **1.** a householder (*TN iv 2*) **2.** a guard dog (*M iii 1*)

housekeeping *noun* hospitality (*TS ii 1*)

house of profession *noun* a brothel (*MM iv 3*)

house of sale *noun* a brothel (*H ii 1*)

housewife, huswife *noun* **1.** the woman who manages a household (*MND ii 1*; *AYLI i 2*) **2.** a prostitute (*2H4 iii 2*; *H5 v 1*; *O iv 1*)

housewifery, huswifery *noun* the task of looking after and managing a household (*H5 ii 3*; *O ii 1*)

hovel post *noun* a heavy wooden post supporting part of a cottage, etc. (*MV ii 2*)

hovering *adjective* indecisive (*WT i 2*)

how

COMMENT: Shakespeare used *how* in ways that are familiar to us, and often more widely too. 'How now?' was a general inquiry, especially about health: Claudius in **Hamlet**, troubled about his wife's distant mood, asks, 'How now, sweet queen'. *How* could be used for astonishment, as when Escalus in **Measure for Measure** hears Elbow say that he detests his wife: 'How, thy wife!' King Lear uses *how* as an angry warning when Cordelia is beginning to displease him: 'How, how, Cordelia! Mend your speech a little'. It was often an abbreviated form of a longer phrase: in **Henry IV Part 2**, 'How a good yoke of bullocks at Stamford fair?' is a way of asking how much they cost. We have extended the word into 'however', but Shakespeare also included the now old-fashioned 'howbeit', 'howsoever', 'howsomever', used as adverbs or conjunctions.

howlet *noun* a baby owl (*M iv 1*)

hox *verb* to cut the tendon at the back of the ankle (*WT i 2*)

hoy *noun* a small single-decked coastal ship (*CE iv 3*)

huddle *verb* **1.** to pile up one thing on top of another (*MA iv 1*) **2.** to crowd together (*MV iv 1*)

hugger-mugger *adverb* secretly (*H iv 5*)

hulk *noun* a large ungainly person (*2H4 i 1*) [From *hulk*, 'a large slow transport ship'.]

hull *verb* (*of a ship*) to lie at anchor (*TN i 5*; *R3 iv 4*)

human, humane *adjective* **1.** behaving in a kind and considerate way (*MND ii 2*; *MV iv 1*; *O ii 1*) **2.** relating to humans (*CE v 1*)

humanity *noun* **1.** humans in general (*KL iv 2*) **2.** human nature (*H iii 2*; *O i 3*)

humble-bee *noun* a bumblebee (*MND iv 1*)

humorous *adjective* **1.** humid (*RJ ii 1*) **2.** temperamental (*H ii 2*; *H5 ii 4*) **3.** fanciful (*AYLI iv 1*)

humour *noun* **1.** a wish for or to do something (*MND i 2*; *MA v 4*; *H5 ii 1*) **2.** a mood (*1H4 iii 1*; *O iii 4*) **3.** a whim (*MV iii 5*) **4.** moisture (*JC i 1*)

COMMENT: *Humour* was essentially a medical term, as in the four humours: an excess of one was thought to cause a bodily imbalance and therefore ill-health. It often meant 'moisture', as with a fluid in the body; Friar Laurence, informing Juliet about the effects of his potion, warns her that 'presently through all thy veins shall run/A cold and drowsy humour'. Since the health of the body has an effect on a person's mood and behaviour, *humour* came to mean a person's disposition or temperament. Shylock, in the trial scene from **The Merchant of Venice**, blocks his enemies' questions about why he insists on having the pound of flesh: 'I'll not answer that-/But say it is my humour'. He means that it is part of his temperament to want to kill Antonio. Today, the meaning of *humour* generally implies comedy and laughter, but we still retain the old meaning, as in phrases like 'She's in a good humour today' or, when used as a verb, 'Let's humour him', implying that a person's difficult mood needs accommodating.

Humphrey Hour *noun* the time of day when a meal was given to beggars, etc. (*R3 iv 4*)

hundred ◇ **Hundred Merry Tales** a contemporary joke book (*MA ii 1*)

hundred-pound *noun* someone pretending to be of noble birth (*KL ii 2*)

hunt counter *noun* when the hunt goes in the wrong direction (*2H4 i 2*)

hunt's up *noun* an early morning song (*RJ iii 5*) [Literally a song sung to waken the huntsmen.]

hurdle *noun* a wooden frame (*RJ iii 5*)

hurling *adjective* threatening (*H i 5*)

hurly, hurly burly *noun* general confusion and commotion (*2H4 iii 1*; *TS iv 1*)

hurricano *noun* a whirling column of water caused by a whirlwind passing over the sea and sucking up water (*KL iii 2*)

hurtle *verb* to make a crashing noise (*AYLI iv 3*; *JC ii 2*)

hurtless *adjective* harmless (*KL iv 6*)

husband *noun* **1.** the man who manages a household (*2H4 v 3*) **2.** a man who manages money etc. (*MM iii 2*; *TS v 1*) ■ *verb*

1. to provide a woman with a husband (*KL v 3*) **2.** to farm an area of land (*2H4 iv 3*)

husbandman *noun* the man who manages a household (*2H4 v 3*)

husbandry *noun* the management of a household or farm (*M ii 1*)

hush *adjective* silent (*H ii 2*)

husks *plural noun* the unwanted parts of something (*H5 iv 2*)

Hybla *noun* a part of Sicily famous for its honey in classical times (*1H4 i 2*; *JC v 1*)

Hydra *noun* in Greek mythology, a many-headed snake, each of the heads producing two more when it was cut off (*1H4 v 4*; *2H4 iv 2*; *O ii 3*)

hyen *noun* a hyena (*AYLI iv 1*)

Hymen, Hymaeus *noun* in Greek mythology, the god of marriage, who carried a burning torch (*AYLI v 4*; *H iii 2*; *MA v 3*)

hyperbole *noun* an exaggerated statement

hyperbolical *adjective* exaggerated, extravagant (*TN iv 2*)

Hyperion *noun* in Greek mythology, the god of the sun (*H i 2*)

Hyrcan *adjective* from **Hyrcania** (*M iii 4*)

Hyrcania *noun* a region of the Caspian Sea, believed to be the home of wild beasts (*H ii 2*)

hyssop *noun* an aromatic herb used in perfumes and medicine. It was thought to be an aphrodisiac. (*O i 3*)

hysterica passio *noun* choking caused by hysteria (*KL ii 4*)

I

Ice *phrase* I shall (*KL iv 6*)

ice brook *noun* the River Salo near Bibilis in Spain (*O v 2*) (NOTE: Cold water was considered the best for making steel and the River Salo was where the best swords were made.)

Iceland dog *noun* a small rough-coated white dog originating from Iceland (a term of contempt) (*H5 ii 1*)

idea *noun* an image (*R3 iii 7*)

ides of March *plural noun* 15th March (*JC i 2*)

idle *adjective* **1.** foolish (*MM iv 1*; *KL i 2*) **2.** mad (*H iii 2*) **3.** worthless (*TN iii 3*; *O i 2*)

idleness *noun* **1.** a pastime (*TN i 5*; *1H4 i 2*; *AC i 3*) **2.** neglect (*H5 v 2*; *O i 3*)

idly *adverb* with little attention or interest (*R2 v 2*)

i'fecks *adverb* in fact (*WT i 2*)

ignis fatuus *noun* will o' the wisp, a faint light seen over marshy ground, caused by the spontaneous ignition of methane (*1H4 iii 3*)

ignoble *adjective* **1.** of low birth (*R3 iii 5*) **2.** behaving dishonourably (*R3 iii 7*; *T i 1*)

ignorant *adjective* **1.** unaware of something (*MM ii 2*) **2.** resulting from being unaware of something (*O iv 2*)

'ild [A shortening of 'yield'.] ◇ **God 'ild you** God reward you (a way of giving thanks) (*AYLI iii 3*; *AYLI v 4*; *H iv 5*; *M i 6*)

ill-beseeming *adjective* unnatural (*2H4 iv 1*; *RJ i 5, iii 3*)

ill-breeding *adjective* bent on making trouble (*2H4 iv 1*)

ill-composed *adjective* made up of evil parts (*M iv 3*)

ill-dispersing *adjective* that spreads evil around (*R3 iv 1*)

ill-divining *adjective* apprehensive (*RJ iii 5*)

ill-erected *adjective* built for evil purposes (*R2 v 1*)

ill-inhabited *adjective* living in poor housing (*AYLI iii 3*)

illness *noun* ruthlessness (*M i 5*)

ill-nurtured *adjective* ill-bred

ill-roasted *adjective* badly cooked (*AYLI iii 2*)

ill-seeming *adjective* ugly (*TS v 2*)

ill sorted *adjective* in bad company (*2H4 ii 4*)

ill-taken *adjective* mistaken (*WT i 2*)

ill-temper'd *adjective* having the bodily humours badly mixed (*JC iv 3*) (NOTE: There were supposed to be four humours corresponding to the four elements (earth, air, fire and water), which governed a person's behaviour and appearance.)

illume *verb* to illuminate something (*H i 1*)

ill-well *adjective* with a convincing imitation of a defect (*MA ii 1*)

imagery *noun* tapestries (*R2 v 2*)

imaginary *adjective* imaginative (*H5 Prol.*)

imagination *noun* something imagined and not actually experienced (*R3 i 4*; *KL iv 6*)

imbar *verb* to secure, defend, or possibly exclude something (*H5 i 2*)

imbrue *verb* **1.** to cover something with blood (*MND v 1*) **2.** to shed blood (*2H4 ii 4*)

immask *verb* to conceal something (*1H4 i 2*)

immediacy *noun* the fact of being closely related to someone in a position of authority (*KL v 3*)

immediate *adjective* **1.** direct (*AC ii 6*) **2.** next in line to succeed someone (*H i 2*; *2H4 v 2*)

immediately *adverb* particularly (*MND i 1*)

immoment *adjective* unimportant (*AC v 2*)

immured *adjective* confined (*MV ii 7*; *R3 iv 1*)

imp *noun* a child, used as a term of affection (*H5 iv 1*) ■ *verb* to graft new feathers onto a hawk's wing to repair it (*R2 ii 1*)

impaint *verb* to portray something (*1H4 v 1*)

impartial *adjective* indifferent (*MM v 1*)

impartment *noun* something to tell (*H i 4*)

impasted *adjective* made into a crust (*H ii 2*) (NOTE: (like pastry))

impawn *verb* **1.** to pledge something (*1H4 iii 3*) **2.** to stake something as in a wager (*WT i 2*) **3.** to risk the safety of someone or something (*H5 i 2*) [Literally 'to give something as security on a loan'.]

impeach *noun* an accusation (*CE v 1*) ■ *verb* to accuse someone of something (*MV iii 3*; *R2 i 1*)

impeachment *noun* **1.** a hindrance (*H5 iii 6*) **2.** an accusation (*R3 ii 2*)

impede *verb* to hold someone back (*M i 5*)

imperfect *adjective* (*of a statement*) unclear (*M i 3*)

imperious *adjective* imperial (*2H4 i 1, iii 1*; *AC iv 1*; *O iii 3*)

impertinency *noun* irrelevance (*L iv 6*)

impertinent, impertinency *adjective* irrelevant (*T i 2*; *MV ii 2*; *KL iv 6*)

impeticos, impetticoat *noun* a word made up by the Fool, possibly meaning to put into the pocket (*TN ii 3*)

impiteous *adjective* relentless and merciless (*H iv 5*)

implorator *noun* someone who implores someone to do something (*H i 3*)

impone, impawn *verb* to stake something in a bet (*H v 2*)

import *verb* **1.** to imply something (*WT i 2*; *RJ v 1*; *H iii 2*) **2.** to state something (*1H4 i 1*; *H i 2*; *O ii 2*) **3.** to be important (*1H4 iv 4*; *AC i 2*) **4.** to be relevant to someone (*O i 3*)

importance *noun* repeated urgent requests (*TN v 1*)

important *adjective* urgent (*CE v 1*; *KL iv 4*)

importing *adjective* significant (*H i 2, v 2*; *O ii 2*)

importunate *adjective* insistent (*H iv 5*; *O iv 1*)

importune *verb* **1.** to urge someone to do something (*MM i 1*) **2.** to harass someone (*AC iv 15*)

importuned *adjective* persistent (*KL iv 4*)

importunity *noun* an insistent request (*H i 3*; *MV iv 1*; *O iii 3*)

impose *noun* a command (*KL ii 4*; *R3 iii 7*) ■ *verb* to place something on someone (*MA v 1*; *H5 iv 1*)

imposition *noun* **1.** a command (*MV iii 4*; *R3 iii 7*) **2.** an accusation (*MM i 2*; *WT i 2*) **3.** a characteristic (*O ii 3*)

impossible *adjective* unbelievable (*MA ii 2*; *TN iii 2*)

imposthume *noun* **1.** an abscess **2.** the undesirable features of government (*H iv 5*)

imprese *noun* an heraldic crest with a motto (*R2 iii 1*)

impress *verb* to call someone up for military service (*H i 1*; *AC iii 7*; *M iv 1*)

impressure *noun* **1.** a stamp or seal (*AYLI iii 5*; *TN ii 5*) **2.** an impression (*TN iv 5*)

imprimis, inprimis *adverb Latin* in the first place (*TS iv 1*)

improve *verb* to make good use of something (*JC ii 1*)

impugn *verb* to question something (*MV iv 1*)

imputation *noun* an opinion (*MV i 3*; *O iii 3*)

incapable *adjective* unable to realise or understand something (*H iv 7*)

incardinate *adjective* used in error for **incarnate** (*TN v 1*; *MV ii 2*)

incarnadine *verb* to dye something red (*M ii 2*)

incarnate *adjective* in human form (*H5 ii 3*)

incarnation *noun* a comic form of **incarnate**, used to refer to the devil (*MV ii 2*)

incense *verb* to annoy someone (*WT v 1*; *JC i 3*)

incertain *adjective* uncertain (*2H4 i 3*; *JC v 1*; *MM iii 1*)

inch *noun* a small island (*M i 2*)

inch-meal ◇ **by inchmeal** gradually (*T ii 2*)

inch-thick *adjective* solid (and therefore certain) (*WT i 2*) [Referring to the standard thickness of a plank of wood.]

incidency *noun* an event (*WT i 2*)

inclination *noun* a nature or attitude (*1H4 iii 2; AC ii 5; H ii 1, iii 3*)

incline *verb* to favour someone or something (*AC iv 6; KL iii 3; MM v 1; O i 1*)

inclining *noun* a group (*O i 2*) ■ *adjective* amenable (*O ii 3*)

inclip *verb* to encircle something (*AC ii 7*)

include *verb* to bring something to an end (*R3 i 1*)

incomprehensible *adjective* beyond all bounds (*1H4 i 2*)

incontinent *adjective* 1. lustful (*AYLI v 2*) 2. immediately, a pun on lustful (*R2 v 6; O iv 3*)

incontinently *adverb* straight away (*O i 3*)

inconvenience *noun* mischief (*H5 v 2*)

inconvenient *adjective* inappropriate (*AYLI v 2*)

incorporal *adjective* incorporeal, without a body (*H iii 4*)

incorpsed *adjective* being in one body with something (*H iv 7*)

increase *noun* 1. reproduction (*KL i 4*) 2. children (*R3 iv 4*) 3. a harvest (*T iv 1*)

incredulous *adjective* unbelievable (*2H4 iv 5; TN iii 4*)

incursion *noun* a raid (*1H4 iii 2*)

indent *noun* a dent (*1H4 iii 1*) ■ *verb* to negotiate with someone (*1H4 i 3*)

indenture *noun* a legal contract. Two copies were made and torn apart, so that when the two parts were fitted together again their validity was proven. (*1H4 ii 4, iii 1*)

indentures tripartite *noun* an agreement between three people (*1H4 iii 1*)

index *noun* a prologue, an opening speech, etc. describing what is to follow (*R3 ii 2; H iii 4; O ii 1*)

Indies *plural noun* the East Indies (*CE iii 2; MV i 3*)

indifferency *noun* normal size (*2H4 iv 3*)

indifferent *adjective* 1. impartial (*H5 i 1*) 2. neither good nor bad (*H ii 2; H5 iv 7*)

indigent *adjective* poor (*H5 i 1*)

indign *adjective* disgraceful (*O i 3*)

indirection *noun* 1. a dishonest practice (*JC iv 3*) 2. a roundabout process (*H ii 1*)

indirectly *adverb* 1. evasively (*MM iv 6*) 2. casually (*1H4 i 3*) 3. wrongly (*H5 ii 4*)

indistinguish'd *adjective* boundless (*KL iv 6*)

individable ◇ **scene individable** where the time and place remains unchanged (*H ii 2*)

inducement *noun* an attraction (*R3 iv 4*)

induction *noun* something done in preparation for something (*1H4 iii 1; R3 i 1*)

indue *verb* 1. to supply something with something (*H iv 7*) 2. to bring something to a particular state (*O iii 4*)

industriously *adverb* intentionally (*WT i 2*)

inexecrable *adjective* unrelenting or cursed (*MV iv 1*)

infallible *adjective* absolutely certain (*MM iii 2; WT i 2*)

infamy *noun* disgrace (*2H4 i 2; MA iv 1; R3 iii 7*)

infant *noun* a young plant (*H i 3*)

infect *verb* to affect someone (*WT i 2*)

infected *adjective* false (*WT iii 2; O iv 1*)

infection *noun* 1. used in error for **affection** (*MV ii 2*) 2. (*of a man*) incompleteness (*R3 i 2*)

infectious *adjective* diseased (*WT iii 2; O iv 1*)

infer *verb* 1. to prove or allege something (*2H4 v 5; H5 i 2; R3 iii 7*) 2. to cause something (*R3 iv 4*)

inference *noun* an allegation (*O iii 3*)

infest *verb* to worry someone or something (*T v 1*)

infinitive *adjective* infinite (*2H4 ii 1*)

inflammation *noun* drunken excitement (*2H4 iv 3*)

influence *noun* the effect of the stars on a person's character and fate (*H i 1; KL i 2, ii 2*)

inform *verb* to take shape (*M ii 1*)

informal *adjective* mad (*MM v 1*)

infuse *verb* to fill someone or something with a quality, idea, etc. (*T i 2; R2 iii 2; JC i 3*)

infusion *noun* a mixture of intrinsic characteristics (*H v 2*)

ingener, inginer *noun* an inventor (*O ii 1*)

ingenious *adjective* 1. quick and sensitive (*KL iv 6; H v 1*) 2. talented (*R3 iii 1*) 3. suitable for a gentleman (*TS i 1*)

ingraft *adjective* ingrained (*JC ii 1; O ii 3*)

ingredience *noun* the ingredients (*M i 7, iv 1*)

ingrossed *adjective* gathered together (*AC iii 7*)

inhabitable *adjective* uninhabitable (*R2 i 1*)

inherit *verb* to put someone in possession of something (*R2 i 1*)

inherited *adjective* realised (*AYLI i 3*)

inhibited *adjective* forbidden by Church law (*O i 2*)

inhibition *noun* a prohibition on performing plays (*H ii 2*)

inhooped *adjective* (*of fighting birds*) kept in confinement to make them aggressive (*AC ii 3*)

iniquity *noun* a comic character of the medieval **morality plays**. He was sometimes called Vice. (*1H4 ii 4; O iv 1*)

initiate *adjective* of a beginner (*M iii 4*)

injoint *verb* to join together (*O i 3*)

injurious *adjective* insulting (*AC iv 1; MM ii 3*)

injury *noun* an insult (*CE v 1; MND ii 1*)

inkle *noun* a type of broad linen tape (*WT iv 4*)

inland *noun* the countryside around the capital (*H5 i 2*) ■ *adjective* sophisticated (*AYLI iii 2*)

inly *adjective* inward (*T v 1; H5 iv Chor.*)

innocent *noun* a person of low mental ability (*KL iii 6*)

innovation *noun* a political upheaval (*H ii 2*)

inoculate *verb* to graft the bud of one plant onto the stem of another (*H iii 1*)

insane *adjective* causing madness (*M i 3*)

insatiate *adjective* incapable of being satisfied sexually (*R3 iii 5, 7*)

insculpe *verb* to engrave something (*MV ii 7*)

insensible *adjective* not perceived by the senses (*1H4 v 1*)

insinewed *adjective* committed to something (*2H4 iv 1*)

insinuate *verb* to talk in an ingratiating or wheedling way (*R2 iv 1; R3 i 4*)

instalment *noun* the ceremony of formally installing someone in an official post (*R3 iii 1*)

instance *noun* **1.** a reason (*H iii 2*) **2.** proof (*2H4 iii 1, iv 1; H iv 5*)

instant *adverb* immediately (*H i 5; O i 2*)

instantly *adverb* at the same time (*1H4 v 2*)

instate *verb* to confer something on someone (*MM v 1*)

instinct *noun* an impulse (*1H4 ii 4; 2H4 i 1; R3 ii 3*)

instruct *verb* to inform someone of something (*TS iv 2; MM i 1*)

instruction *noun* **1.** information (*AC v 1*) **2.** significance (*O iv 1*)

instrument *noun* **1.** the means to do something (*TN v 1; O iv 2*) **2.** a document (*O iv 1*)

instrumental *adjective* useful (*H i 2*)

insubstantial *adjective* imaginary (*T iv 1*)

insufficience, insufficiency *noun* inability (*MND ii 2; WT i 1*)

insulting *adjective* gloating in a sneering manner about a triumph (*R2 iv 1*)

insult on *verb* to gloat about a triumph over someone in a sneering manner (*AYLI iii 5*)

insuppressive *adjective* impossible to suppress (*JC ii 1*)

intelligence *noun* **1.** a communication (*AYLI i 3*) **2.** the action of obtaining secret information (*1H4 iv 3*)

intelligencer *noun* **1.** a spy, an informer (*R3 iv 4*) **2.** a go-between (*2H4 iv 2*)

intelligencing *adjective* involved in passing information between two parties (*WT ii 3*)

intelligent *adjective* informative (*KL iii 5*)

intemperature *noun* lack of moderation (*1H4 iii 2*)

intend *verb* **1.** to pretend to feel something (*MA ii 2; R3 iii 7*) **2.** to incline towards something (*MND iii 2; 2H4 i 2*)

intendment *noun* an intention or aim (*AYLI i 1; H5 i 2*)

intention *noun* an aim (*WT i 2*)

intentively *adverb* attentively (*O i 3*)

interchangeably *adverb* between two parties (*1H4 iii 1; R2 v 2*)

interdiction *noun* renunciation of responsibilty (*M iv 3*)

interessed *adjective* having an involvement in something (*KL i 1*)

interest ◇ **interest of** a right to a share in something (*L i 1*)

interlude *noun* a short, often comic play performed between the main items (*KL v 3*; *MND i 2, v 1*; *TN v 1*)

intermission *noun* a delay between two events (*KL ii 4*; *M iv 3*; *MV iii 2*)

intermit *verb* to stop for a time (*JC i 1*)

interpret *verb* to provide a commentary to something (*H iii 2*; *M iii 6*)

in terram Salicam mulieres ne succedant *phrase Latin* women shall not inherit in Salic lands (*H5 i 2*) (NOTE: The law was created in the 5th century, referring to part of the old Frankish kingdom under Salian rule. Although the Salic lands are now to be found in modern Germany and not France, the law was resurrected by Charlemagne as a way of preventing the King Edward III of England, who was heir through a female line of inheritance, from succeeding to the French throne.)

intertissued *adjective* interwoven (*H5 iv 1*)

intervallum *noun* a period of time during which the law courts have a break from hearing cases (*2H4 v 1*)

intestate *adjective* dying without leaving a will (*R3 iv 4*)

intestine *adjective* domestic (*1H4 i 1*; *CE i 1*)

intimate *verb* to imply something (*TN ii 5*)

intolerable *adjective* excessive (*1H4 ii 4*)

intoxicates *adjective* drunk (*H5 iv 7*)

intranchant *adjective* not able to be cut (*M v 8*)

intrince *adjective* complicated (*KL ii 2*; *AC v2*)

intrinsicate *adjective* entangled (*AC v 2*)

inured *adjective* buried (*H i 4*)

invectively *adverb* with violence and abuse (*AYLI ii 1*)

invention *noun* **1.** inventiveness (*O ii 1*) **2.** a plan (*TS i 1*; *KL i 2*) **3.** a piece of intellectual writing (*TN v 1*)

inventorally *adverb* item by item (*H v 2*)

Inverness *noun* a borough in north-east Scotland (*M i 4*)

invest *verb* **1.** to provide someone with something (*2H4 iv 5*) **2.** to accompany someone (*H5 iv Chor.*)

investments *plural noun* clothes, especially ceremonial robes (*2H4 iv 1*; *H i 3*)

invincible *adjective* invisible (*2H4 iii 2*)

invocate *verb* to appeal to a ghost (*R3 i 1*)

inward *adjective* **1.** intimate (*R3 iii 4*) **2.** secret (*MA iv 1*) ■ *noun* an intimate friend (*MM iii 2*)

inwardness *noun* intimacy (*MA iv 1*)

Io *noun* in Greek mythology, the daughter of a river god and one of Hera's priestesses (*TS Ind. 2*) (NOTE: According to the myth, **Zeus** raped Io when in the form of a cloud. When Hera discovered the liaison, Zeus turned Io into a heifer. She wandered the earth, ending up in Egypt where she was restored to human form.)

ipse *noun Latin* he himself (*AYLI v 1*)

Irish wolves *plural noun* refers to Gaelic (the Irish language) which was supposed to sound like the howling of wolves (*AYLI v 2*)

iron-witted *adjective* unfeeling (*R3 iv 2*)

irreconciled *adjective* not having confessed your sins (*H5 iv 1*)

Isis *noun* the sister and wife of Osiris and the principal goddess of Egypt (*AC i 2, 5, iii 3*) (NOTE: She was the mother of Horus and represented the perfect example of a woman, wife and mother. She was worshipped throughout the Roman world, becoming identified with several Roman goddesses and ultimately as the universal goddess.)

iteration, iterance *noun* **1.** repetition (*O v 2*) **2.** a quotation (*1H4 i 2*)

I wis *phrase* certainly (*MV ii 9*; *R3 i 3*; *TS i 1*) [From Anglo-Saxon *ge-wis.*]

J

Jack *noun* **1.** a servant (*R3 i 3*) **2.** a scoundrel (*1H4 iii 3*) **3.** a short, tight-fitting jacket (*1H4 iv 2*) **4.** a figure that struck the bell of a clock (*R2 v 5*; *R3 iv 2*) **5.** a drinking vessel (*TS iv 1*) ◊ **flouting Jack** a person who makes fun of someone else (*MA i 1*)

Jack-an-apes *noun* a monkey (*H5 v 2*) [Alteration of Jack Napis, nickname of William de la Pole, Duke of Suffolk (1396–1450).]

Jack boy, ho boy news, The cat is well *noun* a song sung as a round (*TS iv 1*)

Jack sauce *noun* a cheeky person (*H5 iv 7*)

Jacob *noun* in the Bible, the son of Isaac who performed twenty years' service to **Laban** to be allowed to marry Laban's daughters, first Leah, then Rachel (Genesis 20–25). A form of James (one of Jesus' apostles), feast day 11 May. (*MV i 3, ii 5*)

jade *noun* a worn-out horse (*TS i 2*) ■ *verb* **1.** to exhaust an animal by driving it hard (*AC iii 1*) **2.** to get the better of somebody or fool them (*TN ii 5*)

jaded lowly, contemptible

jakes *noun* a lavatory (*KL ii 2*)

Janus *noun* in Roman mythology, the two-headed god of the old and new year who guarded the gate of heaven (*MV i 1*; *O i 2*)

Japhet *noun* in the Bible, the youngest son of **Noah** (Genesis 6:9) (*2H4 ii 2*)

jar *noun* **1.** conflict (*AYLI ii 2*) **2.** the tick of a clock (*WT i 2*) **3.** quarrelling (*CE i 1*) ■ *verb* **1.** to tick like a clock (*R2 v 5*) **2.** to produce a discordant sound (*TS iii 1*) **3.** to quarrel

Jason *noun* a hero of Greek mythology who sailed with the Argonauts to recover the Golden Fleece, in order to inherit a kingdom (*MV i 1*)

jaunce *see* **jaunt**

jaunt *noun* a spell of fruitless rushing about (*RJ ii 5*) ■ *verb* **1.** to ramble (*RJ ii 5*) **2.** to spur hard (*R2 v 5*)

jealous *adjective* **1.** concerned about (*H5 iv 1*; *RJ ii 2*) **2.** suspicious (*O iii 4*) **3.** on your guard (*JC i 2*) **4.** fearful (*JC i 2*; *KL v 1*)

jealous-hood *noun* a jealous woman (*RJ iv 4*)

jealousy *noun* apprehension (*MA ii 2*; *TN iii 3*; *O iii 3*)

jennet *noun* a small Spanish horse (*O i 1*)

Jephthah *noun* in the Bible, a judge of Israel who sacrificed his daughter (*H ii 2*)

jesses *plural noun* short straps tied to the legs of a hawk and used to control it (*O iii 3*)

jet *verb* **1.** to strut (*TN ii 5*) **2.** to move forward aggressively (*CE ii 2*; *R3 ii 4*)

Jezebel *noun* in the Bible, the wife of King Ahab (1 Kings 16:31) (*TN ii 5*) (NOTE: According to legend, she was a wicked woman who corrupted her weak husband with pagan beliefs and rituals.)

jig *noun* **1.** a quick dance (*TN i 3*; *MA ii 1*) **2.** a lively dance or comical turn performed during the interval or at the end of a play (*H ii 2*) ■ *verb* to move with rapid jerky movements (*H iii 1*)

jigging *noun* composing jigs (*JC iv 3*)

Jill *noun* a young female servant (*TS iv 1*)

Joan *noun* a general name for a country girl (*TS Ind. 2*)

Job *noun* a biblical character who was a good man, and although he endured considerable suffering, still retained his faith in God (*2H4 i 2*)

Jockey *noun* an affectionate form of the name John or Jack (*R3 v 3*)

John *noun* Little John, one of Robin Hood's men (*2H4 v 3*)

John-a-dreams *noun* a person who daydreams (*H ii 2*)

join *verb* to come together in conflict (*1H4 v 1*; *R3 v 3*)

jointress *noun* a widow owning property that was given to her on her marriage (*H i 2*)

joint-ring *noun* a ring made in two halves (*O iv 3*)

joint-stool *noun* a stool solidly made by inserting the legs into the seat, rather than being simply nailed on (*TS ii 1*; *2H4 ii 4*; *RJ i 5*)

jointure *noun* property given to a wife on her marriage (*AYLI iv 1*; *RJ v 3*; *TS ii 1*)

jollity *noun* sexual pleasure (*CE ii 2*; *MND iv 1, v 1*)

jolly *adjective* **1.** arrogant (*TS iii 2*) **2.** lustful (*R3 iv 3*)

jolt-head *noun* a stupid person (*TS iv 1*)

jordan *noun* a chamber pot, a bowl for use as a toilet at night (*1H4 ii 1*)

journal *adjective* daily (*MM iv 3*)

journey-bated *adjective* tired out by travelling (*1H4 iv 3*)

journeyman *noun* a tradesman who travelled around looking for work (*R2 i 3*; *H iii 2*)

jowl, joul *verb* to hit or knock something (*H v 1*)

Judas Iscariot *noun* one of Jesus' Apostles. In return for thirty pieces of silver he betrayed Jesus to the authorities by identifying him with a kiss. He committed suicide by hanging himself. Traditionally he had red hair. (*AYLI iii 4*)

judgement ◇ **in my judgement** in my opinion (*CE iv 2*; *MND i 1*)

judicious *adjective* just (*KL iii 4*)

Jug *noun* an affectionate form of the name Joan (*KL i 4*)

juggle *verb* to trick someone (*H iv 5*)

juggler *noun* **1.** a trickster (*MND iii 2*) **2.** someone who has sexual intercourse when not married (*2H4 iv 4*)

juggling *noun* deception (*M v 8*)

jump *noun* a risk (*AC iii 8*) ■ *verb* **1.** to risk something (*M i 7*) **2.** to agree, to tally (*MV ii 9*; *TS i 1*; *1H4 i 2*; *TN v 1*) **3.** to have sex vigorously (*WT iv 4*) ■ *adverb* exactly (*H i 1, v 2*; *O ii 3*)

junkets *plural noun* a sweet or other delicacy (*TS iii 2*)

Juno *noun* in Roman mythology, the sister and wife of **Jupiter** to whom peacocks are sacred. She was the queen of heaven and war and protector of women. (NOTE: The Greek equivalent is **Hera**.)

Jupiter, Jove *noun* in Roman mythology, the supreme god in the divine hierarchy (*KL i 1, ii 4*; *T iv 1*; *WT iv 4*; *AYLI ii 4*; *AC iii 2*) (NOTE: The Greek equivalent is **Zeus**.)

just *adjective* **1.** precise (*MA ii 1*; *MV iv 1*; *O i 3*) **2.** loyal (*JC iii 2*) **3.** exactly equal (*2H4 iv 1*)

justice *noun* a toast drunk to someone or something (*O ii 3*) ◇ **the justice, In fair round belly with good capon lin'd** judges who had been bribed with gifts of castrated male chickens (capons) (*AYLI ii 7*)

justicer *noun* a minister of justice (*KL iii 6*)

justified *adjective* proved innocent (*WT i 1, v 3*)

justle *verb* to jostle someone (*T iii 2*)

jut *verb* to intrude (*R3 ii 4*)

jutty *noun* a projecting or overhanging part (*M i 6*) ■ *verb* to overhang (*H5 iii 1*)

juvenal *noun* a youth (*2H4 i 2*; *MND iii 1*)

K

kecksies *plural noun* dried stems of the plant fool's parsley (*H5 v 2*)

keech *noun* a lump of animal fat, used as a term of abuse for a butcher's wife (*2H4 ii 1*)

keep *noun* custody (*TS i 2*) ■ *verb* **1.** to guard something (*WT ii 1*) **2.** to live somewhere (*MV iii 3*; *RJ iii 2*) **3.** to carry on (*CE iii 1*; *TN ii 3*)

keeper *noun* **1.** a guardian angel (*T iii 3*) **2.** a nurse (*2H4 i 1*)

keep time *verb* to keep control (*O iv 1*)

ken *noun* the farthest distance that can be seen (*2H4 iv 1*)

Kendal green *noun* the green cloth of the clothes worn by foresters and associated with Kendal in Cumbria (*1H4 ii 4*)

kennel *noun* a gutter in a street (*TS iv 3*)

kerchief *noun* a headscarf (*JC ii 1*) ◇ **to wear a kerchief** to be ill (*JC ii 1*)

kern *noun* a lightly armed Irish foot soldier (*H5 iii 7*; *M i 2*)

kernel *noun* a pip (*T ii 1*; *WT i 2*)

kettle *noun* a kettledrum, a large bowl-shaped drum (*H v 2*)

key *noun* **1.** control (*H5 ii 2*; *M iii 6*) **2.** a tuning key (*T i 2*)

key-cold *adjective* as cold as a key (*R3 i 2*)

kibe *noun* a sore on a person's heel caused by exposure to cold (a chilblain) (*H v 1*; *T ii 1*)

kickshaw *noun* a thing of little value or significance (*TN i 3*; *2H4 v 1*)

kiln-hole *noun* the oven of a kiln (*WT iv 4*)

kind *noun* **1.** a person's character **2.** instinct **3.** a person's family ■ *adjective* loving ◇ **after kind** in accordance with its nature (*AYLI iii 2*)

COMMENT: *Kind* springs from the Old English word for 'nature'. It is used as a noun, meaning 'type or species', as in 'mankind', and as an adjective, meaning 'affectionate or friendly'.

Hence it would be appropriate for a human being, or of human kind, to show the kindness appropriate to humanity. A person so doing would be behaving properly according to type. 'Kin', meaning 'family', is an associated word, and members of a family would expect to show special kindness to each other. Hamlet in his bitter melancholy plays with both words in his first speech of the play: 'A little more than kin and less than kind'. He means that the King, by marrying Hamlet's mother is now a sort of father and therefore more than simply a relative. But he is 'less than kind' in two senses: he is an inferior type of person and also there is no genuine affection from him. At the end of **The Tempest** Prospero hears Ariel speak sensitively about the suffering of the courtiers who have injured Prospero but who he is struggling to forgive. However, Ariel, not being human, could have no natural impulse of human kindness. Prospero feels shamed at the contrast: 'and shall not myself,/One of their kind, that relish all as sharply/Passion as they, be kindlier moved than thou art?' Prospero is moved to follow Ariel's example into showing the feelings associated with his human species. This verbal link between a species and moral qualities was an impressively instructive and optimistic feature of Shakespeare's thinking.

kindle *verb* **1.** to give birth to a young animal (*AYLI iii 2*) **2.** to bring someone or something (*AYLI i 1*) **3.** to make something (*JC ii 1*)

kindless *adjective* unnatural (*H ii 2*)

kindly *adjective* **1.** natural (*MA iv 1*) **2.** suitable (*AYLI ii 3*) **3.** harmless (*AC ii 5*) **4.** genuine (*2H4 iv 5*) **5.** with an ironic suggestion of kindness (*KL i 5*) **6.** of the same family (*T v 1*) ■ *adverb* **1.** in a relaxed way (*TS Ind. 1*) **2.** precisely (*RJ ii 4*)

kine *noun* cattle (*1H4 ii 4*)

kirtle *noun* a woman's gown or petticoat (*2H4 ii 4*)

kitchened *verb* to entertain someone in the kitchen (*CE v 1*)

kite *noun* **1.** a prostitute (*H5 ii 1*) **2.** a term expressing extreme dislike (*KL i 4*; *AC iii 13*) [From *kite*, 'a hawk-like bird of prey']

knack *noun* a knick-knack (*TS iv 3*)

knap *verb* **1.** to nibble at something (*MV iii 1*) **2.** to hit something sharply (*KL ii 4*)

knell *noun* the tolling of a church bell for the dead (*M v 8*)

knob *noun* a pimple (*H5 iii 6*)

knoll *verb* to toll a bell (*M v 9*)

knot *noun* **1.** a group (*R3 iii 1*; *JC iii 1*) **2.** a flower bed of a complex design in a formal garden (*R2 iii 4*) **3.** the folded position of a person's arms (*T i 2*) ■ *verb* to cluster together (*O iv 2*)

knot-grass *noun* a weed whose stem has many joints. An infusion of it was supposed to stunt growth. (*MND iii 2*)

knot-pated *adjective* stupid (*1H4 ii 4*)

know *verb* **1.** to recognise someone (*JC iv 3*) **2.** to know each other (*WT iv 4*; *AC ii 6*)

knowing *noun* **1.** knowledge (*H v 2*) **2.** experience (*M ii 4*)

knowledge *noun* **1.** familiarity with something (*MM iii 2*; *AYLI i 2*) **2.** a notice (*H ii 1*)

L

Laban *noun* in the Bible, the uncle of **Jacob** (*MV i 3*) (NOTE: He tricked Jacob into working on his lands in exchange for his daughters as wives.)

label *noun* the tag on a document on to which a seal is stuck (*RJ iv 1*) ■ *verb* to add something to the end of a document (*TN i 5*)

laboursome *adjective* elaborate (*H i 2, iii 4*)

lace *noun* a cord for fastening clothing (*WT iii 2*; *R3 iv 1*; *AC i 3*) ■ *verb* **1.** to decorate something (*MA iii 4*; *M ii 3*) **2.** to thread or streak (*RJ iii 5*)

lack *verb* **1.** to do without something (*MA iv 1*; *M iii 4*; *AC i 4*) **2.** to be wanting, to be short of something (*H i 4, 5*)

lack-beard *adjective* too young to have a beard (*MA v 1*)

lack-brain *noun* a fool (*1H4 ii 3*)

lackey *verb* to follow the tide as a servant follows his master (*AC i 4*)

lack-linen *adjective* without a shirt (*2H4 ii 4*)

lack-love *adjective* unloved (*MND ii 2*)

lack-lustre *adjective* dull (*AYLI ii 7*)

lading *noun* the cargo of a ship (*MV iii 1*)

Lady *noun* a name given to a female dog (*1H4 iii 1*; *KL i 4*)

ladybird *noun* a lover (*RJ i 3*)

lady terms *plural noun* effeminate phrases (*1H4 i 3*)

lag, leg *adjective* late (*R3 ii 1*) ■ *preposition* behind (*KL i 2*)

lag-end *noun* the last part (*1H4 v 1*)

lakin *noun* ladykin (a name for the Virgin Mary) (*T iii 3*; *MND iii 1*)

lambkin *noun* a little lamb, used as a term of affection (*2H4 v 3*; *H5 ii 1*)

lame *verb* to make someone lame (*AYLI i 3*)

lamp *noun* an eye (*CE v 1*)

lampass, lampas *noun* a disease of horses in which the roof of the mouth behind the front teeth swells up (*TS iii 2*)

lance, lanch *verb* to pierce something (*R3 iv 4*; *KL ii 1*)

land *noun* a lawn (*T iv 1*)

land-damn *verb* to subject someone to very harsh treatment (*WT ii 1*) [From the idea of creating 'hell on earth' for someone.]

land-service *noun* service in the army (*WT iii 3*; *2H4 i 2*)

language *noun* the ability to speak a foreign language (*T ii 2*)

languish *noun* a prolonged illness (*RJ i 2*; *AC v 2*)

lank *verb* to become hollow and wasted (*AC i 4*)

lanthorn, lantern *noun* **1.** a lantern (*2H4 i 2*; *MND iii 1, v 1*) (NOTE: Thin sheets of horn were used to protect the flame.) **2.** a window turret resembling a lantern (*RJ v 3*)

lap *verb* to wrap someone in something (*R3 ii 1*) ◇ **lapp'd in proof** clothed as if in impenetrable armour (*M i 2*)

Lapland sorcerers *plural noun* Lapland was notorious for witchcraft (*CE iv 3*)

lapse *verb* **1.** to apprehend, detain (*TN iii 3*) **2.** to allow someone time to calm down (*H iii 4*)

lapwing *noun* a small bird that nests on the ground and pretends to be injured to draw attention from its nest (*CE iv 2*; *H v 2*; *MA iii 1*; *MM i 4*)

lard *verb* **1.** to fatten something up (*1H4 ii 2*; *H5 iv 6*) **2.** to decorate something (*H iv 5*) **3.** to elaborate on something (*H v 2*)

lass-lorn *adjective* rejected by your lover (*T iv 1*)

latch *verb* **1.** to shut in (*M iv 3*) **2.** to charm, possibly smear over (*MND iii 2*) **3.** to catch something (*KL ii 1*)

lated *adjective* **1.** coming too late (*AC iii 11*) **2.** belated (*M iii 3*)

latest *adjective* last (*2H4 iv 5*; *H5 iii 3*; *JC v 5*; *O i 3*)

lath *noun* a wooden sword or dagger used as a toy or by an actor (*TN iv 2*; *1H4 ii 4*; *RJ i 4*) [From *lath*, 'a thin strip of wood'.]

laud *noun* a hymn (*H iv 7*)

laughable *adjective* amusing, causing laughter (*MV i 1*)

Laura *noun* the woman whom Petrarch addressed in his sonnets. He met her in the church of St Clara in the French town of Avignon in 1327. According to Petrarch it was this meeting that inspired him to be a poet. (*RJ ii 4*)

lave *verb* to wash something (*M iii 2*; *TS ii 1*)

lavolta, lavolt *noun* a dance for two people that required many turns and high leaps (*H5 iii 5*)

law *noun* the moral law as laid down in the Bible (*R3 i 4*)

law-day *noun* a meeting of a law court (*O iii 3*)

lawn *noun* a fine linen fabric (*O iv 3*)

lay *noun* a bet (*O ii 3*) ■ *adjective* belonging to the people rather than the clergy (*MM v 1*) ■ *verb* **1.** to bet something (*H v 2*) **2.** to bury someone (*TN iv 4*) **3.** to imprison someone (*TN iv 2*; *R3 i 3*) ◇ **lay home** to attack someone (*H iii 4*)

lay on *verb* to begin to fight (*H5 v 2*; *M v 8*)

lazar *noun* a leper (*H5 i 1, ii 1*) [Shortening of *Lazarus*, a character in the Book of Luke who was supposedly a leper.]

lea *noun* **1.** a cultivated field left unplanted (*H5 v 2*) **2.** arable land (*T iv 1*)

lead *noun* **1.** roofs covered with lead rather than tiles or thatch (*R3 iii 7*) **2.** a bullet (*1H4 v 3*) **3.** the lead lining of a coffin (*MV ii 7*)

leading *noun* **1.** the ability to lead people (*1H4 iv 3*) **2.** a command (*H5 iv 3*; *R3 v 3*)

league *noun* **1.** a distance of about 5 km **2.** an alliance ■ *verb* to form an alliance

Leah *noun* in the Bible, the daughter of **Laban** and first wife of **Jacob**. Jacob disliked her and preferred her younger sister Rachel whom he later married. (*MV iii 1*)

leak *verb* to urinate (*1H4 ii 1*)

Leander *noun* in Greek mythology, a young man who swam across the Hellespont to visit his lover, Hero (*AYLI iv 1*; *MA v 2*)

leap-frog *noun* a children's game (*H5 ii 2*)

leaping-house *noun* a brothel (*1H4 i 2*)

learning *noun* **1.** an accomplishment (*H v 2*) **2.** information (*AC ii 2*)

lease ◇ **lease of nature** the allotted span of life (*M iv 1*)

leash *noun* a group of three (*1H4 ii 4*) [From the fact that three greyhounds were usually lead on a single leash.]

leashed *adjective* joined in a group of three (*H5 Prol.*) [See LEASH.]

leasing *noun* the act of telling a lie (*TN i 5*)

leather-coat *noun* a russet apple, which has a rough, rather tough skin (*2H4 v 3*)

leaven *noun* any substance such as yeast which causes fermentation and subsequent rotting

leavened *adjective* showing careful consideration (*MM i 1*)

leavy *adjective* leafy (*MA ii 3*)

lecture *noun* a lesson (*TS iii 1*; *H ii 1*)

Leda *noun* in Greek mythology, the wife of Tyndareus, king of Sparta (*TS i 2*) (NOTE: While she was bathing Zeus came to her in the form of a swan and had sexual intercourse with her. She laid two eggs: from one hatched Castor and Clytemnestra and from the other Pollux and Helen of Troy.)

leer *noun* a person's complexion (*AYLI iv 1*)

leet *noun* a local court under the jurisdiction of the lord of the manor (similar to a modern magistrates' court) (*TS Ind. 1*; *O iii 3*)

leg *noun* a bow made by moving one leg backwards and bending the other (*1H4 ii 4*)

lege, 'lege *verb* to allege (*TS i 2*)

legerity *noun* nimbleness (*H5 iv 1*)

legion *noun* many devils (*T iii 3*; *TN iii 4*) (NOTE: This is a reference to the biblical passage in Mark 5:9.)

legitimate *adjective* reasonable (*TN iii 2*)

leigeman *noun* a subject owing allegiance to a monarch (*WT ii 3*; *1H4 ii 4*; *H i 1*)

leiger, lieger *noun* a resident ambassador (*MM iii 1*)

leman *noun* a lover (*TN ii 3*; *2H4 v 3*)

lend *verb* to give someone something (*WT iv 3*; *JC iii 2*)

lender *noun* a person who lends money (*H i 3*)

lendings *plural noun* **1.** money lent to the king to pay the troops in a time of financial difficulty (*R2 i 1*) **2.** things lent and borrowed (*KL iii 4*)

lenity *noun* leniency (*H5 iii 6*; *MM iii 2*; *RJ iii 1*) *See also* **respective lenity** *at* **respective**

leno *noun* a pimp (*H5 iv 5*)

Lent *noun* the forty days before Easter, commemorating the time Jesus spent in the wilderness. Lent was traditionally a time of fasting, when the eating of certain foods was forbidden. (*2H4 ii 4*; *M iv 3*; *MM i 1*)

lenten *adjective* meagre (*TN i 2*; *H ii 2*) [Referring to the period of Lent in the spring before Easter, when people fasted.]

lenten pie *noun* a pie made without meat (*RJ ii 4*)

leperous, leprous *adjective* causing leprosy (*H i 5*)

lesson *noun* a musical exercise (*TS iii 1*) ■ *verb* to teach someone (*R3 i 4*)

let *noun* a hindrance (*H5 v 2*) ■ *verb* **1.** to hinder someone (*CE ii 1*; *TN v 1*) **2.** to allow someone to stay (*WT i 2*) **3.** to have reason to do something (*H iv 6*) ■ *interjection* let us go! (*MV iii 2*; *1H4 i 1*) ◇ **let me alone** trust me (*TN iii 4*)

let-alone *noun* the power to veto something (*KL v 3*)

lethargied *adjective* dulled (*KL i 4*)

lethargy *noun* a coma (*2H4 i 2*; *O iv 1*; *TN i 5*)

Lethe the mythical river of forgetfulness in Hades, The soul of the dead tasted it and so forgot all that happened during their earthly lives

letter *noun* learning (*T ii 1*; *2H4 iv 1*)

level *noun* **1.** the position of something aimed at by an archer (*WT iii 2*; *RJ iii 3*) **2.** equality (*1H4 iii 2*) ■ *adjective* **1.** well thought-out (*2H4 ii 1*) **2.** easily available (*2H4 iv 4*; *H iv 5*) **3.** direct (*H iv 1*) ■ *adverb* steadily (*TN ii 4*)

level at *verb* to guess at something (*MV i 2*; *AC v 2*)

level with *verb* to be of a standard appropriate to something (*O i 3*)

leven *determiner* eleven (*WT iv 3*; *MV ii 2*)

levity *noun* sexual promiscuity (*MM v 1*; *AC iii 7*)

levy *verb* to raise an army, taxes, etc. (*1H4 i 1*; *2H4 iv 1*; *M iii 2*; *R3 iv 4*)

lewdly *adverb* wickedly (*1H4 ii 4*)

liable to *preposition* dependent on, caused by (*JC i 2*)

libel *noun* a publication that prints lies about someone (*R3 i 1*)

liberal *adjective* **1.** sexually promiscuous (*MA iv 1*; *H iv 7*; *O ii 1*) **2.** having the social graces of a gentleman (*H v 2*) **3.** behaving badly (*MV ii 2*) **4.** unrestrained (*O v 2*) **5.** outspoken (*R2 ii 2*)

liberal arts *noun* education suited to a gentleman (*T i 2*)

libertine ◇ **a chartered libertine** a person who is free to act on their own initiative (*H5 i 1*)

liberty *noun* **1.** freedom (*MM i 3*; *CE i 2*) **2.** individual rights (*JC v 1*) ◇ **writ and liberty** the freedom to alter the text of a play, etc. (*H ii 2*)

Lichas *noun* in Greek mythology, one of Heracles' attendants (*AC iv 1*; *MV ii 1*) (NOTE: Heracles sent Lichas to fetch a clean tunic from Deianera who dipped it in the fatal blood of Nessus. Heracles put on the tunic, and as the poison affected him, he threw Lichas into the sea where he turned into a rock.)

lictor *noun* an officer who attends Roman magistrates or consuls (*AC v 2*)

lie ◇ **to give the lie** to deceive someone (*T iii 2*)

lief ◇ **had as lief** would rather (*H iii 2*)

lieutenancy *noun* authority that is delegated to another (*O ii 1*; *AC iii 11*)

lifelings ◇ **'Od's lifelings** 'God's little children', used as an oath. It may refer to the Massacre of the Innocents (Matthew 2: 16–18). (*TN v 1*)

lifting up *noun* the dawning (*2H4 iv 4*)

lig *verb* to lie (*H5 iii 2*)

light ◇ **set light** to regard something as being of little importance (*O ii 3*)

lighten *verb* **1.** to enlighten someone (*2H4 ii 1*) **2.** to convey a quality or emotion (*R2 iii 3*; *JC i 3*; *RJ ii 2*)

lightness *noun* **1.** immoral behaviour (*2H4 i 1*; *AC i 1*; *MM ii 2*; *TS iv 2*) **2.** a delirium or faint (*H ii 2*)

lightning *noun* a sudden feeling of happiness (*RJ v 3*)

light o' love *noun* a sexually promiscuous woman (*MA iii 4*) [From the name of a dance tune.]

like *verb* **1.** to please someone (*T iv 1*) **2.** to love someone (*CE iii 2*; *RJ i 3*) **3.** to be in good health (*2H4 iii 2*)

likely *adjective* handsome (*MV ii 9*; *2H4 iii 2*)

liking *noun* health (*1H4 iii 3*)

lily-livered *adjective* cowardly (*M v 3*; *KL ii 2*) [From the idea of being pale with fear.]

limbeck *noun* a container used for distilling liquids (*M i 7*)

limber *adjective* unconvincing (*WT i 2*) [From *limber*, 'limp'.]

limbo *noun* **1. limbo patrum** the place of rest for good people who died before the time of Christ (*CE iv 2*) **2.** the region between heaven and hell

lime *noun* **1.** a sticky substance used for catching birds (*MA iii 1*; *H iii 3*; *M iv 2*) **2.** a mixture of lime and horsehair used to bond bricks together (*MND v 1*)

limit *noun* the allotted time (*MM iii 1*; *WT iii 2*; *R2 i 3*; *R3 iii 3*) ∎ *verb* **1.** to decide on a time (*MM iv 2*) **2.** to appoint a person (*CE i 1*; *R3 v 3*)

limn *verb* to draw the outline of something (*AYLI ii 7*)

line *noun* **1.** a fishing line (*MM i 4*; *WT i 2*; *2H4 ii 4, iv 4*) **2.** a plumb line, a weight attached to a string used to determine a vertical line in building (*T iv 1*) **3.** a rank (*1H4 i 3, iii 2*) **4.** a contour (*WT i 2*) **5.** the equator (*T iv 1*) ∎ *verb* **1.** to support or strengthen something (*1H4 ii 3*; *H5 ii 4*; *M i 3*) **2.** to have sexual intercourse with someone (*AYLI iii 2*) ◇ **line of life** in palmistry, the line on a person's hand that indicates how long they will live (*MV ii 2*) ◇ **line their coats** fill their pockets (*O i 1*)

lined *adjective* padded (*2H4 i 3*; *AYLI ii 7, iii 2*)

line grove *noun* a row of lime trees (*T v 1*)

linen *adjective* pale (*M v 3*)

ling *noun* heather (*T i 1*)

link *noun* **1.** a black substance used for colouring and polishing, made from the burnt pitch-soaked rope used for torches (*TS iv 1*) **2.** a torch (*1H4 iii 3*)

linstock *noun* a rod holding the lighted match used for firing a gun (*H5 iii Chor.*)

lip *noun* a contemptuous gesture made by extending your lower lip (*WT i 2*) ∎ *verb* to kiss something (*O iv 1*; *AC ii 5*)

liquor *noun* a liquid with magical properties of prolonging life and turning base metals into gold. To find it was one of the aims of the alchemists. (*T v 1*) ∎ *verb* to rub something with grease (*1H4 ii 1*)

Lispbury pinfold *phrase* a pinfold is 'a cattle pen', so the phrase possibly means 'controlled by a kiss' or 'held between the teeth' (*KL ii 2*)

list *noun* **1.** a wish (*O ii 1*) **2.** a border sewn on to the edge of a piece of fabric to prevent it from fraying (*TS iii 2*) **3.** the enclosed area for a jousting tournament (*M iii 1*) ∎ *verb* **1.** to listen (*TS ii 1*; *WT iv 4*; *1H4 iii 3*; *H i 5*) **2.** to listen to someone or something (*CE iv 1*; *H5 i 1*)

listen ◇ **listen after** to find out about someone or something (*2H4 i 1*)

literatured *adjective* knowledgeable about something (*H5 iv 7*)

little *adjective* in miniature (*MND i 2*) ◇ **in little** high-pitched (*AYLI ii 2*; *H ii 2*)

livelihood *noun* liveliness (*R3 iii 4*)

liver *noun* the liver was considered the centre of violent passions, especially love, courage, and anger. A white liver was a sign of cowardice. (*MV iii 2*; *MA iv 1*; *TN i 1*; *AYLI iii 2*)

livery ◇ **sue my livery** to take legal action to regain an inheritance (*R2 ii 3*; *1H4 iv 3*)

living *noun* a person's possessions (*WT iv 3*; *MV iii 2, v 1*; *RJ iv 5*) ∎ *adverb* during your lifetime (*R2 v 1*) ∎ *adjective* **1.** real (*AYLI iii 2*; *O iii 3*) **2.** lasting (*H v 1*) **3.** life-giving (*M ii 4*)

loach *noun* a small freshwater fish related to the carp. It was supposed to breed prolifically. (*1H4 ii 1*)

lob *noun* a dull person (*MND ii 1*) ∎ *verb* to hang down (*H5 iv 2*)

lobby *noun* an anteroom (*H ii 2, iv 3*)

lock *noun* a curl of hair on a person's forehead or temple (*MA iii 3*)

locusts *plural noun* juice obtained from carob beans, the fruit of a Mediterranean tree that is now used as a chocolate substitute (*O i 3*)

lodestar *noun* the Pole Star (*MND i 1*)

lodge *verb* **1.** to flatten standing corn (*R2 iii 3*; *M iv 1*) **2.** to harbour a feeling (*WT ii 1*; *2H4 iv 5*; *R3 ii 1*)

lodged *adjective* deep-seated (*MV iv 1*)

loff(e) *verb* to laugh (*MND ii 1*)

loggats *noun* a game of throwing small logs at a stake (*H v 1*)

loggerhead *adjective* stupid (*TS iv 1*; *1H4 ii 4*; *RJ iv 4*) [From the idea of having a head like a log.]

logic ◇ **balk logic** to defy reason (*TS i 1*)

loll *verb* to thrust something out (*O iv 1*)

lolling *adverb* with the tongue hanging out (*RJ ii 4*)

long *verb* to belong (*MM iv 2*) ◇ **think long** to become impatient (*RJ iv 5*)

long of *preposition* on account of someone or something (*MND iii 2*)

long purple *noun* an orchid with a purple flower (*H iv 7*)

long purples *plural noun* purple orchids (*Orchis mascula*) (*H iv 7*)

long spoon *noun* a reference to the proverb that you need a long spoon to eat with the devil (*CE iv 3*)

long-staff *noun* a quarterstaff, a pole about 2m long, used as a weapon (*1H4 ii 1*)

long sword *noun* a heavy two-handed sword. This had fallen out of use by Shakespeare's time. (*RJ i 1*)

long-winded *adjective* able to carry out strenuous exercise without getting out of breath (*1H4 iii 3*)

loof *verb* to bring a ship close to the wind (luff) (*AC iii 8 (iii 10)*)

loon *noun* a stupid person (*M v 3*)

loop *noun* a hole (*1H4 iv 1*)

looped *adjective* full of holes (*KL iii 4*)

loose *verb* to fire an arrow (*MND ii 1*; *H5 i 2*) ■ *adjective* careless (*O iii 3*)

loosely *adverb* carelessly (*2H4 ii 2, v 2*)

loosen *verb* to separate two people or things (*KL v 1*)

loose-wived *adjective* having an unfaithful wife (*AC i 2*)

lord *verb* to be elevated to a position of authority (*T i 2*)

lording *noun* a minor noble (*WT i 2*)

lordLiness *noun* a position of authority (*AC v 2*)

lordship *noun* the superior position of a husband (*MND i 1*)

Lord's sake *phrase* for the Lord's sake. The expression was used by those imprisoned for debt when begging. (*MM iv 3*)

lose *verb* **1.** to forget someone or something (*MND i 1*) **2.** to ruin someone's reputation (*1H4 iii 1*; *KL i 1*; *H iii 2*) **3.** to result in someone losing something (*TN ii 2*; *KL i 2*) **4.** to miss something (*AC iv 14*) **5.** to become senile (*AC i 2*)

loss *noun* ruin (*KL iii 6*; *AC iv 12*)

loss of question *noun* the lack of anything to argue about (*MM ii 4*)

lost *adjective* **1.** destroyed (*WT iv 3*; *KL v 3*; *M i 3*) **2.** pointless (*R3 ii 2*; *O v 2*) **3.** bewildered (*H iv 7*; *M ii 2*)

louse *verb* to be infested with lice (*KL iii 2*)

lousy *adjective* contemptible (*H5 v 1*)

Louvre *noun* the palace of the French kings in Paris (*H5 ii 4*) (NOTE: The original building was added to by a succession of French kings and completed by Louis XIV. Napoleon I turned the building into a museum and made further additions.)

love ◇ **to beat love down** to master and subdue love (metaphorically), in a sexual way (*RJ i 4*)

love-in-idleness *noun* the pansy or violet (*MND ii 1*; *TS i 1*)

lower *verb* to glower (*CE ii 1*; *R2 i 3*; *RJ iv 5*)

lowering *adjective* glowering (*R2 i 3*; *RJ ii 5*)

lown *adjective* same as **loon** (*O ii 3*)

lowness *noun* low social rank (*KL iii 4*; *AC iii 11*)

loyal *adjective* legitimate (*KL ii 1*)

lozel *noun* a worthless person (*WT ii 3*)

lubber *noun* a clumsy person (*KL i 1*; *TN iv 1*)

Lucrece, Lucretia *noun* a married Roman woman who was the model of chastity. She committed suicide after she was raped by Tarquin. (*TN ii 5*; *TS ii 1*)

lug *verb* **1.** to drag something roughly (*H iii 4*) **2.** to torment a bear or other animal (*1H4 i 2*)

lull *verb* to lie about (*R3 iii 7*)

lullaby *phrase* goodbye, goodnight (*TN v 1*)

lunes *plural noun* fits of madness, supposedly caused by the moon (*WT ii 2*)

Lupercal *noun* the Roman feast of Lupercus, the Roman god of shepherds, (15 February), associated with fertility rites (*JC iii 2*)

lure *verb* to entice someone (*TS iv 1*; *RJ ii 2*) [From the hunting term for recalling a hawk when it is hunting.]

lust-dieted *adjective* overfed (*KL iv 1*)

lustihood *noun* vitality (*MA v 1*)

lustrous *adjective* shiny (*TN iv 2*)

lusty *adjective* **1.** lively (*AYLI iv 2*; *TS iv 2*) **2.** full of sexual desire (*O ii 1*)

lute *noun* a stringed instrument resembling a pear-shaped guitar (*1H4 i 2, iii 1*; *R3 i 1*; *TS ii 1*)

luxurious *adjective* lustful (*MA iv 1*; *H5 iv 4*)

luxuriously *adverb* lustfully (*AC iii 13*)

luxury *noun* lust (*H i 5*; *H5 iii 5*; *KL iv 6*; *MM v 1*)

lym *noun* a bloodhound (*KL iii 6*)

M

Mab, Queen *noun* the fairies' midwife who delivered men's dreams from their brains (*RJ i 4*) (NOTE: 'Queen' in this context is from the Old English *qun*, 'woman'.)

mace *noun* **1.** an ornamental rod symbolising the authority of an official (*JC iv 3*) **2.** a spice used in cookery (*WT iv 3*)

Machiavel *noun* a ruthless schemer [Referring to a follower of Machiavelli, an Italian politician who wrote works on statecraft and whose name is associated with cunning and trickery.]

machine *noun* a person incapable of acting independently (*H ii 2*)

mackerel *noun* a pimp (*1H4 ii 4*)

mad *verb* to drive someone mad or into a rage (*KL iv 2*) ■ *adjective* immoral (*O iv 3*)

Madam Mitigation *noun* a woman in charge of a brothel (*MM i 2*)

madcap *adjective* reckless, acting without thought for the consequences (*1H4 i 3, iv 1*)

made *adjective* fastened (*CE iii 1*)

madrigal *noun* an unaccompanied song for several voices

maggot-pie *noun* a magpie (*M iii 4*)

magnanimous *adjective* showing great spirit and bravery (*2H4 iii 2*; *H5 iii 6, iv 7*)

magnifico *noun* the powerful men of Venice (*MV iii 2*; *O i 2*)

maidenhead *noun* the early stages of something (*1H4 iv 1*) [From the literal meaning 'virginity'.]

maidenliest star *noun* Venus, the planet of love (*KL i 2*)

maiden-widowed *adjective* having been widowed while still a virgin (*RJ iii 2*)

maidhood *noun* virginity (*TN iii 1*; *O i 1*)

Maid Marian *noun* a traditional character in morris dancing, representing an immoral woman (*1H4 iii 3*)

maid-pale *adjective* as pale as a young girl (*R2 iii 3*)

mailed *adjective* armoured (*1H4 iv 1*)

maim *noun* mutilation, especially as a punishment. Cutting off a person's hand or ear were forms of punishment. (*R2 i 3*; *1H4 iv 4*)

main *noun* **1.** a gambling stake, or a throw of dice (*1H4 iv 1*) **2.** a chance to do something to your own advantage (*2H4 iii 1*) **3.** the mainland (*KL iii 1*) ■ *verb* to maim someone (*O i 3*)

main-course *noun* the mainsail, the largest sail on a ship (*T i 1*)

mainly *adverb* **1.** violently (*1H4 ii 4*) **2.** strongly (*H iv 7*) **3.** completely (*KL iv 7*)

maintain *verb* **1.** to continue something (*TN iv 2*; *MA iv 1*; *KL iii 3*) **2.** to afford something (*TS v 1*)

major *noun* the main part of an argument (the major premise of a syllogism) (*1H4 ii 4*)

make *verb* **1.** to close something (*CE iii 1*; *AYLI iv 1*) **2.** to be concerned with something (*MA iii 3*) **3.** to consider something (*MM v 1*; *TS iii 2*) **4.** to do something (*R3 i 3*; *O iii 4*) **5.** to prove something (*KL v 3*) **6.** to cost an amount (*1H4 iv 2*) **7.** to move something (*CE i 1*; *KL i 1*) **8.** to raise an army (*1H4 iii 1*; *R3 iv 4*)

malady of France *noun* the sexually transmitted disease syphilis (*H5 v 1*)

malapert *adjective* cheeky (*R3 i 3*)

malefaction *noun* a crime (*H ii 2*)

malice *noun* a wretch (*T i 2*)

maliciously *adverb* viciously (*WT i 2*; *AC iii 13*)

malignancy *noun* a harmful state full of hatred (*TN ii 1*)

malignant *adjective* heretical (*O v 2*)

Mall *noun* an affectionate form of the name Mary (*T ii 2*) ◇ **Mistress Mall's picture** possibly a portrait of Mary Frith, who was a notorious thief and was known as Mall Cut-purse (*TN i 3*)

mallard *noun* a wild duck (*AC iii 8 (10)*)

mallecho [From Spanish *malhecho*.] ◇ **miching mallecho** lurking mischief (*H iii 2*)

malmsey-nose *adjective* having a red nose as a result of excessive drinking (*2H4 ii 1*)

malthorse *noun* a stupid person (*CE iii 1*; *TS iv 1*) [From *malthorse*, 'a heavy horse used to pull a brewer's wagon'.]

maltworm *noun* a drunkard (*1H4 ii 1*; *2H4 ii 1*) [From the idea of someone drinking a lot of beer (made from malt).]

mammer *verb* to stand muttering indecisively (*O iii 3*)

mammet *noun* a doll (*1H4 ii 3*; *RJ iii 5*)

man *verb* **1.** to tame a hawk (*TS iv 1*) **2.** to provide someone with a manservant (*2H4 i 2*) **3.** to aim something (*O v 2*) ◇ **a man of wax** a perfect image of a man (*RJ i 3*) ◇ **man of salt** tearful (*L iv 6*) ◇ **the man shall have his mare again** everything will turn out to be alright (*MND iii 2*)

manage *noun* **1.** the taming of a horse (*AYLI i 1*; *R2 iii 3*; *1H4 ii 3*) **2.** control (*T i 2*; *MV iii 4*; *RJ iii 1*) ■ *verb* **1.** to handle or use something (*R2 iii 2*; *RJ i 1*) **2.** to cause something (*O ii 3*)

mandrake *noun* **1.** a poisonous plant that is related to the potato and produces a drug (*2H4 i 2*; *RJ iv 3*) (NOTE: Its forked root resembles a human figure and this gave rise to the belief that it had magical properties and would emit a scream causing madness or death when pulled up.) **2.** the drug produced by the mandrake plant (*O iii 3*; *AC i 5*)

mane *noun* the crest of a wave likened to horse's or lion's mane (*O ii 1*)

mangle *verb* to cut something repeatedly (*H5 iv 4*; *O v 1*)

mangled *adjective* wounded by repeated cuts (*1H4 v 4*)

manikin, manakin *noun* a small man or man-shaped figure (*TN iii 2*)

mankind *adjective* (of a woman) having the ferocity of a man (*WT ii 3*)

manly *adjective* like music to accompany marching (*M iv 3*)

manner *noun* a custom (*MM iv 2*; *CE i 2*; *H i 4*) ◇ **to be taken with the manner** to be caught in the act (*WT iv 3*; *1H4 ii 4*)

mannerly *adjective* respectful (*WT ii 1*; *RJ i 5*) ■ *adverb* respectfully (*MA i 1*; *MV ii 9*)

manners *noun* **1.** respectful behaviour (*TN ii 1*) **2.** moral behaviour (*MV ii 3*; *H5 i 2*) **3.** civil behaviour (*AYLI iv 3*; *TN ii 3*; *1H4 iii 1*)

Manningtree *noun* a place in Essex, famous for cattle (*1H4 ii 4*)

man-queller *noun* a murderer (*2H4 ii 1*)

mansionry *noun* a person's home (*M i 6*)

mantle *noun* the scum on stagnant water (*KL iii 4*) ■ *verb* **1.** to cover something (*T v 1*) **2.** to cover something with a scum (*T iv 1*; *MV i 1*)

manure *verb* to dig or fertilise land (*O i 3*)

map *noun* a true and complete representation of something (*R2 v 1*)

marble *adjective* **1.** merciless (*WT v 2*) **2.** radiant (*O iii 3*)

marble-breasted *adjective* hard-hearted (*WT v 2*)

marble-constant *adjective* hard (*AC v 2*) [Because made completely of marble.]

marcantant, mercatante *noun* a merchant (*TS iv 2*)

March chick *noun* a brash or impertinent person (*MA i 3*) [From the idea of someone born early in the year.]

marches *noun* the border country between England and Wales and between England and Scotland (*H5 i 2, iii 6*; *R3 i 1*)

marchpane *noun* marzipan (*RJ i 5*)

mare *noun* a nightmare (*2H4 ii 1*) ◇ **to ride the wild mare** to play on a see-saw (*2H4 ii 4*) ◇ **Whose mare's dead?** What's the matter? (*2H4 ii 1*)

margent *noun* **1.** the edge of something (*MND ii 1*) **2.** an expression or glance (*RJ i 3*) **3.** comments written in the margin of a page (*H v 2*)

mark *noun* **1.** something used as a guide or example (*WT iv 4*; *2H4 ii 3*) **2.** a target (*MA ii 1*; *AC iii 6*) **3.** notice (*MM v 1*; *O ii 3*) **4.** importance (*1H4 iii 2*) **5.** a sum of money worth 67p (13s. 4d.) (*MM iv 3*; *CE i 1*) ◇ **God save the mark, God bless the mark** used to apologise for something said (*1H4 i 3*; *RJ iii 2*; *O i 1*)

mark prodigious *noun* a birthmark (*MND v 1*)

marl *noun* a clay soil containing a high proportion of limestone and used as a fertiliser (*MA ii 1*)

marmoset *noun* a small South American monkey (*T ii 2*)

marrow *noun* bone marrow (*H i 4*)

Mars *noun* the Roman god of war (*R2 ii 1, 3*; *MV iii 2*; *AC i 1, 5, ii 2, 5*; *H iii 4*; *O v 1*; *M ii 3*; *H5 iv 2*; *1H4 iii 2*)

marshal *noun* **1.** a state official (*1H4 iv 4*; *2H4 i 1, 3, ii 3, iv 1*) **2.** an official in charge of the arrangements for a ceremony (*MM ii 2*) **3.** the highest ranking officer in the French army (*KL iv 3*) ■ *verb* to lead someone (*H iii 4*; *M ii 1*; *O ii 1*)

mart *noun* **1.** a market (*CE i 1*) **2.** the act of bargaining (*TS ii 1*; *H i 1*) ■ *verb* to bargain with someone over something (*JC iv 3*)

martlet *noun* a house martin, a type of bird (*MV ii 9*; *M i 6*) (NOTE: It builds its nest under the eaves of a roof.)

martyr *verb* to mutilate someone (*RJ iv 5*)

marvellous *adverb* extremely (*T iii 3*; *CE iv 3*)

mask, masque *verb* to take part in an entertainment or ball at which masks are worn (*RJ i 5*)

masking, masquing *adjective* **1.** taking part in a **mask** (*MV ii 6*) **2.** used in a **mask** (*TS iv 3*)

Mass *noun* the Holy Communion of the Roman Catholic Church. 'By the Mass!' was used as an expletive. (*2H4 ii 4*; *H v 1*; *MA iii 3*; *RJ iv 4*)

master *verb* to own something (*MV v 1*; *1H4 v 2*)

masterly report *noun* a report on how well a person managed to control a situation (*H iv 7*)

match *noun* **1.** an agreement (*T ii 1*; *TS v 2*; *MV iii 1*) **2.** the act of setting opponents against each other (*H ii 2*) ■ *verb* **1.** to marry (*MA ii 1*; *TN i 3*) **2.** to join together (*MA ii 1*) **3.** to be an equal of something (*MND iii 2*; *H iv 7*) **4.** to be compared or put in competition with someone or something (*O iii 3*; *RJ ii Prol.*) **5.** to be appropriate to someone or something (*H5 ii 4*)
◇ **cry a match** to claim a victory (*RJ ii 4*)
◇ **set a match** to arrange a meeting (*1H4 i 2*)

mate *noun* a contemptible person (*TS i 1*; *2H4 ii 4*; *R3 i 3*) ■ *verb* to shock or bewilder someone (*CE v 1*; *M v 1*)

mate and mate *noun* husband and wife (*KL iv 3*)

material *adjective* of importance or relevance (*AYLI iii 3*; *KL iv 2*; *M iii 1*)

matter *noun* **1.** something important **2.** the true facts of an incident **3.** a reason or cause

mattock *noun* a pickaxe with a flat cutting head, used for breaking up soil (*RJ v 3*)

maugre *conjunction* in spite of (*TN iii 1*; *KL v 3*)

maw *noun* **1.** the mouth (*MM iii 2*; *RJ v 3*; *M iii 4, iv 1*) **2.** the stomach (*CE i 2*; *H5 ii 1*)

May, May-morn *noun* the prime of youth (*MA v 1*; *H5 i 2*)

mazed *adjective* bewildered (*MND ii 1*)

mazzard, mazard *noun* the head (*H v 1*; *O ii 3*)

meacock *adjective* timid and spineless (*TS ii 1*)

mead *noun* same as **meadow** (*TS v 2*; *H5 v 2*)

meadow *noun* an area of land used for grazing animals, especially next to a river

mealed *adjective* speckled (*MM iv 2*) [Literally 'covered in flour (meal)'.]

mean *noun* **1.** the central position (*MV i 2*; *AC ii 7*) **2.** a person singing the musical part between the treble and bass (either alto or tenor) (*WT iv 3*) **3.** a method (*RJ iii 3*; *AC iv 6*) **4.** influence (*MM ii 4*; *R3 i 3*) **5.** an opportunity (*R3 iv 2*; *H iv 6*) **6.** money or wealth (*CE i 2*; *KL iv 1*) ■ *adjective* **1.** poor (*T iii 3*; *CE i 1*) **2.** contemptible (*1H4 iii 2*; *RJ iii 3*) ■ *verb* to complain (*MND v 1*)

meanly *adjective* beneath your social position (*R3 iv 3*) ■ *adverb* moderately (*CE i 1*) [From *mean*, 'a central position'.]

measure *noun* **1.** a stately dance (*MA ii 1*; *RJ i 4*) **2.** a stately way of walking (*MV ii 6*; *WT iv 4*) **3.** a limit (*MA i 3*; *TS i 2*; *RJ iii 2*; *M v 9*; *AC iii 4*) **4.** moderation (*MV iii 2*; *MA ii 1*; *R2 iii 4*) **5.** a punishment (*MM ii 2*) **6.** music, rhythm (*TN v 1*) **7.** any unit of measurement (*M iii 4*; *O ii 3, iv 3*) ■ *verb* **1.** to judge something (*WT ii 1*; *RJ i 1*; *H5 i 2*) **2.** to travel a specified distance (*T ii 1*; *MV iii 4*) **3.** to pace something out (*RJ i 4*)

COMMENT: The various meanings of *measure*, whether as noun or verb, gave Shakespeare excellent scope for puns. He even devoted the word in two of its meanings to the title of a play: **Measure for Measure**, meaning that suitable punishment will be imposed for a course of action: in the specific events of the play, the Duke of Vienna in Act 5 gives judgements on Angelo, Barnadine, and Lucio, who have behaved badly, and on Escalus, the Provost, and Isabella, who have pleased him. *Measure*, here and elsewhere, also implies care or fairness, as today we use the phrase 'in good measure'. Therefore the word is appropriate to describe the fair dealings of any sort of governor, especially a king who wishes to act in a balanced or measured way by avoiding extremes. And this connects with another meaning of *measure*: a stately dance. Judgements on earth were supposed to imitate God's divine sense of justice and His providence was often described in terms of music, as in the music of the spheres, whose cosmic harmony reflected the balance of all parts of the universe cohering in correct order. *Measure* meaning 'dance' is very frequent, especially in early Shakespeare, as at the Capulet's house in Act 1 of **Romeo and Juliet** or Act 2 of **Much Ado About Nothing**. This musical sense can extend to the metre of poetry, as when the soldier Henry V confesses to Katherine that he has 'neither words nor measure'. Even if poems were not specifically written as songs, their words were crafted into rhythmic *measure*. Hence, through apparently diverse meanings of *measure*, Shakespeare makes links between judgement, moderation, fairness and rhythm.

mechanic *adjective* **1.** engaged in manual work (*H5 i 2*; *AC v 2*) **2.** of the working class (*AC iv 4*)

mechanical *noun* a member of the working classes (*MND iii 2*; *JC i 1*)

meddle *verb* **1.** to fight (*TN iii 4*) **2.** to be involved in something (*RJ i 2*) ◊ **meddle with** to mix with (*T i 2*; *MA iii 3*)

meddler *noun* someone who is involved in everything (*MM v 1*)

Medea *noun* in Greek mythology, the daughter of Aetes, king of Colchis (*MV v*

1) (NOTE: She was a sorceress who aided Jason in obtaining the Golden Fleece, and later married him.)

medicinable *adjective* healing (*MA ii 2*)

medicine *noun* **1.** a doctor (*M v 2*) **2.** a love potion (*O i 3*) **3.** a poison (*KL v 3*; *O iv 1*) **4.** the philosopher's stone, a mythical substance believed to be capable of turning base metals into gold (*AC i 5*) ◊ **medicine potable** a drug containing gold (*2H4 iv 5*)

medlar *noun* a tree related to the apple, bearing fruits which are edible only when partly rotten and pulpy; or the male or female genitals. The word seems always to have this double meaning. (*AYLI iii 2*; *MM iv 3*; *RJ ii 1*)

meed *noun* wages (*AYLI ii 3*; *R3 i 4*) ◊ **in his meed** in his pay or employment (*H v 2*)

meet *adjective* suitable (*MV iii 5*) ■ *verb* to be on equal terms with someone (*MA i 1*)

meetly *adjective* adequate (*AC i 3*)

meiny(ie) *noun* the members of a household (*KL ii 4*)

Meisen *noun* a town in Saxony (a region in present-day Germany). It is famous for the manufacture of porcelain. (*H5 i 2*)

member *noun* **1.** a person (*MM v 1*) **2.** someone who has a part in something (*O iii 4*)

memento mori *noun Latin* an object kept as a reminder that you will die one day (*1H4 iii 3*) [Latin, 'a reminder of death'.]

memorize *verb* to make something memorable (*M i 2*)

memory *noun* a reminder (*JC iii 2*; *KL iv 7*) ◊ **of as little memory** as soon forgotten (*T ii 1*)

mend *verb* **1.** to arrange something (*AC v 2*) **2.** to recover your health (*MA v 2*; *2H4 i 2*)

men of hairs *plural noun* men dressed in skins (*WT iv 4*)

men of mould *plural noun* Earth-born men (*H5 iii 2*)

merchant *noun* **1.** a man or boy (*TS iv 2*; *RJ ii 4*) **2.** a merchant ship (*T ii 1*; *2H4 ii 4*)

Mercury *noun* the son of **Jupiter** and Maia and messenger of the gods. He is depicted as having a winged hat and winged sandals and carrying a white baton around which two snakes are entwined. He was also the god of trade and science (particularly medicine) and the patron of travellers and crooks. (*1H4 iv 1*; *TN i 5*; *H iii 4*; *R3 ii 1, iv 3*; *AC iv 15*; *WT iv 3*) (NOTE: The Greek equivalent is **Hermes**.)

mercy *noun* merciful treatment granted by a conqueror or lord

mere *adjective* absolute (*O ii 2*)

mered *adjective* the only or entire (*AC iii 13*)

merit *noun* a reward (*R2 i 3*)

Merlin *noun* the real Merlin was a Welsh bard of the late 5th century who was killed in a battle. His story became mixed with the legends of King Arthur in which he is depicted as a wizard rescued from evil when he was baptised by Blaise. (*1H4 iii 1*; *KL iii 2*)

merriment *noun* **1.** a joke or prank (*TS iv 5*; *2H4 ii 4*) **2.** amusement (*MND iii 2*)

merry *adjective* **1.** pleasant (*CE ii 1*) **2.** favourable (*CE iv 1*) **3.** happy (*O iii 3*) ◊ **rest you merry** may everything go well for you (*AYLI v 1*; *RJ i 2*)

merry men *plural noun* followers (*AYLI i 1*; *TN ii 3*)

mervailous, mervilious *adjective* marvellous (*H5 ii 1*)

mess *noun* **1.** a dish of food (*KL i 1*) **2.** a group of people served together at table, usually four in number (*WT i 2*; *H v 2*) **3.** a small portion (*2H4 ii 1*; *O iv 1*)

Messaline *noun* possibly Marseilles (*TN ii 1*)

metal *noun* **1.** gold (*CE iv 1*; *MV i 3*; *R3 iv 2*) **2.** a substance (*AYLI ii 7*; *MM i 1*; *H5 iii 1*; *KL i 1*) **3.** a person's temperament (*T ii 1*; *TN iii 4*) **4.** spirit or courage (*MA v 1*; *1H4 ii 4, iv 3*; *O iv 2*)

metal of India *noun* a girl worth her weight in gold (*TN ii 5*) [From the idea of gold being precious and from India.]

metaphysical *adjective* not able to be explained by the laws of nature (*M i 5*)

mete *verb* to measure something (*2H4 iv 4*)

mete-yard *noun* a measuring stick (*TS iv 3*)

method *noun* a summary (*TN i 5*)

methought *preposition* it seemed that (*WT i 2*; *R3 i 4*)

metre *noun* poor quality or humorous poetry (*1H4 iii 1*; *MM i 2*)

mettle ◊ **quick mettle** having a lively temperament (*JC i 2*)

mew *verb* to imprison someone (*MND i 1*; *TS i 1*; *R3 i 1, 3*; *RJ iii 4*) [From *mew*, 'a cage for hawks or falcons'.]

mewl *verb* to mew like a cat (*AYLI ii 7*)

micher *noun* someone who plays truant (*1H4 ii 4*)

mickle *adjective* great or much (*CE iii 1*; *H5 ii 1*; *RJ ii 3*)

Midas *noun* in Greek mythology, the king of Phrygia (*MV iii 2*) (NOTE: He asked the gods to give him the power to turn everything he touched into gold. When his food became gold he realised his mistake and prayed for the power to be removed)

mid season *noun* noon (*T i 2*)

might not merit *noun* the intention, not the doing, of a deed (*MND v 1*)

milch *verb* to shed tears (*H ii 2*)

milch-kine *noun* cows producing milk (*TS ii 1*) [From *milch*, 'milk' and *kine*, 'cattle'.]

Mile End *noun* a small village lying a mile east of London in Shakespeare's time. It was situated at the present junction of the Mile End Road and Globe Road. The area around it was used as an exercise ground for the city militia. (*2H4 iii 2*)

milk *noun* used as a symbol for all that is pleasant and maintains life (*RJ iii 3*; *M i 5, iv 3*)

milk-livered *adjective* cowardly (*KL iv 2*)

milky *adjective* cowardly or weak (*KL i 4*; *H ii 2*)

milliner *noun* someone who sells fancy goods from Milan such as gloves, hats, etc. (*WT iv 4*; *1H4 i 3*)

millstones ◊ **to drop** *or* **weep millstones** to be a hardhearted person who never or only rarely cries (*R3 i 3*; *R3 i 4*)

mimic *noun* a comic actor (*MND iii 2*)

mince *verb* to treat something as unimportant (*AC i 1*; *H5 v 1*; *KL iv 6*; *O iii 3*)

mincing *noun* an affected or exaggerated way of walking (*1H4 iii 1*)

mind *noun* **1.** a way of thinking (*JC i 2*) **2.** an attitude towards someone (*AYLI i 2*) **3.** a purpose or wish (*CE iv 1*; *MV ii 8*) **4.** an opinion (*MV iv 1*) ■ *verb* **1.** to remind someone (*WT iii 2*; *H5 iv 3*) **2.** to notice someone (*T ii 2*) **3.** to remember something (*H5 iv Chor.*) **4.** to pay attention to something (*TS i 1*; *RJ iv 1*) ◊ **to my mind** in my judgement (*H i 4*)

minded *adjective* inclined to do something (*T v 1*; *KL iii 1*)

mindless *adjective* careless (*WT i 2*)

mine *noun* **1.** a tunnel dug under enemy fortifications (*H5 iii 2*; *H iii 4*) **2.** a large cave (*O iv 2*) **3.** my property (*TS ii 1*; *WT i 2*) **4.** my concern (*MM ii 2*) ■ *verb* to undermine something (*AYLI i 1*)

mineral *noun* **1.** a poisonous drug made from minerals as opposed to plants (*O ii 1*) **2.** a mine (*H iv 1*)

Minerva *noun* in Roman mythology, the goddess of wisdom. She is said to have sprung from Jupiter's brain clothed in armour. (*TS i 1*) (NOTE: The Greek equivalent is **Athene**.)

mingle *noun* a mixture (*AC i 5, iv 8*)

minikin *adjective* dainty (*KL iii 6*)

minim rest *noun* the shortest rest possible (*RJ ii 4*) (NOTE: In the music of Shakespeare's time, the minim was the shortest note.)

minimus *noun Latin* the smallest (*MND iii 2*)

minion *noun* **1.** a favourite person (*T iv 1*; *TN v 1*; *M i 2*) **2.** an impertinent woman (*CE iii 1*; *O v 1*)

COMMENT: *Minion*, meaning 'a specially favoured servant', is used by the Captain, who praises Macbeth's performance on the battlefield and invents for him the image of 'Valour's minion'. But Macbeth, though impressive, is human and is therefore bound to be inferior to the more grand personification of 'Valour' itself. *Minion* always implies small size. Hence its more widespread use as an insult: 'Minion, thou liest!' Katherine shouts at her sister, Bianca in **The Taming of the Shrew**, frustrated that Bianca, pretty, docile and compliant is her father's favourite daughter. In **Twelfth Night** Orsino, half-jealous, half-scornful, watches Viola leave with Olivia and, thinking she is the boy Cesario, refers to him/her as 'this your minion whom I know you love'. *Minion* here implies darling, as it does in **Othello** when Iago satirically tells Bianca 'Minion, your dear lies dead'. For Iago *minion* implies 'sexual plaything'.

minister *noun* **1.** an agent (*T i 2*; *H iii 4*) **2.** an angel as a messenger of God (*MM v 1*; *H i 4*) **3.** a servant (*O v 2*) ■ *verb* **1.** to perform something (*T iv 1*) **2.** to suggest something (*MM iv 5*)

minnick, minnock *noun* a person who acts the fool (*MND iii 2*)

Minos *noun* a legendary king of Crete. He was known for his just administration and, on his death, was made judge of those who had died, determining their just reward. He owned the labyrinth constructed by Daedalus. The Minoan period of Cretan history (2500–1200 BC) was named after him.

Minotaur *noun* in Greek mythology, a mythical monster with the head of a bull and the body of a man. It was kept in the labyrinth of **Minos**, king of Crete. It fed on human flesh and was sent seven young men and seven young women from Athens each year. The minotaur was killed by **Theseus**.

minutely *adverb* every minute (*M v 2*)

minx *noun* an impertinent or promiscuous woman (*O iii 3, iv 1*; *TN iii 4*)

mire *verb* to make something dirty (*MA iv 1*)

miry *adjective* muddy (*TS iv 1*)

misadventured *adjective* unfortunate (*RJ i Chor.*)

miscarry *verb* **1.** to be destroyed or killed (*MV iii 2*; *H5 iv 1*; *KL v 1*) **2.** to go wrong (*RJ v 3*)

mischief *noun* **1.** evil (*T i 2*) **2.** harm (*MND ii 1*; *2H4 ii 1*; *JC iii 1*; *M i 5*) **3.** a disease (*MA i 3*)

misconster *verb* to misconstrue (*R3 iii 5*)

miscreant *noun* a scoundrel (*R2 i 1*; *KL i 1*)

misdoubt *noun* suspicion (*2H4 iv 1*) ■ *verb* to have suspicions about someone or something (*AC iii 7*; *R3 iii 2*)

Misenum *noun* a promontory in Italy, immediately south of Naples (*AC ii 2*)

miser *noun* a miserable person, not necessarily someone who is mean with money (*1H4 v 4*)

misgovernment *noun* mismanagement (*MA iv 1*)

misgrafted, missgrafted, misgraffed *adjective* wrongly matched (*MND i 1*)

mishaved *adjective* badly behaved (*RJ iii 3*)

mislike *verb* to dislike someone (*AC iii 13*)

misordered *adjective* confused (*2H4 iv 2*)

misprise¹, **misprize** *verb* to despise someone (*MA iii 1*; *AYLI i 1*)

misprise², **misprized** *adjective* mistaken (*MND iii 2*)

misprision *noun* a mistake (*MND iii 2*; *MA iv 1*; *TN i 5*)

misreport *verb* to say unpleasant and untrue things about someone (*MM v 1*)

miss *noun* a disadvantage caused by the absence of someone (*1H4 v 4*) ■ *verb* to be wanting (*RJ i Chor.*)

mis-sheath *verb* to put a knife into something other than its sheath by mistake (*RJ v 3*)

missingly *adverb* sadly because of the absence of someone (*WT iv 2*)

missive *noun* a messenger (*M i 5*; *AC ii 2*)

mist *noun* a state of uncertainty (*CE ii 2*) ■ *verb* to make something opaque (*KL v 3*)

mistake *verb* to find the wrong target (*RJ v 3*)

mistaking *noun* a mistake (*KL i 2*; *MA v 1*; *RJ iii 2*; *TS iv 5*)

mistempered *adjective* made for an evil purpose (*RJ i 1*)

misthink *verb* to think badly of someone (*AC v 2*)

mistreading *noun* an evil deed (*1H4 iii 2*)

mistress *noun* a creator (*H5 i 1*) ■ *adjective* primary (*H5 ii 4*)

misuse *verb* to deceive someone (*MA ii 2*)

moan *noun* grief (*MA v 3*)

mobled *adjective* with the head muffled or tightly covered (*H ii 2*)

mock *verb* 1. to defy someone or something (*MV ii 1*; *M ii 2*; *AC iii 13*) 2. to imitate something (*AC v 1*) ◊ **in mock** scorned (*MM v 1*)

mockable *adjective* worthy of being ridiculed (*AYLI iii 2*)

mocker *noun* someone who deceives someone (*AYLI ii 6*)

mocks ◊ **made mocks with** ridiculed (*O v 2*)

model *noun* 1. a plan (*2H4 i 3*; *R2 iii 4*; *R3 v 3*) 2. a design of a building (*MA i 3*; *2H4 i 3*) 3. a small-scale copy (*R2 i 2*; *H v 2*) 4. a mould (*R2 iii 2*) 5. an imperfect example of something (*H5 ii Chor.*)

modern *adjective* ordinary (*AYLI ii 7*; *M iv 3*; *O i 3*)

moiety *noun* 1. a portion (*1H4 iii 1*; *H i 1*; *H5 v 1*; *MV iv 1*; *R3 ii 2*) 2. a half (*AC v 1*; *R3 i 1*)

moist star *noun* the moon (*H i 1*)

moldwarp *noun* a mole (the animal) (*1H4 iii 1*)

mome *noun* a stupid person (*CE iii 1*)

moment *noun* 1. importance (*R3 iii 7*; *H iii 1*; *O iii 4*) 2. a reason for something (*AC i 2*)

momentany *adjective* momentary (*MND i 1*)

Monmouth cap *noun* a hat of a type commonly worn by soldiers and sailors. The best ones were made in Monmouth. (*H5 iv 7*)

monster *verb* to make something into a monster (*KL i 1*)

monstrous *interjection* outrageous! (*MND iii 1*; *1H4 ii 4*; *KL v 3*)

Montferrat, Monferrato *noun* an independent border region in northwest Italy. It was annexed by the Gonzaga family of Mantua in 1536 and became part of Piedmont (1708). (*MV i 1*)

monument *noun* 1. an ornamental tomb set up in memory of the dead person (*MA iv 1*; *RJ iii 5*; *AC iv 13*) 2. a statue (*MM v 1*) 3. a sign or warning of something (*TS iii 2*)

mood *noun* 1. a fit of passion (*RJ iii 1*) 2. a type (*H i 2*) 3. the key of a piece of music (*2H4 iv 5*)

moon *noun* the symbol of the Roman goddess Diana (*MND i 1*; *1H4 i 2*) ◊ **go by the moon** to move about at night (*1H4 i 2*)

moonbeam *noun see* **beam 2**

mooncalf *noun* a misshapen creature (*T ii 2, iii 2*) [From the belief that a calf born by moonlight was deformed.]

moonish *adjective* changeable, fickle (*AYLI iii 2*)

moonshine *noun* a month (*KL i 2*) ◊ **make a sop o' th' moonshine of** to beat someone to a pulp (*L ii 2*)

moon's men *plural noun* criminals that are active at night (*1H4 i 2*)

Moor *noun* a native of Morocco and the Barbary coast, a black person, a Muslim (*MV iii 5*; *O i 1*)

Moor ditch *noun* a channel running between Bishopsgate and Cripplegate in

Moorsfield in London. The smell, particularly when it was being cleaned, was supposed to bring on depression. (*1H4 i 2*)

mop *noun* a grimace (*T iv 1*)

mope *verb* to wander about in a dazed or aimless manner (*H iii 4*; *H5 iii 7*)

moping *adjective* dazed (*T v 1*)

mopping *noun* the action of grimacing (*KL iv 1*)

moral *noun* 1. a hidden meaning (*MA iii 4*; *TS iv 4*; *H5 iii 6*) 2. a symbol (*H5 iii 6*) ■ *verb* to moralise (*AYLI ii 7*) ■ *adjective* 1. moralising (*MA v 1*; *KL iv 2*) 2. hidden (*MA iii 4*)

morality play *noun* a play intended to teach a moral lesson. The characters were personifications of human virtues and vices, such as Vice, Sloth or Hope.

moraller *noun* someone who complains about moral standards (*O ii 3*)

morris, morris-dance *noun* an English folk dance (*H5 ii 4*) (NOTE: The dance is possibly of **Moorish** origin. It became associated with May Day celebrations and later included characters such as the hobby horse, Robin Hood and Maid Marion who had bells attached to their clothing.) ◇ **nine men's morris, nine men's meril** a game played by two people throwing nine counters to cover the intersection of squares marked on the ground (*MND ii 1*)

morris pike *noun* a spear of Moorish origin (*CE iv 3*)

mortal *adjective* 1. human (*MV ii 7*; *H5 iv 1*; *R2 i 1, iv 1*; *M i 5*) 2. deadly (*CE i 1*; *O iii 3*; *M iv 1*)

mortality *noun* 1. human life (*MM iii 2*; *H5 i 2*; *M ii 3*) 2. death (*MM i 1*) 3. deadliness (*H5 iv 3*)

mortal-living *adjective* condemned to life (*R3 iv 4*)

mortal-staring *adjective* able to kill with a look (*R3 v 3*)

mortified *adjective* deadened (*H5 i 1*; *JC ii 1*; *KL iii 3*; *M v 2*)

mortifying *adjective* dead, unfeeling (*MA i 3*; *MV i 1*)

mortis'd *adjective* secured (*H iii 3*)

mortise ◇ **hold the mortise** to remain with the timber joints held together (*O ii 1*)

mort o' the deer *noun* a hunting call made when a deer had been killed (*WT i 2*)

mose in the chine *noun* the last stages of **glanders**, a disease of horses (*TS iii 2*)

mote *noun* a speck of dust (*H i 1*; *H5 iv 1*; *MND v 1*)

moth *noun* a parasite (*O i 3*)

mother *noun* 1. the head of a female religious community (*MM i 4*) 2. the characteristics typical of a woman (*H5 iv 6*) 3. the prime cause (*R3 ii 2*) 4. a form of hysteria that causes choking, believed to be caused by vapours rising from the womb (*KL ii 4*)

motion *noun* 1. the ability to move (*MM iii 1*; *RJ iii 2*) 2. a move taught in fencing (*TN iii 4*; *H iv 7*) 3. a proposal 4. the act of urging someone to do something (*MM i 4*; *CE iii 2*; *MV v 1*; *JC ii 1*) 5. an insight (*AC ii 3*) 6. a puppet show (*WT iv 3*) 7. a puppet (*MM iii 2*)

COMMENT: *Motion* could apply to many types of movement, some quite stretched from the literal meaning of the word. In Act 5 of **The Merchant of Venice** Lorenzo lectures Jessica and uses the word twice. At first the meaning is literal: even 'the smallest orb…in his motion sings', supporting the theory that the movement of the spheres produced music inaudible to human ears. A few lines later he deplores the unmusical man: 'The motions of his spirit are dull as night', where *motions* is almost a metaphor for inner impulses, the movements inside the heart. A similar meaning, of inclination or desire, appears in **Twelfth Night** when Orsino tells Viola that a lover is 'unstaid and skittish in all motions else,/Save in the constant image of the creature/That is beloved'. *Motion* becomes more metaphorical when the Duke in **Measure for Measure** makes his proposal to Isabella: 'I have a motion much imports your good'. *Motion* is more active than 'idea' or 'notion' would be; the Duke refers to an active impulse in his proposal, which he hopes she will meet with equal energy. A very specialised use of *motion* is when it means a puppet, which moves at the puppet-master's command, but has no independent movement of its own. Lucio uses the phrase 'a motion ungenerative' to describe Angelo, implying that he is an impotent puppet.

motive *noun* someone who starts or causes something (*AC ii 2*; *O iv 2*)

motley *noun* **1.** the multicoloured dress of a court jester (fool) (*AYLI ii 7*; *KL i 4*) **2.** a fool (*AYLI iii 3*)

motley-minded *adjective* foolish (*AYLI v 4*)

mould *noun* **1.** earth (*H5 iii 2*; *TS i 1*) *See also* **men of mould 2.** the form of a person's body (*M i 3*) **3.** a pattern (*H iii 1*)

moulten *adjective* without feathers as a result of having moulted (*1H4 iii 1*)

mounch *verb* to munch (*M i 3*)

mount *verb* to cause something to rise (*H5 iv 2*; *T ii 2*)

mountebank *noun* a fraud (*CE v 1*; *H iv 7*)

mouse *noun* a term of affection (*TN i 5*; *H iii 4*) ∎ *verb* to tear something to pieces with the teeth (*MND v 1*)

mouse-hunt *noun* a man who chases after women (*RJ iv 4*)

mouth *noun* the bark of a hunting dog (*MND iv 1*; *H5 ii 4*)

mouthed *adjective* gaping (*1H4 i 3*)

mouth-honour *noun* flattery (*M v 3*)

mouth-made *adjective* insincere (*AC i 3*)

move *verb* **1.** to suggest something (*MA iv 1*; *H iii 2*; *O iii 4*) **2.** to persuade someone to do something (*CE ii 2*; *O iii 4*) **3.** to cause someone distress (*TS v 2*; *RJ i 1*)

moveable *noun* a piece of furniture (*TS ii 1*)

mow *noun* a grimace (*T iv 1*; *H ii 2*) ∎ *verb* to grimace (*T ii 2*; *KL iv 1*)

moy *noun* an imaginary coin (*H5 iv 4*) [From French *me*.]

mud *verb* to bury someone in mud (*T iii 3*, *v 1*)

muddy *adjective* **1.** mentally confused (*WT i 2*) **2.** bawdy (*2H4 ii 4*)

muddy-mettled *adjective* depressed (*H ii 2*)

muffler *noun* a scarf worn around the neck (*H5 iii 6*)

muleter *noun* someone who drives mules (*AC iii 7*)

mummy *noun* a preparation made from mummified bodies, used in medicine and magic (*M iv 1*; *O iii 4*)

mural, moral *noun* possibly a wall (*MND v 1*)

murdering minister *noun* a murderer or someone who incites someone to murder (*M i 5*)

murdering-piece *noun* a small cannon loaded with small iron balls fired at the same time (*H iv 5*)

mure *noun* a wall (*2H4 iv 4*)

murmur *noun* a rumour (*TN i 2*)

murrain, murrion *noun* a plague (used in oaths) (*T iii 2*) (NOTE: Literally, a disease affecting cattle (possibly foot-and-mouth disease).) ∎ *adjective* diseased (*MND ii 1*)

muscadel *noun* a strong sweet spicy wine (*TS iii 2*)

muse *verb* to wonder (*T iii 3*; *R3 i 3*; *M iii 4*)

Muses *noun* in Greek mythology, the nine daughters of Zeus and Mnemosyne, each identified with a particular art or science (*MND v 1*)

musk-rose *noun* a type of very fragrant white rose (*MND ii 1, 2, iv 1*)

muss *noun* **1.** a children's game in which the players scramble for a prize (*AC iii 1*) **2.** a disturbance (*AC iii 11 (13)*)

mustachio *noun* a moustache (*1H4 ii 1*)

mutine *verb* to rebel (*H iii 4, v 2*) ∎ *noun* a rebel

mutiny *verb* to quarrel (*R2 ii 1*; *AC iii 9*; *O ii 1*)

mutual *adjective* intimate (*MM i 1*)

mutuality *noun* an exchange of confidences (*O ii 1*)

mutually *preposition* together (*MM ii 3*)

Myrmidon *noun* a fierce loyal people. The name of an inn. (*TN ii 3*) (NOTE: According to Greek mythology, the people of the town of Aegina were dying of the plague and King Aeacus prayed to Zeus that he would change the ants emerging from an oak tree into people to replace the population. These people then emigrated to **Thessaly** and followed Achilles to the siege of **Troy**.) [From the Greek, 'ant people'.]

mystery *noun* **1.** a trade or profession (*MM iv 2*; *O iv 2*) **2.** a religious rite (*KL i 1*) **3.** a private secret (*H iii 2*)

mystery play *noun* a play based on a Biblical story. These plays were staged by craft guilds and were performed in cycles on festival days.

N

nag *noun* a prostitute (*AC iii 10*) [Literally 'a small riding horse'.]

nail *noun* a measure of length for cloth, equal to 5.5 cm (*TS iv 3*) ◇ **to blow one's nails** to be patient (*TS i 1*)

naked *adjective* **1.** without any belongings (*R2 i 2*; *H iv 7*) **2.** unarmed (*O v 2*)

nakedness *noun* a state of being without belongings (*MA iv 1*; *H5 iv 1*)

name *noun* **1.** a family **2.** a rightful authority (*T ii 1*; *MA ii 1*; *WT iii 2*; *1H4 iii 2*; *H5 ii 2*; *M ii 1*) **3.** a reputation (*MM i 2*)

nameless *adjective* not worth describing (*R2 ii 2*)

Narcissus *noun* in Greek mythology, a beautiful youth who saw his reflection in a pond. Thinking that it was the nymph that ruled the place he jumped into the water and drowned. (*AC ii 5*)

narrow *adjective* small (*AC iii 4*)

narrowly *adverb* carefully (*MA v 4*; *TS iii 2*)

narrow-prying *adjective* watching closely (*TS iii 2*)

native *adjective* **1.** belonging to naturally (*O ii 1*) **2.** related (*H i 2*) **3.** rightful (by birth) (*R2 ii 2*; *H5 ii 4*)

natural *noun* someone of low mental ability (*T iii 2*; *AYLI i 2*; *RJ ii 4*) ■ *adjective* of low mental ability (*TN i 3*)

COMMENT: *Nature* is identified with life itself and this significance of the word means that *nature* often has a deep impact when it appears in Shakespeare's plays. It could refer simply to human nature itself, as when Kent in **King Lear** declares that 'the open night's too rough/For nature to endure'. It is usually associated with gentle feelings, appropriate to sensitive human nature. Prospero in **The Tempest** condemns his brother Antonio, 'that entertained ambition,/Expelled remorse and nature'; in **Macbeth** Lady Macduff, about to be murdered, feels that her absent husband 'lacks the natural touch'. People have their individual natures from birth, whatever else the workings of fortune may give or take away during their lifetimes. Hamlet knows his mother to be naturally soft, physical, even promiscuous, but he argues that even she could challenge this trait by disciplined habit, 'For use almost can change the stamp of nature'. Contradictions arise when *nature* is applied to communities, such as kingdoms. Is it *natural* for an individual to follow his primal instincts or to observe the social bonds essential to good government? Which is the more *natural* when the two 'natures' collide? In **As You Like It** Oliver schemes against his brother Orlando, but complains to Charles, the wrestler, that Orlando is breaking the bond with 'me, his natural brother'. In **King Lear** there is a complex philosophical issue at the heart of the play, explored by John Danby in **Shakespeare and the Doctrine of Nature**. It centres on Edmund, the bastard, born outside natural wedlock and therefore unable to inherit his father's lands. His first soliloquy begins with an appeal: 'Thou, Nature, art my goddess'. He identifies himself with individual impulses, passion, survival instincts and 'the lusty stealth of nature'. He believes that this type of nature sanctions ruthlessness and cunning, and that he is superior to those, like his brother Edgar, who live within the conventions of what most people consider to be *natural*, the bonds of family and kingdom. When his father, the victim of Edmund's trickery, mistakenly thinks this bastard son has saved his life, he promises, 'and of my land, loyal and natural boy, I'll work the means/To make thee capable'. The irony here is that Gloucester's use of *natural* is opposite to Edmund's and he is unaware of the difference. A specialised meaning of *natural* differs from both

Gloucester's and Edmund's uses: *natural* could be a noun, meaning fool or half-wit. In **As You Like It** Celia sees Touchstone and tells Rosalind, 'Fortune…. hath sent this natural for our whetstone'. In **Twelfth Night** Maria, speaking of Sir Andrew's gifts, assures Sir Toby that 'He hath indeed all, most natural'. She punningly associates the two meanings of idiot and inherently gifted.

naught *noun* wickedness (*MND iv 2*; *R3 i 1*) ■ *adjective* **1.** wicked (*RJ iii 2*; *KL ii 4*; *M iv 3*) **2.** worthless (*MA v 1*; *AYLI iii 2*; *H5 i 2*) **3.** destroyed (*AC iii 10*) ◇ **be naught** to leave quickly (*AYLI i 1*) ◇ **set at naught** to regard something as worthless (*2H4 v 2*)

naughty *adjective* **1.** wicked (*MA iv 2*; *MV iii 3*) **2.** (of the weather) bad (*KL iii 4*)

naughty-house *noun* a brothel (*MM ii 1*)

nave *noun* **1.** the hub of a wheel (*2H4 ii 4*; *H ii 2*) **2.** a person's navel (*M i 2*)

navigation *noun* ships collectively (*M iv 1*)

nayward ◇ **lean to the nayward** tend towards denial or disbelief (*WT ii 1*)

nayword *noun* a byword (*TN ii 3*)

Nazarite *noun* someone from Nazareth (*MV i 3*) (NOTE: Jesus, who lived in Nazareth when he was young, was accepted by the Jews as a prophet but not as the Son of God.)

neaf, neif *noun* a fist (*MND iv 1*; *2H4 ii 4*)

near *adjective* nearer (*M ii 3*; *R2 iii 2*)

near-legged *adjective* having knees which touch when the person is standing upright (*TS iii 2*)

neat *adjective* excessively concerned with your appearance (*WT i 2*; *1H4 i 3*; *KL ii 2*) ■ *noun* a cow or bull with horns (*MV i 1*; *WT i 2*)

neat herd *noun* someone who drives cattle (*WT iv 4*)

neat's foot *noun* a calf's foot preserved in jelly, eaten as a delicacy (*TS iv 3*)

neat's leather *noun* hide from horned cattle e.g. a calf or an ox (*T ii 2*; *JC i 1*)

neb *noun* a bird's beak (*WT i 2*)

necessary *adjective* inevitable (*JC ii 2*; *H iii 2*)

neck ◇ **on one another's neck** in quick succession (*1H4 iv 3*) ◇ **on your neck** (of an accusation) made against you (*O v 2*)

Nedar *noun* The father of Helena (*MND i 1, iv 1*)

need ◇ **for a need** in case of necessity (*R3 iii 5*; *H ii 2*) ◇ **had need** ought to do something (*AYLI ii 7*; *TN ii 3*)

needless *adjective* not in need of anything (*AYLI ii 1*)

needly *adverb* out of necessity (*RJ iii 2*)

neele *noun* a needle (*MND ii 2*)

neeze *verb* to sneeze (*MND ii 1*)

neighbour *noun* a close friend (*R3 iv 2*) ■ *verb* to have something or someone neighbouring you (*WT i 2*; *H5 i 1*)

neighboured *adjective* closely associated (*H ii 2*; *KL i 1*)

neighbourhood *noun* friendly relations (*H5 v 2*)

Nemean *adjective* of the ancient Greek district of Nemea (*H i 4*)

Nemean lion *noun* a lion killed by **Heracles** (*H i 4*)

nephew *noun* a grandchild (*O i 1*)

Neptune *noun* in Roman mythology, the god of the sea. He was the son of **Saturn** and brother of **Pluto** and **Jupiter**. (*T i 2, v 1*; *WT iv 4, v 1*; *R2 ii 1*; *AC ii 7*; *MND iii 2*) (NOTE: The Greek equivalent is **Poseidon**.)

Nereides *plural noun* water nymphs, the fifty daughters of Nereus, the ancient god of the sea (*AC ii 2*)

nerve *noun* a ligament (*H i 4*; *MM i 4*; *T i 2*)

Nervii *plural noun* warriors of ancient Gaul, an ancient region made up of parts of present-day France and Belgium and other neighbouring countries (*JC iii 2*)

Nessus *noun* in Greek mythology, a **centaur** who tried to rape Deianira, Heracles' wife (*AC iv 1*)

nest of spicery *noun* the genitals and pubic area (*R3 iv 4*)

Nestor *noun* the king of Pylos in Greece, who was present at the siege of Troy. He was renowned for his eloquence and wisdom. (*MV i 1*)

net *noun* a complicated argument (*H5 i 2*)

nether *adjective* relating to the earth viewed as below the heavens (*KL iv 2*)

Netherlands *noun* the genitals (*CE iii 2*)

nether-stocks *plural noun* stockings (*1H4 ii 4*) ◊ **wooden nether stocks** the stocks, a wooden frame with holes in which a person's feet, hands, and head were secured as a means of punishment (*L ii 4*)

neuter *adjective* neutral (*R2 ii 3*)

new-fangled *adjective* liking new things (*AYLI iv 1*)

Newgate *noun* prison (*1H4 iii 2*) (NOTE: Newgate Prison in London, built over a gate in the restored Roman city wall, was opened during the reign of King John. It was the main prison for the city and condemned prisoners were executed in the street outside. It was closed in 1880. 'Newgate' became a name applied to prisons in general.)

new-hatched *adjective* newly arrived (*M ii 3*; *H i 3*)

nice *adjective* **1.** trivial (*R3 iii 7*; *RJ iii 1*; *JC iv 3*) **2.** precise (*MV ii 1*; *M iv 3*) **3.** small (*O iii 3*) **4.** precarious (*1H4 iv 1*) **5.** fastidious (*TS iii 1*) **6.** delicate (*2H4 i 1*) **7.** sexually promiscuous (*AC iii 13*)

COMMENT: Early English uses of *nice* were positive, since the word referred to exactness, precision and fastidious judgement, as in the rather rarefied meaning of today when we admire someone for making a 'nice distinction' of argument in debating. This was also Shakespeare's meaning, though generally the implications of the word in his plays are negative. For example, in **Much Ado About Nothing** Leonato despises the elegant niceties of etiquette in swordsmanship when he speaks of Claudio's 'nice-fence and active practice'. The peacekeeper Benvolio in **Romeo and Juliet** urges the Prince 'how nice the quarrel was', implying that the motives were so precise as to be negligible or pointless. This implication of subtlety in *nice* may seem to slide into deceit and therefore *nice* could acquire sexual connotations, as in the phrase 'nice wenches', a euphemism for prostitutes. Shakespeare's use of *nice* was always lively and exact, and therefore quite different from today's bland emptiness, as in 'Have a nice day'.

nice-fence *noun* skill at swordfighting (*MA v 1*)

nicely *adverb* innocently (*R2 ii 1*)

nicenss, nicety *noun* shyness (*MM ii 4*)

Nicholas, St *noun* (fl. 325) Regarded as the prototype of Father Christmas or Santa Claus, little is known of his life except that he was bishop of Myra in Turkey. He is the patron saint of Russia and of scholars, parish clerks, pawnbrokers and small boys. He is supposed to have given three bags of gold to the daughters of a poor man to save them from prostitution, which have been transformed into the three gold balls that are the symbol of a pawnbroker's shop. His feast day is 6 December. (*1H4 ii 1, i v 4*; *TS iv 1*)

Nicholas' clerk *noun* a highwayman (*1H4 ii 1*) [Possibly a play on 'Old Nick' the devil.]

nick *noun* **1.** the neck (*H5 iii 4*) **2.** a reckoning (NOTE: From the practice of keeping records of accounts by cutting notches in sticks.) ■ *verb* to cut something (*AC iii 13*; *CE v 1*) ◊ **in the nick** the right time (*O v 2*)

nickname *verb* to give the wrong name to something (*H iii 1*)

niece *noun* a granddaughter (*R3 iv 1*)

niggard *verb* to put something off (*JC iv 3*)

night-cap, night-cape *noun* a wife (*O ii 1*)

nighted *adjective* dark (*KL iv 5*; *H i 2*)

nightgown *noun* a garment for sleeping in, rather like a modern dressing-gown (*M ii 2*)

nightmare *noun* an evil spirit who was believed to have sexual intercourse with a woman while she slept (*KL iii 4*)

night-rule *noun* lively activity taking place at night (*MND iii 2*)

nill *verb* will not (*H v 1*; *TS ii 1*)

Nilus *noun* the River Nile (*AC i 2, 3, ii 7, v 2*)

nimble-pinioned *adjective* with wings designed for swift flight (*RJ ii 5*)

nine-fold *noun* nine foals or nine familiars (*KL iii 4*)

nine men's morris *noun* see **morris** (*MND ii 1*)

Nine Worthies *noun* famous heroes of the past (*2H4 ii 4*)

Ninus, Ninny *noun* the mythical founder of the ancient city of Nineveh in present-day Iraq (*MND v 1*)

Niobe *noun* in Greek mythology, the wife of the king of Thebes (*H i 2*) (NOTE:

She had fourteen children and derided Latona, the mother of Apollo and Diana for having only two children. In revenge Latona ordered her children to kill Niobe's children. Niobe cried herself to death and was turned into a stone from which flowed a stream of water.)

nip ◇ **nip in the head** to check or halt the progress of something (*MM iii 1*)

Noah *noun* according to the Book of Genesis in the Bible, Noah built a ship (the ark) and with his three sons saved every kind of animal from the flood sent by God to punish the world for its wickedness (*CE iii 2*)

noble *noun* a gold coin worth 33p (6s 8d) (*R2 i 1*; *H5 ii 1*; *R3 i 3*)

noblesse *noun* nobility (*R2 iv 1*)

noddle *noun* a head (*TS i 1*)

noise *noun* **1.** music (*T iii 2*; *AC iv 3*) **2.** a group of musicians (*2H4 ii 4*) **3.** a rumour (*KL iii 6*; *AC i 2*) ◇ **noise it** to cause a disturbance (*AC iii 6*)

nole, nowl *noun* a head (*MND iii 2*)

nonage *noun* the period of time during which a person is under the age of legal adulthood (*R3 ii 3*)

nonce ◇ **for the nonce** for now (*1H4 i 2*; *H iv 7*)

non-come *adjective* confused (*MA iii 5*)

non-pareil *adjective* incomparable, without equal (*AC iii 2*)

non-performance *noun* the fact of not doing something (*WT i 2*)

non-regardance *noun* disregard (*TN v 1*)

non-suit *verb* to reject someone's request for something (*O i 1*)

nook *noun* an inlet or shelter (*T i 2*; *AYLI iii 2*)

nook-shotten *adjective* having many inlets (*H5 iii 5*)

Northampton *noun* the county town of Northamptonshire (*R3 ii 4*)

northern star *noun* the pole star (*JC iii 1*)

Norweyan *adjective* Norwegian (*M i 2, 3*)

nose ◇ **speak in the nose** to sound like a person whose nose has decomposed as a result of the sexually transmitted disease syphilis (*O iii 1*)

nose-painting *noun* reddening of a person's nose as a result of excessive drinking (*M ii 3*)

notable *adjective* noticeable (*O iv 1*)

not a jot *phrase* of little importance (*H v 1*; *MM iv 2*; *O iii 3*; *TS i 1*)

notary *noun* a lawyer's clerk (*MV i 3*)

not a whit *phrase* not at all (*R3 iii 4*)

note *noun* **1.** fame (*M iii 2*; *WT iv 2*) **2.** worthiness **3.** knowledge (*T ii 1*; *KL ii 1*; *WT i 1*) **4.** a sign or indication (*WT i 2, v 2*; *MA iii 2*; *H5 iv Chor.*) **5.** a comment or observation (*AC iii 3*; *TN iii 4*; *RJ i 1*) **6.** a list (*WT iv 3*; *TS i 2*) **7.** an order, bill or invoice (*TS iv 3*; *2H4 v 1*; *MV iii 2*) **8.** a melody (*AYLI ii 5*; *CE iii 2*; *WT i 2*) **9.** a sign of disgrace (*R2 i 1*) ◇ **note of expectation** a list of expected guests (*M iii 3*)

COMMENT: Shakespeare used *note* as we do: in various ways as a noun or a verb. The basic sense is to give a special mark of attention. At a formal occasion courtiers would expect to be especially attentive to their king, but such is Macbeth's mental disorder at his banquet that his wife warns them, 'If much you note him/You shall offend him and extend his passion'. The context can give *note* a high distinction, as when in **Cymbeline** Imogen reads a letter about Iachimo: 'He is one of the noblest note', meaning 'reputation'. The context may also be negative. In **Julius Caesar** Cassius complains that Brutus has 'condemned and noted Lucius Pella/For taking bribes here of the Sardians'. He is referring to a list of criminals. *Note* may also be a musical note and is used in an especially riddling way in **Much Ado about Nothing**. Don Pedro has employed the singer Balthasar, who is excessively wordy in his self-deprecation. Don Pedro tries to stop him: 'if thou wilt hold longer argument,/Do it in notes'.The punning musician replies, 'Note this before my notes:/ There's not a note of mine that's worth the noting'. Each line uses each meaning of *note* twice, and then Don Pedro extends the wordplay further: 'Why these are very crochets that he speaks;/ Note notes forsooth and nothing'. The final word *nothing* plays on its similarity to 'noting', and so draws the audience attention to the play's title, which then comes to mean 'Much Ado About Noting, or observing, since so much of the action is about overhearing and rumour. The play's action, all on the subject of love and marriage, causes much confusion and conflict, but all for nothing. Therefore the wordplay on *note* and *nothing* becomes central to the play's satirical meaning. This is a strong example of how Shakespeare's apparently playful use of language can convey a deeper significance.

noted *adjective* disgraced (*JC iv 3*)

notice *noun* information (*H5 iv 7*; *JC iii 2*)

notify *verb* to give someone information (*O iii 1*)

notion *noun* a person's mind (*KL i 4*; *M iii 1*)

not-pated *adjective* having short hair (*1H4 ii 4*)

noyance *noun* harm (*H iii 3*)

number *noun* a verse of a song or poetry (*TN ii 5*; *RJ ii 4*; *AC iii 2*)

nuncio *noun* a messenger (*TN i 4*)

nunnery *noun* a brothel (*H iii 1*)

nuthook *noun* a term of abuse for a **beadle** (*2H4 v 4*)

nuture *noun* manners (*T iv 1*; *AYLI ii 7*)

nyas *noun* a young hawk (*RJ ii 2*)

nymph *noun* an attractive young woman (*MND ii 1*; *R3 i 1*; *H iii 1*)

O

oak *noun* the oak tree was sacred to the Roman god Jove (*T v 2*; *O iii 3*)

obedient *adjective* having respect for someone ◇ the area in which obedience is required (*1H4 v 1*)

Oberon *noun* the king of the fairies (*MND ii 1, 2, iv 1*)

obligation *noun* a contract (*H i 2, ii 2*)

obliged *adjective* bound by a contract (*MV ii 6*)

oblivious *adjective* causing forgetfulness (*M v 3*)

obscene *adjective* disgusting (*R2 iv 1*; *1H4 ii 4*)

obscuely *adjective* hidden (*JC i 2*)

obscure bird *noun* an owl (*M ii 3*)

obsequious *adjective* **1.** relating to a funeral (*H i 2*) **2.** showing fitting respect and devotion (*MM ii 4*)

> COMMENT: This word was derived from the Latin 'sequor', meaning 'to follow', and therefore *obsequious* meant to comply with something that duty demands. For example, in the second scene of **Hamlet** the king speaks of Hamlet's duty to do 'obsequious sorrow' for his dead father, after which normal life should continue. Today the word has come to imply a slavish and insincere observance to one's superior, generally for some sort of reward. This was not part of the Elizabethan meaning of *obsequious*, even though Hamlet regards the king as a hypocrite. The word was often used in connection with death, since 'obsequies' are funeral rites.

obsequiously *adverb* behaving like a mourner at a funeral (*R3 i 2*)

observance *noun* **1.** the fact of paying attention to someone or something (*AYLI iii 2*; *AC iii 3*; *O iii 3*) **2.** special care (*H iii 2*) **3.** the attention required by respect or love (*AYLI v 2*)

observancy *noun* loving attention (*O iii 4*)

observant *noun* an attentive servant (*KL ii 2*)

observation *noun* **1.** information gathered by observing someone or something (*AYLI ii 7*; *MA iv 1*; *KL i 1*) **2.** a ceremony (*MND iv 1*) **3.** special care (*T iii 3*)

observe *verb* to show respect for someone (*2H4 iv 4*)

observed *noun* someone who is shown respect (*H iii 1*)

obsque hoc nilhil est *phrase Latin* without this there is nothing (*2H4 v 5*)

obstruct *noun* an obstacle (*AC iii 6*)

obstruction *noun* **1.** a lack of light (*TN iv 2*) **2.** the condition of a person's blood ceasing to circulate in their body (*TN iii 4*; *MM iii 1*)

occasion *noun* **1.** something caused by something or someone (*AYLI iv 1*) **2.** a personal need (*MV i 1*; *AC ii 6*) **3.** the course of events (*2H4 iv 1*) **4.** the subject of a debate (*MV iii 5*)

occulted *adjective* hidden (*H iii 2*)

occupy *verb* to have sexual intercourse (*RJ ii 4*; *2H4 ii 4*)

occurrence, occurrent *noun* an event (*TN v 1*; *H v 2*; *H5 v Chor.*)

odd-even *noun* the time between midnight and one in the morning (*O i 1*)

oeilliades *verb* to ogle someone (*KL iv 5*)

o'erblow *verb* to blow something away (*H5 iii 3*)

o'er-crow *verb* to overwhelm something (*H v 2*)

o'er-dyed *adjective* dyed with another colour (*WT i 2*)

o'er-flourished *adjective* decorated on the outside (*TN iii 4*)

o'ergrown *adjective* very large (*MM i 3*)

o'erleap *verb* **1.** to jump across something (*M i 4*) **2.** to jump too far (*M i 7*)

o'erlook *verb* **1.** to examine something (*MND ii 2*; *R3 iii 5*) **2.** to bewitch someone (*MV iii 2*)

o'erlooking *noun* attention (*KL i 2*)

o'er-office *verb* to assume an air of superiority because of your official position (*H v 1*)

o'erperch *verb* to fly over something (*RJ ii 2*)

o'erpictured *adjective* more beautiful than you imagined (*AC ii 2*)

o'er-prize *verb* to exceed something (*T i 2*)

o'er-raught, overraught *adjective* **1.** overtaken (*H iii 1*) **2.** cheated (*CE i 2*; *H v 1*)

o'erset *adjective* overcome (*2H4 i 1*)

o'ershoot *verb* to go too far (*JC iii 2*)

o'er-sized *adjective* covered as if with glue (**size**) (*H ii 2*)

o'erskip *verb* to pass over something (*KL iii 6*)

o'er stare *verb* to outstare someone (*MV ii 1*)

o'erstink *verb* to smell even worse than something (*T iv 1*)

o'ertake *verb* to be made incapable by excessive drinking (*H ii 1*)

o'er-teemed *adjective* exhausted by having given birth to so many children (*H ii 2*)

o'ertrip *verb* to skip over something (*MV v 1*)

o'er watched *adjective* exhausted by keeping watch (*JC iv 3*; *KL ii 2*)

o'erween *verb* to be arrogant (*WT iv 2*)

o'erwhelm *verb* to extend beyond something (*H5 iii 1*)

o'erworn *adjective* **1.** faded (*R3 i 1*) **2.** exhausted

oes *plural noun* circles (*MND iii 2*)

off-cap *verb* to take off your cap as a gesture of respect (*O i 1*)

offence *noun* **1.** harm (*MND ii 2*; *AYLI iii 5*; *JC ii 1*) **2.** disgrace (*TN iv 2*) **3.** discontent (*MV iv 1*)

offenceful *adjective* sinful (*MM ii 3*)

offenceless *adjective* harmless (*O ii 3*)

offend *verb* to obstruct someone (*CE i 1*)

offer *verb* **1.** to attack someone (*2H4 iv 1*) **2.** to dare to do something (*TS v 1*; *WT iv 4*)

offering *noun* **1.** a ritual (*M ii 1*) **2.** a sacrifice (*JC ii 2*)

offering-side *noun* the side that issues a challenge (*1H4 iv 1*)

office *noun* **1.** a task (*R2 ii 2*) **2.** an official (*H iii 1*) **3.** the proper action (*O iii 4*) **4.** a room such as the kitchen in which the daily tasks involved in running a house are carried out (*M ii 1*; *O ii 2*)

officed *adjective* having a particular duty (*WT i 2*; *O i 3*)

old *adjective* **1.** abundant (*TS iii 2*; *RJ iii 3*; *M ii 3*) **2.** in old clothes (*TS iv 1*) ■ *noun* an area of open country (*KL iii 4*) [Alteration of 'wold'.]

Olympus *noun* a mountain in western Thessaly in Greece, believed by the ancient Greeks to be the home of the gods (*H v 1*; *JC iii 1, iv 3*)

omttance *noun* the act of omitting to do something (*AYLI iii 5*)

on *preposition* **1.** of (*T i 2*; *M ii 3, v 1*; *H iii 1*; *KL i 5*) **2.** about (*T v 1*)

one-trunk-inheriting *adjective* having only one trunk of possessions (*KL ii 2*)

oneyers *noun* the meaning is not clear. It may mean clerk of the exchequer, one who has contact with the great, owner, yes-man or simply 'one'. (*1H4 ii 1*)

onion-eyed *adjective* tearful (*AC iv 2*)

onset *noun* a beginning

open *adjective* **1.** public (*MM ii 1*; *RJ v 3*) **2.** obvious (*H5 ii 2*; *R3 iii 5*) **3.** generous (*2H4 iv 4*) ■ *adverb* publicly (*TN iii 3*) ■ *verb* to reveal something (*H5 i 1*; *H ii 2*)

open arse, open et cetera *noun* a fruit of the **medlar** tree (*RJ ii 1*)

open-eyed *adjective* vigilant (*T ii 1*)

operant *adjective* active (*H iii 2*)

operation *noun* the ability to do something (*AC iv 15*)

operative *adjective* able to function (*KL iv 4*)

opinion *noun* **1.** public opinion (*1H4 iii 2*; *2H4 v 2*; *O i 3*) **2.** a reputation (*MV i 1*; *1H4 v 4*; *O ii 3*) **3.** arrogance (*1H4 iii 1*; *AC ii 1*) **4.** criticism (*O iv 2*)

oppose against *verb* to resist something (*WT v 1*; *R2 iii 3*; *KL iv 2*; *H iii 1*)

opposed *noun* an opponent (*H i 3*) ■ *adjective* opposite (*MV ii 9*; *1H4 iii 1*)

opposeless *adjective* too powerful to resist (*KL iv 6*)

opposite *noun* an opposing force (*TN iii 4*; *R3 v 4*; *KL v 3*) ■ *adjective* hostile (*TN ii 5*; *R3 ii 2, iv 4*; *O i 2*)

oppress *verb* to distress someone (*KL v 3*)

oppressed *adjective* distressed (*H i 2*)

oracle *noun* a wise person (*R3 ii 2*; *T iv 1, v 1*)

orb *noun* a dark circle appearing in grass, produced by the growth of mushrooms (*MND ii 1*)

orbed continent *noun* the sun (*TN v 1*)

ordain *verb* 1. to establish something (*TS iii 1*) 2. to design something (*RJ iv 5*)

order *noun* 1. the way in which something occurs (*2H4 iv 4*; *JC i 2, iii 1*) 2. suitable arrangements for doing something (*MM ii 2*; *R2 v 1*; *O v 2*) 3. a plan or method for doing something (*H5 iii 2*; *M v 6*)

ordinance *noun* 1. normal behaviour (*JC i 3*; *H5 ii 4*) 2. a decree (*KL iv 1*; *R3 iv 4, v 5*) 3. *see* **ordnance**

ordinant *adjective* providing for the future (*H v 2*)

ordinary *noun* a meal (*AC ii 2*)

ordinate *adjective* directed (*H v 2*)

ordnance *noun* cannon (*H v 2*; *TS i 2*; *H5 ii 4, iii Chor.*)

orient *adjective* of high quality, like pearls from the Far East (the Orient) (*MND iv 1*; *R3 iv 4*; *AC i 5*)

orison *noun* a prayer (*H5 ii 2*)

Orpheus *noun* in Greek mythology, a poet and musician who could bring inanimate objects to life with his music (*MV v 1*)

ort *noun* a piece of leftover food (*JC iv 1*)

orthography *noun* correct or precise spelling or speaking (*MA ii 3*)

osier *noun* a type of willow used especially for making baskets, etc. (*AYLI iv 3*; *RJ ii 3*)

ostent, ostentation *noun* a display (*MV ii 8*)

othergates *adverb* in a very different way (*TN v 1*)

otherwhere *noun* elsewhere (*CE ii 1*)

ouch *noun* an ornament or jewel (*2H4 ii 4*)

ought *adjective* owed (*1H4 iii 3*)

ounce *noun* a lynx or snow leopard (*MND ii 2*)

ousel *noun* a blackbird (*MND iii 1*; *2H4 iii 2*)

out

COMMENT: *Out* has always performed different functions as a preposition, but its adverbial use was also common and varied in Shakespeare's time. An actor would be described as *out* when he forgot his lines and Leontes in **The Winter's Tale** declares 'O, I am out', meaning 'mistaken', when he alters a word in his attack on Hermione. Sometimes the adverbial *out* requires the verb to be understood, as in **The Merchant of Venice** when Jessica tells Lorenzo that 'Launcelot and I are out', meaning 'fallen out or quarrelled'. In **Henry IV Part 2** a servant 'will not out', in the sense of 'drop out' or leave his master. Today too we use the adverb in an almost wholly verbal sense when gay people urge others to *out* themselves, to acknowledge their homosexuality. *Out* was also a very common exclamation, expressing frustration. In **The Taming of the Shrew** Petruchio is irritated with his servant: 'Out, you rogue! You pluck my foot awry'. Dromio in **The Comedy of Errors** complains, 'Out on thy mistress! I know not thy mistress'.

outbrave *verb* to be braver than someone (*MV ii 1*)

outbreathed *adjective* out of breath (*2H4 i 1*)

outdare *verb* to face something bravely (*R2 i 1*; *1H4 v 1*)

out-dwell *verb* to stay past a particular time (*MV ii 6*)

outface *verb* to defy someone (*AYLI i 3*; *H v 1*; *MV iv 2*)

outfacing *noun* bullying (*MA v 1*)

outjest *verb* to ease something by making a joke of it (*KL iii 1*)

outnight *verb* to mention more nights than someone (*MV v 1*)

outside *noun* outer clothes (*WT iv 4*)

outsleep *verb* to sleep past a particular time (*MND v 1*)

outsport *verb* to go beyond the accepted limits in playing the fool (*O ii 3*)

outstretched *adjective* bloated (*H ii 2*)

outstrike *verb* to strike more rapidly than something (*AC iv 6*)

out-vie *verb* to beat someone by playing a higher card (*TS ii 1*)

out-wall *noun* the exterior (*KL iii 1*)

outwards *adverb* externally (*H ii 2*)

outwork *verb* to be of superior workmanship than something (*AC ii 2*)

overbear *verb* **1.** to flood something (*MND ii 1*) **2.** to suppress something (*MA ii 3*; *H5 iv Chor.*)

overblown *adjective* passed over (*T ii 2*; *TS v 2*; *R2 iii 2*)

over-cloyed *adjective* having eaten too much (*R3 v 3*)

overcome *verb* to take someone by surprise (*M iii 4*)

over-count *verb* **1.** to outnumber someone (*AC ii 6*) **2.** to cheat someone (*AC ii 6*)

over-eye *verb* to observe something critically (*TS Ind. 1*)

over-flourish *verb* to decorate something elaborately (*TN iii 4*)

overflow *noun* an excess (*MA i 1*; *R2 v 3*)

overflown *adjective* covered (*MND iv 1*)

over-fraught *adjective* heavily laden (*M iv 3*)

overgo *verb* to exceed something (*R3 ii 2*)

overlive *verb* to survive something (*2H4 iv 1*)

overlook *verb* **1.** to look down on something (*H5 iii 5*) **2.** to examine something (*H5 ii 4*; *H iv 6*)

overpeer *verb* **1.** to be superior to someone (*MV i 1*) **2.** to rise high above something (*H iv 5*)

overplus *noun* a surplus (*AC iii 7*)

over-posting *verb* to get over easily (*2H4 i 2*)

over-read *verb* to read through something (*MM iv 2*)

over-red *verb* to colour something red (*M v 3*)

over-scutched *adjective* worn out by beatings (*2H4 iii 2*)

overset *verb* to turn something upside down (*RJ iii 5*)

overshine *verb* to surpass someone in a quality

over-shot *adjective* inaccurate (*H5 iii 7*; *JC iii 2*)

overswear *verb* to swear something again (*TN v 1*)

over-topping *noun* the fact of being too ambitious (*T i 2*)

overture *noun* **1.** the revealing of something (*WT ii 1*; *KL iii 7*) **2.** a declaration (*TN i 5*)

overwatch *verb* to stand guard all night (*MND v 1*)

overween *verb* to be arrogant (*2H4 iv 1*)

overwhelming *adjective* overhanging (*RJ v 1*)

overworn *adjective* overused (*TN iii 1*)

Ovid *noun* (43BC –17 AD) a Roman writer, exiled to live amongst the Goths. He is known for his love poems and his works were very popular during the 16th and 17th centuries and greatly influenced contemporary writers such as Shakespeare. (*AYLI iii 3*; *TS i 1*) (NOTE: His full name was Publius Ovidus Naso.)

owe *verb* **1.** to experience an emotion (*AYLI iii 2*; *TN ii 4*) **2.** to have a purpose (*WT iv 4*) **3.** to have complete self-control (*T v 1*)

ox *noun* a fool

Oxford *noun* a city situated between the Rivers Thames and Cherwell. It has been an important commercial centre since pre-medieval times and the site of a university since the 13th century. (*2H4 iii 2*; *R3 ii 1, iv 5, v 3*)

oyster-wench *noun* a woman selling oysters (*R2 i 4*)

P

pace *noun* a way of walking (*R2 v 2*) ■ *verb* to train a horse (*MM iv 3*; *AC ii 2*) ◇ **hold me pace** keep up with me (*1H4 iii 1*)

pack *noun* a gang (*CE iii 2, v 1*; *R3 iii 3*; *KL v 3*) ■ *verb* **1.** to be part of a plot (*CE v 1*; *MA v 1*; *H iii 4*) **2.** to shuffle cards unfairly (*AC iv 12(14)*) **3.** to be off (*CE iii 2*) **4.** to load something (*1H4 ii 1*; *2H4 iv 5*)

packhorse *noun* a menial servant (*R3 i 3*) [From *packhorse*, 'a horse used for carrying loads'.]

packing *noun* plotting (*TS v 1*; *KL iii 1*)

packthread *noun* string for tying up parcels (*TS iii 2*; *RJ v 1*)

paction *noun* a pact (*H5 v 2*)

paddle *verb* to stroke with the fingers (*WT i 2*; *H iii 4*; *O ii 1*)

paddock *noun* **1.** a toad (*H iii 4*) **2.** a familiar spirit like a toad (*M i 1*)

pagan *noun* a prostitute (*2H4 ii 2*)

page *verb* to go after like a page (*T iv 3*)

pageant *noun* **1.** a show or spectacle (*MND iii 2*; *MV i 1*; *AC iv 14*) **2.** deception, a false show (*T iv 1*; *O i 3*) [From *pageant*, 'the cart etc. on which miracle plays were performed'.]

pain *noun* **1.** a punishment (*MM ii 4*; *R2 i 3*) **2.** trouble or effort (*MND v 1*; *R3 iv 4*; *KL iii 1*) ■ *verb* to cause trouble to someone (*MM v 1*)

painful *adjective* laborious (*T iii 1*)

painted *adjective* false (*AYLI ii 1*; *H iii 1*)

painted cloth *noun* a cloth painted with scenes from the Bible, etc. and hung on walls in place of tapestries (*AYLI iii 2*; *2H4 ii 1*)

painting *noun* cosmetics (*WT v 3*)

pair of stairs *noun* a flight of stairs (*AYLI v 2*)

pajock, paiock *noun* a term of abuse (*H iii 2*) [Possibly from 'peacock', a bird which was associated with viciousness in Elizabethan times.]

palabras *plural noun* few words (*MA iii 5*) [From Spanish *pocas palabras*.]

palate *verb* to savour something (*AC v 2*)

pale *noun* **1.** a fence or boundary (*CE ii 1*; *R2 iii 4*; *H i 4*) **2.** an enclosure (*MND ii 1*; *WT iv 3*) **3.** paleness (*WT iv 3*) ■ *verb* **1.** to encircle something (*AC ii 7*) **2.** to make something pale (*H i 5*) ◇ **pale at mine heart** cowardly (*MM iv 3*)

pale-hearted *adjective* cowardly (*M iv 1*)

palfrey *noun* a horse used for riding (*H5 iii 7*)

palisado *noun* a fence of stakes put up as a defence (*1H4 ii 3*)

pall *verb* **1.** to fail (*H v 2*) **2.** to wrap something up (*M i 5*) ◇ **pall'd fortunes** ruined prospects (*AC ii 7*)

pallet *noun* a simple bed, usually filled with straw (*2H4 iii 1*)

palm *noun* a palm leaf as an emblem of victory (*JC i 2*)

palmer *noun* a pilgrim who carried a palm leaf as a sign of having been to the Holy Land (*RJ i 5*)

palm tree *noun* a willow tree, whose branches were used as a substitute for palm leaves (*AYLI iii 2*)

palmy *adjective* victorious (*H i 1*)

palpable *adjective* **1.** able to be seen and touched (*M ii 1*) **2.** obvious (*1H4 ii 4*; *H v 1*; *O i 1*; *R3 iii 6*)

palter *verb* to haggle or stall (*JC ii 1*; *M v 8*; *AC iii 11*)

paltry *adjective* mean (*MV v 1*)

paly *adjective* pale (*RJ iv 1*; *H5 iv Chor.*)

Pandarus *noun* in Greek mythology, the son of Lycaon of Zeleia. He was an ally of the Trojans and fought with them as an archer. (*TN iii 1*)

pander, pandar *noun* a pimp (*MA v 2*; *H5 iv 5*) ■ *verb* to gratify something (*H iii 4*)

pannel *verb* to follow someone submissively, like a dog (*AC iv 12*)

pant *noun* an irregular or fast beating of the heart (*AC iv 8*; *O ii 1*)

pantler *noun* the person in charge of bread and other foodstuffs in a household (*2H4 ii 4*) [From Latin *panis*, 'bread'.]

paper-faced *adjective* having a pale face (*2H4 v 4*)

Paphos *noun* the town in Cyprus where **Venus** was worshipped (*T iv 1*)

paradox *noun* a fact or statement that goes against current thinking (*O ii 1*; *H iii 1*)

paragon *verb* to compare one person with another (*AC i 5*) ■ *noun* a perfect example (*H ii 1*; *T ii 1*) ◇ **to paragon description** to be so perfect that no description could do justice (*O ii 1*)

parallel *verb* **1.** to conform with something (*MM iv 2*) **2.** to make something equal (*M ii 3*) ■ *adjective* having the same purpose (*O ii 3*)

paramour *noun* a lover (*MND iv 2*; *RJ v 3*)

paraquito *noun* a parrot or parakeet (*1H4 ii 3*)

Parca *noun* one of the three **Fates** (*H5 v 1*)

parcel *noun* **1.** a detail (*2H4 iv 2*) **2.** a part (*CE v 1*; *O i 3*) **3.** a group (*MV i 2*) ■ *verb* to add to something (*AC v 2*)

parcel-bawd *noun* a part-time pimp (*MM ii 1*)

parcel-gilt *adjective* partly covered with gold (*2H4 ii 1*)

parcelled *adjective* particular (*R3 ii 2*)

pard *noun* a leopard or panther (*AYLI ii 7*; *T iv 1*)

pardon-me, pardona-mee *noun* someone who is always making excuses (*RJ ii 4*)

'parel *noun* clothing (*KL iv 1*) [Shortening of 'apparel'.]

paring *noun* a small amount trimmed off (*CE iv 3*)

Paris *noun* in Greek mythology, the son of King **Priam** and **Hecuba**. Hecuba believed that her unborn son would destroy his lineage, so when he was born she exposed him on Mount Ida. He was found and brought up by a shepherd. He was asked to make a judgement between the beauty of **Hera**, **Aphrodite** and **Athene**. When he declared in favour of Aphrodite she helped him in the abduction of **Helen** of Troy. He killed **Achilles** at the siege of Troy but was himself wounded by a poisoned arrow fired by Phelactetes.

Paris balls *plural noun* tennis balls (*H5 ii 4*)

parish-top *noun* a spinning top kept to amuse the people of a parish during cold weather (*TN i 3*)

park *noun* an enclosed area of land on which game animals were kept (*1H4 ii 3*; *MND ii 1*; *MV iii 4*; *TS iv 1*)

parle ◇ **brook parle** to allow negotiations to begin (*TS i 1*)

parle(y) *noun* a conversation (*H i 1, i 3*)

parlous *adjective* **1.** dangerous (*MND iii 1*; *R3 iii 1*; *RJ i 3*) **2.** shrewd (*R3 iii 4*)

parmaciti, parmacity, parmaceti *noun* wax from the head of a sperm whale which was mixed with oil and used for healing bruises (*1H4 i 3*)

parrot-teacher *noun* someone who chatters and repeats themselves (*MA i 1*) [From the idea of teaching a parrot to talk.]

partake *verb* **1.** to consume something (*WT ii 1*) **2.** to make something known (*WT v 3*)

parted *adjective* unfocused (*MND iv 1*)

Parthia *noun* an ancient empire corresponding roughly to modern Iraq and Iran (*AC ii 3, iii 1, 6*; *JC v 3*)

Parthian *noun* a fast-running warrior from **Parthia** (*AC i 2, iii 1, iv 1*)

partial ◇ **partial slander** an accusation of being biased in favour of something (*R2 i 3*)

partialize *verb* to be biased in favour of something (*R2 i 1*)

particular *noun* **1.** a detail (*2H4 iv 4*; *H ii 2*) **2.** a personal concern (*AC i 3*) ■ *adjective* personal (*MM iv 4*; *2H4 iv 3*; *H5 iii 2, 7*)

particularities *plural noun* small incidents (*H5 iii 2*)

parti-eyed *adjective* with bleeding eyes (*KL iv 1*) [From the idea of the eyes appearing multicoloured.]

partisan, partizan *noun* a long-handled spear with a head having two axes or spikes (*AC ii 7*; *H i 1*)

Partlet *noun* **1.** a 16th-century piece of clothing designed to cover the shoulders and neck **2.** the name of a hen from Chaucer's *Pertelote* in the *Nun's Priest's Tale* and in the story of *Reynard the Fox*, so called from her ruff (*WT ii 3*; *1H4 iii 3*)

party-verdict *noun* a part played by an individual in making a decision (*R2 i 3*)

pash *noun* the head (*WT i 2*)

pashful *adjective* bashful (*H5 iv 8*)

pass *noun* **1.** a difficult situation (*CE iii 1*; *TS v 2*; *KL iii 4*) **2.** a licence (*MM i 3*) **3.** an error of judgement (*MM v 1*) **4.** a journey (*H ii 2*; *H5 ii Chor.*) **5.** a thrust in fencing (*TN iii 4*; *H v 2*) ■ *verb* **1.** to die (*KL iv 6*) **2.** to exceed something (*MM iv 6*; *H i 2*) **3.** to go through something (*JC i 1*; *M iii 1*; *O i 3*) **4.** to hand over something (*TS iv 4*) **5.** to carry out something (*TS iv 4*) **6.** to pass judgement (*MM ii 1*; *KL iii 7*) **7.** to make a promise (*TN i 5*; *R2 v 3*) **8.** to make a witty remark (*TN iii 1*; *H v 2*) ◇ **pass upon** to take advantage of someone (*TN v 1*) ◇ **pass of pate** a witty remark (*T iv 1*; *H v 2*)

passado *noun* a fencing thrust made by taking a long pace forward (*RJ ii 4, iii 1*)

passage *noun* **1.** passers-by (*CE iii 1*; *O v 1*) **2.** a journey (*R2 i 3*) **3.** a way, course (*WT iii 2*; *RJ Prol.*) **4.** death (*H iii 3, v 2*) **5.** an incident (*H iv 7*) **6.** an action (*TN iii 2*; *1H4 iii 2*; *H5 iii 6*)

passion *noun* **1.** a moving or emotional speech (*MND v 1*; *H iii 2*) **2.** mental or physical pain (*CE v 1*; *1H4 iii 1*; *M iii 4*) **3.** love **4.** Christ's crucifixion (used in oaths) (*TS iv 1*) ■ *verb* to feel sorrow or to grieve (*T v 1*)

passionate *verb* to express something with feeling (*MND iii 2*; *H ii 2*) ■ *adjective* **1.** sorrowful **2.** compassionate (*R3 i 4*)

passport *noun* a document giving permission to travel large distances within a country (*H5 iv 3*)

passy-measures pavin *noun* a slow formal dance of Spanish origin (*TN v 1*)

paste *noun* a covering of pastry (*KL ii 4*)

pastern *noun* the part of a horse's leg between its hoof and its fetlock (*H5 iii 7*)

pastry *noun* a kitchen where pastry is made (*RJ iv 4*)

pasture ◇ **mettle of pasture** the way you were brought up (*H5 iii 1*)

pat *adverb* exactly (*H iii 3*; *KL i 2*; *MND iii 1, v 1*)

patch *noun* a fool (*T iii 2*; *MND iii 3*; *MV ii 5*) ■ *verb* to make something out of small pieces (*AC ii 2*)

COMMENT: *Patch* was a derogatory term often used for a clown or a jester, whose distinctive clothing would

often be made of colourful patches of cloth. The Commedia dell'Arte Harlequin wears a stylish version of patchwork. An alternative origin may be the Italian 'pazzo', meaning 'a fool'. Caliban in **The Tempest** abuses Trinculo the clown as 'Thou scurvy patch'. But the word could be used for low-class fellows who were not professional jesters. In **The Merchant of Venice**, Shylock, with a mixture of indulgence and exasperation, refers to Launcelot: 'The patch is kind enough, but a huge feeder'. Puck, in **A Midsummer Night's Dream** describes Bottom and his friends as 'a crew of patches, rude mechanicals'. Spenser in the 1590s used 'patchocks' to describe low-class Irishmen and Hamlet may be using a version of this word in his over-excited singing after the King has been disturbed by the play: Jove has been usurped and in his place 'now reigns here/A very, very – pajock'.

patched fool *noun* a jester (*MND iv 1*)

pate ◇ **knotty pated** stupid (*1H4 ii 4*)

paten *noun* a thin plate of silver or gold (*MV v 1*)

path *verb* to walk (*JC ii 1*)

pathetical *adjective* contemptible (*AYLI iv 4*)

pattern *noun* an example to follow (*H5 ii 4*) ■ *verb* to be a pattern for something (*MM ii 1*)

pattle *noun* a battle (*H5 iv 7*)

paucas pallabris, porcas palabras *phrase* few words (*TS Ind. 1*)

pauca verba *phrase* Latin few words

paunch *noun* the stomach (*1H4 ii 4*) ■ *verb* to stab in the stomach (*T iii 2*)

pauser *noun* someone who delays (*M ii 3*)

paved bed *noun* a grave covered by a stone slab (*MM v 1*)

pavilion *noun* a large elaborate tent (*H5 i 2, iv 1*)

pavilioned *adjective* set up in pavilions (*H5 i 2*)

pawn *noun* **1.** a glove or other object thrown down as a challenge to fight (*R2 i 1*) **2.** a bet (*KL i 1*) ■ *verb* **1.** to bet or risk something (*WT ii 3*; *MV iii 5*) **2.** to lose something as if in a bet (*R3 iv 4*; *AC i 4*)

pax *noun* a small silver or gold plate engraved with an image of Jesus' crucifixion (an osculatory). It was kissed by people during Mass. (*H5 iii 6* – *Pistol may mean a 'pix' – a small box for carrying the consecrated bread from the Mass*)

pay home *verb* to fully repay something (*WT v 3*; *1H4 i 3*)

peace *verb* to be silent (*T ii 1*; *R2 v 2*; *KL iv 6*) ◇ **keep peace between** to keep one thing separate from another (*M i 5*) ◇ **the peace** the peace of the kingdom, maintained by royal authority (*2H4 iii 2*)

peach *verb* to accuse someone of something, especially a person of high rank or authority (*1H4 ii 2*)

peacock *noun* the showy plumage of the male is used as a symbol of pride (*H5 iv 1*; *T iv 1*)

peak *verb* **1.** to mope about (*H ii 2*) **2.** to grow thin (*M i 3*)

pear *verb* to bear (*H5 iv 8*)

pearl ◇ **kingdom's pearl** the finest members of the nobility (*M v 7*)

peascod *noun* a pea pod (*AYLI ii 4*; *KL i 4*; *TN i 5*)

peascod time *noun* early summer (*2H4 ii 4*) [Referring to the time when peas are growing in their pods.]

pease *plural noun* peas (*T iv 1*)

peat *noun* a darling (*TS i 1*) ■ *verb* to beat (*H5 v 1*)

peculiar *adjective* belonging to you (*H iii 3*; *MM i 2*; *O i 1, iii 3*)

pedant *noun* a teacher (*TN iii 2*; *TS iii 1, iv 2*)

pedascule *noun* a little **pedant** (*TS iii 1*)

pedlar, pedler *noun* someone who travels from place to place carrying a bundle of goods for sale (*TS Ind. 2*)

peer *verb* to appear (*WT iv 3*; *H5 iv 7*)

peerless *adjective* unequalled (*AC i 1*; *M i 4*; *T iii 1*)

peg *noun* the pin holding the string of a musical instrument (*O ii 1*) ■ *verb* to wedge something (*T i 2*)

Peg-a-Ramsey *noun* a popular ballad and dance tune about a woman who interfered with other people's enjoyment (*TN ii 3*)

Pegasus *noun* in Greek mythology, a winged horse, ridden by Perseus (*H5 iii 7*; *TS iv 4*)

peise *verb* to make something heavy and so slow it down (*MV iii 2*) ◇ **peise down** to weigh someone down (*R3 v 3*)

pelf *noun* possessions

pelican *noun* a mythical bird believed to feed its young with blood from its own breast (*H iv 5*; *KL iii 4*) (NOTE: For Christians, it is an emblem of Christ, representing his self-sacrifice. It is also an emblem of piety.)

Pelion *noun* a mountain in central Greece (*H v 1*) (NOTE: In Greek mythology, the giants placed Mount Ossa on Mount Pelion in an attempt to reach the heavens.)

pell-mell *adjective* (of fighting) disorganised or hand-to-hand (*KL iv 6*)

pelt *verb* to throw something (*O ii 1*)

pelting *adjective* of little importance (*MND ii 1*; *MM ii 2*; *R2 ii 1*; *KL ii 3*)

pen *noun* a penis (*MV v 1*)

pencil *noun* an artist's paintbrush (*RJ i 2*)

pendulous *adjective* suspended above (*KL iii 4*)

penetrative *adjective* affecting the deepest emotions (*AC iv 14*)

pennon *noun* a banner (*H5 iii 5*)

pennyworth *noun* a bargain (*MA ii 3*; *WT iv 4*)

pensioner *noun* a bodyguard to the monarch (*MND ii 1*)

pent *adjective* imprisoned (*R3 i 4, iv 1, 3*)

Pentecost *noun* Whitsuntide (forty days after Easter), when the cycle of **mystery plays** was performed (*CE iv 1*)

Penthesilea *noun* in Greek mythology, the queen of the **Amazons** who was killed by Achilles (*TN ii 3*)

penthouse *noun* a small building with a sloping roof, attached to the main building (*MA iii 3*; *MV ii 6*)

penthouse lid *noun* an eyelid (*M i 3*)

pepper *verb* to defeat someone decisively (*TN iii 4*)

peppercorn *noun* **1.** the seed of the pepper plant (*1H4 iii 2*) **2.** something insignificant (*1H4 iii 3*)

pepper-gingerbread *noun* a highly-spiced ginger cake (*1H4 iii 1*)

perch *noun* a measure of land (5.03 metres) (*JC v 1*; *MM ii 1*)

perdu *noun* a sentry in an outlying and therefore dangerous position, who might have little hope of surviving (*KL iv 7*) [French, 'lost'.]

perdurable *adjective* everlasting (*H5 iv 5*; *O i 3*)

perdurably *adverb* for ever (*MM iii 1*)

peremptorily *adverb* decisively (*1H4 ii 4*)

peremptory *adjective* determined (*1H4 i 3*; *H5 v 2*; *TS ii 1*)

perfect *verb* 1. to inform someone about something (*MM iv 3*) 2. to carry out something (*H5 i 1*) ■ *adjective* 1. sound (*CE v 1*; *KL iv 7*) 2. correct (*2H4 iii 1*; *M iii 1*) 3. expert (*1H4 iii 1*; *M iv 2*) 4. fully satisfied (*M iii 4*) 5. certain (*WT iii 3*; *M i 5*) 6. mature (*KL i 2*) 7. ready, prepared (*MM v 1*) ◇ **perfect soul** a clear conscience (*O i 2*)

perfected *verb* skilled (*H5 i 1*; *T i 2*)

perfection *noun* a performance (*MM iii 1*)

perfectness *noun* fullness (*2H4 iv 4*)

perfumer *noun* someone who freshens rooms with perfume (*MA i 3*)

Perigenia *noun* in Greek mythology, the woman loved by King Theseus (*MND ii 1*)

perilous *adjective* 1. cunning (*R3 iii 1*) 2. alarming (*RJ i 3*)

period *noun* a full stop (*MND v 1*)

periwig-pated *adjective* wearing a wig (*H iii 2*)

pernicious *adjective* 1. destructive (*H i 5*; *M iv 3*; *MM ii 4, v 1*; *RJ i 1*) 2. deadly (*KL iii 2*)

perpend *verb* to consider something (*TN v 1*; *H ii 2*; *H5 iv 4*; *AYLI iii 2*)

perpetual wink *noun* death (*WT i 2*)

persever *verb* to continue trying to do something (*AYLI v 2*; *CE ii 2*; *MND iii 2*)

Persian *adjective* richly decorated (*KL iii 6*)

personage *noun* a person's appearance (*MND iii 2*; *TN i 5*)

personal *adjective* physical (*2H4 iv 4*; *JC i 3*)

personate *verb* to describe someone (*TN ii 3*)

perspective *noun* 1. glasses or mirrors cut so as to reflect something as an optical illusion (*TN v 1*) 2. an optical illusion (*H5 v 2*) 3. a picture that makes sense only from a particular angle (*R2 ii 2*)

perspectively *adverb* as if an optical illusion (*H5 v 2*)

persual *noun* a detailed examination (*H ii 1*)

persuasion *noun* 1. a belief or principle (*MND i 1*; *MM iv 1*) 2. the ability to persuade someone (*TN iii 4*)

pert *adjective* cheeky (*MND i 1*)

perturbation *noun* a disturbance (*2H4 i 2, iv 5*; *M v 1*; *MA i 1*)

peseech *verb* to plead with someone (*H5 v 1*) [Alteration of 'beseech'.]

petar *noun* a box containing explosives, used for blowing out doors, etc., rather like a modern hand grenade (a **petard**) (*H iii 4*)

petition *noun* a section of a prayer (*MM i 2*) ■ *verb* to beg for something (*AC i 2*)

petitionary *adjective* begging (*AYLI iii 2*)

pettiness *noun* insignificance (*H5 iii 6*)

pettitoes *plural noun* pig's feet (used as an insult) (*WT iv 3*)

pew *noun* a bench (*KL iii 4*)

pew-fellow *noun* a companion (*R3 iv 4*)

phantasma *noun* a nightmare (*JC ii 1*)

Pharamond *noun* according to the legends of King Arthur, he was the king of the Franks (5th century) and a knight of the Round Table (*H5 i 2*)

Pharaoh *noun* the king of Egypt (*1H4 ii 4*; *MA iii 3*)

Phebe *verb* to treat someone cruelly, like **Phebe** (*AYLI iv 3*)

Philemon *noun* in Roman mythology, a peasant who entertains Jupiter (*MA ii 1*)

Philip and Jacob *noun* the feast of St Philip and St James (1 May) (*MM iii 2*)

Philippi an important city and cultural centre in Macedonia

Philomel(a) A nightingale (NOTE: In Greek mythology, Philomel was turned into a nightingale by the gods after she was raped and had her tongue cut out by Tereus, king of Thrace.)

Phoebe *noun* in Greek mythology, a female Titan and daughter of Uranus and Gaea (*MND i 1*) (NOTE: She is equated with the Roman goddess Diana.)

Phoebus, Phibbus *noun* the Roman god of the sun, or **Apollo**

phoenix *noun* in ancient Egyptian mythology, a bird which burnt itself every 500 years and rose again from its own ashes (*AYLI iv 3*; *T iii 3*) (NOTE: It was a symbol of immortality and uniqueness.)

Phrygia *noun* an ancient region located in what is present-day Turkey, bordered by the Mediterranean in the south and the Black Sea in the north (*TN iii 1*)

physic *noun* a medicine (*2H4 i 1, iv 5*; *AYLI iii 2*; *H iii 3*; *KL iii 4*; *M v 1*; *RJ i 5*, *ii 3*; *TN ii 3*) ■ *verb* to heal something or keep someone healthy (*AYLI i 1*; *M ii 3*)

physical *adjective* good for the health (*JC ii 1*)

pia mater *noun* the whole brain (technically, the membrane covering the brain) (*TN i 5*)

pibble *noun* a pebble (*H5 iv 1*)

pick *verb* to throw something (*JC ii 1*)

picked *adjective* **1.** fussy (*1H4 iii 2*; *H ii 2*) **2.** excessively concerned with your appearance (*H v 1*)

pickers *plural noun* thieves, possibly hands (*H iii 2*)

pick-lock *noun* a tool for picking locks (*MM iii 2*)

pick-thank *noun* a gossip (*1H4 iii 2*)

pie *noun* the book of rules determining the Church service for the day (*2H4 v 1*) [From the black and white of the pages.]

piece *noun* **1.** a coin (*T ii 2*; *1H4 ii 4*) **2.** a masterpiece (*H ii 2*) **3.** a work of art such as a sculpture or painting (*WT v 2*) **4.** a container for wine **5.** an excellent person (*T i 2*) **6.** a person (*WT iv 4*) ■ *verb* **1.** to add to something (*L i 1*; *AC i 5*) **2.** to encourage someone or something **3.** to mend something

pied *adjective* made up of different colours (*MV i 3*)

piedness *noun* the fact of being made up of different colours (*WT iv 4*)

pied ninny *noun* a court jester dressed in a multi-coloured costume (*T iii 2*)

pigeon- liver'd *adjective* docile (*H ii 2*)

pight *adjective* determined (*KL ii 1*)

Pigmies *noun* a legendary race of dwarfs (*MA ii 1*)

pignuts *plural noun* peanuts (*T ii 2*)

Pigrogromitus *noun* an invented name of a star (*TN ii 3*)

pike *noun* **1.** the spike in the centre of a small shield (*MA v 2*) **2.** a long spear carried by foot-soldiers. The bases of the pikes were pushed into the ground in front of the archers to form a defensive barrier against cavalry. (*H5 iv 1*) **3.** a penis (*2H4 ii 4*)

pilcher *noun* **1.** a scabbard for a sword or dagger (*RJ iii 1*) **2.** a pilchard (a type of fish) (*TN iii 1*)

pill *verb* **1.** to steal something (*R2 ii 1*; *R3 i 3*) **2.** to strip the bark off a stick (*MV i 3*)

pillage *noun* stolen items (*H5 i 2*)

pillicock *noun* a penis (*KL iii 4*)

pin *noun* the centre of a target, the bull's eye (*R2 iii 2*; *RJ ii 4*)

pin and web *noun* an eye disease (possibly a cataract) (*WT i 2*; *KL iii 4*)

pinch *noun* a feeling of sadness or remorse (*T v 1*; *KL ii 4*) ■ *verb* to harass someone (*T v 1*; *TS ii 1*; *1H4 i 3*; *AC i 7*)

pinched *adjective* afflicted (*WT ii 1*)

pinch-spotted *adjective* bruised by being pinched (*T iv 1*)

pinfold *noun* an enclosure for cattle that have strayed (*KL ii 2*)

pinion *noun* the flight-feather of a bird's wing (*AC iii 12*)

pink *noun* the best example of something (*RJ ii 4*)

pink eyne *plural noun* half-shut eyes (*AC ii 7*)

pioned *adjective* possibly dug out as a trench, or covered with wild orchids (*T iv 1*) (NOTE: Orchids were known as *pinions* in Stratford (Shakespeare's birthplace).)

pip *noun* a symbol on a playing card (*TS i 2*)

pipes of corn *noun* a musical instrument made from oat, etc. stalks (*MND ii 1*)

piping *adjective* shrill (*MND ii 1*)

piping times *plural noun* times of rural calm (*R3 i 1*)

pippin *noun* a type of apple (*2H4 v 3*)

pire *verb* to peer at something (*MV i 1*)

pismire *noun* an ant (*1H4 i 3*)

pit *noun* a covered hole in the ground forming a trap for animals or enemies (*JC v 5*)

pitch *noun* something evil (*O ii 3*) [From *pitch* meaning 'thick, dark sticky tar or asphalt'.]

pitch and pay *phrase* to pay as you go (*H5 ii 3*)

pitcher *noun* an earthenware jug with handles (*TS iv 4*; *R3 ii 4*)

pith *noun* **1.** vigour (*O i 3*; *H5 iii Chor.*) **2.** importance (*H iii 1*)

pizzle *noun* a penis (*1H4 ii 4*) (NOTE: A dried bull's penis was sometimes used as a whip and might therefore suggest 'thinness'.)

place ◇ **pride of place** the height from which a hawk suddenly flies at its prey (*M ii 4*)

place of resort *noun* a brothel (*MM ii 2*)

plack *adjective* black (*H5 iv 7*)

plackett, placket *noun* a petticoat, or an opening in a petticoat, used to suggest the female genitals (*WT iv 4*; *KL iii 4*)

plain *adjective* **1.** honest or open (*CE ii 2*; *R3 i 1*) **2.** nothing else but (*T v 1*) ■ *verb* to complain about something (*KL iii 1*)

plaining *noun* a complaint (*CE i 1*; *R2 i 3*)

plainness *noun* honesty (*TS iv 4*; *H5 i 2*)

plainsong *noun* a simple song (*MND iii 1*) ◇ **very plainsong** the simple truth (*H5 iii 2*)

plaint *noun* an expression of grief (*R2 v 3*)

plaited *adjective* folded (*KL i 1*)

planched *adjective* made of planks (*MM iv 1*)

plant *noun* the sole of the foot (*AC ii 7*) ■ *verb* to found something (*R2 v 1*)

plantain *noun* a common weed with leaves that lie flattened on the ground. The leaves were used to heal wounds. (*RJ i 2*)

plantation *noun* a settlement of people (*T ii 1*)

plash *noun* a pool (*TS i 1*)

plaster *noun* a dressing for a wound (*MND iii 1*; *T ii 1*)

plate *noun* a coin (*AC v 2*) ■ *verb* to wear armour (*R2 i 3*; *KL iv 6*) ◇ **plated Mars** ready for battle (*AC i 1*)

platform *noun* a gun platform in a fort (*H i 2*; *O ii 3*)

plausible *adjective* willing (*MM iii 1*)

plausive *adjective* pleasing (*H i 4*)

played home *adjective* played to a finish (*WT i 2*)

play off *verb* to drink something in one gulp (*1H4 ii 4*)

pleached *adjective* **1.** made out of interwoven branches (*MA i 2*) **2.** folded (*MA iii 1*; *AC iv 12 (14)*)

pleasing *noun* pleasantness (*R3 i 1*)

pleasure *noun* **1.** desire (*T i 2*; *MM i 1*) **2.** a park (*JC iii 2*) ■ *verb* to please someone ◇ **speak one's pleasure** to express something freely

pledge *noun* **1.** bail (*R2 v 2*) **2.** somebody who agrees to pay somebody else's bail (*TS i 2*) **3.** a drinking toast (*JC iv 3*; *H i 4*; *M iii 4*) ■ *verb* to drink a toast to someone (*AC ii 7*)

plenty *noun* the necessities of life (*H5 v 2*) ■ *adjective* plentiful (*T iv 1*; *1H4 ii 4*)

pless ◇ **God pless** God bless (*H5 iii 6*; *H5 iv 7*; *H5 v 1*)

pleurisy *noun* an excess of something (*H iv 7*)

pliant *adjective* suitable (*O i 3*)

plight *noun* a promise (*KL i 1*) ■ *verb* to promise something (*TN iv 3*; *KL iii 4*)

plighted *adjective* pleated (*KL i 1*)

plod *verb* to move or work slowly (*H5 ii 1*)

plood *noun* blood (*H5 iv 7*)

plow *noun* a blow (*H5 iv 8*) ■ *verb* to blow (*H5 iii 2*)

pluck *verb* **1.** to pull something in a particular direction (*R2 v 2*; *H5 iv Chor.*) **2.** to incite someone to do something (*R3 iv 2*) ◇ **pluck a crow together** to settle a matter (*CE iii 1*) ◇ **pluck up** to rouse yourself (*MA v 1*)

plue *adjective* blue (*H5 iii 6*)

plume *noun* feathers collectively (*T iii 3*)

plume- plucked *adjective* humbled (*R2 iv 1*) [From the idea of having had feathers pulled out.]

plume up *verb* to dress up, to decorate with feathers (*O i 3*)

plummet *noun* a plumb line, a weight attached to a rope used to measure the depth of the sea (*T iii 3, v 1*)

plural

COMMENT: A minor example of the Elizabethan freedom with language – to adapt existing words and to invent new ones – appears in Shakespeare's occasional use of unfamiliar plurals. Shylock in **The Merchant of Venice** is a notable example, when he speaks of his 'monies', when 'money' is the generally unchanging form of the word. He also speaks of 'muttons, beefs and goats'. Both examples occur in his first scene with Antonio and Bassanio; he plays with their awkward responses to him and with his position as an alien Jew in Christian Venice, and so Shakespeare may have wanted an unfamiliar linguistic style to add to these effects. In **Julius Caesar** Brutus speaks of his 'behaviours', when the singular form of 'behaviour' would be generally used. Macbeth, referring to his enemies, acknowledges that 'Revenges burn in them', though perhaps the unusual plural form adds here to the extremes of danger and morality in this play. Sometimes

Shakespeare created unusual or superfluous plurals, and other linguistic eccentricities, to denote regional dialects: 'disparagements', and even 'melancholies', in a Welshman's speech. Often these are for comic effect. However, one must also acknowledge that printing errors were common and that these may account for some oddities in language.

Pluto *noun* in Roman mythology, the god of the underworld and the controller of dead people before they went to Elysium or Tartarus (Hades) (*2H4 ii 4*)

pocketing up *noun* the act of putting up with something (*H5 iii 2*)

pocket up *verb* **1.** to put away and ignore something (*T ii 1*; *AC ii 2*) **2.** to put up with something (*1H4 iii 3*)

pocky *adjective* infected with the sexually transmitted disease syphilis (*H v 1*)

pody *noun* a body (*H5 iv 7*)

poem ◇ **poem unlimited** a drama that does not recognise the limitations of time or space (*H ii 2*)

point *noun* **1.** a full stop (*2H4 ii 4*) **2.** a position of advantage (*MND ii 2*) **3.** a conclusion (*MND i 2*) **4.** the pommel of a saddle **5.** one of the laces for holding up a pair of breeches (*TS iii 2*; *2H4 i 1, ii 4*) **6.** a signal given by a blast of trumpets (*2H4 iv 1*) ◇ **at point 1.** ready (*M iv 3*; *H i 2*) **2.** on the point of doing something (*L iii 1*)

point-devise *adjective* precise or perfect (*AYLI iii 2*) ■ *adverb* precisely or perfectly (*TN ii 5*)

poise *noun* the weight of something (*MM ii 4*; *KL ii 1*; *O iii 3*) ■ *verb* **1.** to estimate something (*RJ i 2*) **2.** to balance something (*O i 3*)

poison *verb* to destroy something (*RJ iii 2*; *O v 2*)

poke *noun* a pocket (*AYLI ii 7*)

poking stick *noun* a small stick used for adjusting the pleats in a ruff (*WT iv 4*)

Polack *noun* a native of Poland (*H i 1, ii 2, iv 4, v 2*)

pole *noun* **1.** a military flag (*AC iv 13*) **2.** the pole star (*H i 1*; *AC iv 15*; *O ii 1*) *See also* **poll**

pole-axe, poll-axe *noun* a long-handled weapon with an axe blade and a spike (*AC iv 1*; *M v 8*)

pole-clipt *adjective* pruned (*T iv 1*)

policy of mind *noun* careful thought (*MA iv 1*)

politic *adjective* **1.** cunning (*AYLI iv 1, v 1*; *H iv 3*; *MA v 1*) **2.** prudent (*KL i 1*; *R3 ii 3*) **3.** concerned with politics (*TN ii 5*)

politician *noun* a political schemer (*TN iii 2*; *1H4 i 3*; *KL iv 6*; *H v 1*)

COMMENT: Shakespeare always used the word negatively, often with a harsh adjective. Hotspur in **Henry IV Part 1** refers to the King as 'that vile politician'. King Lear, seeing the world with fresh eyes in Act 4, satirises 'a scurvy politician'. The politics of England under Elizabeth and James I were dangerous and corrupt; those who succeeded often had to conceal, lie and even murder, but they also had to be talented hypocrites to convince people that they were serving their country rather than themselves. The word *politician* has now come full circle – it was possible in the 19th and 20th century for someone to go into politics as an honourable profession, but a recent newspaper survey has given evidence to show that the general public trust politicians as little as estate agents and journalists.

poll *noun* the head (*2H4 ii 4*; *H iv 5*)

pomander *noun* a ball with holes in it, containing a perfumed substance (*WT iv 4*)

pomgarnet *noun* the name of a room in a tavern (*1H4 ii 4*) [From *pomegranate*.]

pomp *noun* a ceremonial procession (*MND i 1*)

Pompey, the Great *noun* (106–48 BC) a Roman triumvir and famous general. He was initially a triumvir with Julius Caesar, but fell out with him. He is famous for his military campaigns in Spain and the East Mediterranean. (*H5 iv 1*; *MM ii 1, ii 2*; *JC i 1, ii 1, v 1*; *AC i 3, 4, ii 1, 2, 7, iii 2, 4*) (NOTE: His full name was **Gnaeus Pompeius Magnus**.)

pompous *adjective* self-important and flamboyant (*AYLI v 4*)

poor John *noun* dried salted hake (a type of fish) (*T ii 2*; *RJ i 1*)

Poperin pear *noun* the penis and scrotum (*RJ ii 1*) [From the shape of a variety of pear from Poperinghe in Flanders, France.]

popinjay *noun* someone who likes fine clothes and talks about trivial things (*1H4 i 3*) [From *popinjay*, 'a parrot'.]

poppy *noun* the drug opium (*O iii 3*)

popular *adjective* of ordinary people (*T i 2*; *H5 iv 1*)

popularity *noun* contact with ordinary people (*1H4 iii 2*; *H5 i 1*)

poring dark *noun* a dim light that makes you strain your eyes (*H5 iv Chor.*)

porn *adjective* born (*H5 iv 7*)

porpentine *noun* a porcupine (*CE iii 1*; *H i 5*)

porridge *noun* a thick soup (*T ii 1*; *CE ii 2*; *KL iii 4*)

porringer *noun* a **porridge** bowl (*TS iv 3*)

port *noun* **1.** a gate, especially in a city's walls (*R2 i 3*; *2H4 iv 5*; *M i 3*; *AC i 3, iv 4*) **2.** a person's way of standing and walking (*AC iv 14*; *H5 Prol.*) **3.** a wealthy lifestyle (*MV i 1, iii 2*; *TS i 1, iii 1*)

portable *adjective* bearable (*KL iii 6*; *M iv 3*)

portage *noun* a ship's porthole (*H5 iii 1*)

portance *noun* a person's way of standing and walking (*O i 3*)

portcullis *verb* to shut something in (*R2 i 3*) (NOTE: A *portcullis* was a wooden or iron gate, used to prevent people entering or leaving a fortified place such as a castle.) [From *portcullis*, 'a heavy grating that slides vertically and acts as a gate'.]

portend *verb* to indicate something (*TN ii 5*)

portly *adjective* **1.** dignified (*MV i 1*; *1H4 i 3*; *RJ i 5*) **2.** swollen (*MV i 3*)

Poseidon *noun* the Greek equivalent of **Neptune**

position *noun* a confirmation of something (*O i 3, ii 1, iii 3*)

positive *adjective* certain (*H5 iv 2*)

positively *adverb* confidently (*R3 iv 2*; *H ii 2*)

possess *verb* to inform someone about something (*MM iv 1*; *TN ii 3*)

possessed *verb* to be passionate about something (*R2 ii 1*)

possession *noun* control by an evil spirit (*CE v 1*)

posset *noun* hot milk curdled with wine, ale, vinegar, etc. This was used as a treatment for colds, etc. (*M ii 2*) ■ *verb* to curdle something (*H i 5*)

possibility *noun* capability (*2H4 iv 3*)

post *noun* **1.** a messenger (*MV v 1*; *M i 3*; *2H4 Ind.*) **2.** a noticeboard (*TN i 5*; *WT iii 2*) **3.** a doorpost of an inn on which the records of customers' accounts were kept (*CE i 2*)

poster *noun* someone who travels quickly (*M i 3*)

postern *noun* a small gate or door at the side of a building (*MM iv 2*)

post-haste *noun* great speed in preparing for something (*H i 1*) ■ *adverb* as quickly as possible (*R2 i 4*; *O i 2*)

posy *noun* an inscription on the inside of a ring (*MV v 1*; *H iii 2*)

pot *noun* a drinking cup ◇ **little pot and soon hot** a proverb meaning 'small people get angry quickly' (*TS iv 1*)

potation *noun* a drink (*2H4 iv 5*; *O ii 3*)

potential *adjective* powerful (*KL ii 1*; *O i 2*)

pothecary *noun* a person who made and sold medicines, etc. (an **apothecary**) (*RJ v 3*)

pother *noun* a commotion (*KL iii 2*)

potting *noun* the act of drinking alcohol (*O ii 3*)

pottle *noun* a large tankard, containing two quarts (2.25 litres) (*O ii 3*)

pottle-deep *verb* to the bottom of the tankard (*O ii 3*)

poulter *noun* someone who sells poultry and game (*1H4 ii 4*)

pouncet-box *noun* a box with a lid with holes in it, containing a perfumed substance (*1H4 i 3*)

powder *verb* to put salt on something (*1H4 v 4*)

powdered *adjective* treated in a **powdering tub** for a sexually transmitted disease (*MM iii 2*)

powdering tub *noun* a tub in which a person sat and sweated, used as a treatment for sexually transmitted diseases (*H5 ii 1*)

poys *plural noun* boys (*H5 iv 7*)

prabbles *plural noun* squabbles (*H5 iv 8*)

practic *adjective* practical (*H5 i 1*)

practice *noun* **1.** a plot (*TN v 1*; *MM v 1*; *KL i 2*; *H iv 7*) **2.** the carrying out of something (*MA v 1*)

practise *verb* **1.** to play a trick on someone (*KL iii 2*) **2.** to plot something (*AYLI i 1*; *H5 ii 2*; *RJ iii 5*; *O i 2*) **3.** to carry out something (*JC iv 3*)

Praeclarissimus filius noster Henricus, Rex Angliae et haeres Fran-

ciae *phrase Latin* our most dear son Henry, King of England and inheritor of France (*H5 v 2*)

praetor *noun* in ancient Rome, a magistrate, ranking next to a consul (*JC i 3, ii 4*)

pragging *noun* bragging (*H5 v 1*)

prain *noun* the brain (*H5 iv 7*)

praise *noun* something worthy of praise (*MV v 1*) ■ *verb* to assess something (*TN i 5; O v 1*) ◇ **praise in departing** praise given at the end of a performance (*T iii 3*)

prank *noun* a cruel trick (*CE ii 2; H iii 4; O ii 1*) ■ *verb* to dress up or ornament something (*TN ii 4; WT iv 4*)

COMMENT: For Shakespeare, as for us, *prank* was a noun meaning 'a mischievous frolic or trick'. In **The Comedy of Errors** Adriana promises to forgive Antipholus 'of a thousand idle pranks'. But he also uses the verb 'to prank' or 'to prank up' in the sense of its German origin, meaning 'display'. Orsino in **Twelfth Night** makes a rare favourable use of the word when giving high praise of Olivia: 'But 'tis that miracle and queen of gems/That nature pranks her in attracts my soul'. But here it may be that Shakespeare wants to alert us, through *prank*, to criticise Orsino's over-readiness with hyperbole. The modest Perdita in **The Winter's Tale** feels awkward at the country festival when she is 'most goddess-like pranked up'. A similar negative sense appears in **Coriolanus** when the arrogant tribunes enjoy their status: 'They do prank them in authority'. This criticism, generally implicit in the verb, extended to the noun, and both verb and noun imply behaving foolishly for an audience. Therefore there is a very uneasy playfulness in **Othello** when Iago characterises the subtle Venetian women: 'In Venice they do let God see the pranks/They dare not show their husbands'. Venice was known as a self-confident city of inventive display, and so even furtive acts of adultery must have some sort of audience!

prate *verb* **1.** to chatter (*CE ii 2; R3 i 3*) **2.** to speak boastfully (*T ii 1; 2H4 iii 2*) **3.** to speak disrespectfully (*O ii 3; O i 2*)

prater *noun* someone who chatters and repeats themselves (*H5 v 2*)

prattle *verb* to chatter (*MM v 1; O i 1, ii 1; TN i 2*)

prave *adjective* brave (*H5 iii 6*)

prawl *verb* to brawl (*H5 iv 8*)

pray *verb* to invite someone (*MM ii 1*)

pray in aid *verb* to ask for the assistance of someone (*AC v 2*)

pread *noun* bread (*H5 v 1*)

precedence *noun* something that has been said before (*AC ii 5*)

precedent *noun* a rough draft (*R3 iii 1*) ■ *adjective* earlier (*H iii 4*)

precept *noun* **1.** an instruction on how to do something (*T iii 1; H ii 2*) **2.** a written command (*2H4 v 1; H5 iii 3*)

preceptial *adjective* instructive (*MA v 1*)

precious *adjective* **1.** absolute (*O v 2*) **2.** valuable (*RJ ii 3*)

preciously *adverb* as though valuable (*T i 2*)

precipitate *verb* to fall head first (*KL iv 6*)

precise *adjective* very correct or moral (*MM i 3, iii 1; 2H4 ii 3*)

pre-contract *noun* an agreement to be married (*MM iv 1*)

predecessor *noun* an ancestor (*H5 i 2; M ii 4*)

predicament *noun* a situation (not necessarily a bad one) (*MV iv 1; 1H4 i 3; RJ iii 3*)

predominant *noun* the highest or most influential position (*M iii 1; RJ ii 3*)

prefer *verb* **1.** to recommend someone or something (*TS i 1*) **2.** to offer for acceptance (*JC iii 1; O i 3*)

preferment *noun* **1.** a preference (*TS ii 1*) **2.** promotion (*R3 i 3; O i 1*)

preformed *adjective* belonging from birth (*JC i 3*)

pregnancy *noun* intelligence, sharpness of wit (*2H4 i 2*)

pregnant *adjective* **1.** obvious (*MM ii 1; WT v 2; AC ii 1; O ii 1*) **2.** compelling (*KL ii 1*) **3.** significant (*H ii 2*) **4.** cunning (*TN ii 2, iii 1; MM i 1*) **5.** responsive (*TN iii 1*) **6.** inclined (*KL iv 6; H iii 2*)

COMMENT: *Pregnant* came from two different sources, which led to two different meanings, both to be found in Shakespeare's time. One, from 'praegnaere' – 'before bearing' – led to our meaning of a woman about to give birth, but this meaning of *pregnant* does not appear in Shakespeare's plays. The other, from the French 'preindre', meant 'evident or convincing'. In **The Winter's Tale** the Gentleman tells of extraordinary events and assures an astonished listener that they are 'Most true, if ever truth were pregnant by circumstance'. Sometimes *pregnant* stretched its meaning to 'alert' or 'resourceful' as in **Twelfth Night** when Viola sees how the devil, or perhaps Cupid, takes advantage of human situations: 'Disguise, I see thou art a wickedness,/Wherein the pregnant enemy does much'. Hamlet uses this sense of readiness when describing flattering courtiers, who 'crook the pregnant hinges of the knee', as they bow, eager to encourage their lord's generosity.

premises *plural noun* conditions (*T i 2*)

prenominate *adjective* previously mentioned (*H ii 1*)

prenzie *adjective see* **precise**

preordinance *noun* a rule already set down (*JC iii 1*)

preparation *noun* a fighting force (*1H4 iv 1*; *O i 3*)

preposterous *adjective* unnatural (*TS iii 1*)

preposterously *adjective* unnaturally (*MND iii 2*; *H5 ii 2*; *O i 3*)

prerogatife, prerogative *noun* precedence (*T i 2*) ■ *plural noun* privileges that go with your rank or position (*TS iii 1*)

prerogatived *adjective* privileged (*O iii 3*)

presage *noun* a feeling that something, especially something bad, is about to happen (*R2 ii 2*)

prescience *noun* the ability to see the future (*AC i 2*)

prescribe *verb* **1.** to limit something (*KL i 2*) **2.** to give orders, to give somebody an order (*R2 i 1*; *KL i 1*)

prescript *noun* an order (*AC iii 8*)

prescript praise, prescribed praise *noun* praise required by the person receiving it (*H5 iii 7*)

presence *noun* **1.** the room where the king saw his courtiers, etc. (*R2 i 3*; *RJ v 3*) **2.** the assembled people (*R2 iv 1*; *H v 2*) **3.** a person or their appearance (*R2 iii 3*; *1H4 iii 2*)

present *noun* **1.** the matter in hand (*MM iv 2*; *TN iii 4*; *AC ii 6*) **2.** the document to hand (*AYLI i 2*) ■ *verb* **1.** to play the part of someone (*T iv 1*; *MND iii 1*) **2.** to describe something (*O i 3*) ■ *adjective* immediate (*RJ iv 1*; *H iv 3*; *AC ii 2*)

presentation *noun* **1.** a disguise (*AYLI v 4*) **2.** an outward show (*R3 iv 4*)

presentment *noun* a portrait (*H iii 4*)

present money *noun* cash (*CE iv 1*; *MV i 1, iii 2*)

president *noun* a ruler (*AC iii 7*)

press *noun* **1.** a warrant giving the authority to force someone into military service (*1H4 iv 2*) **2.** a crowd (*JC i 2*) ■ *verb* **1.** to burden someone (*RJ i 1*; *KL iv 3*; *O iii 4*) **2.** to force someone into military service (*R2 iii 3*; *1H4 iv 2*) **3.** to push forward (*RJ v 3*) **4.** to crowd around someone (*JC ii 4*) ◇ **pressing to death** torture involving heavy stones being placed on the victim's chest (*MA iii 1*; *MM v 1*; *R2 iii 4*)

press-money *noun* money paid to a soldier or sailor when he was forced into military service. His acceptance of the money was taken as an agreement to serve. (*KL iv 6*)

pressure *noun* an impression or mark made by pressing (*H iii 2*)

prest *adjective* ready (*MV i 1*)

Prester John *noun* a legendary Christian priest-king who was believed to rule over a large kingdom of great wealth in Asia or Africa. He was first mentioned during the 12th century but by the 14th century was referred to as the emperor of Ethiopia. (*MA ii 1*)

pretence *noun* an intention or plan (*M ii 3*) ◇ **pretence of danger** an evil intention (*L i 2*)

pretend *verb* **1.** to intend something (*M ii 4*) **2.** to allege something falsely (*MM iii 1*)

prettily *adverb* skilfully (*MND ii 2*; *R3 iii 1*)

prettiness *adjective* pleasantness (*H iv 5*)

pretty *adjective* clever (*H5 i 2*)

Prevailment *noun* influence (*MND i 1*)

prevent *verb* to escape or avoid something (*R2 iii 2*; *2H4 i 2*)

prevention *noun* the act of anticipating and preventing an event (*H5 i 1, ii 2*; *JC i 1, iii 1*)

Priam *noun* in Greek mythology, the king of Troy when it was under siege by the Greeks (*2H4 i 1*; *H ii 2*) (NOTE: Hector was the eldest of his fifty children.)

prick noun a mark on a sundial (*RJ ii 4*)
■ verb to cross someone off a list (*JC iv 1*)

prick-eared adjective having pointed erect ears (*H5 ii 1*)

prick on verb to spur someone on to do something (*R2 iii 3; 1H4 v 1*)

pricksong noun the written part of a song to be sung, rather than the part to be played on an instrument (*RJ ii 4*)

pride noun 1. sexual desire 2. the stamina or health of a horse (*1H4 iv 3*) ◇ **in pride** (of a female animal) on heat (*O iii 3*)

pridge noun a bridge (*H5 iii 6*)

prig noun a thief (*WT iv 2*)

primal adjective first or primitive (*H iii 3; AC i 4*)

prime adjective lecherous (*O iii 3*)

primo, secundo, tertio adjective Latin firstly, secondly, thirdly (*TN v 1*)

primrose path, primrose way noun the way of pleasure (*H i 3; M ii 3*)

primy adjective at its best (*H i 3*)

principal noun someone who commits or who takes part in a crime (*WT ii 1*)

principality noun a person of the highest quality (*AC iii 13*)

princox noun a conceited young man (*RJ i 5*)

pring verb to bring (*H5 v 1*)

print ◇ **in print** with precision

priser noun someone who fights a boxing match in the hope of winning a prize of a sum of money (*AYLI ii 3*)

pristine adjective 1. previous (*M v 3*) 2. ancient (*H5 iii 2*)

private noun 1. privacy (*TN iii 4*) 2. someone who doesn't hold a public position (*H5 iv 1*) 3. sexual organs (*H ii 2*) ■ adjective alone (*RJ i 1*)

privilege noun 1. a justification for something (*MND ii 1*) 2. a right (*R3 iii 1*)

privily adverb secretly (*KL iii 3; MM i 1*)

prize noun 1. an estimate of a thing's value (*AC v 2*) 2. a contest (*MV iii 2*) ■ verb 1. to value something (*T i 2*) 2. to estimate something (*MA iii 1*) 3. to care about something (*TN iii 4; WT iv 4*)

probal adjective reasonable (*O iii 3*)

probation noun 1. proof (*H i 1*) 2. an investigation (*MM v 1; TN ii 5*)

proceed verb 1. to take place (*R3 iii 2; JC i 2*) 2. to be caused by something (*H5 ii 2*)

proceeder noun someone who quickly succeeds in being awarded a university degree (*TS iv 2*)

process noun 1. an account (*MV iv 1; R3 iv 3; H i 5*) 2. a command to do something (*H iv 3*)

process-server noun a sheriff's officer who carries out arrests, etc. (*WT iv 3*)

proclaim verb 1. to make a public announcement (*MM iv 4*) 2. to denounce someone as being someone or something (*MM ii 4; KL ii 3; O i 1*)

procreant noun 1. someone engaged in sexual intercourse (*O iv 5*) 2. a place to lay eggs (*M i 6*)

Procris, Procrus noun in Greek mythology, the wife of Cephalus, to whom he was completely devoted (*MND v 1*)

procure verb 1. to persuade someone to do something (*RJ ii 2*) 2. to bring someone to a place (*RJ iii 5*) 3. to cause something (*MM v 1; KL ii 4*)

prodigal adjective extravagant (*AYLI i 1; H i 1; MV i 1, ii 6*) ■ noun 1. the Prodigal Son (Luke 15) (*CE iv 3*) 2. someone who spends money extravagantly (*1H4 iv 2; MV ii 5, iii 1; TN i 1*)

prodigious adjective ominous (*JC i 3; MND v 1*)

prodigy noun 1. something abnormal (*R2 ii 2*) 2. an omen (*1H4 v 1; JC i 3*)

proface interjection may it do you good (*2H4 v 3*)

profess verb 1. to claim to have knowledge of something (*AYLI iii 2; TS iv 2; 1H4 v 2*) 2. to do something as a business or job (*MM ii 1*)

professed adjective publicly declared (*RJ iii 3*)

professor noun someone who declares their religion openly (*WT v 1*)

proffer verb to offer something (*1H4 i 3, iv 3; R3 iii 7*)

proficient noun someone who learns quickly (*1H4 ii 4*)

profit noun 1. something of benefit or advantage to someone (*MM i 4; O iii 3*) 2. progress or improvement (*AYLI i 1; TS i 1*)

profited adjective efficient (*1H4 i 2*)

profiting noun progress (*1H4 i 2*)

prognostication noun as forecast in the astrological calendar (*WT iv 4*) ◇ **fruitful prognostication** a forecast of future fertility (*AC i 2*)

progress *noun* a journey through the kingdom made by a monarch (*H iv 3*)

prohibit *verb* to permit something (a misuse of the word) (*MA v 1*)

project *noun* an idea (*2H4 i 1; MA iii 1*) ■ *verb* to present something (*AC v 1*)

projection *noun* a design (*H5 ii 4*)

prolixious *adjective* tiresome (*MM ii 4*)

prolixity *noun* **1.** boredom (*RJ i 4*) **2.** tediousness (*MV iii 1*)

prolong *verb* to put something off (*MA iv 1; R3 iii 4*)

Promethean *adjective* life-giving, from fire (*O v 2*) [Referring to *Prometheus*.]

Prometheus *noun* in Greek mythology, a Titan who supported humankind against the gods (*O v 2*) (NOTE: Zeus deprived humans of fire, which Prometheus restored. As a punishment Zeus chained him to a rock and each day his liver was eaten by an eagle, but each night it was restored.)

promise-crammed *adjective* filled with expectation (*H iii 2*)

prompture *noun* the act of prompting (*MM ii 4*)

promulgate *verb* to announce something (*O i 2*)

prone *adjective* eager (*MM i 2*)

pronounce *verb* to deliver a speech (*MV i 2; H iii 2*)

proof *noun* **1.** an experience (*MA ii 1; R3 ii 3*) **2.** a test (*H iv 7; O v 1*) **3.** armour that has been tested to show that it cannot be pierced (*TS ii 1; R2 i 3*) *See also* **lapp'd in proof** *at* **lap 4.** a result (*TS iv 3; 2H4 iv 3*)

proper *adjective* **1.** your own (*T iii 3; MM i 1, 2; 2H4 v 2; H v 5*) **2.** belonging exclusively to someone (*MM v 1; JC i 2; H5 v Chor.*) **3.** handsome (*AC iii 3; O iv 3*) **4.** excellent (*MA iv 1; M iii 4*) **5.** respectable (*2H4 ii 2*) ◇ **proper false** handsome but deceitful (*TN ii 2*)

COMMENT: Our sense of *proper*, meaning 'socially appropriate', reached the language after Shakespeare's time, though Don John comes near to it in **Much Ado About Nothing** when he sneers at Claudio's social ambitions: 'A proper squire!' Shakespeare used *proper* in its original French sense of 'propre', meaning 'particular to oneself', as in **The Tempest** when Ariel mocks the distressed lords: 'And even with suchlike valour men hang and drown/Their

proper selves'. In **Twelfth Night** Olivia promises to pay for a wedding celebration 'Here at my house and at my proper cost'. In both cases we would use 'own'. The word generally carried a favourable sense: Benedick is 'a very proper man'; Poins in **Henry IV Part 1** justifies himself as being 'a proper fellow of my hands', meaning 'capable with his fists'. The noun *property* continues the same meaning. In **Richard II** Scroop comments on how 'Sweet love...changing his property,/Turns to the sourest and most deadly hate'. He is referring to the very core of love's nature. A specialised use of *property*, also used today, appears in Quince's management of the play in **A Midsummer Night's Dream**: 'I will draw a bill of properties such as our play needs'; 'props' are the accessories appropriate for the acting.

properly *adverb* **1.** accurately (*AYLI i 1*) **2.** personally (*WT ii 1*)

propertied *adjective* **1.** treated as property (*TN iv 2*) **2.** having qualities (*AC v 2*)

properties *plural noun* items used on stage in a play ('props') (*MND i 2*)

property *noun* **1.** a distinctive quality (*2H4 iv 3; AYLI iii 2; H ii 2; MND iii 2; O i 1*) **2.** something used to achieve a goal (*JC iv 1*) ■ *verb* to use of something or someone to achieve a goal (*TN iv 2*)

property of blood *noun* a blood relationship (*KL i 1*)

Propontic *noun* the Sea of Marmara, an inland sea in Turkey leading from the Aegean to the Black Sea (*O iii 3*) [From *pro* ('before') + *pont* ('sea').]

proportion *noun* **1.** poetic rhythm (*MM i 2; R2 v 5*) **2.** supplies and soldiers needed for war (*H5 i 2, ii 4; H i 2*) **3.** the shape or appearance of something (*MV iii 4; R3 i 1*) **4.** an adjustment made in proportion to something (*M i 4*) ■ *verb* **1.** to be in proportion to something (*H5 iii 6*) **2.** to make something be in proportion to something (*AC iv 15*) ◇ **first proportion** the greatest (*1H4 iv 1, 4*)

proportioned *adjective* formed (*RJ iii 5*)

propose *noun* a subject of discussion (*MA iii 1*) ■ *verb* to imagine something (*2H4 v 2*)

proposer *noun* someone who suggests something (*H ii 2*)

proposing *noun* the act of talking together (*MA iii 1*; *O i 1*)

propriety *noun* **1.** someone's personality or identity (*TN v 1*) **2.** the normal or accepted condition (*O ii 3*)

prorogue *verb* **1.** to delay something (*RJ iv 1*) **2.** to suspend something, to put something on hold (*AC ii 1*)

proscription *noun* the act of condemning someone to death without a trial (*JC iv 1, 3*)

prosecution *noun* pursuit (*AC iv 14*)

Proserpina *noun* the daughter of **Ceres** and **Jupiter**

prospect *noun* **1.** the ability to appreciate things (*MA iv 1*) **2.** an aspect (*O iii 3*)

Prosperina same as **Diana**

protester *noun* someone who makes a solemn promise (*JC i 2*)

proud *adjective* **1.** noble (*MA iii 1*) **2.** splendid (*KL iii 4*) **3.** pleased (*R2 v 5*) **4.** having an excess of something (*R2 iii 4*) **5.** overflowing (*MND ii 1*)

proudly *adverb* vigorously (*2H4 v 2*)

proverb *verb* (of a proverb) to give advice to someone (*RJ i 4*)

provided *adjective* ready (*R3 iii 1*; *KL ii 4*)

providence *noun* foresight (*H iv 1*)

provident *noun* careful (*TN i 2*; *H5 ii 4*)

providently *adverb* providentially, happening by an act of God (*AYLI ii 8*)

provincial *adjective* from a particular province (*MM v 1*)

Provincial roses *plural noun* rosettes covering the shoelaces (*H iii 2*)

provost *noun* an officer who arrests and keeps someone in custody (*MM i 4*)

prune *verb* (of a bird) to preen its feathers (*1H4 i 1*)

publican *noun* a Jewish tax collector employed by the Romans occupying the Holy Land (*MV i 3*)

publish *verb* **1.** to proclaim a person's character (*TN ii 1*) **2.** to denounce someone as being someone or something (*WT ii 1*)

published *adjective* publicly declared (*KL iv 6*)

Puck *noun* A mischievous (rather than evil) spirit (*MND ii 1, iv 1, v 1*)

pudder *noun* a commotion (*KL iii 2*)

pudding *noun* a mixture of meat, herbs, etc. stuffed into an animal's stomach or intestine to make a large sausage (*1H4 ii 4*; *H5 ii 1*; *O ii 1*)

puddle *verb* to make something impure (*O iii 4*)

puddled *adjective* made muddy (*CE v 1*)

pugging *noun* pulling, tugging, or stealing. The meaning not is clear. (*WT iv 3*)

puisne, puisny *adjective* unskilled (*AYLI iii 4*)

puissance *noun* **1.** power (*H5 iii Chor.*) **2.** an army (*2H4 i 3*; *H5 ii 2*; *KL v 3*)

puissant *adjective* powerful (*H5 i 2*; *KL v 3*)

puke *verb* to vomit (*AYLI ii 7*)

puke-stocking *noun* a fine woollen stocking, black, purple or reddish brown in colour (*1H4 ii 4*)

puling *noun* whimpering (*RJ iii 5*)

pulpit *noun* the platforms for speakers in the ancient Roman **Forum** (*JC iii 1*)

pulpiter *noun* a preacher (*AYLI iii 2*)

pulsidge *noun* a person's pulse (*2H4 ii 4*)

pump *noun* a light shoe (*RJ ii 4*; *TS iv 1*)

punk *noun* a prostitute (*MM v 1*)

punto reverso *noun* a backward thrust in swordfighting (*RJ ii 4*)

purblind *adjective* totally or partially blind (*RJ ii 1*)

purchase *noun* stolen items (*1H4 ii 1*; *H5 iii 2*) ■ *verb* **1.** to obtain something by some means other than by inheriting it (*2H4 iv 5*; *AC i 4*) **2.** to acquire something (*T iv 1*) ◇ **fourteen years purchase** bought at the cost of fourteen years' rent (the normal price was ten years' rent) (*TN iv 1*) ◇ **purchase out** to make amends for something (*RJ iii 1*)

pure *adverb* simply (*TN v 1*)

purgation *noun* the proof of innocence (*AYLI i 3, v 4*; *H iii 2*) [Literally 'clearing the bowels'.]

purge *noun* the act of removing anything unpleasant (*M v 2*) ■ *verb* **1.** to cleanse or detox the body (*1H4 v 4*) **2.** to prove your innocence (*1H4 iii 2*) **3.** to emit something as a discharge (*H ii 2*) **4.** to reactivate something (*AC i 3*)

purger *noun* someone who cures something by flushing out their system (*JC ii 1*)

purlieu *noun* the land on the edge of a forest that was considered to be part of the forest (*AYLI iv 3*)

purport *noun* **1.** an intention (*KL i 4*) **2.** a meaning (*H i 1*)

purpose *noun* **1.** an intention (*MND iv 1*; *1H4 i 1*) **2.** a meaning (*MM ii 4*) **3.** a conversation (*MA iii 1*) **4.** a plan (*1H4 iv 3*; *AC ii 6*) ■ *verb* **1.** to have the intention to do something (*KL ii 4*) **2.** to intend to go somewhere (*AC iii 1*) ◇ **to any purpose** of any importance (*MA v 4*)

purse *verb* to put something in your pocket (*MV i 3*; *AC ii 2*)

purse-bearer *noun* someone who looks after another person's money (*TN iii 3*)

purse-taker *noun* a highwayman (*1H4 i 2*)

pursue *verb* **1.** to wait on someone (*H iii 2*; *AC iii 12*) **2.** to follow something (*R3 ii 3*) **3.** to follow something with a punishment (*MM v 1*) **4.** to carry on with something (*MV iv 1*; *H i 5*; *AC v 2*)

pursuivant *noun* an official ranking below a herald. He was a messenger with the power to arrest with a warrant. (*R3 v 3*)

pursy *adjective* short of breath (*H iii 4*)

purveyor *noun* an officer who went ahead of an army to arrange lodgings, supplies, etc. (*M i 6*)

push *noun* a term of abuse, scoundrel (*MA v 1*) ◇ **stand the push** to face up to an attack by someone (*1H4 iii 2*)

push against *verb* to strike (*WT iii 2*)

put *verb* **1.** to play a trick (*T ii 2*) **2.** to tell someone a piece of news, etc. (*MM ii 2*; *TN v 1*; *H i 3*) **3.** to blame something on someone (*H ii 1*; *M i 7, ii 4*) **4.** to urge someone to do something (*KL ii 1*) **5.** to

force someone to do something (*MM i 1*) **6.** to thrust something (*O v 1*)

put on *verb* to encourage someone to do something bad (*O ii 3*; *KL i 4*)

putter-on *noun* someone who encourages someone to do something bad (*WT ii 1*)

putter-out *noun* someone who invests money to earn interest on it (*T iii 3*) [Literally 'a traveller who laid bets with a dealer that he would return within a stipulated time'.]

put to *verb* to have sexual intercourse (*WT i 2*)

puttock *noun* a long-tailed bird related to the hawk (a **kite**)

put up *verb* to submit to someone (*O iv 2*)

Pygmalion *noun* in Greek mythology, a king of Cyprus who carved a statue of a woman, which the goddess Aphrodite gave life to (*MM iii 2*)

pyramides *plural noun* pyramids (*AC v 2*)

pyramis *noun* a pyramid (*AC ii 7*)

Pyrrhus *noun* in Greek mythology, the son of Achilles, who killed **Priam** (*H ii 2*)

Pythagoras *noun* (c. 582– c. 507 BC) a Greek philosopher and mathematician who believed that a person's soul could pass into the body of an animal after death, and vice versa (*AYLI iii 2*; *MV iv 1*; *TN iv 2*)

Q

Q *interjection* an actor's cue to do something (*R3 iii 4*)

quail *verb* **1.** to ease off (*AYLI ii 2*) **2.** to overpower someone or something (*MND v 1*; *AC v 5*)

quaint *adjective* **1.** elegant (*TS iv 3*; *MA iii 4*) **2.** dainty (*T i 1*; *MND ii 2*) **3.** complicated (*MND ii 1*)

> COMMENT: Shakespeare uses *quaint* in subtly different ways, but almost always signifying approval. When Prospero in **The Tempest** calls Ariel 'quaint', he refers to his ingenuity and skill. Likewise, Portia, preparing her disguise as a man, in **The Merchant of Venice**, plans to 'tell quaint lies' to deceive people cunningly. In **Much Ado About Nothing** Hero's wedding dress is 'a fine, quaint, graceful and elegant fashion', *quaint* implying tasteful intricacy. A rare perjorative use occurs in **Titus Andronicus** when the rapist Demetrius complains about Lavinia's 'quaint hope' in her chastity. Here *quaint* includes the usual sense of intricate, even cunning, because Demetrius would be brutally dismissive of any argument that supports chastity. There may also be a vulgar play on *quaint* as 'cunt', as Marvell uses it 50 years later when in **To His Coy Mistress** he writes of his lady's 'quaint honour'. Perhaps the **Titus** and Marvell uses also include a sense of 'odd and old-fashioned', which is our meaning of *quaint*.

quaintly *adverb* **1.** skilfully (*H ii 1*) **2.** elegantly (*MV ii 4*)

qualification *noun* the true nature of someone or something (*O ii 1*)

qualify *verb* **1.** to moderate something (*MM i 1*; *KL i 2*) **2.** to calm someone down (*WT iv 4*; *MA v 4*) **3.** to reduce something (*H iv 7*) **4.** to dilute something (*O ii 3*)

quality *noun* **1.** a person's character (*MV iv 1*; *2H4 v 2*; *KL ii 4*) **2.** a rank or position (*2H4 iv 1*; *H5 iv 8*; *KL v 3*) **3.** a profession involving acquired skill (*MM ii 1*; *H ii 2*) **4.** a manner (*MV iii 2*; *KL ii 4*) **5.** a political party (*1H4 iv 3*)

qualm *noun* a sudden feeling of sickness or dizziness (*MA iii 4*)

Qualtitie! Calen o custere me! *interjection* 'Calen o custere me' is the chorus of an Elizabethan song that is a pseudo-Latin translation of the Irish Gaelic 'cailin oc astoir', 'my darling, my treasure' (referring to a young girl) (*H5 iv 4*)

quantity *noun* a tiny piece (*TS iv 3*; *2H4 v 1*) ■ *adverb* in proportion to one another (*MND i 1*; *H iii 2*)

quarrel *noun* **1.** the basis of a quarrel (*H iv 4*; *M i 2*) **2.** a desire to quarrel (*O ii 3*) ■ *verb* to have a difference with someone (*T iii 1*)

quarrelling with occasion *adjective* complaining at every opportunity (*MV iii 5*)

quarry *noun* **1.** a pile of dead animals killed in a hunt (*M iv 3*) **2.** a pile of dead bodies (*H v 2*)

quarter *noun* **1.** an area of a town etc. allocated to troops for lodgings **2.** a relationship (*CE ii 1*; *O ii 3*) ■ *verb* to cut someone into four parts (*JC iii 1*) ◇ **have quarter** to have reliable protection (*AC iv 3*) ◇ **in quarter** on good terms (*O ii 3*)

quat *noun* a pimple (used as a term of abuse) (*O v 1*)

quean *noun* a nagging woman (*2H4 ii 1*)

queasy *adjective* **1.** risky (*KL ii 1*) **2.** disgusted (*AC iii 6*) **3.** fussy (*MA ii 1*)

quell *noun* a murder (*M i 7*) ■ *verb* to kill someone (*MND v 1*)

queller *noun* a killer (*2H4 ii 1*)

quern *noun* a hand-operated mill for grinding corn (*MND ii 1*)

quest *noun* **1.** a group of people set up to make an inquiry (*R3 i 4*; *H v 1*) See also **coroner's quest law 2.** a person or group of people sent out on a search (*O i 2*) **3.** the bark made by dogs when they catch sight of game (*MM iv 1*)

question *noun* a conversation (*AYLI iii 4, v 4*; *2H4 i 1*; *KL iv 3*; *H iii 1*; *MV iv 1*) ■ *verb* **1.** to talk together (*1H4 i 3*) **2.** to determine the guilt of an accused person by making them engage in armed combat (*O i 3*) **3.** to ask about something (*MND i 1*; *H5 ii 4*; *M ii 3*) **4.** to dispute something

questionable *adjective* inviting conversation (*H i 4*)

questrist *noun* someone who is searching for something (*KL iii 7*)

quick *adjective* **1.** alive (*H5 ii 2*; *H v 1*) **2.** fast flowing (*T iii 2*) **3.** hasty (*R3 iv 4*) **4.** pregnant (*AC i 2*) ■ *noun* a sensitive part (*H ii 2*)

quicken *verb* **1.** to bring something to life (*T iii 1*) **2.** to come to life (*KL iii 7*; *AC iv 15*; *O iii 3*) **3.** to stimulate something (*TS i 1*; *MV ii 8*; *R3 iv 4*)

quickening *adjective* the act of coming to life (*MM v 1*)

quiddits *plural noun* arguments based on subtle points (*H v 1*)

quiddity *noun* subtlety (*1H4 i 2*; *H v 1*)

quietus *noun* release from life regarded as a state of slavery (*H iii 1*)

COMMENT: The single Shakespearean use of this word occurs in **Hamlet**, in the prince's most famous soliloquy: 'To be or not to be'. It was taken from the Latin 'quietus est', meaning 'it is at peace', and was used as a formal statement to release an accountant from the particular accounts he was working on. Its context is a good example of Shakespeare's range of language and his readiness to draw words from unusual sources to make a point. In a weighty list of references, Hamlet has just surveyed the pressures and frustrations of a man's life and then points to the simplicity of his committing suicide: 'When he himself might his quietus make/With a bare bodkin'. A simple, small dagger would be enough for the final signing off. The man, or accountant in Shakespeare's image, would need no higher authority: he could do the deed 'himself'. The technical *quietus*, suggesting a complicated contract, refers back to legal language in the preceding lines and contrasts with the simple 'bare bodkin'. 'Quietus' is particularly appropriate for Hamlet himself, a witty intellectual, now in deep despair and longing for the 'quiet' implicit in *quietus*.

quill *noun* **1.** a strong feather (*MND iii 1*) **2.** a spine (*H i 5*)

Quinapalus *noun* an imaginary authority (*TN i 5*)

quince *noun* a round or pear-shaped yellow fruit related to the apple (*RJ iv 4*)

quintain *noun* a post or dummy for thrusting a lance whilst on horseback (*AYLI i 2*)

quintessence *noun* the essential part of something (*AYLI iii 2*; *H ii 2*) (NOTE: In ancient philosophy, the 'quintessence' was the fifth of the five essences or elements, said to make up heavenly bodies. The other four elements were earth, air, fire and water.)

COMMENT: In general, this means 'a perfect or best expression of something' and it sounds as majestic as its meaning. It was believed that all that exists is composed of the four elements (earth, air, fire and water). The *quintessence* (meaning 'fifth essence') is the most specially refined of all. It is a philosophical word and useful for idealists, like lovers. In **As You Like It** Orlando attaches love poems to trees in the forest; in one he says that his girl-friend Rosalind is 'the quintessence' of every spirit that heaven would like to express on earth, therefore Rosalind is unique amongst women. In **Hamlet** the prince describes mankind as 'this quintessence of dust'. Does he mean that, since God made Adam, the first man, from the dust of the earth, mankind is the best of all God's creation? Or is mankind especially dust-like and therefore especially worthless? It's hard to decide. But we do know that he is trying to fool his university friends in the scene where they are all trying to be clever with each other.

quip *noun* a witty remark (*1H4 i 2*; *MA ii 3*)

quire *noun* a group of musicians (*MND ii 1*) ■ *verb* to play music (*MV v 1*)

quirk *noun* **1.** a witty remark (*O ii 1*) **2.** conceit (*MA ii 3*) **3.** an eccentric turn or character (*TN iii 4*)

quit *verb* **1.** to release someone from having to pay a debt, etc. (*TN v 1*; *MV iv 1*; *H5 iii 5*) **2.** to prove someone innocent (*AYLI iii 1*; *1H4 iii 2*; *H5 ii 2*) **3.** to compensate someone for something (*MM v 1*; *RJ ii 4*; *KL iii 7*; *H v 2*) **4.** to be even with someone

(*MA iv 1*; *TS iii 1*) **5.** to pay something off (*CE i 1*) **6.** to play your part (*MM ii 4*) **7.** to do well or badly at something (*KL ii 1*)

quittance *noun* **1.** the act of being released from having to pay a debt (*AYLI iii 5*) **2.** recompense (*2H4 i 1*; *H5 ii 2*)

quiver *adjective* agile (*2H4 ii 4, iii 2*)

quoif, coif *noun* a close-fitting cap (*WT iv 4*; *2H4 i 1*)

quoit *verb* to throw something (*2H4 ii 4*) [From the game where a ring is thrown to fall over a peg.]

quondam *noun* the former (*H5 ii 1*) [Latin, from *quom*, 'when'.]

quote *verb* to observe something (*H ii 1*)

COMMENT: *Quote* was a specialised and rather literary word, taken from the Latin word for marking off a text into chapters and verses to be ready for specific explanations. Therefore the word is appropriate for the occasionally pedantic Polonius speaking of Hamlet: 'I am sorry that with better heed and judgement/I had not quoted him', where *quoted* means 'closely observed'. Boyet, a self-consciously prolix character in **Love's Labours Lost** mocks the King in love: 'His face's own margin did quote such amazes,/That all eyes saw his eyes enchanted with gazes'. The amazement in the King's face *quotes*, or makes a literary reference in the original Latin sense, to the love in his eyes. Later Rosaline, speaking of the lords' serious intentions in love, asserts that 'we did not quote them so'. Her *quote* here describes not the reference made, but the reference interpreted.

quotidian *noun* a fever that recurs daily (*AYLI iii 2*) ◇ **quotidian tertian** a nonsense phrase meaning a daily fever that occurs every other day (*H5 ii 1*)

R

R *noun* dog's letter, sounds like a dog growling (*RJ ii 4*)

rabato *noun* a simple ruff (*MA iii 4*)

rabbit-sucker *noun* a young rabbit (*1H4 ii 4*)

rabblement *noun* a rabble, an unruly crowd of people (*JC i 2*)

race *noun* **1.** a piece of ginger root (*WT iv 3; 1H4 ii 1*) **2.** a flavour (*AC i 3*) **3.** a person's nature (*WT iv 4*) **4.** a herd of animals (*MV v 1*) **5.** lust (*T i 2; MM ii 4*) ■ *verb* to erase something (*M v 3*) ◇ **race of heaven** a taste of heaven (*AC i 3*)

rack *noun* a mass of cloud (*T iv 1; H ii 2*) ■ *verb* **1.** inflate, exaggerate (*MA iv 1*) **2.** to misrepresent someone (*MM iv 1*)

rackets *noun* real tennis, a game played in a walled court, similar to modern squash (*H5 i 2*)

rag *noun* **1.** a tiny amount (*CE iv 4*) **2.** a shabby, worthless person (*TS iv 3; R3 v 3*)

rage *noun* **1.** anger (*MV v 1; 2H4 iv 4*) **2.** madness (*CE iv 3; RJ iv 3; KL iv 5*) **3.** sexual desire (*H iii 3*) **4.** violent action (*R2 i 2*) ■ *verb* **1.** to act madly (*AC iv 1*) **2.** to behave irresponsibly (*MA iv 1*)

raging *adjective* lustful (*R3 iii 5; O i 3*)

raisins o' th' sun *noun* sun-dried grapes (*WT iv 3*)

rake *verb* to cover something over by raking (*KL iv 6*)

rampallian *noun* a scoundrel (*2H4 ii 1*)

ramping *adjective* rearing up (*1H4 iii 1*)

range *noun* the ranks of an army (*AC iii 13*) ■ *verb* **1.** to wander freely (*AYLI i 3; H iii 3*) **2.** to have a particular rank or position (*1H4 i 3*) **3.** to be at the same level as something (*MA ii 2*) **4.** to look around a place (*TN iv 3*) **5.** to be unfaithful (*TS iii 1*) **6.** to be ranked in order (*AC i 1*)

rank *noun* orderly walking in a line (*AYLI iii 2*) ■ *adjective* **1.** foul-smelling (*TN ii 5; H iii 3; AC v 2*) **2.** lustful (*MV i 3; O ii 1*) **3.** unchecked (*H iii 4*) **4.** foul (*2H4 iii 1; H iii 3, 4*) **5.** overfull (*2H4 iv 1*) **6.** fat

(*JC iii 1*) ◇ **ranker rate** a greater price (*H iv 4*)

rankle *verb* to cause an infected wound (*R2 i 3; R3 i 3*)

rankness *noun* insolence (*AYLI i 1*)

rant *verb* to speak loudly and passionately (*H v 1*)

rarely *adverb* splendidly (*MND i 2; MA iii 1; AC iv 4*)

rareness *noun* unusual excellence (*H v 2*)

rarity *noun* same as **rareness** (*KL iv 3; T ii 1*)

rascal *noun* a deer that is the runt of the herd (*AYLI iii 3*) ■ *adjective* worthless (*JC iv 3*)

rase *verb* to lift something off (*R3 iii 2, 4*)

rash *verb* to thrust something sharp into something (*KL iii 7*) ■ *adjective* **1.** having a quick and strong effect (*MM v 1; WT i 2; 2H4 iv 4*) **2.** without proper consideration (*O iii 4*)

rash-levied *adjective* (of an army) raised without proper consideration (*R3 iv 3*)

rate *noun* **1.** an opinion (*T i 2, ii 1*) **2.** an amount (*2H4 iv 1*) **3.** the value of something (*MND iii 1; RJ v 3*) **4.** a way of living (*MV i 1*) ■ *verb* **1.** to scold someone (*TS iv 1; MV i 3; JC ii 1*) **2.** to drive something or someone away by anger (*TS i 1; 1H4 iv 3*) **3.** to calculate something (*2H4 i 3*) **4.** to be worth a certain amount (*AC iii 11*) ■ *adjective* valued (*1H4 iv 4*)

rather ◇ **the rather 1.** the sooner (*TN iii 3*) **2.** the more quickly (*M i 7*) ◇ **me rather had** I had rather (*R2 iii 3*)

ratsbane *noun* arsenic (*2H4 i 2; KL iii 4*) [From the fact that this was used as a rat poison.]

raught *adjective* reached (*AC iv 9*)

ravel *verb* **1.** to unravel something (*R2 iv 1*) **2.** to sort something out (*H iii 4*)

ravelled *adjective* tangled (*M ii 2*)

Ravenspurgh, Ravenspur *noun* a port and castle on the north coast of the Humber estuary in East Yorkshire (*1H4 i 3, iii 2, iv 3*)

ravin *verb* to eat something greedily (*MM i 2; M ii 4*)

ravined *adjective* full up with prey (*M iv 1*)

ravish *verb* **1.** to tear something out (*KL iii 7*) **2.** to abduct and rape someone (*MND ii 1; R3 v 3*) **3.** to overwhelm someone with great joy (*MA ii 3*) ◇ **ravishing strides** in the steps of the person who has abducted and raped someone (*M ii 1*)

ravishing *adjective* seizing violently (*M ii 1*)

raw *adjective* **1.** immature (*R2 ii 3*) **2.** unskilled (*MV iii 3; AYLI iii 2; WT iv 4*)

rawly *adverb* when young (*H5 iv 1*)

rawness *noun* an unprotected state (*M iv 3*)

ray *verb* to make something filthy (*TS iv 1*)

rayed *adjective* afflicted (*TS iii 2*)

raze *verb* **1.** to erase something (*M v 3*) **2.** to pluck something off (*R3 iii 4*) **3.** to lay something flat (*MM ii 2*) **4.** same as **race** (*1H4 ii*)

razed *adjective* slashed (*H iii 2*)

razure *noun* the act of erasing something (*MM v 1*)

re *noun* in music, the second note of an octave (*MND iii 2; RJ iv 5; TS iii 1*)

reach *noun* ability (*H ii 1*) ■ *verb* **1.** to amount to something (*1H4 iv 1*) **2.** to grasp something (*R2 i 3*) **3.** to seize someone (*AC iv 9*) **4.** to struggle for something (*R3 i 1*)

read *verb* to teach someone (*TS iii 1; 1H4 iii 1*)

readiness *noun* efficiency (*MM ii 1*) ◇ **put on manly readiness** to get dressed (*M ii 3*)

re-answer *verb* to compensate for something (*H5 iii 6*)

reaped *adjective* shaved (*1H4 i 3*)

rear *verb* **1.** to raise something (*T ii 1; AC ii 1*) **2.** to stir something up (*R2 iv 1*) **3.** to make something

rearmouse, reremouse *noun* a bat (the animal) (*MND ii 2*)

rearward *noun* the part of an army behind the main body of soldiers (*2H4 iii 2; RJ iii 2*)

reason *noun* **1.** a cause for something (*RJ iv 1; R3 v 3; JC i 3*) **2.** an observation (*AYLI i 3; MM i 2; R3 iv 4*) **3.** the fact of being in keeping with what is reasonable (*MND v 1; O iii 3*) **4.** a reasonable amount (*MA v 4; MV iii 5*) **5.** what is reasonably expected (*T iii 2*) ■ *verb* **1.** to talk with someone (*MV ii 8; RJ iii 1*) **2.** to question something (*1H4 ii 3; R3 i 4*) **3.** to discuss something (*JC v 1; KL i 2, ii 4*)

reasonable shores *noun* the mind (*T v 1*)

reave *verb* to take something from someone by force (*CE i 1*)

rebate *verb* to cause something to lose its sharpness (*MM i 4*)

rebeck *noun* a three-stringed musical instrument resembling a violin. It is used as the name of a musician. (*RJ iv 5*)

rebuke *verb* to drive someone back (*MND iii 2; H5 iii 6; M iii 1*)

rebuse *verb* abuse (*TS i 2*)

receipt *noun* **1.** a container (*M i 7*) **2.** anything that is received (*R2 i 1*)

receive *verb* **1.** to listen to something (*KL v 3; H v 2*) **2.** to believe something (*TN iii 4; H ii 2; M i 7*) **3.** to understand something (*MM ii 4*) **4.** to accept something (*H5 v 2*)

receiving *noun* **1.** understanding (*TN iii 1*) **2.** the fact of being accepted by society (*WT iv 4*)

recheat *noun* a note sounded on a horn to call back the dogs from the wrong scent when hunting (*MA i 1*)

reckoning *noun* **1.** admiration (*RJ i 2*) **2.** a bill (*AYLI iii 4; 1H4 ii 4; 2H4 i 2*) **3.** an assessment of a situation (*TS iv 1*) ◇ **be one reckoning** to be the same (*H5 iv 7*)

reclaim *verb* to bring someone under control (*RJ iv 2*)

reclusive *adjective* preferring to be on your own (*MA iv 1*)

recognizance *noun* **1.** a legal bond defining a debt (*H v 1*) **2.** a token (*O v 2*)

recoil *verb* **1.** to recall something (*WT i 2, ii 3*) **2.** to decline in quality (*M iv 3*)

recollected *adjective* specially composed for the occasion (*TN ii 4*)

recomforture *noun* consolation (*R3 iv 4*)

recommend *verb* **1.** to give something (*TN v 1*) **2.** to inform someone (*O i 3*) **3.** to be pleasant to someone (*M i 6*)

record *noun* **1.** a witness (*R2 i 1*) **2.** a memory (*TN v 1*) ■ *verb* to put something down in a legally binding document (*MV iv 1*) ◇ **in record, upon record** put down in a legally binding document (*R3 iii 1*; *MM ii 2*; *AC iv 14*)

recordation *noun* remembrance (*2H4 ii 3*)

recorder *noun* **1.** a type of flute (*MND v 1*; *H iii 2*) **2.** a lawyer appointed by a town council to note court proceedings and customs and whose verbal statements were treated as the absolute truth (*R3 iii 7*)

recountments *noun* the act of recounting past events (*AYLI iv 3*)

recourse *noun* access (*R3 iii 3*)

recover *verb* **1.** to restore someone to life, health, etc. (*AYLI iv 3*; *WT iv 4*) **2.** to discover something (*MA iii 3*) **3.** to reach something (*T iii 2*; *TN ii 3*) **4.** to rescue someone (*TN ii 1*) **5.** to make someone think well of you again (*O ii 3*) **6.** to resole a shoe (*JC i 1*)

recovery *noun* the process of transferring an estate that cannot be sold (entailed) (*CE ii 2*; *H v 1*)

recreant *noun* **1.** a coward (*MND iii 2*) **2.** a traitor (*R2 i 2*; *KL i 1*) ■ *adjective* **1.** cowardly (*2H4 v 3*) **2.** false (*R2 i 1*)

COMMENT: *Recreant* is one of many French words that enlarged English vocabulary in the early Middle Ages chiefly in areas of law, warfare and chivalry. Literally it means 'going back on one's pledge or belief' and is therefore one of the most powerful words available when accusing an opponent of dishonour, generally of cowardice. **Richard II** opens with Bolingbroke and Mowbray each defending his honour and accusing the other of treachery. Bolingbroke is described as 'A recreant and most degenerate traitor'. Typically, it is a word confined to male aristocracy in a warlike culture, which needed to remain civilised through a high-minded code of conduct. The extreme nature of its meaning made *recreant* a useful word to parody. It sounds eccentrically elevated when Puck in **A Midsummer Night's Dream** imitates Lysander's voice to drive Demetrius into a fury: 'Come, recreant, come, thou child'. There is an absurdity about these two young men throwing wild abuse at each other whilst stumbling about in the wood.

recreation *noun* an entertainer (*TN ii 3*)

recure *verb* to make something whole again (*R3 iii 7*)

redbreast *noun* a robin (*1H4 iii 1*)

rede *noun* a piece of advice (*H i 3*)

redeliver *verb* to repeat something (*H v 2*)

redime te captum quam queas minima *phrase Latin* redeem yourself from captivity at the lowest price (*TS i 1*)

red lattice *noun* the window of a pub (*2H4 ii 2*)

red-lattice *noun* a pub that had the windows painted red (*2H4 ii 2*)

red murrion *noun* a type of plague whose symptoms include sores and boils on the skin (*T i 2*)

redoubted *adjective* feared (*H5 ii 4*; *MV iii 2*; *R3 iv 5*)

red plague *noun* a type of plague whose symptoms included red sores on the skin, in contrast to the bubonic plague whose symptoms included swelling of the lymphatic glands (*T i 2*)

redress *noun* **1.** a solution to a problem (*R2 ii 2, 3*) **2.** a way to set something right (*KL i 4*)

reduce *verb* **1.** to bring something back to its former state (*H5 v 2*; *R3 v 5*) **2.** to bring things together (*R3 ii 2*)

reechy *adjective* dirty (*MA iii 3*; *H iii 4*)

re-edify *verb* to rebuild something (*R3 iii 1*)

reed-voice *noun* a high voice (*MV iii 4*)

reek *noun* a stench ■ *verb* **1.** to stink (*JC iii 2*) **2.** to give something off (*H5 iv 3*)

reeking *adjective* **1.** drifting like smoke (*H5 iv 3*) **2.** vile (*M i 2*)

reeky *adjective* stinking (*RJ iv 1*)

reel *noun* a party (*RJ ii 3*; *H i 4*; *AC ii 7*) ■ *verb* to stagger (*AC i 4*)

reeling-ripe *adjective* drunk enough to stagger (*T v 1*)

refelled *verb* denied (*MM v 1*)

refer ◇ **refer me** submit my case to (*WT iii 2*; *O i 2*)

reference *noun* **1.** a relationship (*AYLI i 3*; *H5 i 2*) **2.** the act of referring something to a third party to decide on (*AC v 2*) **3.** an assignment (*O i 3*)

reflection *noun* a return (*M i 2*)

reflex *noun* a reflection (*RJ iii 5*)

reform *verb* to stop something (*1H4 iv 3*; *H iii 2*)

refuge *noun* an excuse ■ *verb* to hide something (*R2 v 5*)

regard *noun* **1.** your opinion of something (*1H4 iv 3*; *H5 ii 4*; *H iv 7*) **2.** careful consideration (*R2 ii 1*) **3.** a circumstance to be considered (*KL i 1*; *H iii 1*) **4.** a circumstance (*H ii 2*) **5.** an intention (*H5 i 1*; *JC iii 1*) **6.** a look (*TN v 1*; *MM v 1*) **7.** something looked at (*O ii 1*) **8.** attending to duty, heeding (*TS iv 1*; *KL i 4*; *M iii 2*)

regiment *noun* a person's rule over a country or people (*AC iii 6*)

region *noun* the sky (*RJ ii 2*; *H ii 2*)

register *noun* a list (*AC iv 9*)

regreet ◇ **sensible regreets** gifts (*MV ii 9*)

rehearse *verb* to speak (*MND v 1*; *R2 v 3*)

relapse ◇ **in relapse of mortality** with deadly consequences (*H5 iv 3*)

relation *noun* **1.** news that has been passed on (*T v 1*; *WT v 2, 3*; *M iv 3*) **2.** the act of telling something (*T iii 3*) **3.** an application (*MV iv 1*) ◇ **understood relations** connections (*M iii 4*)

relative *adjective* believable (*H ii 2*)

release *verb* to give something up (*R2 iv 1*)

relent *verb* **1.** to dissolve something (*MM iii 1*) **2.** to give up (*MND i 1*)

relenting *adjective* the act of becoming compassionate (*R3 iv 4*)

relic *noun* **1.** a memorial (*JC ii 2*) **2.** an object of historic interest (*TN iii 3*)

relieve *verb* to lift someone again (*T ii 1*)

religious *adjective* conscientious (*TN iii 4*)

religiously *adverb* faithfully (*H5 i 2*)

relish *noun* a characteristic mark or taste (*H iii 3*) ■ *verb* to find something acceptable (*WT v 2*)

reliver *verb* to restore something (*MM iv 4*)

relume *verb* to light something again (*O v 2*)

remain *verb* **1.** to live in a place (*T i 2*; *AYLI iii 2*) **2.** to continue to belong to someone (*KL i 1*) ◇ **make remain** stay with (*M iv 3*)

remained biscuit, remainder biscuit *noun* a ship's biscuit left over after a voyage (*AYLI ii 7*)

remain with *verb* to stay in a person's mind (*T iii 6*)

remediate *adjective* medicinal (*KL iv 4*)

remedy *noun* a solution to a problem (*2H4 i 2*; *RJ ii 3*) ◇ **no remedy** it is unavoidable (*MM ii 2*) ◇ **there is no remedy** it is unavoidable (*MM ii 1*; *TN iii 4*) ◇ **what remedy?** What can be done? (*TN i 5*)

remember *verb* **1.** to commemorate someone (*T i 2*; *1H4 v 4*) **2.** to remind someone of something (*T i 2*; *KL i 4*) **3.** to maintain something (*2H4 v 2*)

remembrance *noun* **1.** something given to remind someone of something (*MV iv 1*; *O iii 3*) **2.** the ability to remember (*T ii 1*) **3.** the act of remembering something (*H i 2*) **4.** a reminder (*2H4 v 2*)

remembrancer *noun* someone who reminds someone about things (*M iii 4*)

remission *noun* a willingness to forgive (*MM v 1*)

remonstrance *noun* a display (*MM v 1*)

remorse *noun* an obligation (*O iii 3*)

remorseful *adjective* full of concern (*R3 i 2*)

remotion *noun* the fact of keeping away (*KL ii 4*)

remove *noun* **1.** the act of moving house, etc. (*KL i 4*; *AC i 2*) **2.** a period of absence (*MM i 1*) **3.** death (*H iv 5*) ■ *verb* **1.** to go elsewhere (*AYLI iii 4*; *M v 3*) **2.** to murder someone (*WT i 2*)

removed *adjective* **1.** separated by time or space (*T ii 1*; *TN v 1*) **2.** distant in relationship (*AYLI v 4*; *WT iv 4*; *RJ iii 3*) **3.** secluded (*MM i 3*; *AYLI iii 2*; *H i 4*) **4.** not very concerned (*1H4 iv 1*)

removedness *noun* absence (*WT iv 2*)

render *verb* **1.** to do something for someone (*MA v 3*) **2.** to give an account of something (*AYLI iv 3*; *H5 i 2*) **3.** to deliver something (*MV iii 4*) **4.** to give something up (*M v 7*; *H i 5*; *AC iii 8, iv 14*)

rendezvous *noun* **1.** a hiding place (*1H4 iv 1*; *H5 v 1*) **2.** a meeting place (*H iv 4*)

renegado *noun* someone who betrays or gives up their religion (*TN iii 2*)

renege *verb* **1.** to deny something (*KL ii 2*) **2.** to give something up (*AC i 1*)

renew *verb* to repeat something (*H5 i 2*)

renowned *adjective* famous (*1H4 iii 2*)

rent *noun* a wound (*JC iii 2*) ■ *verb* to tear something (*MND ii 2*; *R3 i 2*; *M iv 3*)

repair *noun* **1.** the act of coming or going to a place (*MM iv 1*; *H v 2*) **2.** the act of restoring something to a previous state (*WT* *v 1*) ■ *verb* **1.** to return to a place (*MND iv 1*) **2.** to go to a place (*JC i 3*; *AC i 4*) **3.** to set something right (*KL iv 1, 7*)

COMMENT: Shakespeare used the word in our sense of 'to amend or restore', but his more common meaning of *repair* is 'to make one's way'. It derived from the French 'repairer', a version of the Latin 'repatriare', meaning 'to return to one's own country'. *Repair* therefore had a more deliberate and purposeful sense than simply 'go' or 'come'. Hamlet, in his letter to Horatio, asks him to 'repair thou to me with as much speed as thou would'st fly death'. Later, Horatio uses *repair* as a noun when he promises to 'forestall their repair hither'.

repast *verb* to feed a person or animal with something (*H iv 5*) ■ *adjective* past (*R3 iv 4*)

repeal *noun* to recall (from exile, disgrace, etc.) (*JC iii 1*; *KL iii 6*; *O ii 3*)

replenished *adjective* complete (*WT ii 1*; *R3 iv 3*)

replication *noun* **1.** a reply (*H iv 2*) **2.** an echo (*JC i 1*)

reportingly *adjective* according to rumour (*MA iii 1*)

reposal *noun* the act of putting your trust in someone (*KL ii 1*)

repose *verb* to put your trust in someone (*R2 ii 4*)

reprisal *noun* a prize (*1H4 iv 1*)

reproach *verb* to bring disgrace to somebody (*MM v 1*)

reprobance, reprobation *noun* the state of being damned (*O v 2*)

reproof *noun* **1.** shame (*CE v 1*) **2.** the act of denying something (*1H4 iii 2*)

reprove *verb* to disprove something (*MA ii 3*)

repugnant *adjective* refusing to obey (*H ii 2*)

repute *verb* to regard something as being something (*TS iv 2*)

request off *verb* to ask someone to come away (*AC ii 7*)

required *adjective* indispensable (*WT v 3*; *KL iv 3*)

requiring *noun* a demand (*T ii 2*; *MM iii 1*; *H5 ii 4*)

requite *verb* to repay something (*T iii 3*; *O iv 2*)

rescue *verb* to forcibly remove someone from custody (*CE iv 4*; *AC iii 11*)

resemblance *noun* probability (*MM iv 2*)

reservation *noun* the act of claiming a right or privilege (*L i 1*; *L ii 4*)

reserve *verb* **1.** to keep someone or something safe or in a particular state (*H i 3*; *O iii 3*; *TN i 5*) **2.** to keep someone alive (*MM v 1*) **3.** to keep something (*R3 iv 4*)

residence *noun* the act of living in a particular place (*H ii 2*)

resolute *noun* an adventurer (*H i 1*)

resolution *noun* certainty (*KL i 2*)

resolve *verb* **1.** to convince someone (*MM iv 2*; *JC iii 1, 2*) **2.** to melt something (*H i 2*) **3.** to inform someone about something (*T v 1*; *R3 iv 5*; *KL ii 4*) **4.** to make up your mind (*WT v 3*; *M iii 1*) **5.** to decide to go to a place (*2H4 ii 3*) ◊ **resolved correction** intended punishment (*2H4 iv 1*)

resort *noun* a visit made by someone (*H ii 2*)

respect *noun* **1.** a person's reputation or rank (*JC i 2*) **2.** consideration (*H iii 1*) ■ *conjunction* in comparison with (*WT v 1*) ◊ **base respects of thrift** considerations of the profit (*H iii 2*) ◊ **upon respect** after consideration (*L ii 4*) ◊ **without respect** apart from its context (*MV v 1*)

respective *adjective* careful (*MV v 1*; *RJ iii 1*) ◊ **respective lenity** deliberate tolerance (*RJ iii 1*)

respice finem *phrase Latin* be aware of the end (*CE iv 4*)

respite *noun* a delay (*MM ii 3, iv 2*; *R3 v 1*)

responsive *adjective* suited (*H v 2*)

rest *preposition* in the space of ■ *noun* **1.** a final risky action designed to end a matter one way or the other (*CE iv 3*; *MV ii 2*; *H5 ii 1*; *RJ v 3*; *KL i 1*) **2.** peace of mind (*TN v 1*; *MV ii 5*; *WT ii 1*; *KL ii 4*) **3.** renewed strength (*1H4 iv 3*; *JC iv 3*) ■ *verb* **1.** to remain (*M i 6*) **2.** to remain to be done (*TS i 1*; *H iii 3*) [Referring to the stake in the card game *primero* on which the game rests because its loss ends the game.] ◊ **above the rest** especially (*L iv 1*) ◊ **rest you, God rest you (merry** *or* **fair)** I wish you peace and happiness (*AYLI v 1*; *MV i 3, ii 2*; *RJ i 2*; *M iv 3*) ◊ **set up rest** to decide, to make up your mind (*CE iv 3*) ◊ **rest in** to be in the power of someone (*MM i 3*) ◊ **rest on** to rely on something (*H iii 3*)

'rest *verb* to arrest someone (*CE iv 2, 4*)

re-stem *verb* to retrace a course (*O i 3*)

resting *adjective* not able to be moved (*JC iii 1*)

restore *verb* to make amends for something (*MND v 1*)

restrain *verb* **1.** to hold back something from someone (*R3 v 3*) **2.** to pull something tight (*TS iii 2*)

restrained *adjective* forbidden (*MM ii 4*)

restraint *noun* **1.** the act of preventing something (*CE iii 1*) **2.** the imprisonment of someone (*MM i 2*) **3.** self-control (*TN v 1*)

retention *noun* **1.** the imprisonment of someone (*KL v 3*) **2.** a doubt about something (*TN v 1*)

retirement *noun* a place to hide (*1H4 iv 1*)

retort *verb* to reject something (*MM v 1*)

retrait *noun* a retreat (*1H4 v 4*; *2H4 iii 2*)

retreat *noun* the act of calling off a chasing group (*2H4 iv 3*)

retrograde *adjective* contrary (*H i 2*)

return *noun* a reply (*H5 ii 4*) ■ *verb* **1.** to reply (*R2 iii 3*) **2.** to be handed over (*H i 1*)

revengement *noun* a punishment (*1H4 iii 2*)

revengive *adjective* revenging (*KL ii 1*)

reverb *verb* to echo (*KL i 1*)

reverberate *adjective* echoing (*TN i 5*)

reversion *noun* something to be had in the future, or the possibility of having something in the future (*1H4 iv 1*; *R2 i 4*)

revert *verb* to go back (*H iv 7*)

reverted *adjective* opposed (*CE iii 2*)

review *verb* to see something again (*WT iv 4*)

revolt *noun* **1.** a rebel (*KL v 2*) **2.** a reversal of your feelings of love (*RJ iv 1*; *O iii 3*) **3.** disgust at the sight of food (*TN ii 4*) ◇ **give the revolt** to rebel against someone (*M v 4*)

revolted *adjective* **1.** disloyal (*R2 ii 2*; *1H4 i 3*) **2.** unfaithful (*WT i 2*)

revolution *noun* a change made by the turn of Fortune's wheel (*2H4 iii 1*; *H v 1*) ◇ **by revolution** in the course of time (*AC i 2*)

revolve *verb* to think about something (*TN ii 5*)

reward *noun* the parts of an animal killed in a hunt given to the dogs (*1H4 v 4*)

reword *verb* to repeat something (*H iii 4*)

rhapsody *noun* meaningless phrases (*H iii 4*)

Rhenish *noun* a white wine from the Rhine valley in Germany (*H i 4, v 1*)

rhetoric *noun* the art of speaking and debating (*AYLI v 1*; *TS i 1*)

rheum *noun* **1.** a discharge from the mouth, nose or eyes **2.** a disease characterised by a watery discharge from the eyes (*AC iii 2*) **3.** a condition that indicates a disease (*JC ii 1*) **4.** rheumatism (*MND ii 1*; *MM iii 1*) ◇ **void rheum** to spit (*MV i 3*; *H5 iii 5*)

rheumatic *adjective* producing phlegm (*MND ii 1*)

rheumy *adjective* cold and damp and so causing a watery discharge from the mouth, nose or eyes (*JC ii 1*)

Rhodes *noun* a Greek island off the southwest coast of Turkey (*O i 1, 3*) (NOTE: It is a centre of ancient culture and figures in classical and biblical history.)

Rialto *noun* Ponte di Rialto, a bridge and money exchange in Venice (*MV i 3, iii 1*)

rib *verb* to enclose something (*MV ii 7*)

riband *noun* a ribbon (*H iv 7*; *RJ iii 1*)

ribaudred *adjective* rude, obscene (*AC iii 1*) ◇ **ribaudred nag of Egypt** an Egyptian prostitute (*AC iii 10*)

rich *adjective* **1.** experienced (*AYLI iv 1*) **2.** bright red (*1H4 iii 3*) ◇ **rich opinion** a good reputation (*O iii 3*)

rid *verb* to kill someone (*T i 2*; *R2 v 4*)

rider *noun* someone who trains horses (*AYLI i 1*)

ridge *noun* a crossbar (*1H4 i 2*)

rife *adjective* ready (*MND v 1*)

rig *verb* to get something ready (*AC ii 6*)

riggish *adjective* immoral, licentious (*AC ii 2*)

right *adverb* exactly (*MND iv 2*; *CE v 1*)

righteously *adverb* rightly (*AYLI i 2*)

rightful *adjective* just (*MV iv 1*)

rightly *adverb* directly (*R2 ii 2*)

rigol *noun* a crown in the form of a circle (*2H4 iv 5*)

rim, rymme *noun* the membrane lining the abdominal cavity of the body (*H5 iv 4*)

ring ◇ **posy of ring** an inscription on the inside of a ring (*H iii 2*) ◇ **cracked within the ring** a coin made worthless by a crack around the ring surrounding the image of the sovereign's head (*H ii 2*)

ringlet *noun* **1.** a dance performed with the dancers in a ring (*MND ii 1*) **2.** a darker circle produced in grass by the growth of a fungus (a fairy ring) (*T v 1*)

ring-time *noun* a marriage, when rings are exchanged (*AYLI v 3*)

riot *verb* to live immorally (*AC ii 2*)

ripe ◇ **sinking-ripe** ready to sink (*CE i 1*)

ripe sister *noun* an older sister (*AYLI iv 3*)

rivage *noun* a seashore or river bank (*H5 iii Chor.*)

rival *noun* a partner (*H i 1*)

rivality *noun* an equal partnership (*AC iii 5*)

rive *verb* to split open (*AC iv 1*)

riveted trim *adjective* strapped into armour (*AC iv 4*)

rivo *noun* a drinking toast (*1H4 ii 4*)

road *noun* **1.** a suitable place for a ship to anchor (*TS ii 1*; *MV i 1*) **2.** a prostitute (*2H4 ii 2*) ◇ **make road** to carry out a raid (*H5 i 2*)

roan *noun* a dappled brown horse (*1H4 ii 3*)

roar *noun* **1.** a commotion (*T i 2*) **2.** a burst of uncontrolled laughter (*H v 1*)

roarers *plural noun* high waves (*T i 1*)

Robin Goodfellow *noun* same as **Puck**

Robin Hood *noun* a legendary English outlaw who robbed the rich to help the poor. He is generally supposed to have lived in Sherwood Forest in Nottinghamshire. (*2H4 v 3*; *AYLI i 1*)

robustious *adjective* rough or violent (*H5 iii 7*; *H iii 2*)

Rochester *noun* an ancient town on the River Medway in Kent. It has a famous cathedral and was an important centre in medieval times. (*1H4 i 2*)

roe *noun* a female deer (*TS Ind. 2*)

rogue *noun* **1.** a beggar (*WT iv 3*; *KL iv 7*) **2.** a dishonest person (*TS iv 1*; *1H4 ii 4*; *O ii 3*) **3.** a mischievous person (used as a term of affection) (*2H4 ii 4*; *KL v 3*; *O iv 1*)

roguish *adjective* wandering (*KL iii 7*)

roll *noun* **1.** a list (*1H4 iii 1*; *AC v 2*) **2.** a register of troops, etc. (*2H4 iii 2*)

romage *noun* an upheaval (*H i 1*)

Roman hand *noun* italic writing, which replaced the traditional English style (*TN iii 4*)

ronyon *noun* a filthy woman (*M i 3*)

rooky *adjective* full of crows, gloomy, dark (*M iii 2*)

room *noun* a place to be filled or occupied (*TS iii 2*; *R2 v 5*) ◇ **in their rooms** instead of them (*MA i 1*)

root *noun* the depths of something (*AC v 2*) ■ *verb* to fix something firmly (*H i 5*)

rope *noun* a hangman's rope (*T i 1*)

ropery *noun* trickery (*RJ ii 4*)

rope-trick *noun* a trick or act of cheating that deserves hanging (a pun on **rhetoric**) (*TS i 2*)

roping *adjective* in dripping strands (*H5 iii 5, iv 2*)

rose *noun* a woman's virginity (*AYLI iii 2*) ◇ **cakes of roses** packs of rose petals, used as perfume (*RJ v 1*)

Ross *noun* a county in northwest Scotland (*M i 2*)

rotundity *noun* solid roundness (*KL iii 2*)

Rouen *noun* a port on the River Seine in France whose position made it of great strategic importance during the Hundred Years War (*H5 iii 5*)

round *noun* **1.** a circle (*M i 5, iv 1*) **2.** a circular dance (*MND ii 1*; *M iv 1*) **3.** the long way round (*MND iii 1*) **4.** a rung of a ladder (*JC ii 1*) ■ *verb* **1.** to surround something (*MND iv 1*; *R2 iii 2*) **2.** to finish something off (*T iv 1*) **3.** to grow big (*WT ii 1*) **4.** to whisper (*WT i 2*) **5.** to speak freely (*CE ii 1*; *TN ii 3*) ■ *adjective* straightforward (*H5 iv 1*; *KL i 4*; *O i 3*) ■ *adverb* openly (*H ii 2*)

round about *preposition* all over (*MA v 3*)

roundel *noun* **1.** a circular dance (*MND ii 2*) **2.** a rung of a ladder (*JC ii 1*)

roundest *adjective* rudest (*KL i 4*)

round hose *noun* breeches puffed out around the hips (*MV i 2*)

roundly *adverb* unceremoniously (*R2 ii 1*)

rouse *noun* **1.** a full measure or long gulp of a drink (*H i 2, 4*; *O ii 3*) **2.** a drunken party (*H ii 1*) ■ *verb* **1.** to drive something from its hiding place (*R2 iii 3*; *1H4 i 3*) **2.** to lift someone or something up (*2H4 iv 1*; *H5 i 2*; *AC v 2*) **3.** to wake up (*M iii 2*) **4.** to stand on end (*M v 5*)

rout *noun* **1.** a mob (*2H4 iv 2*; *JC i 2*; *TS iii 2*) **2.** a brawl (*O ii 3*)

rover *noun* a scoundrel (*WT i 2*)

royal *noun* a coin worth ten shillings (50p) (*MV iii 2, iv 1*; *1H4 i 2*; *R2 v 5*) (NOTE: In R2 v 5 there is a pun on the value of coins i.e. the royal = 10 shillings, the noble = 6s 8d, with a difference of 40 pence '10 groats'.) ■ *adjective* as wealthy as a king, generous (*JC iii 3*)

royalties *plural noun* the rights and privileges of a king (*T i 2*; *R2 ii 1*)

roynish *adjective* dirty (*AYLI ii 2*)

rub *noun* **1.** an obstacle or hindrance (*R2 iii 4*; *H5 ii 2*; *H iii 1*) **2.** a rough area (*M iii 1*) ■ *verb* to hinder something (*KL ii 2*) [From the idea of a check in the game of bowls.]

rubious *adjective* red (*TN i 4*) [From the idea of being the colour of a ruby.]

ruby *noun* a pimple (*CE iii 2*)

rudder *noun* the backside (*AC iii 11*)

rudely *adverb* **1.** violently or roughly (*1H4 iii 2*; *TN i 5*) **2.** unskilfully (*R3 i 1*)

rudesby *noun* an ill-mannered, rough person (*TS iii 2*; *TN iv 1*)

rue *noun* a strong-smelling Mediterranean shrub which was a symbol of repentance or pity (*H iv 5*; *M iii 6*; *R3 iii 2, 7*) ■ *verb* to regret something (*M iii 6*; *R3 iii 2*; *R3 iii 7*)

ruff *noun* a starched and pleated collar (*2H4 ii 4*; *TS iv 3*)

ruffian *verb* to be wild and stormy (*O ii 1*)

ruffle *verb* **1.** to stir something up (*JC iii 2*) **2.** to be wild and stormy (*KL ii 4*)

ruffling *adjective* frilly (*TS iv 3*)

rug-headed *adjective* rough-haired (*R2 ii 1*)

ruinate *adjective* ruined (*CE iii 2*)

ruinous *adjective* ruined

rule *noun* **1.** a law or principle (*TS iii 1*; *H5 i 2*; *R3 i 2*; *JC v 1*; *O i 3*) **2.** an order (*MV iv 1*; *1H4 iv 3*; *M v 2*) **3.** a person's behaviour (*TN ii 3*) **4.** a measuring rod (*JC i 1*; *AC ii 3, v 2*)

rummage *noun* a commotion (*H i 1*)

rumour *noun* an uproar (*JC ii 4*)

rump-fed *adjective* pampered and well-fed (*M i 3*)

run *verb* **1.** to ride quickly (*T i 2*; *1H4 ii 4*) **2.** to speak without thinking (*R2 ii 1*) **3.** to stab someone (*H5 ii 1*) **4.** to emit something (*H5 ii 1*)

runagate *noun* a homeless person (*R3 iv 4*; *RJ iii 5*)

runaway *noun* **1.** a fugitive (*MND iii 2*; *AYLI ii 2*; *MV ii 6*) **2.** a homeless person (*R3 v 3*; *RJ iii 2*)

rush *noun* something without value or strength (*AYLI ii 2*; *O v 2*)

rush aside *verb* to push something aside (*RJ iii 3*)

rush-candle *noun* a bulrush dipped in animal fat to make a cheap but poor-quality candle (*TS iv 5*)

russet *adjective* **1.** plain or simple (*H i 1*) **2.** grey (*MND iii 2*) [From *russet*, 'a red-brown coloured homespun cloth'.]

rust *noun* corruption (*WT iii 2*)

ruth *noun* pity (*R2 iii 4*) (NOTE: From the Bible story of Ruth, who was devoted and compassionate to her mother-in-law after the death of her husband) [From the story of Ruth in the Book of Ruth in the Bible.]

S

sable *noun* the black fur of a marten, very valuable and used for trimming clothes (*H iii 2, iv 7*) ■ *adjective* black (*H i 2, ii 2*)

sacrament ◇ **receive the sacrament** to confirm your solemn promise (*R3 i 4, v 5*)

sad *adjective* **1.** serious (*TN iii 4; AYLI iii 2; JC i 2; H5 i 2*) **2.** miserable (*MND iii 2; R2 v 5*)

> COMMENT: *Sad* sometimes had our sense of 'unhappy', as in **A Midsummer Night's Dream** when Helena, exhausted in the wood enters 'curst and sad' or in **Much Ado About Nothing** Don John explains his melancholy, 'I must be sad when I have cause'. But *sad* more commonly meant 'serious or grave': in **Henry V** 'the sad and solemn priests' sing masses for Richard II's soul and in **Much Ado About Nothing** the Prince and Claudio enter 'in sad conference'. But given particular contexts, these two meanings, of 'serious' and 'unhappy', can often move very close together. In **Romeo and Juliet** Benvolio asks Romeo to drop his bantering tone: 'Tell me in sadness, who is that you love'. The primary sense here is 'serious', but we remember that Romeo is often very solitary and morose because he suffers from the lover's melancholy. In this sense, if he talks about love his manner is likely to be more miserable than elated. In a similar context, Leonato in **Much Ado** teases Benedick, who has just fallen in love with Beatrice: 'Methinks you are sadder'.

sadly *adverb* seriously (*MA ii 3; 2H4 v 2; RJ i 1*)

sadness *noun* seriousness (*TS v 2; RJ i 1*)

safe *verb* **1.** to make something safe (*AC i 3*) **2.** to provide safe conduct for someone (*AC iv 6*) ■ *adjective* **1.** sound (*JC i 1;*

O iv 1) **2.** trusted (*O ii 3*) ◇ **safe toward** with regard to something (*M i 4*)

sag *verb* to sink (*M v 3*)

sagittary *noun* the name of the Venetian commanding officer's residence, which had a statue of an archer (Sagittarius) over the gate (*O i 1, 3*)

saint *verb* to become a saint (*MM i 4*)

sainted *adjective* **1.** being a saint in heaven (*WT v 1*) **2.** holy (*M iv 3*)

sake ◇ **for the Lord's sake** serving a prison sentence (*MM iv 3*)

Sala *noun* a river in Germany (*H5 i 2*)

salad days *noun* the time when you were young, carefree and inexperienced (*AC i 5*)

salamander *noun* a drunkard's red face (*1H4 iii 3*) [From the myth of the salamander, a lizard that lived in fire that it was able to quench by the coldness of its body.]

salary *noun* a fee (*H iii 3*)

sale *noun* something for sale

sale-work *noun* ready-made goods (*AYLI iii 5*)

Salisbury *noun* a town located south of Salisbury Plain in Wiltshire (*H5 iv 3; R3 iv 4*)

sallet *noun* a rude comment (*H ii 2*)

sallied *adjective* made impure

salt *adjective* immoral (*MM v 1; AC ii 1; O ii 1, iii 4*)

Saltier *noun* a **satyr** (*WT iv 4*)

saltness *noun* the fact of being rancid (*2H4 i 2*)

salt rheum *noun* a cold with a runny nose and eyes (*CE iii 2*)

salvage *noun* a savage (*T ii 2*)

salve *verb* to make something more pleasant (*MA i 1*)

Samingo *noun* San Domingo, the patron saint of drinkers. In Silence's song it may refer to Sir Mingo from a song in Thomas Nashe's 'Summer's Last Will'. (*2H4 v 3*)

samphire *noun* a plant whose leaves were pickled (*KL iv 6*)

sanctified *adjective* holy (*2H4 iv 4*; *AYLI ii 3*; *H i 3*; *O iii 4*)

sanctify *verb* to make something holy (*2H4 iv 5*)

sanctimonious *adjective* holy (*T iv 1*)

sanctimony *noun* **1.** holiness **2.** a sacred bond (*O i 3*)

sanctuarize *verb* to harbour, to give shelter to (*H iv 7*)

sand-blind *adjective* partially blind (as though from having sand thrown in your eyes) (*MV ii 2*)

sanded *adjective* sand-coloured (*MND iv 1*)

sanguine *adjective* blood-red (*1H4 ii 4*) ◇ **sanguine coward** a total coward (*1H4 ii 4*)

sans *conjunction French* without (*AYLI ii 7*)

sap *noun* **1.** life or vitality (*CE ii 2*; *WT iv 4*; *AC iii 13*) **2.** blood (*R3 iv 4*)

sarcenet, sarsenet *adjective* flimsy (*1H4 iii 1*)

Sardis *noun* a town near **Ephesus** in what is modern Turkey (*JC iv 2, v 1, 5*)

Sarum *noun* the town of **Salisbury** (*KL ii 2*)

sate *verb* to satisfy someone sexually to the point of exhaustion (*H i 5*; *O i 3*)

satiety *noun* exhaustion after excessive sexual activity (*O ii 1*)

Saturn *noun* in Roman mythology, a god equated with time (*2H4 iv 3*; *MA i 3*) (NOTE: Saturn was the planet believed to cause evil, depression and vengeance. The Greek equivalent is **Kronos**.)

satyr *noun* in Greek mythology, a god of the woods who was half man and half goat (*H i 2*)

sauce *verb* to scold someone severely (*AYLI iii 5*)

saucy *adjective* **1.** highly flavoured (*TN iii 4*) **2.** sexy (*MM ii 4*) **3.** insolent (*M iii 4*; *O i 1*)

savagery *noun* wild vegetation (*H5 v 2*)

save *verb* to prevent something (*1H4 v 4*)

savour *noun* **1.** a smell (*T ii 2*; *TS Ind. 2*) **2.** the nature of something (*KL i 4*) ■ *verb* **1.** to be of the nature of something (*TN v 1*; *WT ii 3*; *H5 i 2*) **2.** to care for someone (*KL iv 2*)

'sblood *interjection* by God's blood (*H ii 2*)

scab *noun* a scoundrel (*TN ii 5*; *2H4 iii 2*)

scaffold *noun* a stage (*H5 Prol.*)

scald *verb* to get overheated in the sun (*2H4 iv 5*) ■ *adjective* loathsome (*H5 v 1, 5*; *AC v 2*)

scale *noun* a mark on a scale (*AC ii 7*) ■ *verb* to weigh something (*MM iii 1*) ◇ **equal scale** equal, balanced amounts (as on a scale) (*H i 2*)

scales *noun* **1.** an instrument for weighing (*2H4 ii 4*) **2.** balances (*MND iii 2*; *RJ i 1*)

scaly *adjective* made of overlapping metal plates (*2H4 i 1*)

scamble *verb* to grab at something (*MA v 1*; *H5 v 2*) ■ *adjective* disturbing (*H5 i 1*)

scamel *noun* possibly the godwit, a type of bird, or some form of shellfish (meaning not clear) (*T ii 2*)

scan *verb* **1.** to examine something (*CE ii 2*; *M iii 4*; *O iii 3*) **2.** to interpret something (*H iii 3*)

scandal *noun* **1.** a damaging allegation (*WT i 2*; *H ii 1*) **2.** damage to a person's reputation (*CE v 1*; *H i 4*) ■ *verb* to damage the reputation of someone (*JC i 2*)

scandaled *adjective* scandalous (*T iv 1*)

scandalized *adjective* disgraced (*1H4 i 3*)

scant *verb* **1.** to withhold something (*CE ii 2*; *MV v 1*; *KL ii 4*) **2.** to restrict someone (*MV ii 1, iii 2*) **3.** to reduce something (*AC iv 2*) **4.** to ignore something (*O i 3*) ■ *adjective* limited, sparing (*H i 3*)

scantile *noun* a piece (*1H4 iii 1*)

scantly *adverb* contemptuously (*AC iii 4*)

scape *noun* **1.** an escape (*TS v 2*; *O i 3*) **2.** a fling, a brief sexual relationship (resulting in an unwanted child) (*WT iii 3*) ■ *verb* to escape (*MV ii 2*)

scarcity *noun* the fact of being without money, friends, etc. (*T iv 1*)

scarf *noun* **1.** a sash worn by a soldier, often indicating his regiment, rank, etc. (*MA ii 1*) **2.** a sash worn as decoration (*JC i 2*) **3.** a sling for a broken arm (*AYLI v 2*) ■ *verb* **1.** to blindfold someone (*M iii 2*) **2.** to wrap something around someone (*H v 2*)

scarfed *adjective* decorated with flags, etc. (*MV ii 6*)

Scarlet *noun* Will Scarlet, one of Robin Hood's men (*2H4 v 3*)

scathe *verb* to harm someone (*RJ i 5*)

scatheful *adjective* harmful (*TN v 1*)

scattered *adjective* **1.** unexpected (*AYLI iii 5*) **2.** not united (*KL iii 1*)

scattering *adjective* random (*O iii 3*)

scauld *adjective* scabby, scurvy (*H5 v 1*)

scene *noun* **1.** a play or performance (*AYLI ii 7*; *WT iv 1*) *See also* **scene individable** *at* **individable 2.** a stage (*MND iii 2*)

schedule *noun* a piece of paper with writing on it (*2H4 iv 1*; *JC iii 1*; *MV ii 9*; *TN i 5*)

school *noun* **1.** a university (*AYLI i 1*; *H i 2*) **2.** a crowd (*2H4 iv 3*) ■ *verb* **1.** to scold someone (*1H4 iii 1*) **2.** to control someone (*M iv 2*)

schooling *noun* a scold (*MND i 1*)

schoolmaster *noun* a private tutor (*T i 2*; *KL i 4*)

scion *noun* **1.** a shoot cut off to be grafted on to another plant (*WT iv 4*) **2.** an offshoot (*O i 3*)

sconce *noun* **1.** the top of the head (*H v 1*) **2.** a form of protection for the head (*CE ii 2*) **3.** a small fort (*H5 iii 6*) ■ *verb* to settle yourself into a place (*H iii 4*)

scope *noun* **1.** a purpose or objective (*R2 iii 3*; *1H4 iii 1*; *H iii 2*) **2.** freedom (*MM i 2, 3*; *R2 iii 3*)

scorch *verb* to slash something (*CE v 1*)

score *noun* **1.** a record of amounts kept by making notches on a door, etc. (*M v 9*) **2.** twenty (*T v 1*; *TS i 2*; *1H4 ii 4*) ■ *verb* **1.** to keep a record of amounts using notches on a stick, etc. (*TS Ind. 2*) **2.** to run up a debt (*1H4 ii 4*) **3.** to cut something by the strokes of a whip (*AC iv 7*; *O iv 1*) ◇ **on the score** in debt (*TS ii Introd*)

scot and lot *noun* in full (*1H4 v 4*) (NOTE: It refers to an old tax system, the payment of which gave entitlement to vote in parliamentary elections.)

scotch *noun* a cut (*AC iv 7*) ■ *verb* to cut someone (*M iii 2*)

scour *verb* **1.** to scrub something off (*1H4 iii 2*; *H5 i 1*; *M v 3*) **2.** to punish something by a beating (*CE i 2*) **3.** to clean a gun (*H5 ii 1*) **4.** to move quickly (*WT ii 1*)

scout *verb* **1.** to ridicule someone (*T iii 2*) **2.** to keep a lookout on behalf of someone (*TN iii 4*)

scrape *verb* to erase something by scraping (*MM i 2*)

scraping *adjective* mean (*R2 v 3*)

screw *verb* to force someone from a position (*TN v 1*)

scrimer, scrimure *noun* a swordfighter (*H iv 7*)

scrip *noun* **1.** a pouch, usually worn on a belt (*AYLI iii 2*) **2.** a written list (*MND i 2*)

scrippage *noun* the contents of a **scrip** (*AYLI iii 2*)

scriptures *plural noun* writings or letters (*R3 i 3*)

scrivener *noun* someone who draws up contracts, writes letters, etc. (*TS iv 4*)

scrubbed *adjective* stunted (*MV v 1*)

scrupulous *adjective* disagreeing on a small point (*AC i 3*)

scuffle *noun* a small fight (*AC i 1*)

scullion *noun* a menial kitchen servant (*2H4 ii 1*; *H ii 2*)

scuse *noun* an excuse (*MV iv 1*; *O iv 1*)

scutcheon, escutcheon *noun* a shield bearing the coat of arms of a dead person (*AC v 2*)

Scylla *noun* in Greek mythology, a beautiful nymph (*MV iii 5*) *See also* **Charybdis** (NOTE: According to legend, Glaucus was in love with Scylla and asked **Cerce** for a love potion, but Cerce became jealous of Scylla and turned her into a six-headed monster.)

sea-bank *noun* a seashore (*MV v 1*; *O iv 1*)

sea-boy *noun* a young sailor of the lowest rank (*2H4 iii 1*)

sea-coal *noun* coal extracted by mining (in contrast to charcoal) that was transported from Newcastle by sea (*2H4 ii 1*)

seal *verb* to conclude or finish something (*WT i 2*; *AC iii 2*)

sealed quart *noun* a quart measure (1.14 litre), stamped officially (*TS Ind. 2*)

sealed quarts *plural noun* measures that had been officially stamped (*TS Ind. 2*)

sea-like *adjective* seaworthy (*AC iii 13*)

sealing day *noun* the day on which a contract is signed (*MND i 1*)

seal manual *noun* a seal or signature made by the person concerned rather than by a secretary or someone else, indicating absolute authenticity

sea-maid *noun* a mermaid (*MND ii 1*; *MM iii 2*)

sea-mark *noun* a lighthouse (*O v 2*)

sea-mel(l) *noun* a seagull (*T ii 2*)

sea-monster *noun* in Greek mythology, a monster that threatened Hesione, the daughter of Laomedon, king of Troy (*MV iii 2*)

seamy side *noun* the worst aspect of something (*O iv 2*) [Referring to the inside of a garment with the seams showing.]

sear *verb* **1.** to burn a mark on to something (*WT ii 1*) **2.** to dry something out (*R3 iv 1*; *M iv 1*) **3.** to make something useless (*M v 3*) ■ *adjective* same as **sere**

searcher *noun* an officer who reported on the cause of death to the courts, and checked for cases of plague (*RJ v 2*)

searching ◇ **searching wine** strong wine (*2H4 ii 4*)

sea-sick *adjective* tired of being at sea (*RJ v 3*)

season *adjective* in season (*MM ii 2*) ■ *noun* **1.** a preservative such as salt (*MA iv 1*; *M iii 4*) **2.** an opportunity (*CE iv 2*) **3.** bad weather (*KL iii 4*) ■ *verb* **1.** to moderate something (*MV v 1*; *H i 2, ii 1*) **2.** to stimulate something (*MV iv 1*) **3.** to cause something to mature (*H i 3, iii 2*)

second *noun* **1.** a supporter (*KL iv 6*; *H iv 7*) **2.** a deputy (*1H4 i 3*; *2H4 v 2*) ■ *adjective* supportive (*WT ii 3*)

secondary *adjective* lower in rank (*MM i 1*)

secret *adjective* **1.** mysterious (*T i 2*; *M iv 1*) **2.** not giving away secrets (*MA i 1*; *JC ii 1*) **3.** private or personal (*TN i 4*; *R3 iii 5*; *H ii 2*) *See also* **have secret feet** *at* **foot**

sect *noun* **1.** a person's rank or class (*MM ii 2*; *2H4 ii 4*) **2.** a party or group (*KL v 3*) **3.** a shoot cut off (*O i 3*) ◇ **sect and force** division and bitterness (*H i 3*)

sectary astronomical *noun* someone who believes in astrology (*KL i 2*)

secure *verb* **1.** to guard something (*T ii 1*; *H i 5*) **2.** to make someone careless because they have a false sense of being safe (*KL iv 1*; *O i 3*) ■ *adjective* safe ■ *adverb* safely (*1H4 i 2*)

security *noun* carelessness through overconfidence (*R2 iii 2*; *JC ii 3*; *M iii 5*)

sedged *adjective* made of reeds (*T iv 1*)

sedges *plural noun* reeds (*MA ii 1*; *TS Ind. 2*)

See, The *noun* Rome, the centre of the pope's authority (*MM iii 2*)

seedness *noun* sowing with seed (*MM i 4*)

seeing *noun* what can be observed, the appearance of something (*WT v 2*)

seel *verb* to blind a person's eyes (*O i 3, iii 3*; *M iii 2*) [From a hawking term meaning 'to sew up the eyelids of a hawk temporarily'.]

seeming *noun* **1.** the appearance of something (*H iii 2*) **2.** deception (*MM ii 4*; *WT iv 4*; *MA iv 1*; *KL iii 2*) ■ *adjective* apparent (*MV iii 2*; *1H4 v 2*; *AC ii 2*) ■ *adverb* **1.** apparently (*H i 5*) **2.** attractively (*AYLI v 4*)

seething *adjective* boiling hot (*MND v 1*)

segregation *noun* the breaking up of something (*O ii 1*)

seized ◇ **stood seized of** owned (*H i 1*)

seizure *noun* a grasp (*AYLI iii 1*)

Self *adjective* same (*MV i 1*; *KL iv 3*)

self-bounty *noun* natural generosity (*O iii 3*)

self-covered *adjective* with your true feelings masked (*KL iv 2*)

self-reproving *noun* self-reproach (*KL v 1*)

sellingly *adverb* favourably (*H v 2*)

semblable *adjective* similar (*2H4 v 1*; *AC iii 4*; *H v 2*; *H5 v 2*)

semblably *adverb* similarly (*1H4 v 3*)

semblative *adjective* resembling (*TN i 4*)

Semiramis *noun* an Assyrian princess (c. 800 BC). A legend developed that she was the daughter of the goddess Derceto. She married Menones but the Assyrian king Ninus took her from him and Menones hanged himself. Ninus gave her the crown but later Semiramis killed him, only to be killed herself by her son Ninyas. She is sometimes identified with the Babylonian goddess of love and war, Ishtar. (*TS Ind. 2*)

semper idem *phrase Latin* always the same (*2H4 v 5*) (NOTE: The motto of Queen Elizabeth I.)

send *verb* to write to acknowledge something (*AC v 2*)

seniory *noun* seniority (*R3 iv 4*)

sennet *noun* a fanfare of trumpets (often used in stage directions) (*KL i 1*; *M iii 1*)

se'nnight *noun* a week (*AYLI iii 2*; *M i 3*; *O ii 1*) [Literally 'seven nights', from the custom of beginning the day at sunset.]

sense *noun* **1.** sexual desire (*MM i 4, ii 2*) **2.** the mind (*TN iv 1*; *O iii 3*) **3.** the ability to feel or perceive (*H iv 5*; *O v 1*) **4.** a sense organ (*M v 1*; *O iv 3*) **5.** an opinion (*O v 2*) ◇ **let senses rule** keep your wits about you (*H5 ii 3*)

senseless-obstinate *adjective* stupidly obstinate (*R3 iii 1*)

sensible *adjective* **1.** sensitive, capable of feeling or perceiving (*T ii 1*; *MND v 1*; *MV ii 7, 8, 9*; *1H4 v 4*; *JC i 3*; *H i 1*) **2.** capable of being felt (*M ii 1*)

COMMENT: *Sensible* was more literal in its meaning than in our use of the word. Shakespeare used it to refer to the five senses (sight, hearing, touch, smell, taste), rather than, as we would, to intellect, judgement and prudence. In 1600 *sensible* meant having the capacity to feel, or, as we would put it, 'sensitive'. Macbeth thinks he sees a dagger in the air and wonders if his eyes work together with his sense of touch; as he tries to grasp it, he asks, 'Art thou not, fatal vision, sensible/To feeling as to sight?' Strange events also occur in **Julius Caesar**, as when Casca describes the 'common slave' with flames surging up his arm, 'and yet his hand,/Not sensible of fire, remain'd unscorch'd'.

sensibly ◇ **sensibly in grief** affected by grief (*H iv 5*)

sentence *noun* a concise moral saying (*MA ii 3*; *MV i 2*; *O i 3*)

sententious *adjective* full of concise moral sayings (*AYLI v 4*)

sequent *adjective* consequent (*MM v 1*; *KL i 2*; *H v 2*) ■ *noun* one following another (*O i 2*)

sequester *noun* separation (*O iii 4*) ■ *verb* to separate someone from something

sequestered *adjective* separated (*AYLI ii 1*)

sequestration *noun* separation (*H5 i 1*; *O i 3*)

sere, sear *adjective* **1.** ready to happen (*H ii 2*) **2.** withered (*CE iv 2*; *MM ii 4*; *M v 3*) [From *sere*, 'a catch holding a gun at cock or half-cock, ready to be fired'.]

sergeant *noun* a sheriff's officer (*CE iv 2*; *H v 2*)

serpigo *noun* psoriasis, a skin disease producing red, scaly patches (*MM iii 1*)

servant *noun* a man who has declared himself devoted to a woman (*R3 ii 4*)

serve in *verb* to serve up a meal (*TS iii 1*; *MV iii 5*)

service *noun* **1.** the fact of being devoted to a woman (*AYLI v 2*) **2.** everything that is laid on a table in preparation for a meal (*M i 7 – stage direction*) **3.** the various courses of a meal (*H iv 3*)

serviceable *adjective* dedicated to serve someone (*KL iv 6*; *TN v 1*; *TS i 1*)

serving man *noun* a courtier, a male attendant (*2H4 v 3*; *KL iii 4*)

servitor *noun* **1.** an attendant (*MV ii 9*; *R3 iv 3*; *AC iv 2 – stage direction*) **2.** a servant (*O i 3*)

sessa *interjection* stop it! (*KL iii 4*; *TS Ind. 1*)

session *noun* a sitting of a law court (*KL v 3*; *MM v 1*; *O iii 3*)

set *noun* **1.** sunset (*H5 iv 1*; *R3 v 3*; *M i 1*) **2.** a shoot cut off a plant (*O i 3*) ■ *verb* **1.** to regard something in a particular way (*R2 i 3*; *RJ v 3*; *H iv 3*) **2.** (*of the eyes*) to stare (*T iii 2*; *TN v 1*) **3.** to bet something (*1H4 iv 1*; *JC v 1*; *KL i 4*) **4.** to bet against someone (*R2 iv 1*) **5.** to post a guard (*RJ iii 3*; *O ii 3*) **6.** to set words to music (*T i 2*) ◇ **double set** (*of the hands of a clock*) having gone twice round (*O ii 3*)

setter *noun* a spy or informant (*1H4 ii 2*)

settled *adjective* **1.** calm (*MM iii 1*; *H iv 7*) **2.** established (*WT iv 3*; *R2 i 1*) **3.** set, congealed (*2H4 iv 3*; *RJ iv 5*) **4.** decided (*M i 7*)

Seven Stars the Pleiades, a constellation of seven stars (*2H4 ii 4*) (NOTE: The Greeks took the rising of the constellation to indicate the beginning of the season of safe sailing, and after its setting sailing was considered unsafe.)

several *adjective* **1.** different (*T iii 1*; *MND v 1*; *H v 2*; *AC i 5*) **2.** particular (*T iii 3*) **3.** various (*T v 1*; *WT iv 4*) ■ *noun* private property (especially land for grazing) as opposed to common land

severals *plural noun* **1.** individual people (*WT i 2*) **2.** the details of something (*H5 i 1*)

Severn *noun* the longest river in the UK It rises in Wales and runs into the Bristol Channel. It was the boundary between England and Wales and so many battles were fought along its banks. (*1H4 i 3, iii 1*)

sewer *noun* a servant who tasted food before it was given to the monarch, and served it (*M i 7 – stage direction*)

shadow *noun* **1.** shade (*T iv 1*; *R2 iii 4*; *KL v 2*) **2.** a shady place (*AYLI iv 1*) **3.** darkness (*MM iii 1*) **4.** a reflection (*JC i 2*) **5.** protection (*2H4 iv 2*) **6.** a portrait (*MV iii 2*) **7.** a corpse (*R3 i 4*; *AC iv 2*) **8.** a ghost (*MND iii 2, v 1*) ■ *verb* to hide something (*M v 4*)

shadowed *adjective* dark (*MV ii 1*)

shadowing *adjective* overshadowing (*O iv 1*)

Shafalus *noun see* **Cephalus** (*MND v 1*)

shaft *noun* an arrow, as used with a longbow (*2H4 iii 2*; *KL i 1*; *M ii 3*; *MV i 1*)

shag *adjective* shaggy (*MV iv 4*; *M iv 2*)

shake a beard *verb* to treat someone with contempt (*KL iii 7*; *H iv 7*)

shake off *verb* to refuse to accept something (*TN v 1*; *AC iii 7*)

shake up *verb* to scold someone severely (*AYLI i 1*)

shake your ears *verb* to behave like a donkey (*TN ii 3*)

shale *noun* a shell or outer covering (*H5 iv 2*)

shambles *noun* a place where animals are killed (*O iv 2*)

COMMENT: Shakespeare's most famous use of the word comes in a very painful and vivid speech in **Othello** when the hero is obsessed by his wife's supposed adultery. He thinks of her beautiful and sensual flesh and his diseased imagination puts it alongside filthy and poisonous creatures. He imagines 'summer flies' in 'the shambles', meaning 'a slaughter-house or meat-market', which in a hot summer would be swarming with breeding flies. It's perhaps hard for us to imagine the noise and horrible smells that filled the cramped streets of Elizabethan cities. In York an area of the old town is still called 'the shambles' because that was where the butchers used to work. We now use the word to describe general disorder, something more abstract and far less vivid than Shakespeare's meaning.

shame *verb* to be ashamed (*AYLI iv 3*; *H iii 2*; *M ii 2*)

shamefaced, shamefast *adjective* shy (*R3 i 4*)

shank *noun* a shinbone (*AYLI ii 7*; *RJ iv 1*)

shape *noun* **1.** the outward appearance of something (*MA iii 2*) **2.** an imaginary form (*MND v 1*; *TN i 1*; *2H4 iv 3*) ◇ **fit us to our shape** the way we intend to act (*H iv 7*) ◇ **shape of likelihood** the probability of something (*1H4 i 1*)

shapeless *adjective* ugly (*CE iv 2*)

shard *noun* **1.** a piece of pottery (*H v 1*) **2.** a hard case covering a beetle's wing (*AC iii 2*)

shard-borne *adjective* flying like a beetle, using the shards (wing cases) (*M iii 2*)

shark up *verb* to pick up a selection of things quickly and at random (*H i 1*)

sharp *noun* a high note (*RJ iii 5*) ■ *adjective* **1.** hungry (*TS iv 1*) **2.** severe (*MM ii 4*) **3.** subtle

sharp-looking *adjective* hungry-looking (*CE v 1*)

sharply *adverb* keenly (*T v 1*)

sharpness *noun* severity (*KL v 3*; *AC iii 3*)

sharp-provided *adjective* ready (*R3 iii 1*)

she *noun* a woman (*AYLI iii 2*; *WT iv 4*; *H5 ii 1*)

sheal'd *adjective* shelled (*KL i 4*)

sheep-biter *noun* a thief or traitor (*TN ii 5*)

sheep-biting *noun* petty thieving (*MM v 1*)

sheep-cote *noun* a barn for sheltering sheep (*AYLI ii 4*; *WT iv 4*; *KL ii 3*)

sheep-shearing *noun* a celebration held to mark the yearly shearing of sheep (*WT iv 3*)

sheer *adjective* pure (*R2 v 3*)

sheeted *adjective* (of a dead body) wrapped in a sheet (*H i 1*)

shekel *noun* a Middle Eastern gold coin, especially a Jewish one (*MM ii 2*)

shent *adjective* disgraced (*H iii 2*; *TN iv 2*)

sheriff *noun* the chief officer of the Crown in a county (*1H4 ii 3, 4*; *2H4 iv 4*; *TN i 5*)

sheriff post *noun* a post by the sheriff's house, on which he posted notices, etc. (*TN i 5*)

sherris, sherris-sack *noun* a white wine from Jerez in Spain, where sherry is made (*2H4 iv 3*)

shift *noun* **1.** a trick (*CE iii 2*) **2.** something done out of necessity (*AC iii 11*) **3.** a long undergarment like a petticoat **4.**

something improvised (*MA ii 3*; *TS Ind. 1*) ■ *verb* **1.** to set about doing something (*T v 1*; *CE v 1*) **2.** to manage to get something (*MA iii 3*) **3.** to change your clothes (*2H4 v 5*; *KL v 3*) **4.** to leave without being noticed (*M ii 3*; *O iv 1*) **5.** to change places (*MM iii 1*; *TS v 2*) ◇ **make a shift** to work out a way to do something (*MV i 2*; *2H4 ii 2*)

shipped *adjective* provided with a ship (*O ii 1*)

shipping *noun* a voyage (*TS v 1*)

shiver *verb* to smash something into small pieces (*KL iv 6*)

shivering *adjective* shattering (*MND i 2*)

shivers *plural noun* splinters (*R2 iv 1*)

shoals *noun* the shallow waters of the sea (*M i 7*)

shog *verb* to go away (*H5 ii 1*)

shore *noun* **1.** the furthest extent of something (*MM iii 2*) **2.** places (*H5 iv 1*) ■ *verb* **1.** past tense of *shear* meaning 'to cut something' (*MND v 1*) **2.** to put someone ashore (*WT iv 4*) ◇ **the varying shore o' th' world** the variations between countries (*AC iv 15*)

short *adjective* insufficient ◇ **kept short** kept under control (*H iv 1*)

shorten *verb* to cause difficulties with something (*KL iv 7*)

shot *noun* **1.** a marksman (*2H4 iii 2*) **2.** a person's account at a pub (*1H4 v 3*) ◇ **shot free** without paying (*1H4 v 3*)

shotten herring *noun* a herring that has expelled its **roe**, and so is of little value (*1H4 ii 4*)

shough *noun* a shaggy-haired dog (*M iii 1*)

shoulder-clapper *noun* an arresting officer (*CE iv 2*)

shoulder-shotten *adjective* having a dislocated shoulder (*TS iii 2*)

show *verb* **1.** to seem (*AYLI i 3*; *H5 v 1*; *M i 3*) **2.** to display something as an exhibit (*AC iv 12*)

shrewd *adjective* **1.** bad-tempered, shrewish (*MND iii 2*; *MA ii 1*; *TS i 1*) **2.** mischievous, impish (*JC ii 1*) **3.** evil (*AYLI v 5*; *AC iv 9*)

shrewdly *adverb* **1.** intensely (*H5 iii 7*; *JC iii 1*) **2.** sharply (*MA ii 1*; *H5 iii 7*; *H i 4*)

shrift *noun* the act of confessing your sins to a priest and receiving forgiveness for them from him (*RJ ii 3*)

shrill-gorged *adjective* having a high voice (*KL iv 6*) [From French *gorge*, 'throat'.]

shrine *noun* an image of a saint (*MV ii 7*; *RJ i 5*)

shrink *verb* to shiver (*AYLI ii 1*; *R2 ii 2*)

shrive *verb* (of a priest) to hear someone confess their sins and give forgiveness for them (*CE ii 2*; *MV i 1*)

shriving *noun* the act of hearing someone confess their sins and giving forgiveness for them (*R3 iii 2*; *H v 2*)

shroud *noun* a shelter (*AC iii 13*) ■ *verb* to shelter (*T ii 2*)

shuffling *noun* trickery (*H iii 3, iv 7*)

Sibyl, Sibylla *noun* in Greek mythology, a woman was given the gift of seeing the future by Apollo (*TS i 2*)

sicklied o'er *adjective* coloured faintly (*H iii 1*)

sickly coif *noun* a cap worn by an invalid (*2H4 i 1*)

side *noun* **1.** one side of the body, especially that containing the heart (*TN ii 4*; *KL ii 4*) **2.** a geographical region (*WT iv 4*; *AC i 2*) ◇ **carry out my side** achieve my objective (*L v 1*)

side-piercing *adjective* piercing the heart (*KL iv 6*)

side sleeves *plural noun* long wide sleeves (*MA iii 4*)

siege *noun* **1.** a seat (*MM iv 2*) **2.** a rank (*H iv 7*; *O i 2*) **3.** excrement (*T ii 2*)

sieve *noun* a basket (*M i 3*) (NOTE: In M i 3, the magic associated with witches enabled them to float in a sieve.)

Si fortuna me tormente, sperato me contente *phrase Italian* if fortune torments me, hope contents me (*2H4 ii 4, v 5*)

Sigeum, Sigeon an ancient city in Turkey

sight *noun* **1.** an eye (*MND ii 1*) **2.** a visor on a helmet (*2H4 iv 1*)

sightless *adjective* unseen (*M i 5, 7*) [Because it is too dark to see.]

sign *noun* **1.** a manifestation of something (*MA iv 1*; *O i 1*) **2.** a military flag (an **ensign**) (*H5 ii 2*; *JC v 1*; *O i 1*) ■ *verb* **1.** to mark something (*JC iii 1*) **2.** to be a (good or bad) omen of something (*AC iv 3*)

signal *noun* a symbol or sign of something (*JC v 1*; *R3 v 3*; *RJ v 3*; *H5 v Chor.*)

signet *noun* a seal of authority (*H v 2*; *MM iv 2*)

signory *noun* **1.** a state in northern Italy, ruled by a prince (*T i 2*) **2.** an estate (*R2 iii 1*; *2H4 iv 1*) **3.** the governing body of Venice (*O i 2*)

silk *adjective* silky (*AYLI iii 5*)

silken *adjective* effeminate (*R3 i 3*)

silling *noun* a shilling (five pence). There were twenty shillings in the pound. (*H5 iv 8*)

silly *adjective* **1.** pitiful (*R2 v 5*) **2.** plain (*TN ii 4*) **3.** insignificant (*WT iv 3*)

COMMENT: The meaning of *silly* has travelled a steady historical journey from the Middle English 'seli', meaning 'blessed'or innocently happy, to our present unfavourable sense of 'unwise, frivolous, even half-witted'. When in **Twelfth Night** Orsino asks Feste to sing a favourite old song, he describes it as 'silly sooth' – i.e. simple truth, because it is unsophisticated and old-fashioned. The song was written in a happier and more unworldly age. Act 4 of **The Winter's Tale** is set in this sort of unspoiled pastoral countryside, but when the amoral thief Autolycus plans his next trick he says his 'revenue is the silly cheat'. He means that he will cheat the silly peasant coming down the road: here *silly* also means simple, but the word is used in a patronising sense, a little closer to our meaning.

silly-ducking *adjective* the act of bowing in a ridiculous way (*KL ii 2*)

Simois *noun* a river in the ancient Greek city of Troy, in modern Turkey (*TS iii 1*)

simple *noun* a herb used in medicine or cookery (*AYLI iv 1*; *RJ v 1*; *KL iv 4*; *H iv 7*) ■ *adjective* poor or of low status (*WT iv 4*; *TS Ind. 1*; *AC v 2*)

simpleness *noun* **1.** innocence (*MA iii 1*; *MND v 1*; *O i 3*) **2.** stupidity (*RJ iii 3*)

simplicity *noun* stupidity (*MV i 3*)

simular, simulor *noun* someone who pretends to be something or someone they are not (*KL iii 2*)

sinew *noun* a source of strength (*MM iii 1*; *1H4 iv 4*; *H5 i 2*)

singing-man *noun* a member of the choir of a church or cathedral (*2H4 ii 1*)

single *adjective* weak (*T i 2*; *2H4 i 2*; *M i 3, 6*)

singleness *noun* stupidity (*RJ ii 2*)

single-soled *adjective* weak (*RJ ii 4*) [Because a single-soled shoe was of poor quality.]

singular *adjective* expert at something (*WT iv 4*; *RJ ii 4*) ■ *adverb* remarkably (*2H4 iii 2*)

singularities *plural noun* curious things (*WT v 3*)

singularity *noun* the state of being different (*TN iii 4*)

sinister *adjective* **1.** unjust (*H5 ii 4*; *MM iii 2*) **2.** disrespectful (*TN i 5*) **3.** lefthand (*MND v 1*)

sink *noun* a sewer (*H5 iii 5*) ■ *verb* **1.** to be killed or destroyed (*AC iii 7*; *O ii 3*) **2.** to make something to fall (*T ii 1*)

sinking-ripe *adjective* ready to sink (*CE i 1*)

sir-reverence *interjection* begging your pardon (*RJ i 4*; *CE iii 2*) [From the phrase 'save your reverence'.]

sisters three *plural noun see* **Fates** (*MND v 1*)

sit *verb* **1.** (of the wind) to blow from a particular direction (*MV i 1*; *R2 ii 2*; *H5 ii 2*) **2.** to lie heavily on something (*MM v 1*; *R2 i 3*; *R3 v 3*; *H iii 4*) **3.** to hold a council to discuss something (*H5 v 2*; *R3 iii 1*)

sith *conjunction* since that time (*H ii 2*)

sixpenny strikers *plural noun* mean people (*1H4 ii 1*) [From the idea of men who would hold up someone for a small amount of money.]

size *noun* **1.** an amount (*AC iv 15*) **2.** an allowance (*KL ii 4*)

sized *adjective* of a particular size (*H iii 2*)

skainsmate *noun* an associate (*RJ ii 4*) [From the idea of woman who works with another to wind skeins of wool, or man who fights with another, a 'knife–companion'.]

skillet *noun* a small long-handled pan (*O i 3*)

skill-less *adjective* ignorant (*T iii 1*; *TN iii 3*)

skills ◇ **it skills not** it doesn't matter (*TN v 1*)

skimble-skamble *adjective* meaningless (*1H4 iii 1*)

skin *verb* to cover something with or like skin (*MM ii 2*; *H iii 4*)

skipper *noun* a frivolous thoughtless person (*TS ii 1*)

skirr *verb* **1.** to scurry (*H5 iv 7*) **2.** to search a place thoroughly (*M v 3*)

skirt *noun* **1.** the edge (*AYLI iii 2, v 4*; *H i 1*) **2.** the edge of a garment (*MA iii 4*; *TS iv 3*)

slab *adjective* heavy or solid (*M iv 1*)

slack *verb* **1.** to fail to do something or to do something properly (*O iv 3*) **2.** to fail to pay proper attention to someone (*KL ii 4*) ◇ **come slack** fall short of a required standard (*L I 3*)

slander *noun* a spiteful remark (*CE iii 1*) ■ *verb* to accuse someone of something disgraceful (*MA ii 3*; *1H4 i 3*; *H i 3*) ◇ **honest slanders** remarks that damage a woman's reputation without questioning her virginity (*MA iii 1*)

slave *verb* to make a slave of someone (*KL iv 1*)

sleave *noun* a thread of silk made by separating out a thicker strand (*M ii 2*)

sledded *adjective* on sledges (*H i 1*)

sleek *adjective* smooth (*M iii 2*)

sleek-headed *adjective* with the hair neatly combed (*JC i 2*)

sleep *verb* to be inactive (*MM ii 2*; *KL i 4*; *H i 3*)

sleevehand *noun* a wristband (*WT iv 4*)

sleight *noun* an art (*M iii 5*)

sliding *noun* a decline in standards (*MM ii 4*)

slight *verb* to ignore something contemptuously (*JC iv 3*)

sling *noun* a piece of artillery resembling a large crossbow, for hurling heavy objects (*H iii 1*)

slip *noun* **1.** an heir (*MM iii 1*) **2.** a dog's leash (*H5 iii 1*) **3.** a forged coin (*RJ ii 4*) ◇ **let slip** to release the dogs when hunting (*1H4 i 3*; *TS v 2*; *JC iii 1*)

slipper *adjective* slippery (*O ii 1*)

slippery *adjective* unfaithful (*WT i 2*; *AC i 2*)

slipshod *adjective* wearing slippers (*KL i 5*)

sliver *noun* a branch that has been broken off (*H iv 7*) ■ *verb* to break something off (*M iv 1*; *KL iv 2*)

slobbery *adjective* wet and dirty (*H5 iii 5*)

slops *plural noun* wide baggy trousers, worn just above the knee (*2H4 i 2*; *MA iii 2*)

slough *noun* a skin (*H5 iv 1*; *TN ii 5, iii 4*)

slovenly *adjective* dirty (*1H4 i 3*)

slovenry *adjective* the state of being dirty and untidily dressed (*H5 iv 3*)

slow *adjective* dull (*R3 i 2*)

slubber *verb* **1.** to do something carelessly (*MV ii 8*) **2.** to smear something (*O i 3*)

slug, slug-abed *noun* a lazy person (*CE ii 2*; *R3 iii 1*)

sluice *verb* **1.** to channel something (*R2 i 1*) **2.** to seduce someone (*WT i 2*)

slumbery *adjective* sleepy (*M v 1*)

sly *adjective* stealthy (*R2 i 3*)

small *adjective* **1.** shrill (*MND i 2*; *TN i 4*) **2.** little, not much **3.** weak, watered down (drink) (*2H4 ii 2*; *O ii 1*) ■ *noun* (of a period of time) short (*AYLI iv 3*; *H5 ii 4*; *R3 iv 1*)

small beer *noun* weak beer, drunk in quantity (*2H4 ii 2*) ■ *adjective* unimportant (*O ii 1*)

smatch *noun* a taste (*JC v 5*)

smatter *verb* to chatter (*RJ iii 5*)

smilet *noun* a little smile (*KL iv 3*)

Smithfield *noun* a field outside the walls of the City of London, the site of markets, fairs and a weekly horse fair during the 12th century. It was also notorious for its gallows and for executions by burning at the stake (up to c 1611). (*2H4 i 2*) [Alteration of 'smooth field'.]

smock *noun* a woman (*AC i 2*; *MA ii 3*; *O v 2*; *RJ ii 4*) [Because a smock was a woman's petticoat.] ◇ **a shirt and a smock** a man and a woman (*RJ ii 4*)

smoke *noun* a mist (*M i 5*) ■ *verb* **1.** to disinfect something with smoke (*MA i 3*) **2.** to steam something (*KL v 3*)

smooth *verb* **1.** to make something less apparent (*R2 i 3*) **2.** to use flattery (*R3 i 3*; *KL ii 2*) ■ *adjective* **1.** flattering (*AYLI ii 7*) **2.** pleasant (*1H4 i 1*; *2H4 Introd*; *AC i 3*)

smooth-faced *adjective* having a flattering, smarmy expression

smoothing *adjective* flattering (*R3 i 2*)

smother *noun* a thick, suffocating smoke (*AYLI i 2*)

smug *adjective* neat (*1H4 iii 1*; *MV iii 1*)

Smulkin *noun* the name of a demon (*KL iii 4*)

smutched *adjective* smudged (*WT i 2*)

snaffle *noun* a jointed mouthpiece for a horse, giving it more freedom (*AC ii 2*)

snatch *noun* **1.** an excerpt of a song (*H iv 7*) **2.** a small objection (*MM iv 2*)

snatcher *noun* a thief (*H5 i 2*)

Sneak-up, Sneak-cup *noun* someone who sneaks up on people (*1H4 iii 3*)

sneap *noun* a snub (*2H4 ii 1*) ■ *verb* to check, nip (*WT i 2*)

sneck up *interjection* Go and be hanged! (*TN ii 3*)

snipe *noun* someone who is fooled in some way (*O i 3*) [Because a snipe is a wading bird that is easy to catch.]

snorting *noun* snoring (*1H4 iii 4*; *O i 1*)

snuff *noun* a huff (*KL iii 1*) ■ *verb* to take offence at something (*MND v 1*; *1H4 i 3*)

soaking *adjective* quickly taken in (*WT i 2*)

sob *noun* a breathing space (*CE iv 3*)

sobriety *noun* **1.** modesty (*TS i 1*) **2.** proper conduct (*H5 iv 1*)

sociable *adjective* sympathetic (*T v 1*)

sodden *adjective* **1.** boiled (*H5 iii 1*) **2.** worn out by disease (NOTE: This is an allusion to sitting sweating in a tub, a treatment for sexually transmitted diseases.)

soft *adjective* gentle (*H5 iii 3*; *O i 3*) ■ *interjection* go easy! steady! (*T i 2*; *MA v 1*; *RJ i 1*; *H iii 1*; *AC ii 2*; *O v 2*) ■ *adverb* gently (*2H4 v 2*)

soho *noun* a hunting cry made when a hare was surprised out of its hiding place (*RJ ii 4*)

soiled *adjective* well fed on spring grass (*KL iv 6*)

sol *noun* the sun (*KL i 2*; *TS i 2, iii 1*)

sola *interjection* hello there! (*MV v 1*)

solder *verb* to close something up (*AC iii 4*)

sole *adjective* mere (*M iv 3*)

solely *adverb* **1.** totally (*RJ ii 4*; *M i 5*) **2.** only (*MV ii 1*) ■ *adjective* alone (*TS ii 1*; *WT ii 3*; *H5 ii Chor.*)

solemn *adjective* **1.** ceremonious (*AC v 2*) **2.** relating to a festival or ceremony (*TS iii 2*; *M iii 1*) **3.** sombre (*H i 2*)

solemnity *noun* **1.** the performance of customary rituals (*MND iv 1*) **2.** grandeur (*1H4 iii 2*)

sol-fa *verb* to sing from written music (*TS i 2*)

solicit *verb* **1.** to argue your case (*TN iii 1*) **2.** to rouse someone (*R2 i 2*; *H v 2*)

solicitation *noun* courting (*O iv 2*)

soliciting *noun* **1.** courting (*H ii 2*) **2.** urging (*M i 3*)

solus *adjective* Latin alone (*H5 ii 1*)

Solyman *noun* Suleiman (1490–1566), a sultan of the Ottoman Empire. He was famous as a wise ruler and a conqueror. He fought against the Persians (1535). (*MV ii 1*)

something *adjective* some distance away (*M iii 1*)

son *noun* a son-in-law (*TS v 2*; *KL i 1*)

sonance *noun* a sound (*H5 iv 2*)

sonties *plural noun* saints (*MV ii 2*)

sooth *noun* **1.** the truth (*T ii 2*; *MND ii 2*; *WT i 2, iv 3*; *MV i 1*; *H5 iii 6*; *M i 2*) **2.** flattery (*R2 iii 3*) ■ *adjective* true (*M v 5*) ■ *adverb* truly (*TN ii 1*; *WT iv 3*; *O iii 3*)

soothe *verb* to humour someone (*CE iv 4*; *R3 i 3*; *KL iii 4*)

soother *noun* a flatterer (*1H4 iv 1*)

soothsay *verb* to predict the future (*AC i 2*)

sop *noun* a piece of bread or cake soaked in wine (*KL ii 2*; *R3 i 4*; *TS ii 2*) *See also* **make a sop o' th' moonshine of** *at* **moonshine**

sophisticated *adjective* disguised (*KL iii 4*)

Sophy *noun* the former title of the rulers of Persia (*MV ii 1*; *TN ii 5, iii 4*)

sore *noun* a disease (*MA iv 1*; *O iv 2*) ■ *adjective* severe (*T iii 1*; *R3 i 4*; *KL iii 5*) ■ *adverb* severely (*WT v 3*)

sorry *adjective* painful (*O iii 4*)

sort *noun* **1.** a group of people (*MND iii 2*; *R2 ii 4*; *R3 v 3*) **2.** a manner of doing something (*T ii 1*; *MM iii 2*; *MV i 2*; *JC ii 1*) **3.** a rank (*MM iv 4*; *MA i 1*; *H5 iv 7*) ■ *verb* **1.** to happen (*MND iii 2*; *TS iv 3*) **2.** to choose or decide something (*MV v 1*; *R3 ii 2, 3*; *RJ iii 5*) **3.** to be appropriate (*H i 1*) **4.** to class someone as the same as others (*H ii 2*)

sortance *noun* an agreement (*2H4 iv 1*)

sottish *adjective* foolish (*AC iv 15*)

soul *noun* **1.** the source of true feeling (*MM v 1*; *H iii 2*; *O i 3*) **2.** the essential feature of something (*MM iii 1*; *H5 iv 1*; *H ii 2*) **3.** a trace (*H5 iv 1*) ◊ **three souls** according to medieval philosophy, the three principles that make up the human soul, i.e. animal, vegetable and rational (*TN ii 3*)

sound *verb* **1.** to be clear of a sexually transmitted disease (*MM i 2*) **2.** to faint (*RJ iii 2*; *H v 2*)

soundpost *noun* a peg placed under the bridge of a violin (*RJ iv 5*)

soused *adjective* pickled in salt water (*1H4 iv 2*)

south, the *noun* the wind blowing from the south (*2H4 ii 4*; *RJ i 4*)

Southampton *noun* a seaport in Hampshire located between the mouths of the Rivers Test and Itchen. It has been an important port since ancient times. (*H5 v Chor.*)

South Sea *noun* the Pacific Ocean (*AYLI iii 2*)

sovereignly *adjective* supremely (*WT i 2*)

sow-skin *noun* a pig skin (*WT iv 3*)

sowter *noun* someone who makes or repairs shoes (*TN ii 5*)

space *noun* a length of time (*AYLI iv 3*; *KL v 3*; *AC ii 1*)

span *noun* **1.** a short length of time (*O ii 3*) **2.** a unit of measurement based on the distance between the thumb and little finger of the open hand (*AYLI iii 2*)

spaniel *verb* to follow someone in a grovelling manner (*AC iv 10*)

Spanish pouch *noun* a term of contempt for a wine seller (*1H4 ii 4*) [Referring to a type of purse made from Spanish leather and worn by wine-sellers.]

spare *verb* **1.** to avoid doing something (*T ii 1*; *2H4 iii 2*; *R3 i 3*) **2.** to avoid something (*MND ii 1*) **3.** to avoid offending somebody (*MM ii 3*) ■ *adjective* **1.** thin (*2H4 iii 2*; *JC i 2*) **2.** mean (*H5 ii 2*)

sparing *adjective* **1.** tolerant (*R3 iii 7*) **2.** forbearing (*CE iii 1*; *RJ i 1*)

sparrow *noun* a womaniser (*MM iii 2*)

Sparta *noun* one of the dominant city-states of ancient Greece. The inhabitants were noted for their frugal living, discipline and courage. (*MND iv 1*)

spartan kind, spartan dog kind *noun* a breed of bloodhound (*MND iv 1*; *O v 2*)

spavin *noun* a disease of the joints of a horse, causing inflammation and lameness (*TS iii 2*)

spear *noun* a lance (*1H4 i 3*)

speciality *noun* a detailed contract for the payment of money (*TS ii 1*)

speculation *noun* **1.** the act of looking on (*H5 iv 2*) **2.** an observer (*L iii 1*) **3.** the power of seeing combined with understanding (*M iii 4*)

speculative *adjective* with the power of seeing (*O i 3*)

speed *noun* **1.** a person or thing that brings success and wealth (*AYLI i 2*; *1H4 iii 1*; *RJ v 3*) **2.** success (*TS ii 1*; *WT iii 2*) ■ *verb* **1.** to cause someone to succeed (*WT iv 4*; *JC i 2*; *KL iv 6*) **2.** to have success (*TS ii 1*) **3.** to make something go faster (*MM iv 5*; *H5 iii 5*) **4.** to be ruined (*TS iii 2, v 2*) **5.** to be provided for (*MV ii 9*) **6.** to succeed (*R3 iv 3*; *KL i 2*; *O iv 1*) **7.** to kill someone (*RJ iii 1*) ◇ **have the speed of** to be faster than someone (*M I 5*)

speeding *noun* success (*TS ii 1*)

spell backward *verb* to misunderstand someone (*MA iii 1*)

spell-stopped *adjective* stopped by magic (*T v 1*)

spend *verb* **1.** to express a strong emotion (*MND iii 2*) **2.** to use something up (*MA i 1*; *TS v 1*; *R2 i 3*) **3.** to waste something (*O i 2*; *M ii 1*) **4.** to eat something (*2H4 iii 2*; *RJ ii 4*)

spent *adjective* **1.** passed (*R2 i 3*) **2.** exhausted (*M i 2*)

sphere ◇ **the tuned spheres** the sun, moon and the planets were believed to revolve around the earth in concentric spherical orbits producing harmonic sounds (*AC v 2*)

spherical predominance *noun* the influence of the planets (*KL i 2*)

sphery *adjective* star-like (*MND ii 2*)

spicery *noun* spices (*R3 iv 4*)

spices *plural noun* traces (*WT iii 2*)

spies *plural noun* the eyes (*T v 1*)

spill *verb* to kill, destroy (*KL iii 2*; *H iv 5*)

spin *verb* to gush out (*H5 iv 2*)

spinner *noun* a spider (*MND ii 2*; *RJ i 4*)

spinster *noun* a woman who spins (*O i 1*; *TN ii 4*)

spirit *verb* to make something more active (*H5 iii 5*)

spirituality *noun* the clergy (*H5 i 2*)

spirt *verb* to grow rapidly (*H5 iii 5*)

spit ◇ **spit in the hole** to spit on the hands before doing heavy manual work (*TS iii 1*)

splay, spay *verb* to castrate a man (*MM ii 1*)

spleen an organ near the stomach that, in the adult, removes degenerate red blood cells from the body (NOTE: It was thought to be the source of such emotions as anger, malice and sadness (known as melancholy)) ◊ **full of spleen** unpredictable (*TS iii 2*)

COMMENT: Elizabethans believed that strong emotions were created in the *spleen*. If the physical body is out of sorts, then it is likely that behaviour will be disordered and irrational. Shakespeare uses *spleen* or its adjective *splenetive* to describe impulsive behaviour, often angry or malicious. In **Henry IV Part 1** the impulsive young hero Henry Percy, nicknamed Hotspur, is described as 'the hare-brained Hotspur, governed by a spleen'. Most uses of the word describe negative or violent feelings, though sometimes it was used for eagerness or laughter.

splenetive *adjective* impetuous (*H v 1*)

splint, splinter *verb* to join something with a splint (*R3 ii 2; O ii 3*)

split *verb* to make something incomprehensible (*CE v 1; AC ii 7*) ◊ **make all split** to cause an uproar (*MND i 2*)

spoil *noun* 1. destruction (*1H4 iii 3*) 2. stealing on a large scale by an invading army (*MV v 1; H5 iii 3; JC v 3*) 3. a massacre (*JC iii 1*) ■ *verb* to ruin someone (*TS v 1; O v 1*) [From a hunting term meaning 'the dividing of the quarry between the hounds after a hunt'.]

spongy *adjective* 1. moist (*T iv 1*) 2. permanently drunk (*M i 7*)

spoon-meat *noun* delicacies (*CE iv 3*) [Referring to soft food fed to children and invalids with a spoon.]

sport *noun* 1. a pastime (*R2 iii 4; AC i 1*) 2. a theatrical performance (*MND iii 2*) 3. the hunt 4. a joke or the act of joking (*CE iii 2; MA ii 3; MV i 3*) 5. a game of chance (*MV iii 2; AC ii 3*) 6. fighting (*1H4 i 3; H5 iv 2*) 7. sexual intercourse (*O ii 1*) ■ *verb* to have a good time (*T iv 1*) ◊ **make sport** 1. to ridicule someone (*MA iii 1; AYLI i 2*) 2. to play (*CE ii 2; R2 ii 1; H ii 2*)

sportful *adjective* amorous (*TS ii 1*)

sportive *adjective* amorous (*R3 i 1*)

spot *noun* 1. a mark of disgrace (*AC iv 12*) 2. a tick or other mark on a list (*JC iv 1*) 3. a pattern (*O iii 3*)

spotted *adjective* 1. immoral (*MND i 1*) 2. embroidered (*O iii 3*)

spousal *noun* marriage (*H5 iv 2*)

spray *noun* offspring (*H5 iii 5*)

sprightfully *adverb* enthusiastically (*R2 i 3*)

sprighting, spiriting *noun* haunting done by a ghost (*T i 2*)

sprightly, spritely *adjective* 1. lively (*1H4 ii 4; AC iv 14*) 2. cheerful (*AC iv 7*) ■ *adverb* cheerfully (*WT iv 4*)

spring *noun* 1. the beginning (*MND ii 1; 2H4 iv 4*) 2. first love (*CE iii 2*) 3. the source of something (*R2 i 1; 1H4 v 2; M i 2*)

springe *noun* a snare consisting of a noose that will tighten when triggered by an animal (*WT iv 3; H i 3, v 2*)

sprite *noun* a ghost or spirit (*MND v 1*)

spruce *adjective* influenced (*TS iv 1*)

spur *noun* a root (*T v 1*)

spurn *verb* to kick something (*CE ii 1*) ◊ **spurn at** to reject something (*JC ii 1*) ◊ **spurn upon** to trample on someone (*R3 i 2*)

spy *noun* 1. an observer (*T v 1*) 2. an observation (*M iii 1*)

squander *verb* to scatter something (*MV i 3*)

squandering *adjective* random (*AYLI ii 7*)

square *noun* 1. a fair measure 2. a measuring instrument (*WT iv 4*) 3. a piece of material covering a woman's breasts (usually embroidered or smocked) (*WT iv 3*) 4. a military formation (*H5 iv 2; AC ii 11(13)*) 5. a limit of action or conduct (*AC ii 3*) ■ *verb* 1. to quarrel (*MND ii 1; AC ii 1*) 2. to shape something (*MM v 1; WT iii 3*) ■ *adjective* accurate (*AC ii 2*) ◊ **the most precious square** the most valuable part (*L i 1*) ◊ **keep square** to play fairly (*AC ii 3*)

squared *adjective* ruled (*WT iii 3*)

squared me *verb* let myself be ruled by (*WT v 1*)

squarer *noun* someone engaged in a fight (*MA i 1*)

squash *noun* an unripe peapod (*MND iii 1; TN i 5; WT i 2*)

squene *verb* to squint (*KL iii 4*)

squier *noun* a carpenter's ruler (*1H4 ii 2*)

squiny *verb* to squint (*KL iv 6*)

squire *noun* a measuring instrument (*1H4 i 2*)

stablishment *noun* ownership (*AC iii 6*)

staff ◇ **set in staff** to make yourself at home (*CE iii 1*)

stagger in *verb* to be uncertain (*MM i 2; AYLI iii 3*)

staggers *noun* a disease of horses characterised by dizziness and staggering (*TS iii 2*)

stain *noun* disgrace (*MM iii 1*) ■ *verb* **1.** to disfigure something (*R2 iii 1; R3 iv 4*) **2.** to corrupt or taint something (*H iv 4*) **3.** to eclipse, outshine (*AC iii 4; R2 iii 3*)

stale *noun* **1.** a decoy (*T iv 1; TS iii 1*) **2.** a laughing stock (*TS i 1; CE ii 1*) **3.** a prostitute (*MA ii 2, iv 1*) **4.** urine (*AC i 4*) ■ *verb* **1.** to cheapen something (*JC i 2*) **2.** to make something uninteresting (*JC iv 1; AC ii 2*)

COMMENT: When used as an adjective or verb, *stale* carries our sense of unfresh, deteriorating, worn out. Similarly, when *stale* is used as a noun, one of its specialised meanings, used by grooms in the stable, is 'urine'. In **Antony and Cleopatra** Caesar contrasts Antony's glamorous way of life with his former toughness as a soldier: in times of deprivation 'Thou did'st drink the stale of horses'. However, its primary meaning as a noun is as a term from falconry: a lure or decoy. Prospero in **The Tempest** orders Ariel, 'The trumpery in my house, go fetch it hither/For stale to catch these thieves'. Stephano, Trinculo and Caliban are debased to the level of animals and are subject to simple baits, and their human vice of greed and status makes them susceptible to gaudy clothes. In this particular moral context, the noun *stale* perhaps also carries the adjectival meaning of 'worn out rubbish' These two senses of *stale* ('bait' and 'worn out') are present in its more focused meaning of prostitute. Katherine in **The Taming of the Shrew**, rushed by her desperate father into the marriage market, attacks him bitterly: 'I pray you, sir, is it your will/To make a stale of me?' Even stronger is Don Pedro's cutting complaint in **Much Ado About Nothing** that he has been deceived into helping to link his 'dear friend to a common stale'.

stalking-horse *noun* something used to hide someone's real intention (*AYLI v 4*)

stall *verb* **1.** to install someone in a position (*R3 i 3*) **2.** to live (*AC v 1*) **3.** to put a horse in a stall

Stamford *noun* a market town in Lincolnshire (*2H4 iii 2*)

stamp *noun* a coin (*M iv 3*) ■ *verb* **1.** to mark something with a stamp (*R3 i 1*) **2.** to give an impression of being genuine (*O ii 1*)

stanchless *adjective* that cannot be satisfied (*M iv 3*)

standard *noun* a soldier who carries a military flag (a **standard**) (*T iii 2*) ◇ **he's no standard** he cannot stand upright (*T iii 2*)

standing *noun* the time that something lasts (*WT i 2*) ■ *adjective* still (*T ii 1; TN i 5; KL iii 4*)

standing-tuck *noun* a sword standing on its end (a term of abuse) (*1H4 ii 4*)

staniel, stannel *noun* a kestrel (a hawk that hovers) (*T ii 2; TN ii 5*)

star *noun* **1.** a person's condition **2.** the pole star, which has a constant position due north in the northern hemisphere [The planets and constellations of the zodiac were considered to have a great influence on human affairs, hence 'star' frequently refers to a person's state.]

star-blasting *noun* the influence of the stars (*KL iii 4*)

stare *noun* the state of being amazed (*T iii 3*) ■ *verb* to stand on end (*JC iv 3*)

stark *adjective* **1.** rigid (*1H4 v 3; RJ iv 1*) **2.** utterly (*TS iii 2; TN iii 4; CE ii 1*)

starkly *adverb* rigidly (*MM iv 4*)

starred *adjective* destined (*WT iii 2*)

start *noun* **1.** something done or undertaken suddenly (*MV ii 2*) **2.** the advantage of going first (*JC i 2*) ■ *verb* **1.** to alarm (*M v 5*) **2.** to rouse something (*TN iv 1; JC i 2*) **3.** to drive an animal from its lair (*1H4 i 3*) **4.** to disturb something (*O i 1*)

starting-hole *noun* a hiding place (*1H4 ii 4*)

startingly *adverb* in sudden bursts (*O iii 4*)

start-up *noun* an upstart (*MA i 3*)

starved *adjective* **1.** hungry (*MV iv 1*) **2.** thin through lack of food (*2H4 iv 4*) **3.** unimportant (*2H4 iii 2*) **4.** numb with cold

starve-lackey *noun* someone who starves their servants (*MM iv 3*)

starveling *noun* a starving person (*1H4 ii 1, 4*)

state *noun* **1.** a person's social position (*T i 2*; *2H4 v 2*; *R3 iii 7*; *M iv 2*) **2.** the possessions and behaviour indicating a person's social position (*MA ii 1*; *2H4 iii 1*; *H5 i 2*; *JC i 2*; *RJ iv 3*) **3.** a chair of state with a canopy over it (*TN ii 5*; *1H4 ii 4*; *M iii 4*) **4.** the property and land owned by a person (*MV iv 2*; *1H4 iv 1*) **5.** government (*R2 iv 1*; *2H4 v 2*)

station *noun* a way of standing (*H iii 4*; *AC iii 3*)

statist *noun* a statesman (*H v 2*)

statute *noun* a contract by which a debtor mortgaged his land to his creditor (*MM i 3, 4, v 1*; *H v 1*)

stead *verb* to be advantageous to someone (*T i 2*)

stead up *verb* to take someone's place (*MM iii 1*)

steal a marriage *verb* to get married secretly (*TS iii 2*)

stealing *adjective* creeping stealthily (*R3 iii 7*; *H v 1*)

stealth *noun* **1.** the act of creeping stealthily (*MND iii 2*; *TN i 5*) **2.** a dishonest act (*MM i 2*; *KL i 2*) **3.** theft (*KL iii 4*)

steeled *adjective* hardhearted (*MM iv 2*; *H5 ii 2*)

steep *noun* a mountain range (*MND ii 1*)

steerage *noun* control over the direction something takes (*RJ i 4*)

stelled *adjective* fixed (*KL iii 7*)

stem *noun* the front of a ship ∎ *verb* to make progress through something (*JC i 2*)

step-dame *noun* a stepmother (*MND i 1*)

sternage *noun* the collective rear sections (sterns) of the ships of a fleet (*H5 iii Chor.*)

stew *noun* **1.** a large cooking pot (*MM v 1*) **2.** a brothel (*R2 v 3*; *2H4 i 2*)

sticking place *noun* the point at which slipping back is prevented (*M i 7*)

stiff *adjective* **1.** inflexible (*2H4 i 1*; *KL iv 6*) **2.** serious (*AC i 2*)

still conclusion *noun* a settled expression (*AC iv 15*)

stillness *noun* the state of being sober (*H5 iii 7*; *O ii 3*)

still-soliciting *adjective* always begging (*KL i 1*)

still-stand *noun* the time of high or low water when the tide does not move (*2H4 ii 3*)

still-vexed *adjective* always upset by storms (*T i 2*)

stilly *adverb* softly (*H5 iv Chor.*)

sting *noun* sexual desire (*MM i 4*; *AYLI ii 7*; *TS ii 1*; *H i 5*; *O i 3*)

stint *verb* **1.** to stop doing something (*RJ i 3*) **2.** to cause something to stop (*H8 i 2*)

stithy *noun* a blacksmith's forge or smithy (*H iii 2*)

stoccado *adjective* a straight thrust in fencing

stoccata *adjective see* **stoccado** (*RJ iii 1*)

stock *noun* **1.** a stocking (*TN i 3*; *TS iii 2*) **2.** a stupid person (*TS i 1*) ∎ *verb* to punish someone by putting them in the **stocks** (*KL ii 2, 4, iii 4*)

stock-fish *noun* dried cod that was beaten before being boiled (*T iii 2*; *MM iii 2*; *1H4 ii 4*; *2H4 iii 2*)

stockish *adjective* brutal and stupid (*MV v 1*)

stocks *plural noun* a wooden frame with holes in which a person's feet, hands, and head were secured as a means of punishment

stoic *noun* a severe or strict person (*TS i 1*)

stolen *adjective* secret (*O iii 3*)

stomach *noun* **1.** an appetite for food (*CE i 2*; *TS iv 1*; *1H4 iii 3*) **2.** courage (*T i 2*; *2H4 i 1*; *H i 1*) **3.** an inclination for something (*AYLI iii 2*; *TS i 1*; *H5 iv 3*; *JC v 1*) **4.** pride (*TS v 2*) ∎ *verb* to resent something (*AC iii 4*)

COMMENT: The stomach is the place where digestion takes place and the word therefore came to describe the appetite, as when Hotspur's wife in **Henry IV Part 1** asks her husband 'what is it that takes from thee/Thy stomach?' He is certainly not without *stomach* in Shakespeare's very common metaphorical meaning of 'courage or readiness for action'. It was common for parts of the body, like liver and heart, to stand for strong feelings, since these were thought to have a precise physical origin within the body. Shakespeare's use of *stomach* is like our 'guts', both robust words to describe courage. However, someone with 'guts' or *stomach* may be difficult for superiors to deal with, even subversive: Katherine's final speech in **The Taming of the Shrew** urges women to 'vail your stomachs'. She urges them to remove their assertiveness.

stomacher *noun* a quilted covering put over the lower chest for warmth or protection (*WT iv 4*)

stone *noun* **1.** insensitivity and lack of feeling (*TN iii 4*; *R3 iii 7*; *KL v 3*) **2.** a polished crystal (*KL v 5*) **3.** the inability to speak (*AC ii 2*) **4.** a thunderbolt (*O v 2*) ■ *verb* to turn something into stone (*O v 2*)

stone-bow *noun* a crossbow that could fire small stones (*TN ii 5*)

stones *plural noun* the testicles (*MND v 1*; *RJ i 3*)

stonish *verb* to shock someone (*H iii 2*)

stoop *verb* **1.** to be forced to modify something in a humiliating way (*MM ii 4*; *2H4 v 2*) **2.** to bow your head (*R2 iii 1*; *2H4 Ind.*) **3.** (of a falcon) to fly to a lure (*H5 iv 1*)

stop *noun* **1.** a sudden halt of a galloping horse (*MND v 1*) **2.** a punctuation mark (*MND v 1*; *MV iii 1*) **3.** a ridge indicating the position of the fingers on a stringed instrument (*MA iii 2*) **4.** the act of covering a hole on a wind instrument (*H iii 2*; *2H4 Ind.*) ■ *verb* **1.** to fill something in (*AYLI iv 1*) **2.** to fill someone's ears with noise (*R2 ii 1*; *2H4 i 1*)

stop in *verb* to keep something in (*R3 i 4*)

stopple *verb* to stop something up with a plug (*KL v 3*)

store *verb* to populate a country (*H5 iii 5*; *O iv 3*)

stored *adjective* accumulated (*KL ii 4*)

storehouse *noun* a graveyard (*M ii 4*)

story *noun* an object of ridicule (*MM i 4*)

stoup *noun* a jug containing 2.25 litres (*H v 1*; *TN ii 3*)

stoutly *adverb* **1.** boldly (*O iii 1*) **2.** strongly (*O ii 1*)

stover *noun* winter food for cattle (*T iv 1*)

straggler *noun* a homeless person (*R3 v 3*)

straight *adverb* immediately (*MM i 2*; *AC iv 12*; *O iv 1*)

strain *noun* **1.** a person's lineage (*H5 iv 4*; *JC v 1*) **2.** an emotion (*2H4 iv 5*) **3.** a tune or note (*AYLI iv 3*; *JC v 3*) **4.** a characteristic (*KL v 3*) ■ *verb* **1.** to push something to the limit (*MA iv 1*) **2.** to exagger-ate (*WT iii 2*; *1H4 iv 1*) **3.** to limit something (*RJ ii 3, iv 1*)

strain courtesy *verb* to act disrespect-fully (*RJ ii 4*)

strained *adjective* **1.** forced (*MV iv 1*) **2.** excessive (*2H4 i 1*; *KL i 1*)

strait *adjective* **1.** strict (*MM ii 1*; *1H4 iv 3*) **2.** tight-fitting (*H5 iii 7*)

straited *adjective* at a loss (*WT iv 4*)

straitly *adverb* strictly (*R3 i 1, iv 1*)

straitness *noun* strictness (*MM iii 2*)

strange *adjective* **1.** rare or unusual (*T iii 3*; *H i 5*) **2.** unfamiliar (*R2 v 5*; *M i 3*) **3.** foreign (*AYLI iv 1*) **4.** belonging to someone else (*MA v 4*) **5.** ignorant (*CE ii 2*; *M iii 4*) **6.** aloof or reserved (*TN v 1*; *JC i 2*; *RJ iii 2*) ■ *adverb* remarkably (*H i 5*)

strange-achieved *noun* the meaning is obscure. It may mean gained by unusual, wrong means, brought from a foreign country, or collected for another person. (*2H4 iv 5*)

strange-disposed *adjective* of an unusual character (*JC i 3*)

strangely *adverb* **1.** in an exceptional degree (*T iv 1*; *MA iii 2*; *M iv 3*) **2.** as a foreigner (*WT ii 3*) **3.** in a reserved manner (*2H4 v 2*)

strangely-visited *adjective* infected (*M iv 3*)

strangeness *noun* aloofness (*TN iv 1*; *O iii 3*)

strangered *adjective* alienated (*KL i 1*)

strappado *noun* a form of torture in which the arms are tied behind the back and the victim is suspended and dropped suddenly so that the arms are dislocated or broken (*1H4 ii 4*)

stratagem *noun* a violent action (*MV v 1*; *RJ iii 5*)

straw *noun* something of little value (*WT iii 2*; *H iv 4*)

stray *verb* to lead something astray (*CE v 1*) ◇ **make a stray from** to wander away from something (*KL i 1*)

strength *noun* **1.** force (*MV v 1*; *1H4 i 3*; *AC iii 2*) **2.** authority (*JC iii 1*; *KL ii 1*) **3.** an army (*AC ii 1*)

stretch-mouthed *adjective* open-mouthed, suggesting the use of swear-words (*WT iv 4*)

strewing, strewment *noun* flowers placed on a grave (*H v 1*)

stricture *noun* strictness (*MM i 3*)

strife *noun* **1.** the act of striving for something (*MM iii 2*; *RJ ii 2*) **2.** rivalry

strike *verb* **1.** (*of a musician*) to begin to play (*WT v 3*; *R3 iv 4*; *KL v 3*) **2.** to get rid of evil influences (*WT i 2*; *H i 1*) **3.** to give up (*R2 ii 1*; *AC iv 2*) **4.** to fight a battle (*H5 ii 4*) **5.** to open a barrel (*AC ii 7*) [From a nautical term meaning 'to lower the sails'.]

striker *noun* a thief (*1H4 ii 1*)

string *noun* a tendon (*KL v 3*; *H iii 3*; *AC iii 11*)

strond *noun* the seashore (*TS i 1*; *MV i 1*; *1H4 i 1*)

strossers *plural noun* tight trousers (*H5 iii 7*)

'stroy *verb* to destroy something (*AC iii 9*)

struck *adjective* **1.** wounded (*1H4 iv 2*) **2.** (of age) advanced (*TS ii 1*; *R3 i 1*)

strucken *verb* struck (*CE i 2*; *JC ii 2, iii 1*; *RJ i 1*)

strumpet *verb* to make someone a prostitute (*CE ii 2*)

stubborn *adjective* stiff (*H iii 3*)

stubbornness *noun* harshness (*AYLI ii 1*; *O iv 3*)

stuck *noun* a thrust in swordfighting (*TN iii 4*; *H iv 7*)

studied *adjective* **1.** taught (*MV ii 2*; *M i 4*) **2.** disposed to do something (*2H4 ii 2*; *AC ii 6*)

study *noun* **1.** the act of learning a part (*MND i 2*) **2.** hard work and effort (*AYLI v 2*; *KL i 1*) ◼ *verb* to learn something by heart (*AYLI iii 2*; *TN i 5*; *H ii 2*)

stuff *noun* a subject (*H ii 2*) ◼ *verb* to complete something (*KL iii 5*)

stuffed *adjective* **1.** complete (*MA i 1*; *WT ii 1*; *RJ iii 5*) **2.** blocked up (*M v 3*) **3.** having a cold (*MA iii 4*)

stuff-o'-the-conscience *noun* the essence of morality (*O i 2*)

sty *noun* a place of uncontrolled lust (*H iii 4*) ◼ *verb* to lock someone up like a pig in a sty (*T i 2*) [Literally *pig-sty*.]

style *noun* a title

sub-contracted *adjective* engaged to be married for a second time (*KL v 3*)

subdue *verb* to lower the rank or status of someone (*O iii 4*) ◼ *adjective* overwhelmed (*O v 2*)

subject *noun* **1.** an object (*RJ iii 5*) **2.** something that is free and independent (*MM v 1*)

subjection *noun* the act of accepting a superior authority (*KL v 7*; *H5 iv 1*)

submission *noun* an admission of guilt (*1H4 iii 2*; *RJ iii 1*)

submit *verb* to put yourself in a risky situation (*JC i 3*)

suborn *verb* to persuade or bribe someone to commit a criminal or evil act (*CE iv 4*; *R3 iv 3*; *M ii 4*)

subornation *noun* the crime of persuading or bribing someone to commit a criminal act on your behalf (*1H4 i 3*)

subscribe *verb* **1.** to give something up (*TS i 1*; *KL i 2, iii 7*) **2.** to sign something (*R2 i 4*; *AC iv 5*) **3.** to agree to something (*MM ii 4*; *MA v 2*)

subscribe for *verb* to agree to do something on behalf of someone else (*MA i 1*)

subscription *noun* loyalty (*KL iii 2*)

substance ◇ **sightless substances** invisible shapes (*M i 5*)

substractor *noun* a critical person (*TN i 3*)

subtle *adjective* **1.** cunning (*TN i 5*; *1H4 i 3*) **2.** fine, rarefied (*T ii 1*)

subtle knee *noun* an insincere display of humility (*R2 i 4*)

subtlety *noun* a fantastic illusion (*T v 1*)

subtly, subtilly *adverb* treacherously (*H5 iv 1*; *RJ iv 3*)

suburbs *noun* the outskirts of a city, where the brothels were situated (*JC ii 1*)

succeed *verb* **1.** to inherit something (*MM ii 4*) **2.** to be inherited by someone (*O v 2*) ◼ *noun* something which happens (*KL i 2*)

success *noun* **1.** the process of inheriting something (*WT i 2*; *2H4 iv 2*) **2.** a result of something (*AC iii 5*; *O iii 3*) ◇ **success of mischief** disastrous consequences (*2H4 iv 2*)

COMMENT: *Success*, coming from the verb 'to succeed', basically means whatever follows, whether the results are good or bad. We use 'succession' to describe a new king following on from his father: his reign is the result of his father's death. 'Success', for Shakespeare, was therefore neutral in its meaning, whereas for us it refers only to happy or prosperous results. A striking example occurs in **Othello** when Iago protests that he wants no 'vile success' in his investigations about Desdemona's possible affair with Cassio. **In Much Ado**

About Nothing the Friar tries to re-assure Leonato: 'and doubt not but success/Will fashion the event in better shape'. Although he wants 'success' in our happy sense, his word *success* means 'succession', what follows in the passage of time.

successfully ◇ **looks successfully** looks as though he will succeed (*AYLI i 2*)

succession *noun* the future (*CE iii 1*; *H ii 2*)

successively *adverb* by right of inheritance (*2H4 iv 5*; *R3 iii 7*)

sudden *adjective* **1.** immediate (*MM ii 2*; *H v 2*; *O iv 2*) **2.** unpredictable (*AYLI ii 7*; *R2 ii 1*; *2H4 iv 4*; *M iv 3*; *O ii 1*) **3.** hasty (*AYLI v 2*; *JC iii 1*)

suddenly *adverb* at once (*AYLI ii 4*; *1H4 i 3*)

suerly *adjective* surely (*H5 iii 2*)

suffer *verb* **1.** to put up with something (*T iii 2*; *MV iv 1*; *KL iii 4*; *O v 2*) **2.** to allow someone to do something (*MND iii 2*) **3.** to be affected by something bad (*H v 2*) ◇ **to be suffered** to go unchecked (*2H4 ii 3*; *KL i 2*)

sufferance *noun* **1.** tolerance (*MA i 3*; *MV i 3*; *H5 iii 6*) **2.** permission (*AYLI ii 2*; *H5 ii 2*) **3.** the condition of suffering pain (*MM ii 4*; *MA v 1*; *JC ii 1*) **4.** the fact of experiencing death (*H5 ii 2*) **5.** damage (*O ii 1*)

sufficiency *noun* the quality of being suitable for a position (*MM i 1*; *O i 3*)

sufficient *adjective* **1.** able (*MM ii 1*; *2H4 iii 2*; *O iii 4*) **2.** able to pay your debts (*MV i 3*)

suggest *verb* **1.** to lead someone astray (*R2 iii 4*; *H5 ii 2*; *O ii 3*) **2.** to incite someone to do something (*R2 i 1*)

suggestion *noun* **1.** a temptation (*T iv 1*) **2.** an incitement (*R3 iii 2*; *M i 3*; *KL ii 1*)

suit *noun* **1.** clothing (*TS Ind. 1*; *MV ii 2*; *H i 2*) **2.** attendance at court (*MM iv 4*; *AYLI i 2*) **3.** a request (*KL ii 2*; *O iii 1*) ▪ *verb* **1.** to correspond to something (*TN i 2*; *H5 i 2*; *M ii 1*) **2.** to dress yourself (*AYLI I 3*; *H5 iv 2*)

suited *adjective* dressed (*TN v 1*; *MV i 2*; *KL iv 7*)

sullens *noun* depression (*R2 ii 1*) ▪ *adjective* **1.** dull (*1H4 i 2*) **2.** dismal (*R2 v 6*; *2H4 i 1*; *RJ iv 5*) **3.** depressing (*O iii 4*)

sumless *adjective* not able to be calculated (*H5 i 2*)

summer *adjective* welcome (*WT iv 3*; *1H4 iii 1*; *R3 iv 3*)

summered *adjective* well kept (like land used by animals for grazing in the summer) (*H5 v 2*)

summer-house *noun* a country house in which to spend the summer (*1H4 iii 1*)

summer-seeming *adjective* short-lived (like the English summer) (*M iv 3*)

summoner *noun* an official who formally accused people in a church court (*KL iii 2*)

sumpter *noun* a drudge (*KL ii 4*) [From *sumpter*, 'a pack horse'.]

sun ◇ **in the sun** leading an idle, care-free life (*AYLI ii 5*; *RJ iii 1*; *H i 2*)

sunburnt *adjective* unattractive (*MA iv 3*) (NOTE: For the Elizabethans and until the later part of the 20th century, to be sunburnt meant you were poor enough to have to work out in the sun and so it made you look like a peasant.) [From *son*, i.e. a man, and *burnt*.]

superflux *noun* an excess of something (*KL iii 4*)

super-serviceable *adjective* doing more than is necessary or asked for in a job (*KL ii 2*)

supervise *noun* an examination of something (*H v 2*)

supervisor *noun* a spectator (*O iii 3*)

suppliance *noun* a pastime (*H i 3*)

supply *verb* **1.** to please someone (*MM v 1*; *O iv 1*) **2.** to strengthen something (*M i 2*)

support *verb* to endure with something (*KL v 3*; *O i 3*)

supportable *adjective* able to be endured (*T v 1*)

supportance *noun* **1.** the act of keeping a promise (*TN iii 4*) **2.** support (*R2 iii 4*)

supposal *noun* an estimate (*H i 2*)

suppose ◇ **counterfeit supposes** deceptive substitutions (*TS v 1*)

supposition *noun* a belief (*CE iii 2*) ◇ **in supposition** in doubt (*MV i 3*)

surcease *noun* an ending (*M i 7*) ▪ *verb* to stop (*RJ iv 1*)

surety *noun* **1.** someone who guarantees to do something if another person fails to fulfil an undertaking (*T i 2*; *MV i 2*) **2.** a guarantee (*H5 v 2*) **3.** certainty (*O i 3*)

surfeit-swelled *adjective* swollen by excess eating and drinking (*2H4 v 5*)

surly *adjective* haughty (*TN ii 5*; *JC i 3*; *H5 i 2*)

surmise *noun* speculation (*M i 3*; *R3 ii 1*) ■ *verb* to imagine (*H ii 2*)

surprise *verb* to capture someone (*1H4 i 1*)

sur-reined *adjective* ridden too much (*H5 iii 5*)

surspire *verb* to breathe (*2H4 iv 5*)

survey *verb* to notice something (*M i 2*)

suspect *noun* suspicion (*CE iii 1*)

suspiration *noun* breathing (*H i 2*)

sustain *verb* to have a place (*O v 2*)

sutler *noun* someone who sold food, etc. to soldiers in a camp (*H5 iii 1*)

swabber *noun* someone who washed the decks of a ship (*T ii 2*; *TN i 5*)

swaddling clouts *noun* the cloths in which a newborn baby is wrapped (*H ii 2*)

swag-bellied *adjective* with a sagging stomach (*O ii 3*)

swagger *verb* to bully using threatening language (*TN v 1*; *2H4 ii 4*; *KL iv 6*; *O ii 3*)

swaggerer *noun* someone who bullies using threatening language (*AYLI iv 3*; *2H4 ii 4*)

swaggering *noun* bullying using threatening language (*2H4 ii 4*)

swain *noun* 1. a young man in love 2. a peasant from the country (*AYLI ii 4*; *WT iv 4*; *MND iv 1*)

swan *noun* according to legend, a swan would sing just before its death (*AC iii 2*; *O v 2*; *RJ i 2*)

swart *adjective* with a dark complexion (*CE iii 2*)

swarth *noun* a pile (*TN ii 3*)

swasher *noun* a loud, boisterous bully (*H5 iii 2*)

swashing *adjective* 1. the actions of a loud, boisterous bully (*AYLI i 3*) 2. staggering (*RJ i 1*)

swathe, swath *noun* the corn or grass cut by a single stroke of a scythe (*TN ii 3*)

sway *noun* the realm (*JC i 3*) ■ *verb* to move (*2H4 iv 1*; *M v 3*)

swayed *adjective* with a bent back (*TS iii 2*)

sweat *noun* a disease whose symptoms included heavy sweating (either malaria or a form of plague) (*MM i 2*)

sweeting *noun* 1. darling (a term of affection) (*TS iv 3*; *TN ii 3*; *O ii 3*) 2. a sweet variety of apple (*RJ ii 4*)

sweetmeat *noun* a piece of fruit preserved in sugar (*MND i 1*; *RJ i 4*)

sweetness, saucy *noun* frivolous pleasure (*MM ii 4*)

swelling *adjective* 1. overflowing (*1H4 iii 1*) 2. developing (*M i 3*; *H5 iv Chor.*)

sweltered *adjective* sweated out (*M iv 1*)

swerve *verb* to become distracted (*WT iv 4*)

swerving *noun* an error (*AC iii 11*)

swift *adjective* quick-witted (*AYLI v 4*; *TS v 2*)

swim *verb* to float (*AYLI iv 1*; *JC v 1*)

swinge *verb* to beat someone with a stick or whip (*2H4 v 4*)

swinge-buckler *noun* a noisy, boisterous person (*2H4 iii 2*)

swinish *adjective* coarse, like a pig (*H i 4*; *M i 7*)

switch and spurs *adjective* as fast as possible (*RJ ii 4*) [From the idea of using spurs and whip to make a horse go faster.]

Swithold *noun* St Withold (St Vitalis), called on to protect someone from nightmares (*KL iii 4*)

Switzers *noun* a Swiss bodyguard (*H iv 5*)

swoond *verb* fainted (*JC i 2*; *AC iv 9*)

swoopstake *adverb* indiscriminately (*H iv 5*) (NOTE: From the idea of taking the whole stake at once in a gambling game.) [From the idea of taking the whole stake at once in a gambling game.]

sword-and buckler *adjective* common (*1H4 i 3*) [Because a sword and small shield were the arms of a common soldier.]

sword Philippian *noun* the sword Anthony used at the victory at **Philippi** (*AC ii 5*)

sworn *adjective* confirmed (*TN iii 4*)

syllable ◇ **by** *or* **to the syllable** exactly (*T i 2*) ◇ **to the last** *or* **utmost syllable** to the absolute limit (*M v 5*)

syllogism *noun* a method of reasoning in logic (*TN i 5*)

sympathize *verb* 1. to have a similar nature to something (*1H4 v 1*; *H5 iii 7*) 2. to correspond to something (*R2 v 1*)

sympathized *adjective* in which everyone has shared (*CE v 1*)

sympathy *noun* **1.** correspondence (*O ii 1*) **2.** equality of rank (*MND i 1*; *R2 iv 1*)

synod *noun* **1.** a council of the gods (*AYLI iii 2*) **2.** a legislative assembly (*AC iii 10*; *CE i 1*; *H ii 2*)

Syracuse, Syracusa *noun* an ancient Greek town founded (c. 734 BC) on the small island of Ortygia off the southeast coast of Sicily (*CE i 1, v 1*) (NOTE: It was a famous centre of culture.)

Syria *noun* a country on the east coast of the Mediterranean. Its capital is Damascus. The ancient country was larger than modern Syria. (*AC iii 1, 6*)

syrup *noun* a medicine sweetened to mask its unpleasant taste (*O iii 3*)

T

table *noun* **1.** a notebook (*2H4 ii 4*; *H i 5*) **2.** in the Bible, the tablets of stone on which the Ten Commandments were written (Exodus 19) (*MM i 2*; *R3 i 4*) **3.** a written or printed record (*WT iv 4*; *H ii 2*) **4.** in palmistry, the figure formed by the crossing of the lines on the palm of a hand (*MV ii 2*)

table-book *noun* a notebook (*WT iv 4*; *H ii 2*)

tabor a small drum, usually held in one hand

taborer *noun* someone who plays the **tabor** (*T iii 2*)

tabourine, taborin(e) *noun* a **tabor** with a long body (*AC iv 8*)

tackled stair *noun* a rope ladder (*RJ ii 4*)

taffeta *noun* a fine shiny silk fabric (*1H4 i 2*; *TN ii 4*)

tag, tag-rag *noun* a rabble (*JC i 2*)

tail *noun* **1.** the female genitals (*TS ii 1*) **2.** the penis (*O iii 1*)

tailor *interjection* used as a crude interjection (*MND ii 1*) *See also* **tail**

taint *noun* **1.** decay (*KL i 1*) **2.** a stain (*H ii 1*; *M iv 3*; *AC v 1*) ■ *verb* **1.** to hinder or damage something (*TN iii 4*; *O i 3, iv 2*) **2.** to treat something as being of no value (*TN v 1*; *O ii 1*) **3.** to corrupt someone (*H i 5*) **4.** to become faint as a result of something (*M v 3*) ◇ **fall into taint** to become spoilt (*L i 1*)

tainted *adjective* infected with a sexually transmitted disease

take 1. to infect someone with a disease (*AC iv 2*) **2.** to bewitch someone (*T v 1*; *WT iv 4*; *H i 1*) **3.** to hit someone (*MM ii 1*; *TN ii 5*; *H5 iv 1*) **4.** to meet someone (*CE iii 2*; *H5 iv 1*) **5.** to hide in a place (*CE v 1*) **6.** to hear or believe something (*TS ii 1*; *KL iv 6*) **7.** to agree a truce (*RJ iii 1*) **8.** to catch fire (*H5 ii 1*) **9.** to put up with something (*KL ii 2*; *H ii 2*) ◇ **take me with you** help me to understand you (*RJ iii 5*; *1H4 ii 4*) ◇ **taken-off** killed (*O v 2*)

◇ **ta(k)'en out** copied (*O iii 3*) ◇ **take on** to rage at someone (*MND iii 2*) ◇ **take out** to copy something (*O iii 3*) ◇ **take thought** to be sad (*JC ii 1*)

COMMENT: This word had various meanings in Shakespeare's time, as it does nowadays. However, one of the most specialised, and unfamiliar to us, is 'to bewitch or infect'. In the first scene of **Hamlet**, Marcellus is relieved as the dawn replaces a threatening night: 'Then no planets strike,/No fairy takes, nor witch hath power to charm'. When King Lear is reminded of Goneril he urges the vengeance of Heaven to 'strike her young bones,/You taking airs, with lameness'. Both contexts refer to mysterious worlds beyond human understanding. This use of *take* is thought to derive from an early, primitive culture, from the Gaelic word 'tachd'.

take up *verb* to sort out a quarrel (*TN iii 4*) ◇ **take up short** put a stop to someone (*H5 ii 4*)

taking *noun* **1.** an agitated state **2.** sinister influence (*KL iii 4*)

taking off *noun* a murder (*KL v 1*; *M i 7*)

taking up *noun* the act of obtaining something on credit (*2H4 i 2*)

talk *verb* to talk nonsense (*WT iii 2*; *M iv 2*; *O iv 3*)

talker *noun* someone who talks but doesn't act (*MV i 1*; *R3 i 3*)

tall *adjective* **1.** lively **2.** spirited **3.** courageous **4.** impressive

tallow *noun* animal fat (*1H4 ii 4*; *CE iii 2*)

tallow catch, tallow ketch *noun* a pan for catching the fat from roasting meat (*1H4 ii 4*)

tallow face *noun* a face the colour of tallow (*RJ iii 5*)

'tame, attame *verb* to break into something (*H5 i 2*)

tang *noun* a twanging sound, sting (*T ii 2*) ■ *verb* to make a loud clanging noise (*TN ii 5, iii 4*)

tangle *verb* to trap something in a snare (*AYLI iii 5*)

taper *noun* a candle, usually a thin one (*JC ii 1, iv 3*; *O i 1*)

taphouse *noun* a pub (*MM ii 1*)

tardiness *noun* diffidence (*KL i 1*)

tardy *verb* to delay something (*WT iii 2*) ■ *adjective* surprised (*R3 iv 1*) ◇ **come tardy off** to fail to do something properly (*H iii 2*)

tardy-apish *verb* to imitate fashions that are out of date (*R2 ii 1*)

tardy-gaited *adjective* walking slowly (*H5 iv Chor.*)

Tarquin, Tarquinius *noun* an early Roman king (*JC ii 1*; *M ii 1*) (NOTE: Tarquinius Superbus (d. 510 BC) was the last king of Rome. As a result of his tyrannical rule he was overthrown and a Republic was established. His son, Tarquinius, raped Lucrece)

tarre *verb* to provoke someone into a fight (*H ii 2*)

tarry *verb* **1.** to stay in a place (*MV iv 2*) **2.** to stay for something (*2H4 iii 2*)

tart *adjective* **1.** distressing (*KL iv 2*) **2.** acid (*AC ii 5*)

Tartar *noun* **1.** a native of Tartary, a large area of northern Asia and eastern Europe formerly controlled by the Mongols (*M iv 1*; *MND iii 2*; *RJ i 1*) **2.** hell (*CE ii 2*; *H5 ii 2*; *TN ii 5*) (NOTE: According to the writings of **Homer**, Tartarus was a place which was as far below **Hades** as the earth was below heaven, and was where the people in Hades who had done wrong were sent.)

Tartar's painted bow *noun* the bow-like outline of the upper lip (*RJ i 4*) (NOTE: The **Tartars** were generally nomadic people and expert horsemen. They were also noted for their archery skills on horseback, using short bows shaped like an upper lip.)

tartly *adverb* acidly (*MA ii 1*)

tartness *noun* acidity

task *verb* **1.** to place a heavy demand on something (*H5 i 2*; *O ii 3*) **2.** to challenge someone to do something (*T i 2*; *1H4 iv 1*) **3.** to force someone to do something **4.** to tax something (*1H4 iv 3*) **5.** to criticise

someone for something (*KL iii 2*) ◇ **at task** blamed (*L i 4*)

tasking *noun* a challenge (*1H4 v 2*)

tassel-gentle, tercel gentle *noun* a male goshawk (a short-winged hawk used for hunting geese, etc.) (*RJ ii 2*)

taste *noun* **1.** a test (*2H4 ii 2*; *KL i 2*) **2.** a small sample that is tasted (*AYLI iii 2*; *JC iv 1*; *H ii 2*) **3.** the act of tasting something (*R2 ii 1*) **4.** the act of experiencing something (*1H4 iii 1*; *H5 ii 2*) ■ *verb* **1.** to experience something (*T v 1*; *MND v 1*; *WT iii 2*; *RJ ii 3*) **2.** to test something (*TN iii 1, 4*; *1H4 iv 1*; *2H4 iv 1*)

Taurus *noun* **1.** the sign of the zodiac represented by a bull (*TN i 1*) *See also* **Europa 2.** a mountain range in southern Turkey (*MND ii 2*)

Tavy *noun* an affectionate form of the names Davy or David (*H5 iv 7*)

tawdry-lace *noun* a cheap lace collar or scarf (*WT iv 4*) (NOTE: Such cheap items could be bought at an annual fair dedicated to st Audrey, from which the word 'tawdry' is derived.)

taxation *noun* **1.** satire (*AYLI i 2*) **2.** a demand for something (*TN i 5*)

tax home *verb* to criticise someone for something (*H iii 3*)

taxing *noun* criticism (*AYLI ii 7*)

tear *verb* to erase something (*RJ ii 2*)

Te Deum *noun* the *Te Deum laudamus* (We praise thee O Lord), a hymn usually sung during the morning church service (matins) (*H5 iv 8*)

teem *verb* **1.** to produce something (*H5 v 2*; *M iv 3*) **2.** to give birth to children (*KL i 4*)

teeming-date *noun* the time for giving birth to children (*R2 v 2*)

teen *noun* distress (*T i 2*; *R3 iv 1*)

Telamon *noun* in Greek mythology, the father of the hero **A**jax (*AC iv 1*)

tell *verb* **1.** to count the number of something **2.** to say the prayers using rosary beads

Tellus, Terra *noun* in Greek mythology, Mother Earth, the first creature to be born from the primeval Chaos (*H iii 2*) (NOTE: The Greek equivalent is **Gaea** (**Ge**).)

temper *noun* the hardness and flexibility of steel (*R2 iv 1*) ■ *verb* **1.** to mould something (*H5 ii 2*) **2.** to prepare something (*MA ii 2*; *RJ iii 5*) **3.** to modify something (*RJ ii Prol.*) **4.** to soften something by warming it (*2H4 iv 3*) **5.** to moisten something (*KL i 4*)

temperance *noun* **1.** a climate (*T ii 1*) **2.** the state of not being sexually active or promiscuous (*AC iii 13*)

temperate *adjective* moderate, restrained, not sexually active or promiscuous (*T iv 1*; *TS ii 1*)

temporal *adjective* not having to do with the church (*MM ii 2*; *MV iv 1*; *H5 i 1*)

temporary *adjective* concerned with worldly things (*MM v 1*)

temporize *verb* to compromise (*MA i 1*)

temporizer *noun* someone who compromises (*WT i 2*)

tempt *verb* to risk something (*JC ii 1*)

tench *noun* a freshwater fish related to the carp (*1H4 ii 1*) (NOTE: The reference may be to the sensory barbs (that look like stings) hanging from the mouth or to the red spots on the body that look like insect bites.)

tend *verb* to refer to something (*JC iii 2*)

tendance *noun* care

tender *noun* **1.** something offered in payment (*MND iii 2*) **2.** an offer to accept something (*RJ iii 4*; *H i 3*) **3.** care or consideration (*1H4 v 4*; *KL i 4*) ■ *verb* **1.** to be concerned about something (*RJ iii 1*) **2.** to display something (*H i 3*) **3.** to put down money, etc. as payment (*MM ii 4*) ■ *adjective* **1.** precious (*M i 7*) **2.** (of the weather) mild (*T ii 1*) **3.** sensitive (*MND iv 1*)

tender-hefted *adjective* mounted in a delicate handle, possibly moved by tender emotions (*KL ii 4*)

tending *noun* the act of attending to someone (*M i 5*)

tennis *noun see* **rackets** (*H ii 1*)

tenor *noun* a legal term for the summary of a document

tent *noun* a canopy over a bed (*TS ii 1*) ■ *verb* to probe or examine someone (*H ii 2*) (NOTE: A 'tent' was an instrument for cleaning and exploring wounds.)

tenure *noun see* **tenor** (*H v 1*)

term *noun* the time during which the law courts sat (*AYLI iii 2*; *2H4 v 1*)

Termagant *noun* a violent abusive woman (*H iii 2*) [According to the Crusaders, Termagant was an idol worshipped by the Saracens. He was introduced into morality plays as a violent evil person dressed in long flowing robes and this dress led to his being regarded as a woman.]

termination *noun* the final words of a sentence (*MA ii 1*)

terrene *adjective* relating to the earth (*AC iii 13*)

tertian *noun* a fever that recurs every other day, probably malaria (*H5 ii 1*)

test *noun* evidence (*O i 3*)

testament *noun* a will (*AYLI i 1*; *H5 i 1, iv 6*; *JC iii 2*)

tested *adjective* refined (*MM ii 2*)

tester, testril *noun* a sixpence (2.5p) (*2H4 iii 2*)

testimony *verb* to prove something (*MM iii 2*)

testril *noun see* **tester** (*TN ii 3*)

testy *adjective* irritable (*JC iv 3*; *MND iii 2*; *R3 iii 4*)

tetchy *adjective* irritable (*RJ i 3*)

tetter *noun* a skin condition such as eczema (*H i 5*)

text *noun* a quotation (*TN i 5*; *KL iv 2*; *RJ iv 1*) ■ *verb* to write something clearly in capital letters (*MA v 1*)

thanks ◇ **to con thanks** to give thanks for something

thatched *adjective* covered (*T iv 1*)

Theban *noun* an inhabitant of **Thebes** (*KL iii 4*)

Thebes *noun* an ancient Egyptian city extending about 37km along the banks of the Upper Nile, in the area of the Valley of the Kings (*MND v 1*)

theft *noun* **1.** the act of creeping away stealthily (*M ii 3*) **2.** something stolen (*H iii 2*)

theme *noun* **1.** a conversation (*CE v 1*; *WT v 1*) **2.** an undertaking (*2H4 i 2*)

theoric *noun* a theory (*O i 1*)

there *pronoun* that (*AYLI i 3*) ■ *conjunction* **1.** at that (*MV ii 8*; *KL iv 3*; *H ii 1*) **2.** by that (*AC ii 5*) **3.** in that (*KL iv 6*; *RJ iii 3*; *H iii 1*) **4.** with that (*MA v 2*)

thereabout *pronoun* that part (*H ii 2*)

thereabouts *adverb* near to that (*WT i 2*; *AC iii 10*)

thereafter as *conjunction* according to how (*2H4 ii 2*)

therefore *conjunction* for that (*T iii 3*; *MND iii 2*; *1H4 i 1*)

thereto, thereunto *adverb* besides (*WT i 2*; *O ii 1*)

therewithal *adverb* also (*M iii 1*)

Theseus *noun* in Greek mythology, the son of Aegeus and king of Athens, who killed the minotaur and fought against the **Amazons**, taking their queen, Hippolyta as his wife. He was murdered by Lycomedes at Scyros. The character as depicted by Shakespeare differs from that of mythology.

Thessalian *adjective* of Thessalia (**Thessaly**) (*MND iv 1*)

Thessaly, Thessalia *noun* a province in central Greece (*AC iv 1*; *MND iv 1*)

Thetis *noun* a sea nymph, the mother of **Achilles** (*AC iii 7*)

The Turk *noun* the Sultan of Turkey (*H5 v 2*; *O i 3*)

thick *adjective* (of a person's sight) poor (*2H4 iii 2*; *JC v 3*) ■ *adverb* quickly (*2H4 ii 3*; *AC i 5*)

thicken *verb* to become dim (*M iii 2*)

thick-eyed *adjective* having poor sight (*1H4 ii 3*)

thick-pleached *adjective* made up of closely intertwined branches (*MA i 2*)

thick-skin *noun* a stupid person (*MND iii 2*)

thievish *adjective* surrounded by thieves (*RJ iv 1*)

thill-horse *noun* a horse attached to a wagon to pull it as part of a team (*MV ii 2*)

thing *noun* **1.** a creature (*M v 4*) **2.** something (*RJ iv 1*; *O iii 3*) **3.** all creation (*KL iii 1*; *M iii 2*) **4.** the genitals (*1H4 iii 3*)

third *noun* the essential part (*T iv 1*) [From a thread, something which holds things together.]

thirdborough *noun* a local constable (*TS Ind. 1*)

thirsty *adjective* causing thirst (*MM i 2*)

thisne *adverb* in this way (*MND i 2*)

thorough *preposition* through (*MND ii 1*)

thou *noun* 'you' in a poetical or solemn sense (*CE v 1*; *TN i 1*)

COMMENT: One effect of the French influence on medieval English was to extend the language of address between two people. Just as the French had 'tu' and 'vous' as singular forms of *you*, English came to have *you* and *thou*. This choice could denote different levels of rank and intimacy. *You* was generally more respectful: the prince Hamlet tells his scholar/friend Horatio, 'Thou art e'en as just a man', and Horatio promises him to be 'at your service'. Children would usually address their parents with the respectful *you* and receive *thou* in reply. Courtiers, mindful of mutual high status would often use *you*, whilst it was common for lower classes to give each other *thou*. We will not find these distinctions used as invariable rules in Shakespeare's plays, but particular scenes are often enriched in their impact if we observe characters' use of *you* and *thou*, especially scenes of shifting emotions between two people. In the first scene of **King Lear**, Goneril, Regan and Cordelia all use the respectful *you* to their father. In keeping with the scene's national significance, he addresses all three formally and as *you*. When Goneril and Regan please him with their answers, he switches to a more intimate 'thee' and 'thine'. But when Cordelia angers him, 'thy truth then be thy dower' sounds like a violent shift to dismissing an inferior. Most shocking of all is Kent's unprecedented intervention with *thou*, instead of the proper *you* to his king: 'What would'st thou do, old man?' Everything about Kent's speech in its context is insolent and dangerous. A more complex exchange of *you* and *thou* is found in **Much Ado About Nothing** after the crisis in the church. Benedick and Beatrice are alone and he tentatively begins to declare his love for her. She is moved by this but furious at what has happened to her cousin, Hero. She always uses *you* to him, but he switches between *you* and *thou*, depending on whether he feels encouraged or rebuffed. When he undertakes to challenge Claudio, he reverts to the formal *you*, indicating the serious issue of honour that is at stake.

thou-est *verb* to address someone as 'thou' (i.e. as an inferior) (*TN iii 2*)

though *interjection* so what! (*AYLI iii 3*)

thought *noun* sad pondering (*AYLI iv 1*; *H iii 1, iv 5*) ■ *adverb* in silence (*R3 iii 6*) ◇ **upon** *or* **with a thought** instantly (*1H4 ii 4*; *JC v 3*; *M iii 4*)

thought-executing *adjective* carried out as quickly as thought (*KL iii 2*)

thought-sick *adjective* sick with worry (*H iii 4*)

Thracian *adjective* of Thrace (*AC iii 6*; *MND v 1*)

Thracian poet, Thracian singer *noun* *see* **Orpheus** (*MND v 1*)

thraldom *noun* slavery (*R3 i 5*)

thrall *noun* a slave (*H iii 4*; *M iii 6*; *R3 iv 1*; *TS i 1*)

thrasonical *adjective* in the boastful manner of Thraso, a soldier in Terence's *Eunuch* (*AYLI v 2*)

thread *noun* the course of life (*MND v 1*; *H5 iii 6*; *O v 2*) ■ *verb* to pass through something like a thread goes through the eye of a needle (*R2 v 5*; *KL ii 1*)

threaden *adjective* woven (*H5 iii Chor.*)

three-inch fool *noun* a man with a short penis (*TS iv 1*)

three-man beetle *noun* a heavy ram for driving in large posts, requiring three men to lift it (*2H4 i 2*)

three-man-song *noun* a lively song for treble, tenor and bass voices (*WT iv 3*)

three-nooked *adjective* three-cornered (*AC iv 6*) [From the view of the world being divided into the continents of Europe, Africa and Asia.]

three-piled *adjective* (of velvet) very high quality, thick and luxurious (*MM i 2*)

three-pile velvet *noun* a velvet with a very thick raised surface made from three-stranded thread and therefore very expensive (*WT iv 2*)

three-suit *noun* a servant's annual clothes allowance given in kind or as cash (*KL ii 2, iii 4*)

thrice-crowned *noun* a reference to the Roman goddess Diana ruling on earth (as Diana), in heaven (as Cynthia) and in the underworld (as Hecate) (*AYLI iii 2*)

thrice-driven *adjective* made with the lightest feathers that had been separated three times by blasts of air (*O i 3*)

thride *noun* a thread (*T iv 1*)

thrift *noun* **1.** a profit (*WT i 2*; *MV i 3*; *H iii 2*) **2.** an advantage (*MV i 1*)

thriftless *adjective* **1.** pointless (*TN ii 2*; *M ii 4*) **2.** wasteful (*R2 v 3*)

thrilling *adjective* extremely cold (*MM iii 1*)

throat *noun* a person's voice (*AYLI ii 5*; *O iii 3*)

throe *verb* **1.** to cause someone pain (*T ii 1*) **2.** to produce something (*AC iii 7*)

thronging *adjective* enclosing (*MA i 1*; *R3 iv 4*)

throstle *noun* a thrush (*MND iii 1*; *MV i 1*)

throw *noun* a throw of a dice (*TN v 1*; *MV ii 1*)

thrum *noun* the tufted end of a weaver's thread (*MND v 1*) ◇ **thrum and thread** good and bad (*MND v 1*)

thrusting on *noun* a driving force (*KL i 2*)

thumb ◇ **bite one's thumb at** an insulting gesture involving flicking the thumb forwards from the back of the upper teeth (*RJ i 1*)

thumb-ring *noun* a ring worn on the thumb (*1H4 ii 4*)

thunder-stone *noun* a thunderbolt (*JC i 3*)

thwart *adjective* awkward (*KL i 4*)

tib *noun* a working-class, common woman

tickle *verb* **1.** to beat someone with a stick or whip (*TN v 1*) **2.** to serve someone well (*1H4 ii 4*) **3.** to caress something with the fingers ■ *adjective* unstable (*MM i 2*) ◇ **tickle o' the sere** easily set off, susceptible (*H ii 2*)

tickle-brain *noun* strong drink (*1H4 ii 4*)

tick-tack *noun* sexual intercourse (*MM i 2*) [From *tick-tack*, a game similar to back-gammon, using pegs in holes to score.]

tide *noun* **1.** a flow of tears **2.** a season (*RJ iii 5*) **3.** the passage of time (*JC iii 1*) **4.** a large number or amount (*R2 ii 2*)

tide life, tide death *phrase* come life, come death (*MND v 1*)

tidy *adjective* plump and so ready to kill (*2H4 ii 4*)

tight *adjective* **1.** (of a ship) not leaking (*T v 1*) **2.** fast (*AC iv 4*)

tike, tyke *noun* a mongrel dog (*H5 ii 1*; *KL iii 6*)

tilly-fally, tilly-vally *interjection* rubbish! (*TN ii 3*; *2H4 ii 4*)

tilt *verb* to fight on horseback with a lance in a competition (*1H4 ii 3*)

tilter *noun* a fighter (*MM iv 3*; *AYLI iii 4*)

timeless *adjective* at the wrong time (*R3 i 2*; *RJ v 3*)

timely *adjective* **1.** early (*CE i 1*) **2.** in good time (*M iii 3*)

time-pleaser *noun* someone who changes their opinions and conduct according to the circumstances (*TN ii 3*)

timorous *adjective* terrified (*O i 1*)

tinct *noun* **1.** same as **tincture 1** (*H iii 4*) **2.** the golden colour given to base metals by the alchemists' elixir (*AC i 5*)

tincture *noun* **1.** a colour (*WT iii 2*) **2.** a stain on a handkerchief that had been dipped in a martyr's blood and was kept because regarded as sacred (*JC ii 2*)

tinder *noun* dry material for starting a fire from a spark (*O i 1*)

tine *noun* the vetch plant (*O i 1*) ■ *adjective* very small (*2H4 v 1*; *KL iii 2*)

tinsel *noun* a cloth made to glitter by having fine strips of gold or silver woven in it (*MA iii 4*)

tire *noun* a headdress (*AC ii 5*; *MA iii 4*)

tiring *noun* the act of styling your hair (*CE ii 2*)

tiring-house *noun* the dressing room of a theatre (*MND iii 1*)

tirrits *plural noun* terrors (*2H4 ii 4*)

tissue *noun* a fine fabric with strips of gold or silver woven into it (*AC ii 2*)

Titans *plural noun* in Greek mythology, the twelve giant children of Uranus and Gaea (NOTE: There were six males and six females who were noted for their strength and lawlessness. The poets Virgil and Ovid refer to the sun as a titan.)

tithe the tenth part of one's income, etc., which was paid to the church ■ *noun* a tenth (*1H4 iii 3*; *H iii 4*)

tithe-pig *noun* a pig paid to a parish priest as a **tithe** (*RJ i 4*)

tithing *noun* a district containing ten households, with each responsible for the rest (*KL iii 4*)

title *noun* **1.** a name (*R3 iv 4*; *M v 7*) **2.** a possession (*M iv 2*) **3.** a share in something (*R3 ii 2*) ◇ **make title** to state that you have a claim to something (*H5 i 2*)

toad-spotted *adjective* foul (*KL v 3*)

toasts-and-butter *plural noun* pampered weaklings, fed on buttered toast (*1H4 iv 2*)

toaze *verb* to tease something out of someone (*WT iv 4*)

todpole *noun* a tadpole (*KL iii 4*)

toged *adjective* robed (*O i 1*)

toil *noun* a trap (*H iii 2*) ■ *verb* to make something work hard (*MND v 1*; *H i 1*)

token *noun* a mark on the body caused by a disease such as the plague (*AC iii 10*)

toll *verb* to collect a tax (*2H4 iv 5*)

tombless *adjective* without a headstone or monument (*H5 i 2*)

Tom o' Bedlam *noun* a mentally ill beggar discharged from the Hospital of St Mary of Bethlehem (known as Bedlam) which was a hospital for the mentally ill in London (*KL i 2*)

tongs *noun* a simple metal percussion instrument (*MND iv 1*)

tongue *noun* a language (*MA v 1*; *1H4 iii 1*) ■ *verb* to scold someone (*MM iv 4*)

tonight *adverb* last night (*MA iii 5*; *MV ii 5*; *RJ ii 4*)

tool *noun* a weapon (*RJ i 1*)

tooth *noun* bite (*AYLI ii 7*; *M iii 2*) ◇ **flout me in the tooth** to your face (*1H4 v 2*; *H iv 7*) ◇ **from his tooth** not deeply felt (*AC iii 4*)

tooth-picker *noun* a toothpick (*MA ii 1*)

top *noun* **1.** a spinning top (*WT ii 1*) **2.** a lock of hair hanging over a person's forehead (*MA i 2*) **3.** the supreme example of something (*MM ii 2*) **4.** the topsail, the sail above the lowest one on a sailing ship (*MV i 1*) ■ *verb* **1.** to be better than someone at something (*H iv 7*) **2.** to have sexual intercourse with someone (*O v 2*) ◇ **in top of** above all others (*H ii 2*; *AC v 1*)

top gallant *noun* the highest point (*RJ ii 4*) [From the nautical term meaning 'the highest point of the sails on a ship'.]

topped *verb* expected (*H iv 7*)

toss *verb* to carry about impaled on the point of a sharp object (*1H4 iv 2*)

tosspot *noun* a drunkard (*TN v 1*)

tottered *adjective* in ruins (*R2 iii 3*; *1H4 iv 4*)

touch *noun* **1.** a stone used for testing gold and silver by the mark they leave on it (a **touchstone**) (*1H4 iv 4*) **2.** the stroke of a brush (*T i 1*) ■ *verb* **1.** to have sexual intercourse with someone (*MM v 1*; *O iv 2*) **2.** to test something with a touchstone (*O iii 3*) **3.** to wound someone (*1H4 ii 4*) **4.** to make a brief reference to something (*R3 iii 5, 7*; *AC ii 2*) ◇ **of noble touch** excellent (*1H4 iv 4*)

touse, touze *verb* to tear someone apart (*MM v 1*)

toward *adjective* compliant (*TS v 2*)

towards *adverb* in the course of preparation (*RJ i 5*)

tower *verb* to soar like a bird of prey (*M ii 4*)

towering *adjective* **1.** furious (*H v 2*) **2.** circling at a height (*M ii 4*)

town clerk *noun* a parish clerk (*MA iv 2*)

town-crier *noun* a man who shouts out the news, etc. in a town (*H iii 2*)

town of war *noun* a fortified town where an army is lodged or based (*H5 ii 4; O ii 3*)

toy *noun* **1.** nonsense (*O i 3*) **2.** a whim (*MND v 1; R3 i 1; H i 4; O iii 4*) **3.** a worthless trinket (*TN iii 3; WT iv 4*)

trace *verb* **1.** to go or travel over something (*MND ii 1; MA iii 1*) **2.** to follow someone (*M iv 1; H v 1, 2*)

tract *noun* an orbit (*R2 iii 3; R3 v 3*)

tractable *adjective* willing (*1H4 iii 2; R3 iii 1*)

trade *noun* **1.** a custom (*MM iii 1*) **2.** an occupation (*TN iii 1; H iii 2*) **3.** a track or way (*R2 iii 3; 2H4 i 1*) ■ *verb* **1.** to go in a particular direction (*MV iii 4*) **2.** to have dealings with someone (*M iii 5*)

traded *adjective* experienced

trade-fallen *adjective* out of work (*1H4 iv 2*)

traduced *verb* criticized (*H i 4; O v 2*)

traffic *noun* **1.** a business (*CE i 1; TN iii 3; TS i 1*) **2.** an occupation (*RJ Prol.*)

train *noun* **1.** a troop of soldiers (*2H4 iv 2; H5 iii 3*) **2.** something designed to tempt someone (*M iv 3*) ■ *verb* to tempt someone (*CE iii 2; 1H4 v 2*)

traject *noun* a ferry, a way across (possibly a bridge) (*MV iii 4*) [From Italian *tragetto*.]

trammel up *verb* to catch something in a fishing net (*M i 7*)

trance *noun* delight (*TS i 1*)

tranced *adjective* in a trance (*KL v 3*)

tranquil *adjective* calm or peaceful (*O iii 3*)

tranquillity *noun* people who live free from any anxiety (*1H4 ii 1*)

translate *verb* **1.** to transform someone or something (*2H4 iv 1; AYLI ii 1, v 1; H iii 1*) **2.** to explain something (*H iv 1*)

transmigrate *adjective* (of a person's soul) passing to the body of someone else after death (*AC ii 7*)

transmutation *noun* a change in status (*TS Ind. 2*)

transport *verb* **1.** to transform someone (*MND iv 2*) **2.** to kill someone (*MM iv 3*)

transported *adjective* overcome by passion or ecstasy (*M iv 3*)

trans-shape *verb* to distort something (*MA v 1*)

trapped *adjective* lavishly decorated (*TS Ind. 2*)

trapping *noun* an attendant (*TN v 1; H i 2*)

trash *verb* **1.** to control someone (*O ii 1*) **2.** to hold someone back (*T i 2*) **3.** to hold back a dog by its leash (*TS Ind. 1*) [From *trash*, 'the weights hung around a dog's neck to restrain it'.]

travailer, traveller *noun* a labourer (*MM iv 2*)

travel of regard *noun* a look around (*TN ii 5*)

traverse *verb* **1.** to march backwards and forwards (a military command) (*2H4 iii 2; O i 3*) **2.** (*in jousting*) to break your lance by a misplaced thrust across your opponent's body (*AYLI iii 4*)

tray-trip *noun* a dice game in which winning depends on throwing a three (*TN ii 5*) [Alteration of French *trois*, 'three'.]

treacher *noun* a traitor (*KL i 2*)

treasury *noun* treasure (*WT iv 4; KL iv 6*)

treatise *noun* a statement (*MA i 1; M v 5*)

treble-sinewed *adjective* three times as strong (*AC iii 13*)

tremor cordis *phrase* Latin a condition in which the heart beats too quickly or irregularly (*WT i 2*) [Latin, 'trembling of the heart'.]

trench *verb* **1.** to divert something into a new channel (*1H4 iii 1*) **2.** to cut something deeply (*M iii 4*)

trencher *noun* a wooden plate (*AC iii 1; RJ i 5; T ii 2*)

trencher-man *noun* someone who likes their food (*MA i 1*)

tribunal *noun* a platform (*AC iii 4*)

tributary *noun* someone who worships another (*JC i 1; H v 2; AC iii 13*) ■ *adjective* flowing (*RJ iii 2*)

trick *noun* **1.** a custom (*MM v 1; H iv 7*) **2.** a distinctive look, voice, or other feature (*WT iii 3; 1H4 iii 4, v 2; KL iv 6*) **3.** a trinket (*TS iv 3; WT ii 1*) **4.** a skill (*H v 1*) ■ *verb* **1.** to make something more elaborate (*H5 iii 6*) **2.** to cover something (*H ii 2*) [From *trick*, the heraldic term for black and white shading used to indicate colour.]

COMMENT: *Trick* may well mislead the modern reader of Shakespeare because it rarely contained our meaning of 'a deception'. It generally had the sense of a surface detail, a habit or peculiarity. Paulina in **The Winter's Tale** shows the lords that the baby girl is 'a copy of the father': she has 'the trick of's frown'. In **The Tempest** the storm-beaten sailors 'played/ Some tricks of desperation', meaning that their appearance and behaviour were typical of terrified people. Perhaps *trick* moves a little way towards our meaning when Berowne in **Love's Labours Lost** complains that Boyet 'knows the trick/To make my lady laugh'. *Trick* here means 'a way or knack'. When Shakespeare coins the adjective 'tricksy' to describe the riddling words of the clown Launcelot in **The Merchant of Venice** and the ingenuity of the 'tricksy spirit' Ariel in **The Tempest**, we may well feel that the contexts are moving the word towards its later meaning of 'deceit'.

tricks eleven and twenty long *noun* a card game in which one and thirty are winning numbers (*TS iv 2*)

tricksy *adjective* mischievous (*T v 1*; *MV iii 5*)

trifle *verb* **1.** to waste time (*MV iv 1*) **2.** to treat something as being of little importance (*M ii 4*)

trigon ◇ **the fiery trigon** a conjunction of the three 'fire' signs of the zodiac, i.e. Aries, Leo and Sagittarius (*2H4 ii 4*)

trill *verb* to trickle (*KL iv 3*)

trim *adjective* **1.** (*of a ship*) having the sails up and ready to sail (*T v 1*; *CE iv 1*) **2.** pretty or fine (*MND iii 2*; *1H4 v 1*) ■ *noun* a fine array (*1H4 iv 1*; *H5 iv 3*) ■ *verb* to provide someone with something (*2H4 i 3*) ■ *adverb* neatly (*RJ ii 1*)

trip *noun* a throw in wrestling that unbalances your opponent (*TN v 1*) ■ *verb* to interrupt or slow something (*2H4 v 2*)

tripe-visaged *adjective* having a pale wrinkled face resembling tripe (*2H4 v 4*)

triple *noun* the third, or one of three (*AC i 1*)

triplex *noun* triple time in music (*TN v 1*)

tristful *adjective* sad (*1H4 ii 4*; *H iii 4*)

triumph *noun* a trump card (*AC iv 20*)

triumphant *adjective* **1.** celebrating a public festival (*R3 iv 4*) **2.** magnificent (*RJ v 3*; *AC ii 2*)

triumphantly *adverb* merrily (*MND iv 1*)

Trojan *noun* a close friend (*1H4 ii 1*; *H5 v 1*)

COMMENT: Curiously, *Trojan* was not used in an elevated way to refer to the heroes of Troy. It was a slang word, used in rough male company, to mean a good, cheerful fellow. It has been thought to derive from a Celtic word meaning 'to fight or quarrel'. In **Henry IV Part 1** just before the robbery Gadshill speaks of 'other good Troyans' on their way; here, they are 'good' because they are reliable thieves, part of a London underworld and therefore far from an accepted heroic status. Costard in **Love's Labours Lost** urges Armado to 'play the honest Troyan' and marry the pregnant Jacquenetta. A few lines later Armado appears before the courtiers dressed as Hector. He is ludicrously inappropriate for the role and the King says: 'Hector was but a Troyan in respect of this'. He is entertaining the rest of the audience by punning on *Troyan* as literally the heroic Hector and *Troyan* in its common slang meaning.

troll *verb* to sing something (*T iii 2*)

trol(l)-my-dames *noun* a game played by women which involved rolling balls through hoops set in a board (*WT iv 3*) [From French *trou-madame*.]

troop *verb* to accompany something (*KL i 1*; *RJ i 5*)

trophy *noun* a memorial (*H iv 5*; *H5 v Chor., 1*)

tropically *adverb* figuratively (*H iii 2*)

trot *noun* an old woman (*TS i 2*; *MM iii 2*)

troth *noun* truth (*MND ii 2*)

COMMENT: *Troth* is connected with 'truth', but means something far more important than our meaning of 'accuracy'. It signifies a person's integrity and is therefore the basic component of honour. It was much used in medieval chivalric literature and is at the heart of several of Chaucer's Canterbury Tales. A man would pledge his troth to his feudal overlord or to the woman he intended to marry. To break his troth would be a deep dishonour. In **Troilus and Cressida**, Agamemnon welcomes Hector, his heroic opponent, and in linking 'faith and troth' he finds words that he intends to overcome all division or threat of treachery. In **A Midsummer Night's Dream** Lysander escapes with Hermia to the wood and, wanting to sleep beside her, he tries to overcome her anxiety: 'One heart, one bed, two bosoms and one troth'. *Troth* coming at the end of his list suggests a sense of honour that is more solemn and binding than mere terms of affection. *Troth*, like variants of 'God', are often used in swearing, because the speaker wishes to intensify what he is about to say. 'By my troth' or simply 'Troth' were used because this type of oath needs a reference point in something the speaker holds very dear.

trothed *adjective* engaged (*MA iii 1*)

troth-plight *noun* an engagement (*WT i 2, v 3*)

trow *verb* **1.** to know (*KL i 4*) **2.** to believe (*KL i 4*)

Troy *noun* a walled town on the south side of the Dardanelles at the entrance to the Sea of Marmara (*2H4 i 1, ii 4*; *JC i 2*)

truant *noun* an idle person who begs for money even though they don't actually need to (*MA iii 2*) ∎ *verb* to be unfaithful to someone (*CE iii 2*)

truckle-bed *noun* a low bed on wheels that could be pushed under another bed (*RJ ii 1*)

trudge *verb* to walk about, walk off (*CE iii 2*; *RJ i 2, 3*)

true-derived *adjective* honestly obtained (*R3 iii 7*)

truepenny *noun* an honest person (*H i 5*)

trull *noun* a prostitute (*AC iii 6*)

trumpet *noun* a trumpeter (*H5 iv 2*)

truncheon *noun* a stick carried by military officers (*H i 2*; *MM ii 2*) ∎ *verb* to beat someone with a truncheon (*2H4 ii 4*)

trundle-tail, trindle-tail *adjective* having a long, drooping tail (*KL iii 6*)

trunk sleeve *noun* a full, baggy sleeve (*TS iv 3*)

trunk-work *noun* some underhand activity involving the use of a trunk (*WT iii 3*)

truss *verb* to stuff someone into something (*2H4 iii 2*)

trust *noun* **1.** a belief (*TN iv 3*) **2.** belief that someone will pay for an item sold to them at a later date (*MV i 1*)

truster *noun* someone to whom money is owed (*H i 2*)

trustful *adjective* faithful (*1H4 ii 4*)

try *verb* **1.** to improve something (*MV ii 1*) **2.** to prove something (*MA i 1*; *RJ iv 3*; *H i 3*) ◇ **bring to try** to sail a ship as close to the wind as possible (*T i 1*)

tub *noun* **1.** a sweating tub used in the treatment of sexually transmitted diseases (*MM iii 2*) **2.** a barrel for preserving beef in salt (*H5 ii 1*)

tuck *noun* a thin light sword (*TN iii 4*; *1H4 ii 4*)

tucket *noun* a fanfare of trumpets (*MV v 1 – stage direction*; *H5 iv 2*; *KL ii 1*)

tuft *noun* a group of trees (*AYLI iii 5*; *R2 ii 3*)

tuition *noun* protection (*MA i 1*)

tumble *verb* **1.** to roll about (*AC i 4*; *M iv 1*; *R3 iii 4*) **2.** to have sexual intercourse with someone (*WT iv 3*)

tun *noun* **1.** a large barrel holding 216 gallons (972 litres) of ale or 252 gallons (1134 litres) of wine (*1H4 ii 4*; *H5 i 2*) **2.** a measure of liquid

tun-dish ◇ **filling a bottle with a tun-dish** having sexual intercourse with someone (*MM iii 2*)

tune *noun* a mood (*MM iii 2*; *KL iv 3*; *H v 2*)

tupping *noun* the mating of sheep (*O i 1*)

Turk Gregory *noun* the Turkish people and Pope Gregory XIII had a reputation for ferocity (*1H4 v 3*)

Turkish tapestry *noun* embroidery imitating Turkish carpets (*CE iv 1*)

turlygod *noun* a name given to mentally ill beggars released from **Bedlam** (*KL ii 3*)

Turnbull Street, Turnmill Street *noun* a street in east London. It was called Trimillstrete (Three Mill Street) in the 14th century after three water mills on the River Fleet. It was notorious for the thieves, prostitutes, etc. who lived there. (*2H4 iii 2*)

turncoat *noun* someone who changes sides (*MA i 1*)

turn Turk *verb* to change for the worse (*H iii 2*; *MA iii 4*) (NOTE: From the idea of a Christian converting to Islam.) [From the idea of a Christian converting to Islam.]

turpitude *noun* immorality (*AC iv 6*)

turtle *noun* a turtle dove. It mates for life and is a symbol of faithfulness. (*TS ii 1*)

tway *noun* two (*H5 iii 2*)

twelve score *noun* 240 yards (216 metres), the firing range of a cannon (*1H4 ii 4*; *2H4 iii 2*)

twice double *noun* a ghost (*1H4 v 4*)

twiggen-bottle *noun* a bottle in a wicker basket (*O ii 3*)

twilled *adjective* woven, possibly tangled with reeds (*T iv 1*)

twine *noun* thread (*MA iv 1*)

twist *verb* to spin something into a thread (*MA i 1*)

U

umber *noun* a brown powder made from the oxides of iron and manganese, used in painting (*AYLI i 3*)

umber'd *adjective* darkened (*H5 iv Chor.*)

umbrage *noun* a shadow (*H v 2*)

unable *adjective* powerless (*TS v 2*; *KL i 1*)

unaccommodated *adjective* in a natural unadorned state (*KL iii 4*)

unaccustomed *adjective* unusual (*JC ii 1*; *RJ iii 5*)

unadvised *adjective* not thought out (*RJ ii 2*)

unadvisedly *adverb* thoughtlessly (*R3 iv 4*)

unaneled *adjective* without having received the last rites from a priest (*H i 5*)

unapt *adjective* **1.** unsuitable (*TS v 2*) **2.** unwilling (*1H4 i 3*)

unarm *verb* to take off your armour and weapons (*2H4 i 3*)

unattained *adjective* not favouring one side or the other in an argument (*RJ i 2*)

unavoided *adjective* unavoidable (*R3 iv 1, 4*)

unbacked *adjective* (of a horse) not having been ridden before (*T iv 1*)

unbanded *adjective* without a hatband (*AYLI iii 2*)

unbated *adjective* **1.** undiminished (*MV ii 6*) **2.** (of a sword) not having a knob on the end to make it blunt for use when practising (*H iv 7, v 2*)

unbend *verb* to weaken something (*M ii 2*)

unbitted *adjective* uncontrolled (*O i 3*) [From the idea of a horse without a bit.]

unblessed, unblest *adjective* cursed (*O iii 3, v 1*)

unbolted *adjective* coarse (*KL ii 2*) [From the literal use referring to flour, meaning 'unsifted'.]

unbonneted *adjective* on equal terms (*KL iii 1*; *O i 2*) [From the idea of removing your hat as a respectful gesture on meeting someone.]

unbookish *adjective* untrained in the ways of society (*O iv 1*)

unbraced *adjective* having your doublet undone (*JC i 3, ii 1*; *H ii 1*)

unbraided *adjective* unused (*WT iv 4*)

unbreathed *adjective* unused (*MND v 1*)

unbreeched *adjective* young and inexperienced (*WT i 2*) [Literally 'not yet wearing breeches'. Young boys wore some form of skirt, like a girl, until they were 4–5 years old.]

unbuckle *verb* to snatch off a helmet during a fight (*AC iv 4*)

uncase *verb* to undress yourself (*TS i 1*)

uncharge the practice *verb* to fail to recognise the plot (*H iv 7*)

unchary *adverb* rashly unguarded (*TN iii 4*)

unchecked *adjective* not contradicted (*MV iii 1*)

unclasp *verb* to reveal something (*1H4 i 3*; *MA i 1*; *TN i 4*)

uncleanly *adjective* improper (*AYLI iii 2*; *O iii 3*)

uncoined *adjective* genuine (*H5 v 2*) ◊
uncoined constancy pure metal does not need a stamp to prove its worth (*H5 v 2*)

uncolted *adjective* without a horse (*1H4 ii 2*)

unconfirmed *adjective* inexperienced (*MA iii 3*)

unconstant *adjective* erratic (*KL i 1*)

uncouple *verb* to release the dogs in a hunt (*MND iv 1*)

uncouth *adjective* unfamiliar and terrifying (*AYLI ii 6*)

uncovered *adjective* not hidden (*MA iv 1*)

unction *noun* an ointment (*H iii 4, iv 7*)

uncurbable *adjective* not able to be controlled (*AC ii 2*)

uncurrent *adjective* **1.** worthless (*TN iii 3*; *H ii 2*) **2.** unnatural (*WT iii 2*)

uncurse *verb* to remove a curse from something (*R2 iii 2*)

undeaf *verb* to bring back the power of hearing to a person's ears (*R2 ii 1*)

undeeded *adjective* having done nothing (*M v 7*)

under *preposition* **1.** by the authority of someone (*TS v 1*; *KL ii 2*) **2.** pretending to be (*MV ii 4*) ■ *adjective* that is the earth (*MM iv 3*; *KL ii 2*)

underbearing *noun* endurance (*R2 i 1*)

underborne *adjective* trimmed around the lower edge (*MA iii 4*)

undergo *verb* **1.** to risk something (*MA v 2*; *1H4 i 3*) **2.** to perform a task (*WT iii 3*; *JC i 3*) **3.** to endure something (*MM i 1*; *H i 4*)

undergoing *adjective* enduring (*T i 2*)

underling *noun* an underdog (*JC i 2*)

underskinner *noun* a junior wine waiter (*1H4 ii 4*)

understand *verb* to stand underneath someone (*CE ii 1*; *TN iii 1*)

undertake *verb* **1.** to make approaches to someone (*TN i 3*) **2.** to attempt something (*KL iv 2*) **3.** to do something on behalf of someone else (*O ii 3*)

undertaker *noun* someone who takes on a matter, especially on behalf of someone else (*TN iii 4*; *O iv 1*)

undisposed *adjective* miserable (*CE i 2*)

undistinguished *adjective* infinite (*KL iv 6*)

undo *verb* **1.** to defy something (*WT v 2*) **2.** to destroy someone (*AC ii 5*) **3.** to prevent something (*KL iv 1*)

undone *adjective* destroyed

undoubted *adjective* fearless

unequal *adjective* unjust (*2H4 iv 1*)

uneven *adjective* embarrassing (*1H4 i 1*)

unexpressive *adjective* of such quality that words can not describe it (*AYLI iii 2*)

unfashioned *adjective* ugly (*R3 i 1*)

unfathered *adjective* illegitimate (*2H4 iv 4*)

unfellowed *adjective* none like him (*H v 2*)

unfelt *adjective* **1.** not felt deeply (*R3 i 4*; *M ii 3*) **2.** not expressed visibly (*R2 ii 3*)

unfix *verb* to dislodge something, to cause something to move or come free (*2H4 iv 1*; *M i 3, iv 1*)

unfledged *adjective* inexperienced (*WT i 2*; *H i 3*) [Literally 'not having left the nest'.]

unfold *verb* **1.** to open something (*H v 1*) **2.** to betray someone (*AC v 2*; *O iv 2, v 1*)

unfolding *noun* an explanation (*O i 3*)

unfolding star *noun* the star that orders shepherds to put their sheep out to graze (*MM iv 2*)

unfortified *adjective* weak (*H i 2*)

unfurnished *adjective* **1.** unmatched (*MV iii 2*) **2.** not decorated with hanging tapestries (*R2 i 2*) **3.** undefended (*H5 i 2*) **4.** unprepared (*RJ iv 2*)

ungalled *adjective* **1.** unspoilt (*CE iii 1*) **2.** uninjured (*H iii 2*)

ungartered *adjective* untidily dressed, because of not having garters to hold up your stockings (*AYLI iii 2*)

ungenitured *adjective* impotent (*MM iii 2*)

ungored *adjective* uninjured (*H v 1*)

ungot, ungotten *adjective* unborn (*MM v 1*; *H v 2*)

ungracious *adjective* wicked (*R2 ii 3*; *1H4 ii 4*; *H i 3*)

unhandled *adjective* untamed (*MV v 1*)

unhandsome *adjective* **1.** not handsome (*AYLI v 4*; *MA i 1*) **2.** indecent (*1H4 i 3*) **3.** unskilled (*O iii 4*)

unhappily *adverb* **1.** unluckily (*MM i 2*) **2.** with the intention of doing evil (*KL i 2*)

unhappiness *noun* an evil character (*R3 i 2*)

unhappy *verb* to make someone unhappy (*R2 iii 1*) ■ *adjective* miserable (*MV v 1*; *CE iv 4*; *O ii 3*)

unhatched *adjective* **1.** unused (*TN iii 4*) **2.** not yet fully developed (*H i 3*; *O iii 4*)

unhoused *adjective* without any responsibilities at home (*O i 2*)

unhouseled *adjective* without receiving the Christian ceremony of the sacrament (*H i 5*)

unhurtful *adjective* gentle (*MM iii 2*)

unicorn *noun* a mythical animal with the body and head of a horse, the tail of a lion, the legs of a deer and a single horn in the centre of its head (*JC ii 1*) (NOTE: The unicorn was very fierce, but became very docile in the presence of a virgin. In Christian symbolism, the unicorn represents Christ, with the horn being truth.)

unimproved *adjective* yet to have shape or purpose (*H i 1*)

unintelligent *adjective* unaware (*WT i 1*)

union *noun* a large valuable pearl (*H v 2*)

unjointed *adjective* incoherent (*1H4 i 3*)

unjust *adjective* **1.** untrue (*MA v 1*) **2.** dishonest (*WT iv 4*; *1H4 iii 3, iv 2*)

unkennel *verb* to reveal something (*H iii 2*)

unkind *adjective* unnatural (*JC iii 2*; *KL iii 4*)

unkindness *noun* **1.** hostility (*TS iv 3*; *JC iv 3*) **2.** ingratitude (*KL iii 2*)

unkiss *verb* to resolve something with a kiss (*R2 v 1*)

unknown *adjective* that cannot be spoken of (*R3 i 2*)

unlace *verb* to destroy something (*O ii 3*) [Literally 'to undo'.]

unlike *adjective* unlikely (*AC i 5*; *MV ii 9*; *O i 1*; *TS iii 2*)

unlimited *see* **poem unlimited**

unlineal *adjective* unrelated (*M iii 1*)

unlooked for *adjective* **1.** unexpected (*R3 i 3*; *RJ i 5*) **2.** ignored (*1H4 v 3*)

unmake *verb* to destroy someone (*M i 7*)

unmanned *adjective* (*of a hawk*) untamed (*RJ iii 2*; *M iii 4*)

unmannerly *adjective* rude (*1H4 i 1*; *KL i 1*) ■ *adverb* rudely (*M ii 3*)

unmastered *adjective* uncontrolled (*H i 3*)

unmeet *adjective* **1.** unsuitable (*MA iv 1*) **2.** not ready (*MM iv 3*)

unmeritable *adjective* undeserving (*R3 iii 7*)

unminded *adjective* unnoticed (*1H4 iv 3*)

unmitigable *adjective* not able to be calmed (*T i 2*)

unmuzzle *verb* to let something loose (*AYLI i 2*)

unnecessary *adjective* useless, needless (*H5 iv 2*; *KL ii 2*)

unordinate *adjective* excessive (*O ii 3*)

unpay *verb* to set something right (*2H4 ii 1*)

unpinked *adjective* without a decorative pattern of punched holes (*TS iv 1*)

unpitied *adjective* without mercy (*MM iv 2*)

unpolicied *adjective* unskilled in politics (*AC iv 2*)

unpossessing *adjective* having no right to inherit your father's estate (*KL ii 1*)

unpregnant *adjective* **1.** not well disposed towards something (*MM iv 4*) **2.** having no interest in something (*H ii 2*)

unprevailing *adjective* unproductive (*H i 2*)

unprizeable *adjective* worthless (*TN v 1*)

unprized *adjective* priceless (*KL i 1*)

unproper *adjective* not owned by one person only (*O iv 1*)

unproportioned *adjective* excessive (*H i 3*)

unprovide *verb* to unsettle something (*O iv 1*)

unqualitied *adjective* no longer having the necessary qualities (*AC iii 11*)

unquestionable *adjective* unwilling to talk (*AYLI iii 2*)

unreasonable *adjective* not able to reason (*RJ iii 3*)

unreclaimed *adjective* untamed (*H ii 1*)

unrespective *adjective* inattentive (*R3 iv 2*)

unreverend *adjective* disrespectful (*MM v 1*)

unrolled *adjective* struck off a list (*WT iv 2*)

unroosted *adjective* henpecked (*WT ii 3*)

unrough *adjective* having smooth cheeks (*M v 2*)

unsanctified *adjective* wicked (*KL iv 6*; *M iv 2*)

unseam *verb* to cut someone open (*M i 2*)

unseminared *adjective* castrated (*AC i 5*)

unshape *verb* to upset someone (*MM iv 4*)

unshaped *adjective* imperfect (*H iv 5*)

unshapen *adjective* deformed (*R3 i 2*)

unshunnable, unshunned *adjective* inevitable (*MM iii 2*; *O iii 3*)

unsifted *adjective* inexperienced (*H i 3*)

unsisting *noun* unresisting or persistent (meaning not clear) (*MM iv 2*)

unskilful *adjective* foolish (*H iii 2*; *O i 3*)

unskilfully *adverb* foolishly (*MM iii 2*)

unsorted *adjective* not well chosen (*1H4 ii 3*)

unsought *adjective* unexplored (*CE i 1*)

unspeakable *adjective* too great to be spoken of (*CE i 1*)

unstaid *adjective* **1.** not kept in check (*TN ii 4*; *R2 ii 1*) **2.** unstable or unrestrained (*TN ii 4*; *R2 ii 1*) (NOTE: [all senses] Women of the period wore tight corsets (**stays**).)

unstanched *adjective* incontinent (*T i 1*)

unstate *verb* to strip someone of their status and the honour associated with it (*KL i 2*)

unswayed *adjective* uncontrolled (*R3 iv 4*)

untainted *adjective* not accused of something (*R3 iii 6*)

untaught *adjective* ill-bred (*MM ii 4*; *1H4 i 3*; *RJ v 3*)

untempering *adjective* unappealing (*H5 v 2*)

untented *adjective* (of a wound) that has not been cleaned and so is likely to become infected (*KL i 4*)

unthrift *noun* a lazy person who spends money extravagantly (*R2 ii 3*; *MV v 1*)

unthrifty *adjective* **1.** extravagant and lazy (*MV i 3*) **2.** unwilling to increase (*WT v 2*) **3.** unlucky (*RJ v 3*)

untoward *adjective* impolite (*TS iv 5*)

untowardly *adverb* badly (*MA iii 2*)

untread *verb* to go back along a path (*MV ii 6*)

untreasured *adjective* robbed of something valuable (*AYLI ii 2*)

untrussing *noun* the act of undressing by unlacing your stockings (*MM iii 2*)

untruth *noun* disloyalty (*R2 ii 2*)

untunable, untuneable *adjective* out of tune (*AYLI v 3*)

untuned *adjective* **1.** out of tune (*R2 i 3*; *KL iv 7*) **2.** changed from its usual tone (*CE v 1*)

untwind *verb* to destroy someone (*2H4 ii 4*) [Literally 'to unravel'.]

unvalued *adjective* **1.** priceless (*R3 i 4*) **2.** worthless (*H i 3*)

unwashed hands *plural noun* without delay (*1H4 iii 3*)

unwedgeable *adjective* not able to be split (*MM ii 2*)

unweighing *adjective* thoughtless (*MM iii 2*)

unwholesome *adjective* defective (*O iv 1*)

unwish *verb* to wish that someone did not exist (*H5 iv 3*)

unwonted *adjective* unusual (*T i 2*; *MM iv 2*)

unwrung *adjective* not rubbed by a badly fitting saddle (*H iii 2*)

unyoke *verb* to remove a burden from someone (*H v 1*)

unyoked *adjective* unrestrained (*1H4 i 2*)

uproar *verb* to throw something into chaos (*M iv 3*)

up-spring *noun* a boisterous dance, or possibly a newly-introduced dance (*H i 4*)

up-staring *adjective* standing on end (*T i 2*)

up-swarm *verb* to cause something to rise up in a swarm (*2H4 iv 2*)

upward *noun* the top of something (*KL v 3*)

urchin *noun* **1.** a goblin (*T i 2, ii 2*) **2.** a hedgehog

urinal *noun* a doctor's glass jar for testing urine

usance *adjective* interest on money lent, usually charged at an excessive rate (*MV i 3*)

use ◊ **in use** in trust (*MV iv 1*)

usurer's chain *noun* a gold chain worn by merchants, bankers, etc. (*MA ii 1*)

usurp *verb* to exert an evil influence on something (*H iii 2*)

usurp'd beard *noun* a beard recently grown as part of a disguise (*O i 3*)

usury *noun* the practice of lending money at an excessive interest rate (*MM iii 2*)

ut *noun* the lowest musical note in the scale (*TS iii 1*)

utensil *noun* a feature or part of the body (*TN i 5, iii 2*)

utis *noun* noisy celebrating (*2H4 ii 4*) (NOTE: The literal meaning refers to the time between the beginning and the eighth day of a festival.)

utter *verb* **1.** to give off something (*MND iv 2*) **2.** to pass something from one person to another (*WT iv 4*; *RJ v 1*)

utterance [From French *outrance*.] ◊ **to the utterance** to the death (*M iii 1*)

V

vacancy *noun* a period of spare time (*AC i 4, ii 2; TN v 1*)

vade *verb* to fade (*R2 i 2*)

vagabond *adjective* moving from place to place (*AC i 4*) [From *vagabond* meaning 'an unlicensed traveller'.]

vagrom *noun* a homeless person (*MA iii 3*)

vail *verb* to lower something (*2H4 i 1; TS v 2*)

vailful *adjective* advantageous (*MM iv 6*)

vain *adjective* **1.** stupid (*CE iii 2; 1H4 iii 2; KL iv 2*) **2.** devious (*CE iii 2*) ◇ **for vain** pointlessly (*MM iii 4*)

vainly *adverb* wrongly (*2H4 iv 5*)

valanced *adjective* having a beard (*H ii 2*) [Literally 'fringed'.]

valance of Venice *noun* a fringed canopy decorated with Venetian embroidery (*TS ii 1*)

validity *noun* **1.** a value (*TN i 1; KL i 1*) **2.** strength (*H iii 2*)

valuation *noun* judgement (*2H4 iv 1*)

valued file *noun* a list of gifts with the value of each noted down (*M iii 1*)

vane *noun* a weather vane (*MA iii 1, 3*)

vanish *verb* to escape (*RJ iii 3*)

vanities *noun* the behaviour and customs of someone who is excessively concerned with their appearance (*R2 iii 4; 1H4 v 4; H5 ii 4*)

vanity *noun* **1.** a wicked character in **morality plays** (*KL ii 2*) **2.** an illusion (*T iv 1*)

vant *noun* the front part of something (*AC iv 6*) [Shortening of 'vanguard'.]

Vapians *noun* an invented astrological term (*TN ii 3*)

vapour *noun* in Elizabethan medicine, a gas given off by a diseased organ that affected the rest of the body (*2H4 iv 3*)

variable *adjective* various (*H iii 1, iv 3; MV ii 8; RJ ii 2*)

varlet *noun* a knight's servant (a **squire**) (*H5 iv 2*)

varletry *noun* a mob (*AC v 2*)

varnish *noun* gloss, polish (*H iv 7*)

varnished faces *plural noun* faces with makeup on (*MV ii 2*)

vassal *noun* **1.** a servant (*2H4 iv 5; AC ii 6, v 1; MM v 1; T i 1*) **2.** a wretch (*R3 i 1*) ■ *adjective* grovelling (*1H4 iii 2; H5 iii 5*)

vast *noun* a dreary stretch of sea (*WT i 1*)

vastidity *noun* infinite space (*MM iii 1*)

vast of night *noun* the depths of night (*T i 2; H i 2*)

vasty *adjective* vast (*1H4 iii 1; H5 Prol., ii 4*)

vault *noun* **1.** a roof, ceiling (*KL v 3*) **2.** the sky (*M ii 3; T v 1*) ■ *verb* to leap (*H5 v 2*)

vaultages *plural noun* underground rooms with arched roofs (*H5 ii 4*)

vaulting *adjective* soaring, confident (*M i 7*)

vaulty *adjective* arched (*RJ iii 5*)

vaunt *verb* to boast (*R3 v 3*)

vaunt-couriers *plural noun* forerunners (*KL iii 2*) [From French *avant-courriers*.]

vaward *noun* the vanguard, the front section of an army (*2H4 i 2; H5 iv 3; MND iv 1*)

vaward of the day *noun* early in the day (*MND iv 1*)

velure *noun* velvet (*TS iii 2*)

velvet *adjective* expensively dressed (*AYLI ii 1*)

velvet-guard *noun* women wearing clothes with velvet trimming (*1H4 iii 1*)

velvet-guards *plural noun* velvet trimmings and the people who wear them (*1H4 iii 1*)

velvet patch *noun* a patch worn to cover a scar (*MM i 2*)

vendible *adjective* suitable for marriage (*MV i 1*)

venge *verb* to take revenge for something (*H5 i 2; KL iv 2; RJ iii 5*)

vengeance *noun* damage (*AYLI iv 3*)

vent *noun* a flow of something (*AC v 2*) ■ *verb* **1.** to utter something (*T i 2; TN iv*

1) **2.** to get rid of something (*T ii 2*) ◇
vent of hearing an ear (*2H4 Introd*)

ventages *plural noun* the holes in a flute (*H iii 2*)

Venus *noun* in Roman mythology, the goddess of sexual love and beauty (NOTE: The Greek equivalent is **Aphrodite**.)

verdure *noun* freshness (*T i 2*)

verge *noun* the limit of a law court's authority (*R2 ii 1*)

verily *adverb* truly (*AYLI iv 3*; *H5 v 1*; *T ii 1*)

verity *noun* truthfulness (*AYLI iii 4*)

veronesa *noun* a ship fitted out at the port of Verona in northern Italy (*O ii 1*)

versal *adjective* universal (*RJ ii 4*)

verse *verb* to write a poem about something (*MND ii 1*)

very *adjective* **1.** real (*MA iv 1*; *H ii 2*) **2.** absolute (*TN i 3*; *TS v 2*) **3.** mere (*TS iv 3*; *H iii 4*) ■ *adverb* exactly (*MM iv 3*; *KL v 3*; *O i 1*) ■ *noun* himself (*T ii 2*; *WT iii 3*)

vesper *noun* evening (*AC iv 1*)

vestal *noun* a virgin (*AC iii 12*; *MND ii 1*) ■ *adjective* pure (*RJ ii 2, iii 3*) (NOTE: The priestesses of Vesta, the goddess of the hearth, were vowed to chastity and kept the vestal fire burning.)

vesture *noun* the human body (*MV v 1*; *O ii 1*) [From the idea that the body is the clothing of the soul.]

via *interjection* go on! (used to express encouragement) (*MV ii 2*)

viage *noun* a voyage (*H iii 3*)

vial *noun* a small glass bottle (*AC i 3*; *H i 5*; *RJ iv 1, 3*)

vice *verb* to force someone to do something (*WT i 2*) [From the idea of being held in a vice tightened with a screw.]

Vice *noun* a clown character who performed during the play's interludes (*TN iv 2*; *R3 iii 1*; *2H4 iii 2*)

COMMENT: The allegorical figure of the *Vice* appeared in 16th century morality plays which dramatised the perpetual struggle between good and evil for the possession of the human soul. Human virtues battled with vices, often derived from the Seven Deadly Sins to give these plays a strong, and often complicated, didactic effect. The Vice could appear in various forms, often noisy, robust, irreverent and comic; he provided dramatic variety and ensured that the moral lessons were not too solemn. Feste, the jester in **Twelfth Night**, associates himself with the Vice when he mocks Malvolio in prison: 'I am gone, sir,/And anon, sir,/I'll be with you again,/In a trice/Like to the old Vice,/Your need to sustain'. He is a lively, anarchic musical outsider goading the solemn, unmusical puritan. Feste/Vice is far more appealing to an audience than the 'virtuous' steward Malvolio. Their conflict lies at the heart of this play and helps to show how complicated morality drama can become when vice has more dramatic charisma than virtue. Similar complications occur when an audience responds to Iago in **Othello** and Edmund in **King Lear**, both derived from the Vice; both characters are cruel, but also lively and capable of charm. In the bedchamber scene of **Hamlet** the prince tells his mother that King Claudius is 'a vice of kings', using *vice* to imply buffoonery rather than deep wickedness; a few lines later he is 'a king of shreds and patches', which would remind an audience of a jester's costume. In **Henry IV Part 1** Shakespeare makes the reference to the old morality plays especially clear. Falstaff and Hal improvise a play in the pub that seems to be a rehearsal for the prince's imminent interview with the king. However, it becomes an investigation into a prince's education for kingship through the attractions and dangers of anarchy. At the end of the 'play' Hal enacts his father and attacks all that Falstaff stands for. A list of grotesque physical descriptions ends with a series of neat paradoxes: 'that reverend vice, that grey iniquity, that father ruffian, that vanity in years'. One would expect *vice*, 'iniquity' 'ruffian' and 'vanity' all to be characteristics of youth, not of age. Therefore, Shakespeare, through Hal's paradoxes, directs us to the moral and dramatic ambiguities of Falstaff/Vice.

vicious *adjective* **1.** defective (*H i 4*) **2.** mistaken (*O iii 3*)

COMMENT: For Shakespeare the word *vicious* had a less intense meaning than it has for us. It could mean something as slight as 'a fault or mistake', as when Iago proposes an idea to Othello of Desdemona's adultery and then qualifies it by saying 'though I perchance am vicious in my guess'. However, modern audiences may infer irony because they also know that Iago's hidden intentions are indeed *vicious* in our sense of 'depraved or eager to hurt'. When Hamlet speaks to Horatio of men 'who have some vicious mole of nature in them' he uses the word lightly to mean simply some defect; his *vicious* does not even imply guilt. But Cordelia in **King Lear** probably implies more weight in the word when she asks her father to be fair about what she is guilty of: 'It is no vicious blot, murder or foulness'. 'Murder' and unchaste 'foulness' seem here to be specific examples of the more general 'vicious blot'.

videlicet *conjunction Latin* that is to say (*MND v 1*)

vie *verb* to compete with or outdo someone (*TS ii 1; AC v 2*) [Literally 'to make a bet at cards'.]

view *noun* 1. an inspection (*TN ii 2*) 2. the external appearance of something (*MV iii 2; RJ i 1*)

viewless *adjective* invisible (*MM iii 1*)

vigil *noun* the evening before a feast day (*H5 iv 3*)

vigitant *adjective* vigilant (*MA iii 3*)

vile *adjective* 1. poor quality, suitable for somebody of low rank (*MV ii 4; 2H4 i 2; H5 iv 4*) 2. evil (*R3 iii 2; JC ii 1; M iii 1*)

vilely *adverb* meanly (*2H4 ii 2*)

villagery *noun* a group of villages (*MND ii 1*)

villainous *adjective* terrible (*1H4 ii 1, 4*) ■ *adverb* horribly (*T iv 1*)

viol-de-gamboys, viol de gama *noun* a musical instrument resembling a cello (*TN i 3*)

viperous *adjective* poisonous

virginal *verb* to tap the fingers as if playing a keyboard instrument (a **virginal**) (*WT i 2*) [The virginal is an instrument with a single keyboard by which the strings are plucked.]

virgin-knot *noun* virginity (*T iv 1*)

virgin patent *noun* the privilege of liberty of a girl who is a virgin (*MND i 1*)

virtuous *adjective* 1. powerful (*MND iii 2; MM ii 2; O iii 4*) 2. necessary (*2H4 iv 5*)

visage *noun* a facial expression (*O i 1*)

visit *verb* 1. to afflict someone with a disease, especially the plague (*1H4 iv 1; M iv

3) **2.** to punish someone for something (*MV iii 5; H5 iv 1*)

visitings *plural noun* attacks (*M i 5*)

visitor *noun* someone who comes to comfort a sick person (*T ii 1*)

visor, vizor, vizard *noun* a mask covering the whole face and kept in place by a peg held in the mouth (*MA ii 1; R3 ii 2; RJ i 5; M iii 2*)

vistation *noun* 1. an attack of the plague (*T iii 1*) 2. a sudden onset (*2H4 iii 1*) 3. a visit (*WT i 1; R3 iii 7*)

voice *noun* 1. words spoken but not listened to (*H5 v 2; H i 2*) 2. a vote (*MND i 1; JC iii 1; H v 2*) 3. rumour, opinion (*TN i 5; 2H4 iv 1; JC ii 1*) ◇ **in my voice** 1. in my opinion (*AYLI ii 4*) 2. in my name (*MM i 2*)

void *verb* 1. to vomit something (*MV i 3; H5 iii 5*) 2. to abandon something (*H5 iv 7*) 3. to empty something (*JC ii 4*)

volk *noun* folk, people (*KL iv 6*)

volley *noun* a shot or missile fired from a gun (*AC ii 7; H v 2*)

vor *verb* to guarantee the truth of something to someone (*KL iv 6*)

votaress *noun* a woman who has taken religious vows to become a nun (*MND ii 1*)

votarist *noun* someone who has taken vows to follow a religious life (*MM i 4; O iv 2*)

vouch *noun* a piece of evidence (*MM ii 4; O ii 1*) ■ *verb* 1. to confirm the truth of something (*MM v 1; O i 3*) 2. to witness something (*O i 3*)

vouched *adjective* proven (*T ii 1*)

voucher *noun* someone who is called to confirm the truth of a person's claim to something (*H v 1*)

Vulcan *noun* in Roman mythology, the god of fire and metal-workers (*H iii 2; MA i 1; TN v 1*) (NOTE: His wife was **Venus** and because of her affair with Mars, Vulcan is the patron of men whose wives have been unfaithful to them. The Greek equivalent is **Hephaestus**.)

vulgar *noun* the common people (*JC i 1*) ■ *adjective* 1. common soldiers (*H5 iv 7*) 2. common or well-known (*1H4 iii 2; 2H4 i 1; AC iii 13; CE iii 1; H i 1; TN iii 1*)

vulgarly *adverb* publicly (*MM v 1*)

vulgo *adjective* in the speech of the common people (*TN i 3*)

vurther *adjective* further (*KL iv 6*)

W

wad *verb* would (*H5 iii 2*)

wafer-cake *noun* a biscuit (*H5 ii 3*)

waft *verb* **1.** to beckon (*CE ii 2*; *MV v 1*; *H i 4*) **2.** to turn your eyes away (*WT i 2*)

waftage *noun* travel by boat (*CE iv 1*)

wafting *noun* shifting (*WT i 2*)

wafture *noun* a wave of the hand (*JC ii 1*)

wag *verb* to go about your business (*AYLI ii 7*; *MA v 1*)

wage *verb* **1.** to risk something (*1H4 iv 4*; *O i 3*) **2.** to bet something (*KL i 1*; *H v 2*) ◇ **waged equal** having met on equal terms (*AC v 1*)

waggish *adjective* cheeky (*MND i 1*)

waggon *noun* a carriage (*WT iv 4*)

waggoner *noun* a charioteer (*RJ i 4, iii 2*)

wagtail *noun* a grovelling person (*KL ii 2*) [From the idea of dog who wags its tail to its master.]

wain *noun* a wagon, especially one used for carrying hay (*1H4 ii 1*) *See also* **Charles' wain**

wainscot *noun* the wooden panelling on the wall of a room (*AYLI iii 2*)

waist *noun* the middle section of a ship (*T i 2*)

wait *verb* to be with someone to look after them and carry out their orders (*RJ i 3*; *1H4 i 2*)

wake *noun* **1.** the evening before the feast of a holy day (*KL iii 6*) **2.** a late party (*WT iv 2*; *H i 4*)

walk *noun* **1.** a course taken by a person (*MND iii 1*) **2.** a path ■ *verb* to go away (*WT i 2*; *KL iv 7*)

walk about *verb* **1.** to form a couple for a dance (*MA ii 1*; *RJ i 5*) **2.** to take part in a bout of swordfighting practice (*RJ iii 1*)

wallet *noun* a sagging lump (*T iii 3*)

wall-eyed *adjective* savage-looking [Because the iris of the eye is whitened.]

wall-newt *noun* a lizard (*KL iii 4*)

wan *verb* to turn pale (*H ii 2*; *AC ii 1*) ■ *adjective* pale and sickly (*CE iv 4*; *1H4 i 1*)

waned *adjective* shrunken (*AC ii 1*)

want *verb* **1.** to be without something (*T iii 3*; *R3 v 3*; *RJ ii 2*) **2.** to be insufficient (*KL iv 6*) **3.** to miss something (*O iii 3*)

wanton *noun* **1.** a lively mischievous person (*RJ i 4*) **2.** a promiscuous woman (*MA iv 1*) **3.** a spoilt child, effeminate person (*H v 2*) ■ *verb* to be playful or flirtatious ■ *adjective* **1.** unrestrained (*MV v 1*) **2.** frivolous (*1H4 v 1*; *2H4 iv 1*) **3.** lush (*MND ii 1*; *R2 i 3*; *RJ ii 5*) **4.** effeminate (*1H4 iii 1*; *2H4 i 1, iv 4*)

COMMENT: *Wanton* originated from two Anglo-Saxon words, which meant 'lacking in education'. Education is supposed to bring thoughtful restraint to people as they grow up, and so *wanton* in Shakespeare's time came to describe youthful and undisciplined behaviour. In **The Merchant of Venice**, Lorenzo tells Jessica of 'a wild and wanton herd...of youthful and unhandled colts' which need the educative power of music to control them. Young animals also feature in **Henry IV Part 1** in Vernon's simile describing the Prince and his friends: they are 'wanton as youthful goats'. However, *wanton* is more commonly associated with sportive sexual behaviour: Iago anticipates Othello's wedding night when he tells Cassio, 'He hath not yet made wanton the night with her'. Perhaps the darkest meaning of the word occurs in **King Lear** when the blind and outcast Gloucester complains, 'As flies to wanton boys are we to th'gods;/They kill us for their sport'. *Wanton* here implies irresponsibility, of great power engaged in cruel frivolity. This is a terrifying thought, given that human beings would like to imagine the gods as infinitely wise.

wantonness *noun* playful behaviour (*1H4 v 2*; *H iii 1*)

wan(n)y *adjective* pale (*RJ iv 1*)

ward *noun* **1.** an area of a town **2.** a defensive position in swordfighting (*T i 2*; *WT i 2*; *1H4 i 2*, *ii 4*) **3.** a prison (*MM iv 3*, *v 1*; *H ii 2*) ■ *verb* to protect someone (*R3 iv 3*)

warden *noun* a variety of pear which kept well and was used particularly in cooking (*WT iv 3*)

warder *noun* **1.** a guardian (*M i 7*) **2.** a ceremonial staff (*R2 i 3*; *2H4 iv 1*)

warm *adjective* well cared for (*1H4 iv 2*)

warn *verb* to call troops to battle (*JC v 1*; *RJ v 3*) ◇ **God warn us** God preserve us (*AYLI iv 1*)

warp *verb* **1.** to distort something (*KL iii 6*) **2.** to change something (*AYLI ii 7*; *WT i 2*) **3.** to stray from something (*MM i 1*)

war-proof *noun* tested in war (*H5 iii 1*)

warrant *noun* **1.** a promise or guarantee **2.** justification (*M ii 3*) ■ *verb* **1.** to give someone a guarantee of something (*CE i 1*) **2.** to protect someone (*MND v 1*; *AYLI iii 3*) ◇ **of warrant** allowed (*H ii 1*) ◇ **out of warrant** not allowed (*O i 2*)

warranted *adjective* **1.** needing a guarantee (*MM iii 2*) **2.** justified (*M iv 3*)

warrantise, warrantize *noun* the authority to do something (*H v 1*)

warranty *noun* permission (*O v 2*)

warren *noun* an area of parkland for game (*MA ii 1*)

washing *adjective* (of a blow) slashing (*RJ i 1*)

waspish-headed *adjective* hot-headed (*T iv 1*)

wasp-stung *adjective* irritable (*1H4 i 3*)

wassail *noun* **1.** a noisy celebration (*2H4 i 2*; *H i 4*) **2.** spiced ale (*M i 7*)

wassail-candle *noun* an expensive candle used at a feast (*2H4 i 2*)

waste *verb* **1.** to spend (*AYLI ii 4*; *2H4 iv 1*; *H ii 2*) **2.** to damage (as an estate by its owner) (*R2 ii 1*)

wasted *adjective* **1.** burnt out (*MND v 1*) **2.** (*of time*) past (*O i 3*)

wasteful *adjective* destructive (*AYLI iii 2*; *H5 i 2*, *iii 1*; *M ii 3*)

watch *noun* **1.** a clock or watch (*T ii 1*; *TN v 1*; *R2 v 5*) **2.** officers who patrolled the streets at night (*MA iii 3*; *1H4 ii 4*; *RJ v 3*) **3.** an interval of time (*R2 v 5*) **4.** one of the three or four parts into which the night was divided (*2H4 iv 5*) **5.** the state of being awake and unable to sleep (*H5 iv 1*; *H ii 2*) **6.** a candle marked to measure the time (*R3 v 3*) **7.** a call by a watchman during the night (*M ii 1*) ■ *verb* **1.** to be or stay awake (*TS iv 2*; *KL ii 2*; *M v 1*) **2.** to look forward to something (*MND ii 1*; *MV ii 6*; *JC iv 3*) **3.** to tame a hawk by keeping it awake (*TS iv 1*; *O iii 3*)

watch-case *noun* a sentry box (*2H4 iii 1*)

watchful *adjective* **1.** causing lack of sleep (*2H4 iv 5*; *JC ii 1*) **2.** used by the watchmen (*H5 iv Chor.*)

watching *plural noun* one night's sentry duty, meaning a lack of sleep (*MA ii 1*)

watchman *noun* a sentry, an officer who patrolled the streets at night (*MA iii 3*)

water *noun* **1.** tears **2.** urine (*TN iii 4*) **3.** the reflective quality of a diamond ◇ **to raise waters** to make someone cry (*MV ii 2*) ◇ **for all waters** fit for anything (*TN iv 2*)

water-fly *noun* a vain person pretending to be busy (*H v 2*; *AC v 2*) [From the idea of a dragon-fly, hovering over water.]

watering *noun* the act of urinating (*1H4 ii 4*)

waterish *adjective* **1.** watery (*O iii 3*) **2.** weak (*KL i 1*)

water-rat *noun* a pirate (*MV i 3*)

water-rug *noun* a rough-haired type of dog (*M iii 1*)

water-work *noun* a watercolour painting on a wall (*2H4 ii 1*)

watery arch *noun* a rainbow (*T iv 1*)

watery star *noun* the moon (*WT i 2*)

waul, wawl *verb* to cry like a baby (*KL iv 6*)

wave *verb* **1.** to beckon someone (*H i 4*) **2.** to nod the head (*H ii 1*)

waxen *verb* to increase (*MND ii 1*) ■ *adjective* **1.** easily moulded (*TN ii 2*) **2.** easily pierced (*R2 i 3*) **3.** easily erased (*H5 i 2*)

wayward *adjective* **1.** uncooperative (*R2 ii 1*) **2.** perverted (*M iii 5*)

weak *adjective* **1.** unimportant (*MND v 1*; *H5 iii 6*; *O iii 3*) **2.** foolish (*T ii 2*; *MA iii 1*; *RJ ii 4*)

weal *noun* **1.** welfare (*H iii 3*) **2.** the state (*KL i 4*; *M iii 4*)

weal-balanced *adjective* taking into account the welfare of all (*MM iv 3*)

wealth *noun* prosperity (*MV v 1*; *H iv 4*)

weapon *noun* a penis (*RJ i 1*)

wear *noun* the fashion (*MM iii 2; AYLI ii 7*) ■ *verb* **1.** to own someone (*MA v 1; H5 v 2*) **2.** to carry (*MV ii 2*) ◇ **wear to** to conform to (*TN ii 4*)

wearer *noun* an owner (*MV ii 9*)

weasel *noun* a sly argumentative person (*1H4 ii 3; AYLI ii 5; H iii 2; H5 i 2*) [From *weasel*, 'a small carnivore that is blood thirsty and attacks prey even when it is not hungry'.]

weather *noun* a storm (*T i 1; MV ii 9*)

weather-fend *verb* to protect something from bad weather (*T v 1*)

web ◇ **web and the pin** a cataract of the eye (*L iii 4*)

weed *noun* a horse in poor condition (*MM i 3*) ■ *verb* to eradicate, to weed out (*R2 ii 3*)

weet *verb* to know (*AC i 1*)

weird

> COMMENT: Shakespeare used the word in just one play, but very intriguingly. The witches in *Macbeth* describe themselves as 'the weird sisters'. The word probably has our modern sense of 'disturbingly odd', but more important is its Anglo-Saxon origin: 'wyrd' meant 'destiny or fate', and the weird sisters speak of the hero's destiny as king and so help to bring about all the terror and violence that fill this play.

weird sisters *noun* the **Fates** (*M i 3*)

welfare *noun* a person's health (*MV v 1*)

welkin *noun* the sky (*T i 2; TN iii 3; WT i 2*)

well *adjective* happy (*WT v 1; RJ v 1; AC ii 5*)

well-a-day *interjection* alas! (*TN iv 2; RJ iii 2*)

well-advised *adjective* **1.** sane (*CE ii 2*) **2.** wary (*R3 iv 4*)

well-appointed *adjective* well equipped (*2H4 i 1*)

well-beseeming *adjective* orderly (*1H4 i 1*)

well-favoured *adjective* handsome (*MA iii 3; KL ii 4*)

well-given *adjective* favourably disposed (*JC i 2*)

well-graced *adjective* popular (*R2 v 2*)

well-painted *adjective* convincingly acted (*O iv 1*)

well-respected *adjective* carefully considered (*1H4 iv 3*)

well-seen *adjective* highly skilled (*TS i 2*)

well to live *adjective* wealthy (*WT iii 3; MV ii 2*)

well-wished *adjective* popular (*MM ii 4*)

Welsh hook *noun* a long-handled battleaxe with a long curved blade (*1H4 ii 4*)

wen *noun* a cyst or a tumour on the skin (*2H4 ii 2*)

Westward-ho *noun* the cry of the men rowing the ferries on the Thames (*TN iii 1*)

wether *noun* a castrated ram (*T iv 1; MV iv 1*)

wezand *noun* the windpipe (*T iii 2*)

wharf *noun* a riverbank (*H i 5*)

wheel *noun* **1.** a spinning wheel, a device for spinning yarn from wool (*AYLI i 2; H iv 5*) **2.** the wheel of fortune, representing how a person's luck can change from good to bad and back again (*KL v 3*) ■ *verb* to turn around (*R3 iv 4*) ◇ **turn in the wheel** to turn a roasting spit like a trained dog (*CE iii 2*)

wheeling *adjective* wandering (*O i 1*)

wheel of fire *noun* a form of torture in hell (*KL iv 7*)

wheeson *noun* the Christian festival of Whitsun (**Pentecost**), held on the seventh Sunday after Easter (*2H4 ii 1*)

whelk *noun* a pimple (*H5 iii 6*)

whelked *adjective* twisted like a seashell (*KL iv 6*)

whe'r *conjunction* whether (*T v 1; CE iv 1*)

where *interjection* what are you suggesting? (*AYLI v 2*) ■ *adverb* wherever (*MND v 1; KL iv 5*)

whereabout *noun* an intention (*M ii 1*)

whereas *conjunction* where

whet *verb* to incite someone (*R3 i 3; JC ii 1*)

whetstone *noun* a stone for sharpening swords, etc. (*AYLI i 2; M iv 3*)

whey-face *adjective* pale faced (*M v 3*) [From the colour of whey, the liquid remaining after the curds have been removed from milk in making cheese.]

whiffler *noun* someone who goes in front of a procession to clear a way through a crowd (*H5 v Chor.*)

while *noun* the passage of time ■ *conjunction* until (*M iii 1*; *R2 i 3*) ◇ **as while** while (*2H4 i 1*) ◇ **the while** meanwhile (*AYLI ii 5*)

while-ere *adverb* not long ago (*T iii 2*)

whiles *conjunction* while (*T i 2*; *TN iv 3*) ◇ **the whiles** meanwhile (*TS iii 1*)

whilst ◇ **the whilst 1.** meanwhile (*R2 v 2*) **2.** while (*H iii 2*)

whip *noun* drat! (a mild expletive) (*O i 1*)

whipping-cheer *verb* to be whipped (*2H4 v 4*)

whipster *noun* a useless beginner (*O v 2*)

whirligig *noun* a spinning top (*TN v 1*)

whist *adjective* quiet (*T i 2*)

whistle ◇ **go whistle** get lost! (*WT iv 4*) ◇ **worth the whistle** worth noticing (*L iv 2*)

whistle her off *verb* to let a hawk fly from your wrist (*O iii 3*)

whistle of *verb* to speak secretly of something (*WT iv 4*)

white *noun* the centre of an archery target (*TS v 2*) ■ *adjective* (*of fish*) fresh (*KL iii 6*) (NOTE: Contrasted with a red (or smoked) herring.) ◇ **spit white** to spit out white froth (*2H4 i 2*)

white-livered *adjective* cowardly (*H5 iii 2*; *R3 iv 4*) (NOTE: The liver (which is very red in colour) was considered to be the centre of courage.)

Whitsun pastorals *plural noun* entertainments held at Whitsun, usually involving idyllic rural themes (*WT iv 4*)

whole *adjective* solid (*MND iii 2*; *M iii 4*)

wholesome *adjective* **1.** healthy (*KL i 4*; *H i 5, iii 2*; *M iv 3*) **2.** health-giving (*CE v 1*) **3.** sensible (*H ii 2, iii 2*; *O iii 1*) **4.** beneficial (*KL ii 4*; *O i 1*)

whoobub *noun* a hubbub (*WT iv 3*)

whoop *noun* a shout of excitement or joy (*WT iv 4*; *KL i 4*)

whore ◇ **whore of Babylon** the Roman Catholic Church (an anachronism), referred to in Revelation 17–18 (*H5 ii 3*)

whoreson *noun* a bastard (used as a term of abuse) (*KL i 1*) (NOTE: Literally, the son of a prostitute.)

COMMENT: *Whoreson* is very common among the many Shakespearean terms of abuse. Literally it means 'son of a whore (or prostitute)', but was often used in vulgar banter simply to emphasise or intensify something, as 'bloody' is today. The low-life scenes in **Henry IV Part 1** are full of competitive abuse, especially between Falstaff and Prince Hal; for example, Falstaff is very fat and Hal mocks him as 'you whoreson round man'. This is typical of the sense of rough affection when the word is used, though it also provides irony in the first scene of **King Lear**. The Earl of Gloucester cheerfully confesses to Kent that his son Edmund, present in the scene, is illegitimate: 'The whoreson must be acknowledged', he says. In Elizabethan times illegitimate children, who therefore might be literally sons (or daughters) of whores, would forfeit any rights of inheritance. Gloucester may joke of his sexual exploits, but 'the whoreson' Edmund's sense of unfair discrimination leads to horrible consequences for his father.

wicked *adjective* **1.** harmful (*T i 2*; *KL ii 1*) **2.** unlucky (*MND ii 2*)

wide *adjective* mistake (*KL iv 7*) ■ *adverb* misguidedly (*MA iv 1*; *H ii 2*) [From the idea of shooting an arrow wide of the mark or target.]

wide-chapped *adjective* open-mouthed (*T i 1*)

wide-enlarged *adjective* generously given (*AYLI iii 2*)

widow *verb* to give a wife rights to property, etc. when she is widowed (*MM v 1*)

widowhood *noun* property inherited by a woman from her husband (*TS ii 1*)

wield *verb* to manage to say something (*RJ i 1*; *KL i 1*)

wife *noun* a woman (*TN v 1*; *H5 v Chor.*)

wight *noun* a person (*H5 ii 1*; *O ii 1, 3*)

wild *noun* **1.** a wilderness (*MV ii 7, iii 2*) **2.** wooded countryside (*1H4 ii 1*) ■ *adjective* rash (*WT ii 1*)

wilderness *noun* infertility (*MM iii 1*)

wildfire *noun* gunpowder (*1H4 iii 3*)

wild-goose chase *noun* a horse race across open country, in which the other horses have to follow the course set by the leader (*RJ ii 4*)

wild-mare ◇ **to ride the wild-mare** to play on a seesaw (*2H4 ii 4*)

wildness *noun* madness (*H iii 1*)

wilful *adjective* **1.** keen (*MND v 1*; *RJ i 5*) **2.** stubborn (*MV i 1*; *R3 iii 7*) ■ *adverb* stubbornly (*WT i 2*)

wilful-blame *adjective* to blame for being too stubborn (*1H4 iii 1*)

will *noun* **1.** sexual desire (*MM ii 4*; *KL iv 6*; *AC iii 13*) **2.** the male or female sex organ (*AC ii 5*) ◇ **of thine own good will** freely (*R2 iv 1*)

willow *noun* a willow garland was worn as a symbol of grief or lost love (*MA ii 1*; *TN i 5*; *O iv 3*)

win *verb* to defeat someone (*AC ii 4*)

wince *verb* to kick out in pain (*H iii 2*)

Wincot *noun* Wilmecot, the home of Shakespeare's mother (*TS Ind. 2*)

wind *verb* **1.** to blow a horn (*MND iv 1*; *MA i 1*; *TS Ind. 1 Stage direction*) **2.** to make a horse turn around (*JC iv 1*; *1H4 iv 1*) **3.** to use a subtle argument (*MV i 1*) **4.** to ingratiate yourself (*KL i 2*) **5.** to scent ◇ **down the wind** to fly into the wind (*O iii 3*) ◇ **on the wind** freely (*AC iii 6*) ◇ **sit in the wind against** to oppose somone (*AC iii 10*) ◇ **recover the wind of** to get the better of someone (*H iii 2*)

windgall *noun* a tumour on a horse's leg (*TS iii 2*)

windlass *noun* a roundabout way of doing things (*H ii 1*)

window *noun* an eyelid (*R3 v 3*; *RJ iv 1*; *AC v 2*)

windowed *adjective* **1.** seated at a window (*AC iv 14*) **2.** full of holes (*KL iii 4*)

windring *adjective* winding, wandering (*T iv 1*)

Windsor *noun* a town on the River Thames 32 km west of London, home of the royal castle founded by William I (*1H4 i 1*; *2H4 ii 1, iv 4*)

windy *adjective* (*of speech*) long-winded (*R3 iv 4*)

windy side *noun* the safe side (*TN iii 4*)

winged *adjective* protected on each side by additional troops (*R3 v 3*)

wink *noun* a small distance (*T ii 1*) ■ *verb* **1.** to glance at someone as a way of conveying a message (*H5 iv 2*) **2.** to be blind (*CE iii 2*) ◇ **wink at** to pretend not to see something (*M i 4*)

winking *noun* a period of being blind (*H ii 2*)

winnowed *adjective* with the worthless material removed (*H v 2*) [From the idea of separating the dry outer coverings from grain.]

wintered *adjective* as worn in the winter (*AYLI iii 2*)

wisdom *noun* sanity (*M iv 4*) ◇ **wisdom of nature** knowledge about nature (*L i 2*)

wise *adjective* sane (*KL i 5*; *O iv 1*)

wise-woman *noun* a witch (*TN iii 4*)

wish *verb* to recommend someone (*TS i 1, 2*)

wishtly, wistly *adverb* longingly (*R2 v 4*)

wit *noun* **1.** intelligence **2.** wisdom **3.** understanding **4.** quickness of perception

COMMENT: *Wit* had a basic meaning of 'intelligence or good sense', as when Leonato in **Much Ado Ado About Nothing** asks his brother about the source of some overhearing: 'Has the fellow any wit that told you this?' He is not here intending our sense of quick, amusing comments. However, the Elizabethan *wit* did extend its meaning to ingenuity and is a word often associated with jesters who professionally had to entertain kings and courtiers. Feste, Touchstone and Lear's Fool play cleverly with words, even to the extent of confusing and distorting their basic meaning. In **Twelfth Night** at the opening of Act 3 Feste and Viola discuss this dangerous potential in a jester's wit. Feste, wittily disparaging his profession, complains: 'To see this age! A sentence is but a cheveril glove to a good wit – how quickly the wrong side may be turned outward'. *Wit* typically includes word-play, puns, paradoxes and many types of verbal surprise. The Metaphysical poets of the early 17th century valued witty conceits as a way of illuminating a new angle of their topic and thereby surprising their readers. Such ingenuity was highly prized too within the group known as the University Wits and the young lawyers, such as John Donne, in Shakespeare's London. Intellectual status was important, and competitive *wit* could sometimes drive out concern for others' feelings. At the end of **Love's Labours Lost** Rosaline reviews Berowne's habits and life-style and will marry him only if he removes the cruelty in his intellectual exuberance: she declares him to be 'full of comparisons and wounding flouts,/Which you on all estates will execute/That lie within the mercy of your wit': In short, Berowne must lose his superficial cleverness and gain wisdom. But *wit* can also mean wisdom, as when Polonius in **Hamlet** states that 'Brevity is the soul of wit'. Since *wit* is derived from the Anglo-Saxon word 'witan', 'to know', it is not surprising that the word, like knowledge itself, can be used in many different contexts.

with *preposition* being greeted with (*M iii 6*)

withal *adverb* **1.** at the same time **2.** besides ■ *preposition* with ◇ **could not do withal** I could not help it (*MV iii 4*)

withering out *noun* the act of using something up (*MND i 1*)

withers *noun* the ridge between the shoulder blades of a horse, which gets rubbed by the saddle (*1H4 iii 1; H iii 2*)

withold *verb* to keep someone back (*MND ii 1*)

without-book *adjective* without a script (*RJ i 4*)

without-door *adjective* external (*WT ii 1*)

wit snapper *noun* someone who has a quick answer to everything (*MV iii 5*)

wittily *adverb* wisely (*TN iv 2*)

witty *adjective* **1.** wise (*TN i 5; O ii 1*) **2.** cunning (*MA iv 2; R3 iv 2*)

wo ha ho *noun* a call to attract attention (*MV v 1*) [From the call of a falconer to his hawk.]

woman *noun* a wife (*1H4 ii 3*) ◇ **woman of the world** a married woman (*AYLI v 3*)

woman'd *adjective* accompanied by a woman (*O iii 4*)

woman-queller *noun* someone who has murdered women (*2H4 ii 1*)

woman-tired *adjective* henpecked (*WT ii 3*)

womb *noun* **1.** a hollow space (*R2 ii 1; RJ v 1*) **2.** the stomach (*2H4 iv 3*) ■ *verb* to enclose something (*WT iv 3*)

womby *adjective* hollow (*H5 ii 4*)

wondered *adjective* working wonders (*T iv 1*)

wont *noun* a habit (*T iv 1*) ■ *verb* to be in the habit of doing something (*CE iv 4*) ■ *adjective* tended to do something (*R3 i 4; H ii 2*)

wood *adjective* mad (*MND ii 1*)

woodbine *noun* the honeysuckle or bindweed, both of which are climbing plants found in hedgerows (*MA ii 1, iii 1, iv 1*)

woodcock *noun* a stupid person (*MA v 1; TS i 2; H i 3*) [Because a woodcock is a bird related to snipe that is easy to catch]

wooden *adjective* **1.** stupid (*H5 Prol., iv 4; KL ii 3*) **2.** insensitive (*T iii 1*)

wooden O *noun* **1.** a round or octagonal wooden theatre, e.g. The Globe (*H5 Prol.*) **2.** anything round (*AC v 2; MND iii 2*)

woodman *noun* a man who seduces women (*MM iv 3*)

woollen *adjective* covered with a woollen cloth (*MV iv 1*) ◇ **to lie in the woollen** to sleep between rough blankets, without sheets, possibly to be buried (*MA ii 1*)

woolsack *noun* a sack of wool (*1H4 ii 4*)

woo't *interjection* will you? (*H v 1; AC iv 15*)

word *noun* a password (*MV iii 5; KL iv 6; H i 5*) ■ *verb* to urge someone to do something (*AC v 2*) ◇ **at a word** on little evidence (*JC i 2*)

work *noun* a fortification (*O iii 2*) ■ *verb* to have an effect on someone (*T iv 1; M i 3; O v 2*) ◇ **make work** to cause confusion

working *noun* **1.** an effort (*AYLI i 2; 2H4 iv 2*) **2.** an activity (*MM ii 1; H ii 2*) **3.** an action (*2H4 v 2*)

working-day *adjective* ordinary (*AYLI i 3*)

working-house *noun* a factory (*H5 v Chor.*)

worky-day *adjective* ordinary (*AC i 2*)

world *noun* **1.** existence (*MM v 1; RJ iii 1; H iv 5*) **2.** a representation of something in miniature (*KL iii 1*) ◇ **a world to see** a wonder to see (*MA iii 5; TS ii 1*) ◇ **to go to the world** to be married (*MA ii 1*)

worm *noun* **1.** a pathetic person (*KL iv 1*) **2.** a snake (believed to cause tooth decay) (*MND iii 2; MM iii 1; M iii 4; AC v 2*) **3.** a creature (*T iii 1*) **4.** a form of skin parasite (*RJ i 4*)

wormwood *noun* a bitter plant that was used medicinally (*H iii 2; RJ i 3*)

worry *verb* to hug someone tightly (*WT v 2*) [Literally 'to strangle'.]

worship *verb* to honour something (*H5 i 2*)

worth *noun* **1.** merit (*MM i 1*) **2.** wealth (*KL iv 4*; *RJ ii 6*) *See also* **worth the whistle** *at* **whistle**

worthy *noun* a valued person or thing ■ *verb* to make someone appear worthy of honour (*KL ii 2*) ■ *adjective* **1.** suitable for something (*JC v 5*; *M i 2*) **2.** valuable (*T i 2*; *AYLI iii 3*; *JC iii 1*) **3.** deserved (*R2 v 1*; *R3 i 2*) **4.** justifiable (*1H4 iii 2*; *O iii 3*)

woundless *adjective* not able to be damaged (*H iv 1*)

wrack *noun* **1.** a ruin (*M i 3*) **2.** a wreck (*T i 2*; *H5 i 2*; *CE v 1*; *O ii 1*) **3.** a ruined person (*TN v 1*; *R3 i 4*) ■ *verb* **1.** to ruin someone (*R3 iv 1*; *H ii 1*) **2.** to wreck (*T i 2*; *MM iii 1*; *MV iii 1*)

wrangle *verb* dispute, argue (*T v 1*)

wrangler *noun* an opponent (*H5 i 2*) (NOTE: This was a term used in tennis.)

wrath *noun* passion (*AYLI v 2*) ■ *adjective* angry (*MND ii 1*)

wrathful *adjective* angry (*2H4 iii 2*; *KL iii 2*; *M iii 5*)

wreak *verb* to take revenge for something (*RJ iii 5*)

wrenching *adjective* the act of being pulled and moulded into shape (*2H4 iii 1*)

wrest *verb* to misinterpret something said (*MA iii 4*; *H5 i 2*)

wretch *noun* a term of affection (*RJ i 3*; *AC v 1*; *O iii 3*)

wring *verb* **1.** to writhe about in pain (*MA v 1*) **2.** to force something to turn in a particular direction (*T i 2*) **3.** to force something out of someone (*MM v 1*; *H i 2*; *O v 2*)

wringing *noun* pain (*H5 iv 1*)

writ *noun* **1.** a document (*H v 2*) **2.** the scriptures of the Bible (*R3 i 3*; *O iii 3*) ◇ **writ and liberty** the parts of London under the authority of the sheriff (the 'law of writ') and where the performance of plays was controlled, and the areas outside the sheriff's authority (**liberty**) where the conventional rules of drama need not apply (*H ii 2*)

write *verb* to put something in writing (*H i 2, iv 5*) ◇ **write against** to condemn something (*MA iv 1*)

write over *verb* to copy something out (*R3 iii 6*)

writer *noun* a clerk with the authority to carry out certain legal actions, especially the drawing up of legal documents (*MA iii 5*)

wrong ◇ **do oneself wrong** to be mistaken (*T i 2*; *MM i 2*) ◇ **have wrong** to experience injustice or loss (*2H4 v 1*; *JC iii 2*)

wrong-incensed *adjective* angered by a crime or offence (*R3 ii 1*)

wroth *noun* misery (*MV ii 9*)

wrung *adjective* **1.** rubbed (*H i 2*; *MV ii 8*) **2.** sore from being rubbed (*1H4 ii 1*)

wry-necked *adjective* having a twisted neck (*MV ii 5*) (NOTE: This is a reference to the fact that a fife (a type of flute) is played with the head turned sideways.)

XYZ

Xanthippe *noun* the ancient Greek philosopher Socrates' bad-tempered wife (*TS i 2*)

yard *noun* a stick used for measuring, one yard (0.9 metres) long (*TS iv 3; 1H4 ii 4*)

yare *adjective* ready (*T v 1; TN iii 4; AC iii 7; MM iv 2*)

yarely *adverb* briskly (*T i 1; AC ii 2*)

Yaughan *noun* an innkeeper (*H v 1*)

yaw *verb* to follow an erratic course, like a ship not responding properly to its steering (*H v 2*)

yawn *noun* an earthquake which often occurs when the sun or moon is in eclipse (*H iii 2*) ■ *verb* **1.** to open wide (*MA v 3; JC ii 2; H5 iv 6*) **2.** to gape in surprise (*H iv 5; O v 2*)

yea-forsooth ◇ **yea-forsooth knave** always agreeing unquestioningly with your superiors (*2H4 i 2*)

yearn *verb* to distress someone (*H5 iv 3; R2 v 5; JC ii 2*)

years *adjective* of mature age (*1H4 ii 4; O i 2*)

yeast *noun* foam (*WT iii 3*)

yeasty *adjective* **1.** foamy (*M iv 1*) **2.** superficial (*H v 2*)

Yedward *noun* Edward (*1H4 i 2*)

yellow *noun* jealousy (*WT ii 3*)

yellows *noun* the disease jaundice in horses (*TS iii 2*)

yeoman *noun* **1.** a man who owns rather than rents land (*1H4 iv 2; H5 iii 1; KL iii 6*) **2.** a court official (*TN ii 5*)

yeoman service *noun* excellent and loyal service (*H v 2*) [From the reputation of yeomen during wartime.]

yerk *verb* to stab someone (*O i 2*) ◇ **yerk out** to lash out (*H5 iv 7*)

yerwhile *adverb* just now (*AYLI iii 5*)

yesty *adjective* foaming (*WT iii 3; M iv 1; H v 2*) [From the way yeast foams when it ferments.]

yield *verb* **1.** to state something (*TN iii 2; AC ii 5*) **2.** to give birth (*T ii 1; AYLI ii 3*) **3.** to reward someone for something (*AC iv 2*) *See also* **yield the crow a pudding** *at* **crow**

yolk *noun* a pair of oxen (*2H4 iii 2; H5 ii 2*) ■ *verb* to join together in marriage (*O iv 1*)

young *adjective* inexperienced (*AYLI i 1; M iii 4*)

young bones *noun* an unborn child (*KL ii 4*)

younger *noun* a younger son (*MV ii 6*)

youngling *noun* a youth (*TS ii 1*)

younker *noun* **1.** a young inexperienced man (*1H4 iii 3*) **2.** a younger son (*MV ii 6*)

zany *noun* a professional jester's stooge (*TN i 5*)

zed *noun* the letter of the alphabet that is most ignored (*KL ii 2*)

zenith *noun* the most successful stage of life (*T i 2*)

Zeus *noun* the Greek equivalent of **Jupiter**

zodiac *noun* **1.** the belt in space in which the the sun, moon and planets appear to move (*T ii 1*) **2.** a year (*MM i 2*) (NOTE: The new moon occurs on the same day every nineteen years.)

zounds *noun* by God's wounds (used as an oath) (*O i 1*)

SUPPLEMENTS

English Kings and Queens 1327–1603
Shakespeare's Life and Times
A Chronological List of Shakespeare's Plays
Dramatis Personae
Filmography

English Kings and Queens 1327–1603

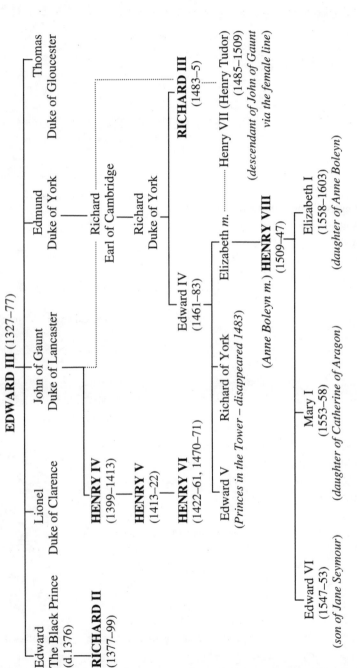

EDWARD III (1327–77)

Edward
The Black Prince
(d.1376)

Lionel
Duke of Clarence

John of Gaunt
Duke of Lancaster

Edmund
Duke of York

Thomas
Duke of Gloucester

RICHARD II
(1377–99)

HENRY IV
(1399–1413)

HENRY V
(1413–22)

HENRY VI
(1422–61, 1470–71)

Richard
Earl of Cambridge

Richard
Duke of York

RICHARD III
(1483–5)

Henry VII (Henry Tudor)
(1485–1509)
(descendant of John of Gaunt via the female line)

Edward IV
(1461–83)

Edward V
Richard of York
(Princes in the Tower – disappeared 1483)

Elizabeth *m.* ....

Elizabeth *m.*
(Anne Boleyn m.) **HENRY VIII**
(1509–47)

Edward VI
(1547–53)
(son of Jane Seymour)

Mary I
(1553–58)
(daughter of Catherine of Aragon)

Elizabeth I
(1558–1603)
(daughter of Anne Boleyn)

Names in capitals indicate the subjects of plays by Shakespeare

Shakespeare's Life and Times

1558	Elizabeth I crowned Queen of England
1564	William Shakespeare born
1576	The opening of The Theatre, the first purpose-built theatre in London since Roman times
1582	William Shakespeare marries Anne Hathaway
1583	Birth of Shakespeare's daughter, Susanna
1585	Birth of Shakespeare's son, Hamnet. The Queen's Men perform in Stratford
1590	Shakespeare working in London, writing and acting with Burbage's company of players at The Theatre
1592	First performances of Shakespeare's *Henry VI, Parts One and Two* in London
1592–94	An outbreak of plague closes the London theatres
1593	Christopher Marlowe dies
1593–94	Shakespeare's poems *Venus and Adonis* and *The Rape of Lucrece* published
1596	Hamnet Shakespeare dies. The Shakespeare family is granted a coat of arms
1597	Shakespeare buys New Place, the second largest house in Stratford
1598	The building of the Globe Theatre begins
1599	The Globe Theatre opens
1601	Shakespeare's father, John Shakespeare, dies
1603	Queen Elizabeth I dies. James I crowned King of England
1605	The Gunpowder Plot, a failed attempt to blow up the Houses of Parliament
1607	Shakespeare's daughter, Susanna, marries John Hall
1608	Shakespeare's mother, Mary Arden, dies
1609	Shakespeare's *Sonnets* published
1610–11	Shakespeare writes his last play, *The Tempest*
1613	The Globe Theatre burns to the ground
1614	The rebuilt Globe Theatre reopens
1616	Shakespeare's daughter, Judith, marries Thomas Quiney
	Shakespeare writes his will
	Shakespeare dies
1619	Richard Burbage dies
1623	Shakespeare's wife Anne dies
	The *First Folio* edition of Shakespeare's plays published

A Chronological List of Shakespeare's Plays

While there are some records that give us the dates of first performances of Shakespeare's plays, it is difficult to be precise about when the plays were actually written and there is considerable debate among scholars on the subject. The table below lists the plays in the order in which they were probably written, together with the probable dates of their composition.

The Two Gentlemen of Verona	1590–91
The Taming of the Shrew	1590–93
Henry VI, Part One	1590–91
Henry VI, Part Two	1590–92
Henry VI, Part Three	1590–92
Titus Andronicus	1590–93
The Reign of Edward III	1592–93
Richard III	1592–93
The Comedy of Errors	1593–94
Love's Labour's Lost	1594–95
Richard II	1595
Romeo and Juliet	1591–96
King John	1591–96
A Midsummer Night's Dream	1594–96
The Merchant of Venice	1596–98
Henry IV, Part One	1596–98
The Merry Wives of Windsor	1596–98
Henry IV, Part Two	1597–98
Much Ado About Nothing	1598
Henry V	1598–99
Julius Caesar	1599
As You Like It	1598–1600
Hamlet	1599–1601
Twelfth Night	1599–1601
Troilus and Cressida	1600–02
Measure for Measure	1603–04
Othello	1603–04
All's Well That Ends Well	1603–05
Timon of Athens	1605
King Lear	1605–06
Macbeth	1606
Antony and Cleopatra	1606–08
Pericles	1606–08
Coriolanus	1607–08
The Winter's Tale	1609–10
Cymbeline	1606–10
The Tempest	1610–11
King Henry VIII	1612–13
The Two Noble Kinsmen	1613–14

Dramatis Personae

Antony and Cleopatra

Mark Antony, Octavius Caesar and M. Aemilius Lepidus, triumvirs
Domitius Enobarbus, Ventidius, Eros, Scarus, Dercetas, Demetrius and Philo,
    friends to Antony
Maecenas, Agrippa, Dolabella, Proculeius, Thidias and Gallus, friends to Caesar
Menas, Menecrates and Varrius, friends to Pompey
Taurus, Lieutenant-General to Caesar
Canidius, Lieutenant-General to Antony
Silius, a Roman officer under Ventidius
A Schoolmaster
Alexas, Mardian, Seleucus and Diomedes, attendants on Cleopatra
A Soothsayer
A Clown
Cleopatra, Queen of Egypt
Octavia, sister to Caesar and wife to Antony
Charmian and Iras, attendants on Cleopatra
Officers, Soldiers, Messengers, Attendants
Scene: various parts of the Roman Empire

As You Like It

Duke, living in exile in the Forest of Arden
Frederick, his brother and usurper of the dukedom
Amiens and Jaques, lords attending on the banished Duke
Le Beau, a courtier attending on Duke Frederick
Charles, wrestler to Duke Frederick
Oliver, Jaque de Boys and Orlando, sons of Sir Rowland de Boys
Adam and Dennis, servants to Oliver
Touchstone, a clown
Sir Oliver Martext, a vicar
Corin and Silvius, shepherds
William, a country fellow in love with Audrey
Hymen
Rosalind, daughter to the banished Duke
Celia, daughter to Duke Frederick
Phebe, a shepherdess
Audrey, a country wench
Lords, Pages, Foresters, Attendants
*Scene: Oliver's orchard near his house; afterwards in the Usurper's Court and the
    Forest of Arden*

Dramatis Personae *continued*

Hamlet
Claudius, King of Denmark
Hamlet, son to the late, and nephew to the present king
Polonius, Lord Chamberlain
Horatio, friend to Hamlet
Laertes, son to Polonius
Voltimand, Cornelius, Rosencrantz, Guildenstern, Orsic and A Gentleman, courtiers
A Priest
Marcellus and Barnardo, officers
Francisco, a soldier
Reynaldo, servant to Polonius
Players, Two Clowns, grave-diggers
Fortinbras, Prince of Norway
A Captain
English Ambassadors
Gertrude, Queen of Denmark and mother to Hamlet
Ophelia, daughter to Polonius
Lords, Ladies, Officers, Soldiers, Sailors, Messengers and other Attendants
Ghost of Hamlet's Father
Scene: Elsinore, Denmark

Henry IV Part 1
King Henry the Fourth
Henry, Prince of Wales and John of Lancaster, sons to the King
Earl of Westmoreland
Sir Walter Blunt
Thomas Percy, Earl of Worcester
Henry Percy, Earl of Northumberland
Henry Percy, surnamed Hotspur, his son
Edmund Mortimer, Earl of March
Richard Scroop, Archbishop of York
Archibald, Earl of Douglas
Owen Glendower
Sir Richard Vernon
Sir John Falstaff
Sir Michael, a friend to the Archbishop of York
Poins, Gadshill, Peto, Bardolph
Lady Percy, wife to Hotspur, and sister to Mortimer
Lady Mortimer, daughter to Glendower and wife to Mortimer
Mistress Quickly, hostess of the Boar's Head Tavern in Eastcheap
Lords, Officers, Sheriff, Vintner, Chamberlain, Drawers, two Carriers, Travellers
    and Attendants
Scene: England

Dramatis Personae *continued*

Henry IV Part 2

Rumour, the Presenter
King Henry the Fourth
Henry, Prince of Wales, afterwards King Henry V
Thomas, Duke of Clarence, son of Henry the Fourth
Prince John of Lancaster, son of Henry the Fourth
Prince Humphrey of Gloucester, son of Henry the Fourth
Earl of Warwick
Earl of Westmoreland
Earl of Surrey
Gower
Harcourt
Blunt
Lord Chief-Justice of the King's Bench
A Servant of the Chief-Justice
Earl of Northumberland
Richard Scroop, Archbishop of York
Lord Mowbray
Lord Hastings
Lord Bardolph
Sir John Colevile
Travers and Morton, retainers of Northumberland
Sir John Falstaff
His Page
Bardolph, Pistol, Poins, Peto
Shallow and Silence, country justices
Davy, servant to Shallow
Mouldy, Shadow, Wart, Feeble and Bullcalf, recruits
Fang and Snare, sheriff's officers
Lady Northumberland
Lady Percy
Mistress Quickly, hostess of a tavern in Eastcheap
Doll Tearsheet
Lords and Attendants, Porter, Drawers, Beadles, Grooms etc.
A Dancer, speaker of the epilogue
Scene: England

Dramatis Personae *continued*

Henry V

King Henry the Fifth
Duke of Gloucester and Duke of Bedford, brothers to the King
Duke of Exeter, uncle to the King
Duke of York, cousin to the King
Earls of Salisbury, Westmoreland and Warwick
Archbishop of Canterbury
Bishop of Ely
Earl of Cambridge
Lord Scroop
Sir Thomas Grey
Sir Thomas Erpingham, Gower, Fluellen, MacMorris and Jamy, officers in the King's army
Bates, Court and Williams, soldiers in the same
Pistol, Nym and Bardolph
Charles the Sixth, King of France
Lewis, the Dauphin
Dukes of Burgundy, Orleans and Bourbon
The Constable of France
Rambures and Grandpre, French Lords
Governor of Harfleur
Montjoy, a French Herald
Ambassadors to the King of England
Isabel, Queen of France
Katharine, daughter to Charles and Isabel
Alice, a lady attending on her
Hostess of a tavern in Eastcheap, formerly Mistress Quickly, now married to Pistol
Chorus, Boy, Herald, Lords, Ladies, Officers, Soldiers, Citizens, Messengers and Attendants
Scene: England and France

Julius Caesar

Julius Caesar
Octavius Caesar, Marcus Antonius and M Aemilius Lepidus, triumvirs after the death
   of Julius Caesar
Cicero, Publius and Popilius Lena, senators
Marcus Brutus, Caius Cassius, Casca, Trebonius, Ligarius, Decius Brutus, Metellus
   Cimber and Cinna, conspirators against Julius Caesar
Flavius and Marullus, tribunes
Artemidorus, a sophist of Cnidos
A Soothsayer
Cinna, a poet; another poet
Lucilius, Titinius, Messala, Young Cato and Volumnius, friends to Brutus and Cassius
Varro, Clitus, Claudius, Strato, Lucius and Dardanius, servants to Brutus
Pindarus, servant to Cassius
Calpurnia, wife to Caesar
Portia, wife to Brutus
Commoners, or Plebeians, of Rome; Senators, Guards, Attendants etc.
Scene: Rome, Asia Minor and the plains near Philippi, in Macedonia

Dramatis Personae *continued*

King Lear

Lear, King of Britain
King of France
Duke of Burgundy
Duke of Cornwall
Duke of Albany
Earl of Kent
Earl of Gloucester
Edgar, son to Gloucester
Edmund, bastard son to Gloucester
Curan, a courtier
Oswald, steward to Goneril
Old Man, tenant to Gloucester
Doctor
Fool
An Officer, employed by Edmund
A Gentleman, attendant on Cordelia
A Herald
Servants to Cornwall
Goneril, Regan and Cordelia, daughters to Lear
Knights of Lear's train, Officers, Messengers, Soldiers and Attendants
Scene: Britain

Macbeth

Duncan, King of Scotland
Malcolm and Donalbain, his sons
Macbeth and Banquo, generals of the King's army
Macduff, Lennox, Ross, Menteth, Angus and Cathness, noblemen of Scotland
Fleance, son to Banquo
Siward, Earl of Northumberland, general of the English forces
Young Siward, his son
Seyton, an officer attending on Macbeth
Boy, son to Macduff
An English Doctor, a Scotch Doctor, a Captain, a Porter and an Old Man
Lady Macbeth
Lady Macduff
Gentlewomen attending on Lady Macbeth
Hecate and Three Witches
Banquo's Ghost and other Apparitions
Lords, Gentlemen, Officers, Soldiers, Murderers, Attendants and Messengers
Scene: Scotland and England

Dramatis Personae *continued*

Measure for Measure

Vincentio, the Duke
Angelo, Lord Deputy in the Duke's absence
Escalus, an Ancient Lord, joined with Angelo in the deputation
Claudio, a young Gentleman
Lucio, a Fantastic
Two other Gentlemen
Varrius, a Gentleman attending on the Duke
Provost
Thomas and Peter, two Friars
A Justice
Elbow, a simple Constable
Froth, a foolish Gentleman
Pompey, Tapster to Mistress Overdone
Abhorson, an Executioner
Barnardine, a dissolute Prisoner
Isabella, sister to Claudio
Mariana, betrothed to Angelo
Juliet, beloved of Claudio
Francisca, a Nun
Mistress Overdone, a Bawd
Lords, Officers, Citizens, Boy and Attendants
Scene: Vienna

A Midsummer Night's Dream

Theseus, Duke of Athens
Egeus, father to Hermia
Lysander and Demetrius, in love with Hermia
Philostrate, master of the revels to Theseus
Quince, a carpenter
Snug, a joiner
Bottom, a weaver
Flute, a bellows-mender
Snout, a tinker
Starveling, a tailor
Hippolyta, queen of the Amazons, bethrothed to Theseus
Hermia, daughter to Egeus, in love with Lysander
Helena, in love with Demetrius
Oberon, king of the fairies
Titania, queen of the fairies
Puck, or Robin Goodfellow
Peaseblossom, Cobweb, Moth and Mustardseed, fairies
Other fairies attending their King and Queen, and attendants on Theseus and Hippolyta
Scene: Athens and a wood nearby

Dramatis Personae *continued*

Much Ado About Nothing

Don Pedro, prince of Aragon
Don John, his bastard brother
Claudio, a young lord of Florence
Benedick, a young lord of Padua
Leonato, governor of Messina
Antonio, his brother
Balthasar, attendant on Don Pedro
Conrade and Borachio followers of Don John
Friar Francis
Dogberry, a constable
Verges, a headborough
A Sexton
A Boy
Hero, daughter to Leonato
Beatrice, niece to Leonato
Margaret and Ursula, attendants to Hero
Messengers, Watch, Attendants etc.
Scene: Messina

Othello

Othello
Brabantio, a Senator and father to Desdemona
Cassio, an honourable lieutenant
Iago, a villain, ('ancient' or standard-bearer, and third in command to Othello)
Roderigo, a gulled gentleman
Duke of Venice
Senators
Montano, Governor of Cyprus
Gentlemen of Cyprus
Lodovico and Gratiano, two noble Venetians; kinsmen to Brabantio
Clown, in Othello's retinue
Desdemona, wife to Othello
Emilia, wife to Iago
Bianca, a courtesan
Sailors, Messengers, Herald, Officers, Musicians and Attendants
Scene: Venice and a sea-port in Cyprus

Dramatis Personae *continued*

Richard II

King Richard the Second
John of Gaunt, Duke of Lancaster, uncle to the King
Edmund of Langley, Duke of York, uncle to the King
Henry, surname Bolingbroke, Duke of Hereford, son to John of Gaunt, afterwards King Henry IV
Duke of Aumerle, son to the Duke of York
Thomas Mowbray, Duke of Norfolk
Duke of Surrey
Earl of Salisbury
Lord Berkeley
Bushy, Bagot and Green, servants to King Richard
Earl of Northumberland
Henry Percy, surnamed Hotspur, his son
Lord Ross, Lord Willoughby and Lord Fitzwater
Bishop of Carlisle
Abbot of Westminster
Lord Marshal
Sir Stephen Scroop
Sir Pierce of Exton
Captain of a band of Welshmen
Queen to King Richard
Duchess of York
Duchess of Gloucester
Lady attending on the Queen
Lords, Heralds, Officers, Soldiers, two Gardeners, Keeper, Messenger, Groom, other Attendants
Scene: England and Wales

Richard III

King Edward the Fourth
Edward, Prince of Wales; afterwards King Edward the Fifth and Richard, Duke of York, sons to the King
George, Duke of Clarence and Richard, Duke of Gloucester, afterwards King Richard the Third, brothers to the King
A young son of Clarence
Henry, Earl of Richmond; afterwards King Henry the Seventh
Cardinal Bourchier, Archbishop of Canterbury
Thomas Rotherham, Archbishop of York
John Morton, Bishop of Ely
Duke of Buckingham
Duke of Norfolk
Earl of Surrey, his son
Earl Rivers, brother to King Edward's Queen
Marquess of Dorset and Lord Grey, her sons
Earl of Oxford
Lord Hastings
Lord Stanley, also called Earl of Derby
Lord Lovel

Dramatis Personae *continued*

Richard III *continued*

Sir Thomas Vaughan
Sir Richard Ratcliff
Sir William Catesby
Sir James Tyrrell
Sir James Blount
Sir Walter Herbert
Sir Robert Brakenbury, Lieutenant of the Tower
Sir William Brandon
Christopher Urswick, a Priest
Another priest
Lord Mayor of London, Sheriff of Wiltshire
Tressel and Berkeley, gentlemen attending on Lady Anne
Elizabeth, Queen of King Edward the Fourth
Margaret, widow of King Henry the Sixth
Duchess of York, mother to King Edward the Fourth, Clarence and Gloucester
Lady Anne, widow of Edward, Prince of Wales, son to King Henry the Sixth;
    afterwards married to the Duke of Gloucester
Lady Margaret Plantagenet, a young daughter of Clarence
Lords and other Attendants, two Gentlemen, a Pursuivant, Scrivener, Citizens,
    Murderers, Messengers, Ghosts of those murdered by Richard the Third, Soldiers
Scene: England

Romeo and Juliet

Escalus, prince of Verona
Paris, a young nobleman
Montague and Capulet, heads of warring households
Old man, cousin to Capulet
Romeo, son to Montague
Mercutio, kinsman to the prince and friend to Romeo
Benvolio, nephew to Montague and friend to Romeo
Tybalt, nephew to Lady Capulet
Friar Laurence and Friar John, Franciscans
Balthasar, servant to Romeo
Sampson and Gregory, servants to Capulet
Peter, servant to Juliet's nurse
Abraham, servant to Montague
An Apothecary
Three Musicians
Page to Paris, another Page and an Officer
Lady Montague, wife to Montague
Lady Capulet, wife to Capulet
Juliet, daughter to Capulet
Nurse to Juliet
Chorus, Citizens of Verona, Maskers, Guards, Watchmen and Attendants
Scene: Verona and Mantua

Dramatis Personae *continued*

The Taming of the Shrew

A Lord, Christopher Sly, Hostess, Page, Players, Huntsmen and Servants, persons in the Induction

Baptista, a rich gentleman of Padua

Vincentio, an old gentleman of Pisa

Lucentio, son to Vincentio, in love with Bianca

Petruchio, a gentleman of Verona, a suitor to Katharina

Gremio and Hortensio, suitors to Bianca

Tranio and Biondello, servants to Lucentio

Grumio and Curtis, servants to Petruchio

A Pedant

Katharina, the shrew and Bianca, daughters to Baptista

Widow

Tailor, Haberdasher and Servants attending on Baptista and Petruchio

Scene: Padua and Petruchio's country house

The Comedy of Errors

Solinus, Duke of Ephesus

Aegeon, a Merchant of Syracuse

Antipholus of Ephesus and Antipholus of Syracuse, twin brothers; sons to Aegeon and Aemilia

Dromio of Ephesus and Dromio of Syracuse, twin brothers; slaves to the two Antipholuses

Balthazar, a Merchant

Angelo, a Goldsmith

A Merchant, friend to Antipholus of Syracuse

A second Merchant, to whom Angelo is a debtor

Dr Pinch, a Schoolmaster and a Conjurer

Aemilia, wife to Aegeon, an Abbess at Ephesus

Adriana, wife to Antipholus of Ephesus

Luciana, sister to Adriana

Luce, servant to Adriana

A Courtesan

Gaoler, Officers and other Attendants

Scene: Ephesus

Dramatis Personae *continued*

The Merchant of Venice

The Duke of Venice
The Prince of Morocco, suitor to Portia
The Prince of Arragon, suitor to Portia
Antonio, a merchant of Venice
Bassanio, his friend, suitor likewise to Portia
Salanio, Salarino, Gratiano and Salerio, friends to Antonio and Bassanio
Lorenzo, in love with Jessica
Shylock, a rich Jew
Tubal, a Jew, his friend
Launcelot Gobbo, the clown, servant to Shylock
Old Gobbo, father to Launcelot
Leonardo, servant to Bassanio
Balthasar and Stephano, servants to Portia
Portia, a rich heiress
Nerissa, her waiting maid
Jessica, daughter to Shylock
Magnificos of Venice, Officers of the Court of Justice, Gaoler, servants to Portia
Scene: Venice and Belmont, the seat of Portia, on the Continent

The Tempest

Alonso, King of Naples
Sebastian, his brother
Prospero, the right Duke of Milan
Antonio, his brother, the usurping Duke of Milan
Ferdinand, son to the King of Naples
Gonzalo, an honest old councillor
Adrian and Francisco, lords
Caliban, a savage and deformed slave
Trinculo, a jester
Stephano, a drunken butler
Master of a ship
Boatswain
Mariners
Miranda, daughter to Prospero
Ariel, an airy spirit
Iris, Ceres, Juno, Nymphs and Reapers, spirits
Scene: a ship at sea and a remote island

Dramatis Personae *continued*

Twelfth Night

Orsino, Duke of Illyria
Sebastian, brother to Viola
Antonio, a sea captain and friend to Sebastian
A Sea Captain, friend to Viola
Valentine and Curio, gentlemen attending on the Duke
Sir Toby Belch, kinsman of Olivia
Sir Andrew Aguecheek, suitor of Olivia
Malvolio, steward to Olivia
Fabian, an attendant to Olivia
The Clown Feste, Olivia's fool
Olivia, a countess
Viola, in love with the Duke; sister to Sebastian
Maria, Olivia's gentlewoman
Lords, a Priest, Sailors, Officers, Musicians and other attendants
Scene: Illyria and the coast nearby

The Winter's Tale

Leontes, King of Sicilia
Mamillius, young Prince of Sicilia
Camillo, Antigonus, Cleomenes and Dion, four lords of Sicilia
Hermione, Queen to Leontes
Perdita, daughter to Leontes and Hermione
Paulina, wife to Antigonus
Emilia, a lady
Polixenes, King of Bohemia
Florizel, Prince of Bohemia
Old Shepherd, reputed father of Perdita
Clown, his son
Autolycus, a rogue
Archidamus, a lord of Bohemia
Mopsa and Dorcas, shepherdesses
Other Lords, Gentlemen and Servants
Shepherds and Shepherdesses
A Mariner
A Gaoler
Ladies attending the Queen
Satyrs for a dance
Time, as Chorus
Scene: Sicilia and Bohemia

Filmography: a selected list of film and TV adaptations of Shakespeare's plays

Note: Television adaptations of all the titles below were made for the *BBC Television Shakespeare* series (1978 to 1985) produced by Cedric Messina, Jonathan Miller and Shaun Sutton. The entire cycle is now available on video under the title *The Complete Dramatic Works of William Shakespeare*. These productions are explicitly mentioned below only if there is no other version available: see **www.wikipedia.org/wiki/BBC_Television_Shakespeare** for details of the other plays.

Antony and Cleopatra

Cleopatra (1963) USA. Directed by Joseph L. Mankiewicz, with Elizabeth Taylor and Richard Burton. Loosely based on Shakespeare's play.

Antony and Cleopatra (1972) USA. Directed by and starring Charlton Heston as Antony.

Antony and Cleopatra (1974) UK. Directed by Trevor Nunn, with Janet Suzman and Richard Johnson.

As You Like It

As You Like It (1936) UK. Directed by Paul Czinner, with Laurence Olivier. J.M. Barrie adapted the script.

As You Like It (1953) UK. TV version directed by Peter Ebert, with Laurence Harvey and Margaret Leighton.

As You Like It (1963) UK. TV version directed by Michael Elliott, with Vanessa Redgrave and Patrick Wymark.

As You Like It (1992) UK. Modern-dress version directed by Christine Edzard: the Forest of Arden becomes the banks of the Thames. With Cyril Cusack and Griff Rhys Jones.

The Comedy of Errors

The Boys from Syracuse (1940) USA. Musical based on the story, directed by A. Edward Sutherland.

The Comedy of Errors (1964) UK. TV version directed by Peter Duguid and Clifford Williams, with Ian Richardson, Diana Rigg and Donald Sinden.

The Comedy of Errors (1978) UK. RSC version directed by Trevor Nunn, with Judi Dench.

Hamlet

Le Duel d'Hamlet (1900) France. Directed by Clément Maurice, with Sarah Bernhardt as Hamlet.

Hamlet (1907) France. Directed by Georges Méliès.

Hamlet (1948) UK. The famous Laurence Olivier version, one of the definitive Hamlets.

Hamlet (1964) UK. Directed by John Gielgud (who also plays the Ghost), with Richard Burton.

Filmography *continued*

Hamlet *continued*

Hamlet (1966) Russia. Directed by Gregory Kozintsev.

Hamlet (1969) UK. Directed by Tony Richardson, with Nicol Williamson, Anthony Hopkins and Marianne Faithfull.

Hamlet (1976) UK. Directed by Celestino Coronada, with Quentin Crisp and Helen Mirren.

Hamlet (1990) USA. Directed by Franco Zeffirelli, with Mel Gibson, Glenn Close and Helena Bonham Carter in an acclaimed but controversial version.

Discovering Hamlet (1990) USA. Documentary about Kenneth Branagh's first performance as Hamlet, directed by Derek Jacobi.

Hamlet (1990) USA. Kevin Kline stars in and directs a version for the New York Shakespeare Festival.

Hamlet (1996) UK. Directed by and starring Kenneth Branagh in a full uncut four-hour version, with Kate Winslet, Derek Jacobi, Robin Williams, Julie Christie, Jack Lemmon, Ken Dodd, Billy Crystal, and Charlton Heston

Hamlet (2000) USA. Modern adaptation set in New York. Directed by Michael Almereyda with Ethan Hawke, Bill Murray and Kyle MacLachlan.

Henry IV Part One *and* Part Two

Chimes at Midnight (1966) USA. Directed by and starring Orson Welles, telling Falstaff's story by taking scenes from the three plays he appears in.

My Own Private Idaho (1991) USA. Starring Keanu Reeves as a modern American 'Prince Hal'.

Henry V

The Chronicle History of King Henry the Fifth with his Battell at Agincourt in France (1944) UK. Better known as *Henry V*, the famous morale-raising film made during World War II by Laurence Olivier.

Henry V (1989) UK. Directed by and starring Kenneth Branagh, and less jingoistic than Olivier's version.

Henry V at Shakespeare's Globe (1997) UK. Film of a live performance at the Globe Theatre directed by Richard Olivier and Steve Ruggi, with Mark Rylance.

Julius Caesar

Julius Caesar (1950) USA. Directed by David Bradley, with Charlton Heston.

Julius Caesar (1953) USA. Directed by Joseph L. Mankiewicz, with Marlon Brando, James Mason, and John Gielgud.

An Honourable Murder (1959) UK. Modern adaptation directed by Geoffrey Grayson, with Norman Woodland.

Julius Caesar (1970) USA. Directed by Stuart Burge, with Charlton Heston, John Gielgud and Jason Robards.

Filmography *continued*

King Lear

The Yiddish King Lear (1934) USA. Yiddish language adaptation set in the immigrant community of New York, directed by Harry Thomashefsky.

King Lear (1953) USA. TV version directed by Andrew McCullough, with Orson Welles and Alan Badel.

Korol Lir (1969) USSR. Directed by Grigori Kozintsev, translated by Boris Pasternak.

King Lear (1971) UK/Denmark. Directed by Peter Brook, with Paul Scofield and Tom Fleming.

King Lear (1974) USA. TV version directed by Edwin Sherin, with James Earl Jones.

King Lear (1984) UK. TV version directed by Michael Elliott ,with Laurence Olivier, Leo McKern and Dorothy Tutin.

Ran (1985) Japan/France. The *King Lear* story transposed to feudal Japan. Directed by Akira Kurosawa.

King Lear (1997) UK. TV version directed by Richard Eyre, with Ian Holm and David Burke.

King of Texas (2002) USA. TV adaptation set in 19th-century America. Directed by Uli Edel, with Patrick Stewart.

Macbeth

Macbeth (1948) USA. Directed by and starring Orson Welles.

Throne of Blood (1957) Japan. *Macbeth* transposed to medieval Japan. Directed by Akira Kurosawa, with Toshiro Mifune.

Macbeth (1971) USA. Directed by Roman Polanski, with Jon Finch and Francesca Annis.

Macbeth (1979) UK. TV version directed by Trevor Nunn, with Ian McKellen and Judi Dench.

Men of Respect (1991) USA. Modern version of *Macbeth.* Directed by William Reilly, with John Turturro.

Macbeth on the Estate (1997) UK. Modern-dress TV adaptation set among drug-dealers. Directed by Penny Woolcock, with Ray Winstone.

Macbeth (1998) UK. TV version directed by Michael Bogdanov, with Sean Pertwee and Greta Scacchi.

Makibefo (1999) UK. Directed by Alexander Abela. Filmed in Madagascar using local people as actors.

Measure for Measure

Measure for Measure (1994) UK. Modern-dress TV version directed by David Thacker, with Corin Redgrave and Tom Wilkinson.

Filmography *continued*

The Merchant of Venice

The Merchant of Venice (1969) USA. TV version directed by and starring Orson Welles.

The Merchant of Venice (1973) UK. TV version directed by Jonathan Miller, with Laurence Olivier.

The Merchant of Venice (1996) UK. TV version directed by Alan Horrox, with Bob Peck and Hadyn Gwynne.

The Merchant of Venice (2001) UK. National Theatre production, directed by Trevor Nunn and set in 1930s Germany.

Te Tangata Whai Rawa o Weniti (2002) New Zealand (Maori title). Directed by Don Selwyn. Translated into Maori and set in New Zealand/Maori culture.

The Merchant of Venice (2004) USA/UK. Directed by Michael Radford, starring Jeremy Irons, Al Pacino, Joseph Fiennes and Lynn Collins

A Midsummer Night's Dream

A Midsummer Night's Dream (1935) USA. Directed by William Dieterle and Max Reinhardt, with James Cagney, Mickey Rooney and Olivia de Havilland.

A Midsummer Night's Dream (1968) UK. Directed by Peter Hall, with Helen Mirren, Ian Holm, and Diana Rigg.

A Midsummer Night's Dream (1996) UK. RSC version directed by Adrian Noble, with Lindsay Duncan and Alex Jennings.

William Shakespeare's A Midsummer Night's Dream (1999) USA. Set in *fin de siècle* Italy. Directed by Michel Hoffman, with Michelle Pfeiffer, Calista Flockhart, Kevin Kline and Rupert Everett.

The Children's Midsummer Night's Dream (2001) UK. Astonishing film entirely acted by children. Directed by Christine Edzard.

Much Ado About Nothing

Much Ado About Nothing (1967) UK. Directed by Franco Zeffirelli, with Derek Jacobi and Maggie Smith.

Much Ado About Nothing (1993) USA/UK. Directed by and starring Kenneth Branagh, with Emma Thompson, Denzel Washington and Keanu Reeves.

Othello

The Tragedy of Othello: The Moor of Venice (1952) USA. Famous version directed by and starring Orson Welles.

Othello (1991) UK. TV version directed by Trevor Nunn, with Ian McKellen, Imogen Stubbs and Willard White.

Othello (1995) USA/UK. Directed by Oliver Parker with Laurence Fishburne and Kenneth Branagh.

Kaliyattam (1997) India. Adaptation directed by Jayaraaj.

Othello (2001) USA/UK/Canada. TV version set in the modern police. Directed by Geoffrey Sax, with Christopher Eccleston as 'Ben Jago'.

Filmography *continued*

Richard II

The Tragedy of King Richard II (1970) UK. Directed by Richard Cottrell, with Ian McKellen and Timothy West.

Richard II (1997) UK. Filmed for TV. Directed by Deborah Warner, and notable for Fiona Shaw's playing of Richard II.

Richard III

Richard III (1955) UK. Famous and seminal version directed by and starring Laurence Olivier.

Tower of London (1962) USA. 'Horror' adaptation directed by Roger Corman, with Vincent Price.

Richard III (1995) UK/USA. Set in the 1930s. Directed by Richard Loncraine, with Ian McKellen and Kristin Scott Thomas.

Looking for Richard (1996) USA. Documentary by Al Pacino about his production of *Richard III,* with Kevin Spacey and Winona Ryder.

Romeo and Juliet

Romanoff and Juliet (1961) USA. Comedy adaptation set during the Cold War. Directed by and starring Peter Ustinov.

West Side Story (1961) USA. Film of the musical by Leonard Bernstein, based on *Romeo and Juliet* but set in gangland New York. Directed by Jerome Robbins and Robert Wise.

Romeo and Juliet (1968) UK/Italy. Directed by Franco Zeffirelli, and famous for the youth of the two lead actors (Olivia Hussey and Leonard Whiting).

Romeo + Juliet (1996) USA. Baz Luhrmann's blockbuster version in modern setting, with Leonardo DiCaprio and Claire Danes.

Shakespeare in Love (1998) USA/UK. Fictional account of the inspiration for *Romeo and Juliet*. Directed by John Madden, with Joseph Fiennes and Gwyneth Paltrow.

The Taming of the Shrew

The Taming of the Shrew (1929) USA. Directed by Sam Taylor, with Mary Pickford and Douglas Fairbanks.

Kiss Me Kate (1953) USA. Musical based on the play, directed by George Sidney.

The Taming of the Shrew (1967) Italy/USA. Zeffirelli's version with Elizabeth Taylor and Richard Burton.

Ten Things I Hate About You (1999). USA. Set in a modern American high school. Directed by Gil Junger, with Julia Stiles.

Filmography *continued*

The Tempest

Forbidden Planet (1956) USA. Classic sci-fi based on the story of *The Tempest*. Directed by Fred M.Wilcox, with Walter Pidgeon.

The Tempest (1968) UK. TV version directed by Basil Coleman, with Michael Redgrave.

The Tempest (1979) UK. Controversial version directed by Derek Jarman, with Heathcote Williams and Toyah Willcox.

Prospero's Books (1991) UK. Directed by Peter Greenaway, with John Gielgud.

Twelfth Night

Twelfth Night (1987) Australia. Directed by Neil Armfield, with Geoffrey Rush and Gillian Jones.

Twelfth Night (1988) UK. TV version directed by Kenneth Branagh, with Caroline Langrishe and Richard Briers.

Twelfth Night (1996) UK. Directed by Trevor Nunn and set in the 1800s, with Imogen Stubbs, Helena Bonham Carter and Nigel Hawthorne.

Twelfth Night (1998) USA. Directed by Nicholas Hytner, with Helen Hunt and Philip Bosco.

The Winter's Tale

The Winter's Tale (1968) UK. Directed by Frank Dunlop, with Laurence Harvey and Jane Asher.

Conte d'hiver (1992) France. Directed by Eric Rohmer, including scenes showing a performance of *The Winter's Tale*.

The Winter's Tale (1998) UK. RSC production directed by Gregory Doran, with Anthony Sher. Interspersed with the cast discussing the ideas in the play.

General

Ian McKellen: Acting Shakespeare (1982) UK. The great actor performs monologues.

The Wars of the Roses (1989) UK. TV series directed by Michael Bogdanov, showing all the history plays.